CWNA™

Certified Wireless Network Administrator
Official Study Guide

(Exam PW0-100)

SECOND EDITION

Planet3 Wireless

McGraw-Hill/Osborne
New York Chicago San Francisco Lisbon London Madrid
Mexico City Milan New Delhi San Juan Seoul Singapore Sydney Toronto

McGraw-Hill/Osborne
2600 Tenth Street
Berkeley, California 94710
U.S.A.

To arrange bulk purchase discounts for sales promotions, premiums, or fund-raisers, please contact McGraw-Hill/Osborne at the above address. For information on translations or book distributors outside the U.S.A., please see the International Contact Information page immediately following the index of this book.

**CWNA Certified Wireless Network Administrator
Official Study Guide (Exam PW0-100) Second Edition**

1234567890 JPI JPI 019876543

ISBN 0-07-222902-0

Publisher Brandon A. Nordin	**Editorial Director** Gareth Hancock	**Indexer** Jack Lewis
Vice President & **Associate Publisher** Scott Rogers	**Technical Editor** Devin Akin	**Computer Designers** Scott Turner
Acquisitions Editor Timothy Green	**Copy Editor** Kevin Sandlin	**Illustrator** Scott Turner
Project Editor Kevin Sandlin	**Proofreader** Kevin Sandlin	**Series Design** Scott Turner

CWNP™ Certification Program

The Certified Wireless Network Professional Training & Certification Program is intended for individuals who administer, install, design, and support IEEE 802.11 compliant wireless networks. Because the CWNP program is vendor neutral, candidates who achieve the different levels of CWNP Certification will be trained and qualified to administer and support many different brands of wireless LAN hardware. Although there are many manufacturers of wireless LAN hardware, the technologies behind the hardware – Radio Frequency and Local Area Networking – are the same for each piece of gear. Each manufacturer approaches these technologies in different ways.

The CWNP program consists of 4 levels of certification:

Administrator – Site survey, installation, and management of 802.11 compliant wireless LANs

Security Professional – Design and implementation of 802.11 security techniques, processes, hardware, and software

Integrator – Design, management, QoS, advanced site surveying, advanced RF theory, and vertical market analysis of 802.11 compliant wireless LANs

Expert – Wireless LAN packet analysis and troubleshooting using the latest software tools

We at Planet3 Wireless would like to dedicate this book to our Lord Jesus Christ. It is through Him that we have had the talent, time, encouragement, and strength to work many long months in preparing this text. Our goal through the creation of this book and through all things that He allows us to do going forward is to glorify Him. We acknowledge His hand in every part of our company, our work, and our friendships. We would also like to thank our families who have been amazingly supportive, our friends who have encouraged us and everyone that contributed to this book in any way.

"I can do all things through Christ, who strengthens me." – Philippians 4:13

Acknowledgements

Planet3 Wireless, Inc. would like to acknowledge and thank the following people for their tireless contributions to this work:

Devin Akin, whose knowledge of wireless LANs, networking, and radio frequency surprised even us. His talents to convey, teach, write, and edit were essential in making this the most accurate and comprehensive writing on wireless LANs in today's market.

Scott Turner, who constantly keeps us in line and focused on what is important. Scott's work in formatting, framing, content organization, and graphics creation was indispensable. Scott's eye for detail and his motivation for perfection in everything he does keep us in awe.

Kevin Sandlin, for his intellect to make difficult concepts sound simple, his skill to write and edit the most difficult material, and his ability to motivate every member of the team to do their best and to keep their eyes on the sometimes moving target.

Robert Nicholas, for his ability to conceptualize and create difficult graphics and radio frequency concepts, his savvy in presentation of difficult material, and his ability to find the answer to even the most vague concepts through diligent research and study.

Jeff Jones and **Josh McCord,** who have been with Planet3 since the beginning of this project. Their willingness to volunteer as much time and effort as was needed to make all of it possible has been amazing. They have been an inspiration to the entire team. Their relentless pursuit of perfection in support of Planet3's mission is recognized and greatly appreciated.

Stan Brooks, **Bill Waldo**, and **Barry Oxford**, each of whom brought a unique set of skills to the review and quality assurance process for this publication. Their time, effort and eye for necessary changes were immeasurable, and helped to publish this book in a timely manner.

Contents at a Glance

Contents

Introduction

This Official CWNA Study Guide is intended first to help prepare you to install, manage, and support wireless networks, and second to prepare you to take and pass the CWNA certification exam. As part of the CWNP Training and Certification program, the CWNA certification picks up where other popular networking certification programs leave off: *wireless LANs.*

Your study of wireless networking will help you bring together two fascinating worlds of technology, because wireless networks are the culmination of Radio Frequency (RF) and networking technologies. No study of wireless LANs would be complete without first making sure the student understands the foundations of both RF and local area networking fundamentals.

For that reason, we recommend that you obtain a basic level of networking knowledge, as exhibited in the CompTIA Network+™ certification. If you have achieved other certifications such as CCNA, MCSE, or CNE, then you most likely already have the understanding of networking technologies necessary to move into wireless.

By purchasing this book, you are taking the first step towards a bright future in the networking world. Why? Because you have just jumped ahead and apart from the rest of the pack by learning wireless networking to complement your existing networking knowledge.

The wireless LAN industry is growing faster than any other market segment in networking. Many new careers will be presenting themselves in support of the added responsibilities network administrators must deal with when they add wireless LANs to their networks. Getting a head start on wireless technology now will enable you to compete effectively in tomorrow's marketplace.

Who This Book Is For

This book focuses on the technologies and tasks vital to installing, managing, and supporting wireless networks, based on the exam objectives of the CWNA certification exam. You will learn the wireless technology standards, governing bodies, hardware, RF math, RF behavior, security, troubleshooting, and site survey methodology. After you achieve your CWNA certification, you will find this book to be a concise compilation of the basic knowledge necessary to work on wireless LANs.

The best method of preparation for the CWNA certification exam is attending an official CWNA training course. If you prefer to study and prepare at your own pace, then this book and a practice exam should adequately prepare you to pass the exam.

New To Wireless

If you've been working on networks – LANs, MANs, WANs, etc. – but not yet taken on wireless, then this book and the subsequent certification exam are great introductions into wireless LAN technology. Be careful not to assume that wireless is just like any other form of networking. While they certainly serve as an extension to wired LANs, wireless LANs are a field of study all their own. An individual can spend many more than the standard 40 hours in a week learning and using wireless LAN technology. With wireless LAN security now clearly in focus, the industry is piling on knowledge requirements that wireless LAN administrators must master quickly in order to keep pace. Wireless LANs are reaching into new areas with each passing month that nobody thought they would ever reach. If you administer LANs, there's simply no avoiding wireless. Wireless is here to stay.

Wireless Experts

If you are experienced in wireless networking already, there is substantial material covered in this book that will benefit you. Most people who attend a CWNA class marvel from the first day about how much they *don't* know. If you have been working with wireless LANs for years, be careful you don't assume that you know all there is to know about them. Even experts who spent 12 hours each day studying wireless material in order to stay up-to-date cannot keep up with the technology. Many new solutions, both for seamless connectivity and for security, are released each week. There are new solutions that are designed each month and before you can blink, there are 3 or 4 companies producing products supporting these new technologies. This book will be kept up-to-date as the wireless industry progresses so that the reader always knows that they are receiving the latest information.

While our program was still in its infancy, we were privileged to have some industry experts take part in our testing. We found out very quickly that their status of "expert" was in question. There is such a broad base of knowledge required to be a wireless expert that it will likely feel overwhelming at times. As you will soon see, this book is geared toward the beginner and intermediate reader alike. We hope that it will take you further than you had expected to go when you first picked it up, and we hope that it will open your eyes to a wonderful new field of study.

RF Experienced

Some of you may have worked with RF for years, perhaps in the military, and have moved into the networking industry. Your knowledge and experience is right on track with the evolution of wireless LAN technology, but you have probably never measured your knowledge of these two technologies by taking a certification exam. This measurement is the purpose of the CWNA certification exam. Fields of study like Electrical Engineering, RF Metrology, Satellite Communications, and others typically provide a solid background in radio frequency fundamentals. In this book, we will address specific topics that you may or may not be familiar with, or you may just have to dust off that portion of your memory. Many people have crossed over from careers in radio frequency to careers in Information Technology (IT), but never dreamed where the two fields of study might meet. Wireless LAN technology is the meeting place.

New to Networking

Finally, if you are stepping into the networking world for the very first time, please make sure you have a basic understanding of networking concepts, and then jump right in! The wireless LAN industry is growing at a phenomenal rate. Wireless networking is replacing and adding to the mobility of conventional network access methods very quickly. We won't pretend to know which technology will ultimately hold the greatest market share. Instead, we cover all currently available wireless LAN technologies. Some technologies, like 802.11b, hold a tremendous market share presently, and those will be covered at length in this book.

Again, as the industry and market place change, so will this book in order to stay current.

How Is This Book Organized?

This Official CWNA Study Guide is organized in the same manner as the official CWNA course is taught, starting with the basic concepts or building blocks and developing your knowledge of the convergence of RF and networking technologies.

Each chapter contains subsections that correspond to the different topics covered on the CWNA exam. Each topic is explained in detail, followed by a list of key terms that you should know after comprehending each chapter. Then, we close each chapter with comprehensive review questions that cause you to apply the knowledge you've just gained to real world scenarios.

Finally, we have a complete glossary of wireless LAN terms for continual reference to you as you use your new wireless LAN knowledge on the job.

Why Become CWNA Certified?

Planet3 Wireless, Inc. has created a certification program, not unlike those of Cisco, Novell, and Microsoft, that gives networking professionals a standardized set of measurable wireless LAN skills and employers a standard level of wireless LAN expertise to require of their employees.

Passing the CWNA exam proves you have achieved a certain level of knowledge about wireless networking. Where Cisco and Microsoft certifications will prove a given level of knowledge about their products, the CWNA exam is proof of achievement about wireless technology that can be applied to any vendor's products. The wireless LAN industry is still in its infancy, much like the world of networking LANs and WANs was in the early 1990s. Learning wireless networking sets you apart from your peers and your competition.

For some positions, certification is a requirement for employment, advancement, or increases in salary. The CWNP program is positioned to be that certification for wireless networking. Imagine if you had CCIE, MCSE, or CNE in 1993! Advancement in wireless technologies will follow the same steps as other certifications – an increase in responsibilities within your organization, perhaps followed by increases in salary.

How Do You Get CWNA Certified?

The CWNP program consists of multiple levels of certification, beginning with CWNA. You can become CWNA certified by passing one written exam. The CWNA exam is currently available at all Prometric Testing Centers worldwide.

The best way to prepare for the CWNA exam is to attend a CWNA training course or to study at your own pace with this book. The CWNA practice exam will provide you with a good idea of the types of questions that can be found on the real exam. The CWNA practice exam is available at http://www.boson.com. Complete information on available training for the CWNA certification is available at http://www.cwne.com.

As you prepare for the CWNA exam, and the other, more advanced CWNP certifications, we highly recommend that you practice with wireless LAN gear. The best part of that recommendation is that wireless LAN gear is plummeting in price. As of the writing of this book, you can get a basic wireless LAN (Access Point, USB Client, PC Card, PCI Card) for less than $500 retail.

Exam Objectives

The CWNA certification covering the 2002 objectives will certify that successful candidates know the fundamentals of RF behavior, can describe the features and functions of wireless LAN components, and have the skills needed to install, configure, and troubleshoot wireless LAN hardware peripherals and protocols. A typical candidate should have the CompTIA Network+ certification or equivalent knowledge, although Network+ certification is not required.

The skills and knowledge measured by this examination are derived from a survey of wireless networking experts and professionals. The results of this survey were used in weighing the subject areas and ensuring that the weighting is representative of the relative importance of the content.

This section outlines the exam objectives for the CWNA exam.

 The objectives for the CWNA exam can change at any time. For the most current objectives visit www.cwne.com.

Radio Frequency (RF) Technologies – 24%

1.1. RF Fundamentals

1.1.1. Define and apply the basic concepts of RF behavior

- Gain
- Loss
- Reflection
- Refraction
- Diffraction
- Scattering
- VSWR
- Amplification & attenuation

1.1.2. Understand the applications of basic RF antenna concepts

- Visual LOS
- RF LOS
- The Fresnel Zone
- Intentional Radiator
- EIRP
- Wave propagation

1.2. RF Math

1.2.1. Understand and apply the basic components of RF mathematics

- Watt
- Milliwatt
- Decibel (dB)
- dBm
- dBi

1.3. Spread Spectrum Technologies

1.3.1. Identify some of the different uses for spread spectrum technologies

- Wireless LANs
- Wireless PANs
- Wireless WANs

1.3.2. Comprehend the differences between, and apply the different types of spread spectrum technologies

- FHSS
- DSSS

1.3.3. Identify and apply the concepts which make up the functionality of spread spectrum technology

- Co-location
- Channels

- Dwell time
- Throughput
- Hop time

1.3.4. Identify the laws set forth by the FCC that govern spread spectrum technology, including power outputs, frequencies, bandwidths, hop times, and dwell times.

Wireless LAN Technologies – 17%

2.1. 802.11 Network Architecture

2.1.1. Identify and apply the processes involved in authentication and association

- Passive scanning
- Active scanning
- Authentication
- Association
- Open system authentication
- Shared key authentication
- Secret keys and certificates
- AAA Support

2.1.2. Recognize the following concepts associated with wireless LAN service sets

- BSS
- ESS
- IBSS
- SSID
- Infrastructure mode
- Ad-hoc mode
- Roaming

2.1.3. Understand the implications of the following power management features of wireless LANs

- PSP Mode
- CAM
- Beacons

- TIM
- ATIM
- ATIM Windows

2.2. Physical and MAC Layers

2.2.1. Understand and apply the following concepts surrounding wireless LAN Frames

- The difference between wireless LAN and Ethernet frames
- Layer 3 Protocols supported by wireless LANs

2.2.2. Specify the modes of operation involved in the movement of data traffic across wireless LANs

- DCF
- PCF
- CSMA/CA vs. CSMA/CD
- Interframe spacing
- RTS/CTS
- Dynamic Rate Selection
- Modulation and coding

Wireless LAN Implementation and Management – 30%

3.1. Wireless LAN Application

3.1.1. Identify the technology roles for which wireless LAN technology is an appropriate technology application

- Data access role
- Extension of existing networks into remote locations
- Building-to-building connectivity
- Last mile data delivery
- Flexibility for mobile users
- SOHO Use
- Mobile office, classroom, industrial, and healthcare

3.2. Hardware Management

3.2.1. Identify the purpose of the following infrastructure devices and explain how to install, configure, and manage them

- Access points
- Wireless bridges
- Wireless workgroup bridges

3.2.2. Identify the purpose of the following wireless LAN client devices and explain how to install, configure, and manage them

- PCMCIA cards
- Serial and Ethernet converters
- USB devices
- PCI/ISA devices

3.2.3. Identify the purpose of the following wireless LAN gateway devices and explain how to install, configure, and manage them

- Residential gateways
- Enterprise gateways

3.2.4. Identify the basic attributes, purpose, and function of the following types of antennas

- Omni-directional/dipole
- Semi-directional
- High-gain

3.2.5. Describe the proper locations and methods for installing antennas.

3.2.6. Explain the concepts of polarization, gain, beamwidth, and free-space path loss as they apply to implementing solutions that require antennas.

3.2.7. Identify the use of the following wireless LAN accessories and explain how to install, configure, and manage them

- Power over Ethernet devices
- Amplifiers
- Attenuators
- Lightning arrestors
- RF connectors and cables
- RF splitters

3.3. Troubleshooting Wireless LAN Installations

3.3.1. Identify, understand, correct or compensate for the following wireless LAN implementation challenges

- Multipath
- Hidden node
- Near-Far
- RF interference
- All-band interference
- System throughput
- Co-location throughput
- Weather

3.3.2. Explain how antenna diversity compensates for multipath.

3.4. RF Site Survey Fundamentals

3.4.1. Identify and understand the importance and process of conducting a thorough site survey.

3.4.2. Identify and understand the importance of the necessary tasks involved in preparing to do an RF site survey

- Gathering business requirements
- Interviewing management and users
- Defining security requirements
- Site-specific documentation
- Documenting existing network characteristics

3.4.3. Identify the necessary equipment involved in performing a site survey

- Wireless LAN equipment
- Measurement tools
- Documentation

3.4.4. Understand the necessary procedures involved in performing a site survey

- Non-RF information
- Permits and zoning requirements
- Outdoor considerations
- RF related information
- Interference sources
- Connectivity and power requirements

3.4.5. Identify and understand site survey reporting procedures

- Requirements
- Methodology
- Measurements
- Security
- Graphical documentation
- Recommendations

Wireless LAN Security – 16%

4.1. Protection

4.1.1. Identify the strengths, weaknesses and appropriate uses of the following wireless LAN security techniques

- WEP
- AES
- Filtering
- Emerging security techniques

4.2. Attacks

4.2.1. Describe the following types of wireless LAN security attacks, and explain how to identify and prevent them

- Passive attacks (eavesdropping)
- Active attacks (connecting, probing, and configuring the network)
- Jamming
- Man-in-the-middle

4.3. Security Solutions

4.3.1. Given a wireless LAN scenario, identify the appropriate security solution from the following available wireless LAN security solutions

- WEP key solutions
- Wireless VPN
- Key hopping
- AES based solutions
- Wireless gateways
- 802.1x and EAP

4.3.2. Explain the uses of the following corporate security policies and how they are used to secure a wireless LAN

- Securing sensitive information
- Physical security
- Inventory and audits
- Using advanced solutions
- Public networks

4.3.3. Identify how and where the following security precautions are used to secure a wireless LAN

- WEP
- Cell sizing
- Monitoring

- User authentication
- Wireless DMZ

Wireless LAN Industry and Standards – 13%

5.1. Standards

    5.1.1. Identify, apply and comprehend the differences between the following wireless LAN standards

- 802.11
- 802.11b
- 802.11a
- 802.11g
- Bluetooth
- HomeRF

5.2. Organizations & Regulations

    5.2.1. Understand the roles of the following organizations in providing direction and accountability within the wireless LAN industry

- FCC
- IEEE
- The Wi-Fi Alliance
- WLANA
- IrDA
- ETSI

    5.2.2. Identify the differences between the ISM and UNII bands

    5.2.3. Identify and understand the differences between the power output rules for point-to-point and point-to-multipoint links

    5.2.4. Identify the basic characteristics of infrared wireless LANs

Where do you take the CWNA Exam?

You may take the CWNA exam at any one of the Prometric Testing Centers worldwide. For the location of a testing center near you, call 800-639-3926 or visit http://www.2test.com. The CWNA Exam is exam number **PW0-100**. The exam cost is $175.00 worldwide.

Once you register for the exam, you will be given complete instructions for where to go and what to bring. For cancellations, please pay close attention to the procedures, which can be found at the following URL:

http://www.cwne.com/cwnp/exam_policy.html

Tips for successfully taking the CWNA Exam

The CWNA exam consists of 90 questions, and you will have 90 minutes to complete the exam. You may schedule and take the exam the next day.

Following are some general tips for success on the CWNA Exam:

- Take advantage of the CWNA Practice exam so you will be familiar with the types of questions that you will see on the real exam.

- Arrive at least 15 minutes earlier than your scheduled exam time, and preferably 30 minutes early, so you can relax and review your study guide one last time.

- Read every question very carefully.

- Don't leave any unanswered questions. These count against your score.

Once you have completed the CWNA exam, you will be provided with a complete Examination Score Report, which shows your pass/fail status section by section. Your test scores are sent to Planet3 Wireless, Inc. within 10 working days. If you pass the exam, you will receive a CWNA Certificate within 3 weeks.

Contact information

We are always eager to receive feedback on our courses and training materials. If you have specific questions about something you have read in this book, please use the information below to contact Planet3 Wireless, Inc.

Planet3 Wireless, Inc.
P.O. Box 412
Bremen, Georgia 30110
866-GET-CWNE
http://www.cwne.com

Direct feedback via email:
feedback@cwne.com

Introduction to Wireless LANs

CWNA Exam Objectives Covered:

❖ Identify the technology roles for which wireless LAN technology is an appropriate application:

- Data access role

- Extension of existing networks into remote locations

- Building-to-building connectivity

- Last mile data delivery

- Flexibility for mobile users

- SOHO Use

- Mobile office, classroom, industrial, and healthcare

In This Chapter

The Wireless LAN Market

Applications of Wireless LANs

In this section, we will discuss the wireless LAN market, an overview of the past, present, and future of wireless LANs, and an introduction to the standards that govern wireless LANs. We will then discuss some of the appropriate applications of wireless LANs. In closing, we will introduce you to the various organizations that guide the evolution and development of wireless LANs.

The knowledge of the history and evolution of wireless LAN technology is an essential part of the foundational principles of wireless LANs. A thorough understanding of where wireless LANs came from and the organizations and applications that have helped the technology mature will enable you to better apply wireless LANs to your organization or your client's needs.

The Wireless LAN Market

The market for wireless LANs seems to be evolving in a similar fashion to the networking industry as a whole, starting with the early adopters using whatever technology was available. The market has moved into a rapid growth stage, for which popular standards are providing the catalyst. The big difference between the networking market as a whole and the wireless LAN market is the rate of growth. Wireless LANs allow so many flexibilities in their implementation that it's no wonder that they are outpacing every other market sector.

History of Wireless LANs

Spread spectrum wireless networks, like many technologies, came of age under the guidance of the military. The military needed a simple, easily implemented, and secure method of exchanging data in a combat environment.

As the cost of wireless technology declined and the quality increased, it became cost-effective for enterprise companies to integrate wireless segments into their network. Wireless technology offered a relatively inexpensive way for corporate campuses to connect buildings to one another without laying copper or fiber cabling. Today, the cost of wireless technology is such that most businesses can afford to implement wireless segments on their network, if not convert completely to a wireless network, saving the company time and money while allowing the flexibility of roaming.

Households are also benefiting from the low cost and subsequent availability of wireless LAN hardware. Many people are now creating cost-effective wireless networks that take advantage of the convenience of mobility and creating home offices or wireless gaming stations.

As wireless LAN technology improves, the cost of manufacturing (and thus purchasing and implementing) the hardware continues to fall, and the number of installed wireless LANs continues to increase. The standards that govern wireless LAN operation will increasingly stress interoperability and compatibility. As the number of users grows, lack of compatibility may render a network useless, and the lack of interoperability may interfere with the proper operation of other networks.

Today's Wireless LAN Standards

Because wireless LANs transmit using radio frequencies, wireless LANs are regulated by the same types of laws used to govern such things as AM/FM radios. The Federal Communications Commission (FCC) regulates the use of wireless LAN devices. In the current wireless LAN market there are several accepted operational standards and drafts in the United States that are created and maintained by the *Institute of Electrical and Electronic Engineers (IEEE)*.

These standards are created by groups of people that represent many different organizations, including academics, business, military, and the government. Because standards set forth by the IEEE can have such an impact on the development of technology, the standards can take many years to be created and agreed upon. You may even have an opportunity to comment on these standards at certain times during the creation process.

The standards specific to wireless LANs are covered in greater detail in Chapter 6 (Wireless LAN Organizations and Standards). Because these standards are the basis upon which the latest wireless LANs are built, a brief overview is provided here.

IEEE 802.11 - the original wireless LAN standard that specifies the slowest data transfer rates in both RF and light-based transmission technologies. This standard was ratified by IEEE in 1997.

IEEE 802.11b – describes somewhat faster data transfer rates and a more restrictive scope of transmission technologies. This standard is also widely promoted as Wi-Fi™ by the Wi-Fi Alliance. This standard was ratified by IEEE in 1999 as an amendment to the original IEEE 802.11 standard.

IEEE 802.11a - describes much faster data transfer rate than (but lacks backwards compatibility with) IEEE 802.11b, and uses the 5 GHz UNII frequency bands. This standard was ratified by IEEE in 1999 as an amendment to the original IEEE 802.11 standard.

IEEE 802.11g - the most recent draft based on the 802.11 standard that describes data transfer rates equally as fast as IEEE 802.11a, and boasts the backward compatibility to 802.11b required to make inexpensive upgrades possible. This draft has not been ratified by the IEEE, but should be early in 2003.

Emerging technologies will require standards that describe and define their proper behavior. The challenge for manufacturers and standards-makers alike will be bringing their resources to bear on the problems of interoperability and compatibility.

Applications of Wireless LANs

When computers were first built, only large universities and corporations could afford them. Today you may find 3 or 4 personal computers in your neighbor's house. Wireless LANs have taken a similar path, first used by large enterprises, and now available to us all at affordable prices. As a technology, wireless LANs have enjoyed a very fast adoption rate due to the many advantages they offer to a variety of situations. In this section, we will discuss some of the most common and appropriate uses of wireless LANs.

Access Role

Wireless LANs are mostly deployed in an access layer role, meaning that they are used as an entry point into a wired network. In the past, access has been defined as dial-up, ADSL, cable, cellular, Ethernet, Token Ring, Frame Relay, ATM, etc. Wireless is simply another method for users to access the network. Wireless LANs are Data-Link layer networks like all of the access methods just listed. Due to a lack of speed and resiliency, wireless networks are not typically implemented in Distribution or Core roles in networks. Of course, in small networks, there may be no differentiation between the Core, Distribution, or Access layers of the network. The Core layer of a network should be very fast and very stable, able to handle a tremendous amount of traffic with little difficulty and experience no down time. The Distribution layer of a network should be fast, flexible, and reliable. Wireless LANs do not typically meet these requirements for an enterprise solution. Figure 1.1 illustrates mobile clients gaining access to a wired network through a connection device (access point).

FIGURE 1.1   Access role of a wireless LAN

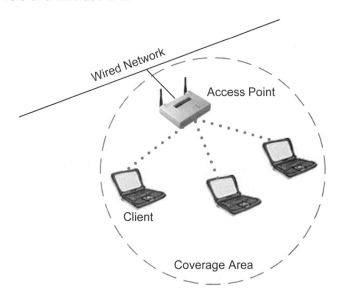

Wireless LANs offer a specific solution to a difficult problem: mobility. Without a doubt, wireless LANs solve a host of problems for corporations and home users alike, but all of these problems point to the need for freedom from data cabling. Cellular solutions have been available for quite some time, offering users the ability to roam while staying connected, at slow speeds and very high prices. Wireless LANs offer the same flexibility without the disadvantages. Wireless LANs are fast, inexpensive, and they can be located almost anywhere.

When considering wireless LANs for use in your network, keep in mind that using them for their intended purpose will provide the best results. Administrators implementing wireless LANs in a Core or Distribution role should understand exactly what performance to expect before implementing them in this fashion to avoid having to remove them later. The only distribution role in a corporate network that is definitely appropriate for wireless LANs is that of building-to-building bridging. In this scenario, wireless *could* be considered as playing a distribution role; however, it will always depend on how the wireless bridging segments are used in the network.

There are some Wireless Internet Service Providers (WISPs) that use licensed wireless frequencies in a distribution role, but almost never unlicensed frequencies such as the ones discussed at length in this book.

Network Extension

Wireless networks can serve as an extension to a wired network. There may be cases where extending the network would require installing additional cabling that is cost prohibitive. You may discover that hiring cable installers and electricians to build out a new section of office space for the network is going to cost tens of thousands of dollars. Or in the case of a large warehouse, the distances may be too great to use Category 5 (Cat5) cable for the Ethernet network. Fiber might have to be installed, requiring an even greater investment of time and resources. Installing fiber might involve upgrades to existing edge switches.

Wireless LANs can be easily implemented to provide seamless connectivity to remote areas within a building, as illustrated by the floor plan image in Figure 1.2. Because little wiring is necessary to install a wireless LAN, the costs of hiring installers and purchasing Ethernet cable might be completely eliminated.

FIGURE 1.2   Network Extension

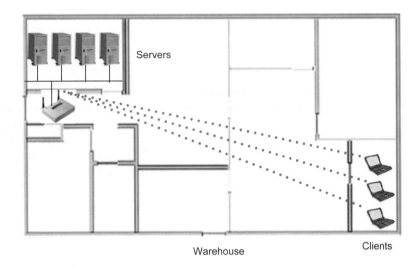

Building-to-Building Connectivity

In a campus environment or an environment with as few as two adjacent buildings, there may be a need to have the network users in each of the different buildings have direct access to the same computer network. In the past, this type of access and connectivity would be accomplished by running cables underground from one building to another or by renting expensive leased-lines from a local telephone company.

Using wireless LAN technology, equipment can be installed easily and quickly to allow two or more buildings to be part of the same network without the expense of leased lines or the need to dig up the ground between buildings. With the proper wireless antennas, any number of buildings can be linked together on the same network. Certainly there are limitations to using wireless LAN technology, as there are in any data-connectivity solution, but the flexibility, speed, and cost-savings that wireless LANs introduce to the network administrator make them indispensable.

There are two different types of building-to-building connectivity. The first is called point-to-point (PTP), and the second is called point-to-multipoint (PTMP). Point-to-point links are wireless connections between only two buildings, as illustrated in Figure 1.3. PTP connections almost always use semi-directional or highly directional antennas at each end of the link.

FIGURE 1.3 Building-to-building connectivity

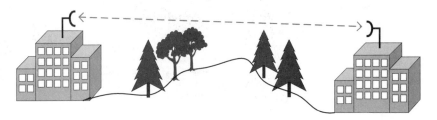

Point-to-multipoint links are wireless connections between three or more buildings, typically implemented in a "hub and spoke" or star topological fashion, where one building is the central focus point of the network. This central building would have the core network, Internet connectivity, and the server farm. Point-to-multipoint links between buildings typically use omni-directional antennas in the central "hub" building and semi-directional antennas on each of the outlying "spoke" buildings. Antennas will be covered in greater detail in Chapter 5.

There are many ways to implement these two basic types of connectivity, as you will undoubtedly see over the course of your career as a wireless LAN administrator or consultant. However, no matter how the implementations vary, they all fall into one of these two categories.

Last Mile Data Delivery

Wireless Internet Service Providers (WISPs) are now taking advantage of recent advancements in wireless technology to offer last mile data delivery service to their customers. "Last mile" refers to the communication infrastructure—wired or wireless—that exists between the central office of the telecommunications company (telco) or cable company and the end user. Currently the telcos and cable companies own their last mile infrastructure, but with the broadening interest in wireless technology, WISPs are now creating their own wireless last mile delivery service, as illustrated in Figure 1.4.

FIGURE 1.4   Last Mile Service

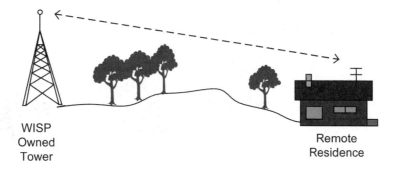

Consider the case where both the cable companies and telcos are encountering difficulties expanding their networks to offer broadband connections to more households or businesses. If you live in a rural area, chances are you do not have access to a broadband connection (cable modem or xDSL), and probably will not for quite some time. It is much more cost effective for WISPs to offer wireless access to these remote locations because WISPs will not encounter the same costs a cable company or telco would incur in order to install the necessary equipment.

WISPs have their own unique set of challenges. Just as xDSL providers have problems going further than 18,000 feet (5.7 km) from the central office and cable providers have issues with the cable being a shared medium to users, WISPs have problems with rooftops, trees, mountains, lightning, towers, and many other obstacles to connectivity. Certainly WISPs don't have a fail-proof solution, but they have the capability to offer broadband access to users that other, more conventional technologies cannot reach.

Mobility

As an access layer solution, wireless LANs cannot replace wired LANs in terms of data rates (100BaseTx at 100Mbps versus IEEE 802.11a at 54Mbps). A wireless environment uses intermittent connections and has higher error rates over what is usually a narrower bandwidth. As a result, applications and messaging protocols designed for the wired world sometimes operate poorly in a wireless environment. The wireless expectations of end users and IT manager are set by the performance and behaviors of their wired networks. What wireless LANs do offer is an increase in mobility (as can be seen in Figure 1.5) as the trade off for speed and quality of service.

For example, a parcel delivery company uses wireless technology to update parcel-tracking data immediately upon the arrival of the delivery vehicle. As the driver parks at the dock, the driver's computer has already logged onto the network and transferred the day's delivery data to the central network.

FIGURE 1.5   Mobility

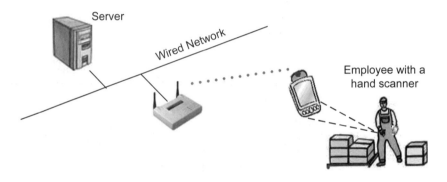

In warehousing facilities, wireless networks are used to track the storage locations and disposition of products. This data is then synchronized in the central computer for the purchasing and shipping departments. Handheld wireless scanners are becoming commonplace in organizations with employees that move around within their facility processing orders and inventory.

In each of these cases, wireless networks have created the ability to transfer data without requiring the time and manpower to input the data manually at a wired terminal. Wireless connectivity has also eliminated the need for such user devices to be connected using wires that would otherwise get in the way of the users.

Some of the newest wireless technology allows users to *roam,* or move physically from one area of wireless coverage to another without losing connectivity, just as a mobile telephone customer is able to roam between cellular coverage areas. In larger organizations, where wireless coverage spans large areas, roaming capability has significantly increased the productivity of these organizations, simply because users remain connected to the network away from their main workstations.

Small Office-Home Office

As an IT professional, you may have more than one computer at your home. And if you do, these computers are most likely networked together so you can share files, a printer, or a broadband connection.

This type of configuration is also utilized by many businesses that have only a few employees. These businesses have the need for the sharing of information between users and a single Internet connection for efficiency and greater productivity.

For these applications – small office-home office, or SOHO – a wireless LAN is a very simple and effective solution. Figure 1.6 illustrates a typical SOHO wireless LAN solution. Wireless SOHO devices are especially beneficial when office workers want to share a single Internet connection. The alternative of course is running wires throughout the office to interconnect all of the workstations. Many small offices are not outfitted with pre-installed Ethernet ports, and only a very small number of houses are wired for Ethernet networks. Trying to retrofit these places with Cat5 cabling usually results in creating unsightly holes in the walls and ceilings. With a wireless LAN, users can be interconnected easily and neatly.

FIGURE 1.6   SOHO Wireless LAN

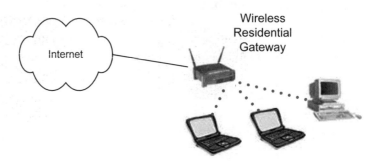

Mobile Offices

Mobile offices or classrooms allow users to pack up their computer equipment quickly and move to another location. Due to overcrowded classrooms, many schools now use mobile classrooms. These classrooms usually consist of large, movable trailers that are used while more permanent structures are built. In order to extend the computer network to these temporary buildings, aerial or underground cabling would have to be installed at great expense. Wireless LAN connections from the main school building to the mobile classrooms allow for flexible configurations at a fraction of the cost of alternative cabling. A simplistic example of connecting mobile classrooms using wireless LAN connectivity is illustrated in Figure 1.7.

Temporary office spaces also benefit from being networked with wireless LANs. As companies grow, they often find themselves with a shortage of office space, and need to move some workers to a nearby location, such as an adjacent office or an office on another floor of the same building. Installing Cat5 or fiber cabling for these short periods of time is not cost-effective, and usually the owners of the building do not allow for the installed cables to be removed. With a wireless network, the network components can be packed up and moved to the next location quickly and easily.

FIGURE 1.7   A school with mobile classrooms

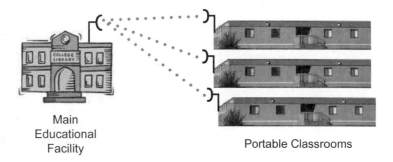

Main
Educational
Facility

Portable Classrooms

There are many groups that might use movable networks effectively. Some of these include the Superbowl, the Olympics, circuses, carnivals, fairs, festivals, construction companies, and others. Wireless LANs are well suited to these types of environments.

Hospitals and other healthcare facilities benefit greatly from wireless LANs. Some valuable uses of wireless LANs within these facilities include doctors using wireless PDAs to connect to the networks and mobile diagnostic carts that nurses can move from room to room to connect to the patient and the network. Wireless networks allow doctors and nurses to perform their jobs more efficiently using these new devices and associated software.

Industrial facilities, such as warehouses and manufacturing facilities, utilize wireless networks in various ways. A good example of an industrial wireless LAN application is shipping companies whose trucks pull into the dock and automatically connect to the wireless network. This type of networking allows the shipping company to become automated and more efficient in handling the uploading of data onto the central servers.

Summary

Wireless technology has come a long way since its simple military implementations. The popularity and level of technology used in wireless LANs continues to grow at an incredible rate. Manufactures have created a myriad of solutions for our varying wireless networking needs. The convenience, popularity, availability, and cost of wireless LAN hardware provide us all with many different solutions.

With the explosive expansion of wireless technology, manufacturers, and hardware, the role of organizations such as the FCC, IEEE, the Wi-Fi Alliance, and WLANA will become increasingly important to the removal of barriers of operation between solutions. The laws put in place by regulatory organizations like the FCC along with the standards provided by promotional and other organizations like IEEE, WLANA, and the Wi-Fi Alliance will focus the wireless LAN industry and provide a common path for it to grow and evolve over time.

Key Terms

Before taking the exam, you should be familiar with the following terms:

access layer

core layer

distribution layer

FCC

IEEE

IEEE 802.11

IEEE 802.11a

IEEE 802.11b

IEEE 802.11g

last mile

SOHO

WISP

Review Questions

1. Which one of the following does a wireless LAN provide that a wired network does not?

   A. Mobility

   B. Centralized security

   C. Reliability

   D. VPN security

2. Which one of the following would not be an appropriate use of a wireless LAN?

   A. Connecting two buildings together that are on opposite sides of the street

   B. Connecting two computers together in a small office so they can share a printer

   C. Connecting a remote home to a WISP for Internet access

   D. Connecting two rack-mounted computers together

3. Why is a wireless LAN a good choice for extending a network? Choose all that apply.

   A. Reduces the cost of cables required for installation

   B. Can be installed faster than a wired network

   C. Hardware is considerably less expensive than wired LAN hardware

   D. Eliminates a significant portion of the labor charges for installation

4. Wireless ISPs provide which one of the following services?

    A. Small office/home office services

    B. Connectivity for large enterprises

    C. Last mile data delivery

    D. Building-to-building connectivity

5. Wireless LANs are primarily deployed in which one of the following roles?

    A. Backbone

    B. Access

    C. Application

    D. Core

6. Why would a mobile office be a good choice for using a wireless LAN? Choose all that apply.

    A. Wireless LANs take less time to install than wired LANs

    B. Wireless LAN equipment could be easily removed if the office moves

    C. Wireless LANs do not require administration

    D. Wireless LANs take a more centralize approach over wired LANs

7. Which one of the following is the IEEE family of standards for wireless LANs?

    A. 802.3

    B. 803.5

    C. 802.11

    D. 802.1x

8.   As a consultant, you have taken a job creating a wireless LAN for an office complex that will connect 5 buildings in close vicinity together. Given only this information, which one of the following wireless LAN implementations would be most appropriate for this scenario?

   A.   Last mile data service from a WISP

   B.   Point-to-point bridge links between all buildings

   C.   Point-to-multipoint bridge link from a central building to all remote buildings

   D.   One central antenna at the main building only

9.   Which of the following are challenges that WISPs face that telephone companies and cable companies do not? Choose all that apply.

   A.   Customers located more than 18,000 feet (5.7 km) from a central office

   B.   High costs of installing telephone lines or copper cabling

   C.   Trees as line of sight obstructions

   D.   Rooftop access for antenna installation

10.   In what organization did the use of spread spectrum wireless data transfer originate?

   A.   The Wi-Fi Alliance

   B.   WLANA

   C.   FCC

   D.   U.S. Military

11. Which one of the following is the most recently approved IEEE standard for wireless LANs?

    A. 802.11a

    B. 802.11b

    C. 802.11c

    D. 802.11g

12. Which one of the following IEEE standards for wireless LANs is *not* compatible with the standard currently known as Wi-Fi™?

    A. 802.11

    B. 802.11g

    C. 802.11a

    D. 802.11b

13. Which one of the following IEEE 802.11 standards for wireless LANs utilizes the 5 GHz UNII bands for its radio signal transmissions?

    A. 802.11b

    B. Bluetooth

    C. 802.11

    D. 802.11g

    E. 802.11a

14. A WISP would take advantage of which one of the following applications for wireless LANs?

    A. Last Mile data delivery

    B. Building-to-building bridging

    C. Classroom connectivity

    D. Home network connectivity

15. Who makes the regulations that govern the technical requirements, licensing, and usage of wireless LANs in the United States?

    A. IEEE

    B. The Wi-Fi Alliance

    C. FCC

    D. ETSI

Answers to Review Questions

1. A. The most alluring feature of a wireless network is the freedom to move about while remaining connected to the network. Wired networks cannot offer this feature.

2. D. Generally speaking, computers that are rack-mounted together are servers, and servers should be connected to a high-speed, wired backbone. Wireless networks are meant for mobile access rather than server room connectivity.

3. A, B, D. Cabling a facility is a time-consuming and expensive task. Wireless networks can quickly and inexpensively be installed and configured.

4. C. Wireless Internet Service Providers (WISPs) provide last mile data delivery service to homes and businesses. In this fashion, they compete directly against wired ISPs such as telephone and cable companies.

5. B. The *access* layer of the industry standard design model is where users attach to the network. Wireless network devices are most generally installed in this capacity. There are times when wireless networks may be used in a distribution role, such as building-to-building bridging, but a very large percentage of wireless networks are used strictly for access.

6. A, B. In the setup and teardown of a mobile office, cabling is the most significant task. In a small office, many of the common problems of a wireless network are not experienced so time-consuming tasks such as site surveys are not required. Centralized connection points (called access points) are minimal so wiring is minimal.

7. C. The 802.11 family of standards specifically address wireless LANs. There are many flavors of standards addressing many types of wireless technologies and various topics related to wireless technologies. For example, 802.11, 802.11b, 802.11g, and 802.11a are all specifications of wireless LANs systems whereas 802.11f addresses inter-access point protocol and 802.11i addresses wireless LAN security. The 802.1x standard is for port-based network access control.

8. C. Since using a single antenna would likely have severe problems with coverage and many point-to-point bridge links (forming a partial or full mesh) would be highly expensive, the only logical alternative is to use point-to-multipoint bridge connectivity between buildings. This is an economically sound and highly effective solution.

9. C, D. Wireless Internet Service Providers (WISPs) face problems with line of sight limitations of 2.4 GHz and 5 GHz wireless LAN systems. Antennas must be installed on rooftops or higher if possible in most cases. Trees and hills both pose problems to WISPs for the same reason.

10. D. During WWII, actress Hedy Lamarr and composer George Antheil co-invented the frequency hopping communications technique. The U.S. military began using frequency hopping spread spectrum communications in 1957 well before the broad commercial use that spread spectrum systems enjoy today.

11. A. The first wireless LAN standard was the 802.11 standard using the 2.4 GHz ISM band, approved in 1997. Following 802.11 was 802.11b raising the top speed to 11 Mbps and limiting use to DSSS technology only. Following 802.11b was 802.11a, which uses the 5 GHz UNII bands. The 802.11g standard is in draft form, and has not yet been completed.

12. C. Wi-Fi is the hardware compatibility standard created and maintained by the Wi-Fi Alliance for 802.11b devices. IEEE 802.11g devices use the 2.4 GHz ISM band are backwards compatible with 802.11b. 802.11a devices use a different set of frequencies and a different modulation type from 802.11b, and are thus incompatible.

13. E. The IEEE 802.11, 802.11b, 802.11g, Bluetooth, and HomeRF all use the 2.4 GHz ISM bands, whereas the 802.11a standard uses the 5 GHz UNII bands.

14. A. WISPs are direct competitors for telephone companies and cable companies in providing last mile connectivity to businesses and residences in the broadband Internet services market.

15. C. The Federal Communications Commission (FCC) makes the laws regarding frequency band usage (licensed and unlicensed) in the United States. The IEEE makes standards regarding wireless LANs, which use RF frequencies. The Wi-Fi Alliance makes the hardware compatibility standard called Wi-Fi, and ETSI publishes communications standards for Europe.

Radio Frequency (RF) Fundamentals

CWNA Exam Objectives Covered:

❖ Define and apply the basic concepts of RF behavior:

- Gain
- Loss
- Reflection
- Refraction
- Diffraction
- Scattering
- Absorption
- VSWR
- Amplification & attenuation

❖ Identify and understand application of basic RF antenna concepts:

- Visual LOS
- RF LOS
- The Fresnel Zone
- Intentional Radiator
- EIRP
- Wave propagation

❖ Understand and apply the basic components of RF mathematics:

- Watt
- Milliwatt
- Decibel (dB)
- dBm
- dBi

In order to understand the wireless aspects of a wireless LAN, an administrator must have a solid foundation in the fundamentals of radio frequency (RF) theory. In this chapter we will discuss the properties of RF radiation and how its behavior in certain situations can affect the performance of a wireless LAN. Antennas will be introduced to create a good understanding of their uses and properties. We will discuss the mathematical relationships that exist in RF circuits and why they are important, as well as how to perform the necessary RF math calculations.

To a wireless LAN administrator, an understanding of RF concepts is essential to the implementation, expansion, maintenance, and troubleshooting of the wireless network.

Radio Frequency

Radio frequencies are high frequency alternating current (AC) signals that are passed along a copper conductor and then radiated into the air via an antenna. An antenna converts/transforms a wired signal to a wireless signal and vice versa. When the high frequency AC signal is radiated into the air, it forms radio waves. These radio waves propagate (move) away from the source (the antenna) in a straight line in all directions at once.

If you can imagine dropping a rock into a still pond (Figure 2.1) and watching the concentric ripples flow away from the point where the rock hit the water, then you have an idea of how RF behaves as it is propagated from an antenna. Understanding the behavior of these propagated RF waves is an important part of understanding why and how wireless LANs function. Without this base of knowledge, an administrator would be unable to locate proper installation locations of equipment and would not understand how to troubleshoot a problematic wireless LAN.

FIGURE 2.1   Rock into a pond

RF Behaviors

RF is sometimes referred to as "smoke and mirrors" because RF seems to act erratically and inconsistently under given circumstances. Things as small as a connector not being tight enough or a slight impedance mismatch on the line can cause erratic behavior and undesirable results. The following sections describe these types of behaviors and what can happen to radio waves as they are transmitted.

Gain

Gain, illustrated in Figure 2.2, is the term used to describe an increase in an RF signal's amplitude. Gain is usually an active process; meaning that an external power source, such as an RF amplifier, is used to amplify the signal or a high-gain antenna is used to focus the beamwidth of a signal to increase its signal amplitude.

FIGURE 2.2 Power Gain

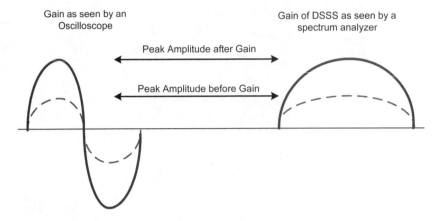

However, passive processes can also cause gain. For example, reflected RF signals can combine with the main signal to increase the main signal's strength. Increasing the RF signal's strength may have a positive or a negative result. Typically, more power is better, but there are cases, such as when a transmitter is radiating power very close to the legal power output limit, where added power would be a serious problem.

Loss

Loss describes a decrease in signal strength (Figure 2.3). Many things can cause RF signal loss, both while the signal is still in the cable as a high frequency AC electrical signal and when the signal is propagated as radio waves through the air by the antenna. Resistance of cables and connectors causes loss due to the converting of the AC signal to heat. Impedance mismatches in the cables and connectors can cause power to be reflected back toward the source, which can cause signal degradation. Objects directly in the propagated wave's transmission path can absorb, reflect, or destroy RF signals. Loss can be intentionally injected into a circuit with an RF attenuator. RF attenuators are accurate resistors that convert high frequency AC to heat in order to reduce signal amplitude at that point in the circuit.

FIGURE 2.3   Power Loss

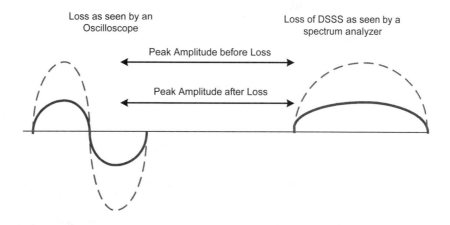

There are many things that can affect an RF signal between the transmitter and receiver. In order for gains or losses to be relevant to the implementation of wireless LANs, they must be quantifiable. The section in this chapter about RF mathematics will discuss quantifiable loss and gain and how to calculate and compensate for them.

Being able to measure and compensate for loss in an RF connection or circuit is important because radios have a receive sensitivity threshold. A sensitivity threshold is defined as the point at which a radio can clearly distinguish a signal from background noise. Since a receiver's sensitivity is finite, the transmitting station must transmit a signal with enough amplitude to be recognizable at the receiver. If losses occur between the transmitter and receiver, the problem must be corrected either by removing the objects causing loss or by increasing the transmission power.

Reflection

Reflection, as illustrated in Figure 2.4, occurs when a propagating electromagnetic wave impinges upon an object that has very large dimensions when compared to the wavelength of the propagating wave. Reflections occur from the surface of the earth, buildings, walls, and many other obstacles. If the surface is smooth, the reflected signal may remain intact, though there is some loss due to absorption and scattering of the signal.

FIGURE 2.4   Reflection

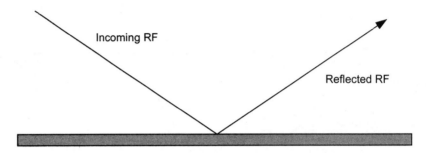

RF signal reflection can cause serious problems for wireless LANs. This reflecting of the main signal from many objects in the area of the transmission is referred to as *multipath*. Multipath can have severe adverse affects on a wireless LAN, such as degrading or canceling the main signal and causing holes or gaps in the RF coverage area. Surfaces such as lakes, metal roofs, metal blinds, metal doors, and others can cause severe reflection, and hence, multipath.

Reflection of this magnitude is never desirable and typically requires special functionality (antenna diversity) within the wireless LAN hardware to compensate for it. Both multipath and antenna diversity are discussed further in Chapter 9 (Troubleshooting).

Refraction

Refraction describes the bending of a radio wave as it passes through a medium of different density. As an RF wave passes into a denser medium (like a pool of cold air lying in a valley) the wave will be bent such that its direction changes. When passing through such a medium, some of the wave will be reflected away from the intended signal path, and some will be bent through the medium in another direction, as illustrated in Figure 2.5.

FIGURE 2.5   Refraction

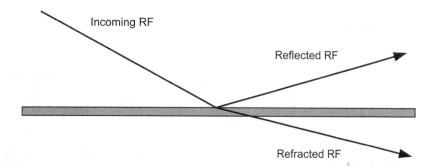

Refraction can become a problem for long distance RF links. As atmospheric conditions change, the RF waves may change direction, diverting the signal away from the intended target.

Diffraction

Diffraction occurs when the radio path between the transmitter and receiver is obstructed by a surface that has sharp irregularities or an otherwise rough surface. At high frequencies, diffraction, like reflection, depends on the geometry of the obstructing object and the amplitude, phase, and polarization of the incident wave at the point of diffraction.

Diffraction is commonly confused with and improperly used interchangeably with *refraction*. Care should be taken not to confuse these terms. Diffraction describes a wave bending around an obstacle (Figure 2.6), whereas refraction describes a wave bending through a medium. Taking the rock in the pond example from above, now consider a small twig sticking up through the surface of the water near where the rock hit the water. As the ripples hit the stick, they would be blocked to a small degree, but to a larger degree, the ripples would bend around the twig. This illustration shows how diffraction acts with obstacles in its path, depending on the makeup of the obstacle. If the object was large or jagged enough, the wave might not bend, but rather might be blocked.

FIGURE 2.6 Diffraction

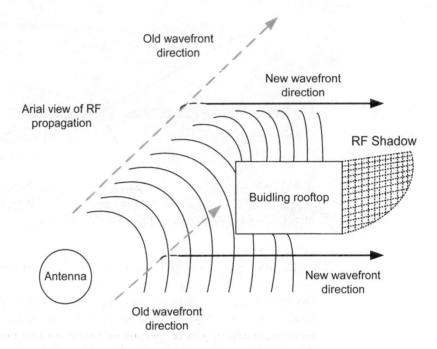

Diffraction is the slowing of the wave front at the point where the wave front strikes an obstacle, while the rest of the wave front maintains the same speed of propagation. Diffraction is the effect of waves turning, or bending, around the obstacle. As another example, consider a machine blowing a steady stream of smoke. The smoke would flow straight until an obstacle entered its path. Introducing a large wooden block into the smoke stream would cause the smoke to curl around the corners of the block causing a noticeable degradation in the smoke's velocity at that point and a significant change in direction.

Scattering

Scattering occurs when the medium through which the wave travels consists of objects with dimensions that are small compared to the wavelength of the signal, and the number of obstacles per unit volume is large. Scattered waves are produced by rough surfaces, small objects, or by other irregularities in the signal path, as can be seen in Figure 2.7.

FIGURE 2.7   Scattering

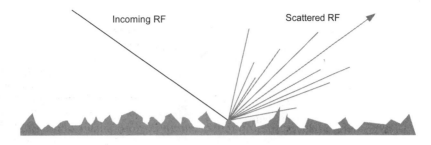

Some outdoor examples of objects that can cause scattering in a mobile communications system include foliage, street signs, and lampposts. Scattering can take place in two primary ways.

First, scattering can occur when a wave strikes an uneven surface and is reflected in many directions simultaneously. Scattering of this type yields many small amplitude reflections and destroys the main RF signal. Dissipation of an RF signal may occur when an RF wave is reflected off sand, rocks, or other jagged surfaces. When scattered in this manner, RF signal degradation can be significant to the point of intermittently disrupting communications or causing complete signal loss.

Second, scattering can occur as a signal wave travels through particles in the medium such as heavy dust content. In this case, rather than being reflected off an uneven surface, the RF waves are individually reflected on a very small scale off tiny particles.

Absorption

Absorption occurs when the RF signal strikes an object and is absorbed into the material of the object in such a manner that it does not pass through, reflect off, or bend around the object, as shown in Figure 2.8.

FIGURE 2.8 Absorption

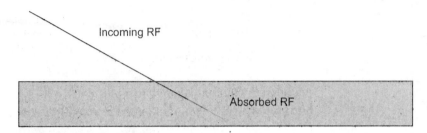

Voltage Standing Wave Ratio (VSWR)

VSWR occurs when there is mismatched *impedance* (resistance to current flow, measured in Ohms) between devices in an RF system. "Mismatched", in this context, means that one piece of equipment has a greater or lesser impedance than the piece of equipment to which it is connected. VSWR is caused by an RF signal reflected at a point of impedance mismatch in the signal path. VSWR causes *return loss*, which is defined as the loss of forward energy through a system due to some of the power being reflected back towards the transmitter. If the impedances of the ends of a connection do not match, then the maximum amount of the transmitted power will not be received at the antenna. When part of the RF signal is reflected back toward the transmitter, the signal level on the line varies instead of being steady. This variance is an indicator of VSWR.

As an illustration of VSWR, imagine water flowing through two garden hoses. As long as the two hoses are the same diameter, water flows through them seamlessly. If the hose connected to the faucet were significantly larger than the next hose down the line, there would be backpressure on the faucet and even at the connection between the two hoses. This standing backpressure illustrates VSWR, as can be seen in Figure 2.9. In this example, you can see that backpressure can have negative effects and not nearly as much water is transferred to the second hose as there would have been with matching hoses screwed together properly.

FIGURE 2.9   VSWR - like water through a hose

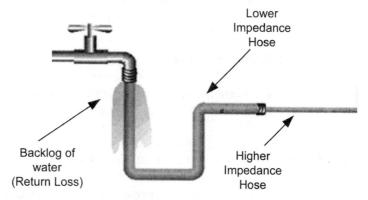

VSWR Measurements

VSWR is a ratio, so it is expressed as a relationship between two numbers. A typical VSWR value would be 1.5:1. The two numbers relate the ratio of impedance mismatch against a perfect impedance match. The second number is always 1, representing the perfect match, where as the first number varies. The lower the first number (closer to 1), the better impedance matching your system has. For example, a VSWR of 1.1:1 is better than 1.4:1. A VSWR measurement of 1:1 would denote a perfect impedance match and no voltage standing wave would be present in the signal path.

Effects of VSWR

Excessive VSWR can cause serious problems in an RF circuit. Most of the time, the result is a marked decrease in the amplitude of the transmitted RF signal. However, since some transmitters are not protected against power being applied (or returned) to the transmitter output circuit, the reflected power can burn out the electronics of the transmitter. VSWR's effects are evident when transmitter circuits burn out, power output levels are unstable, and the power observed is significantly different from the expected power. The methods of changing VSWR in a circuit include proper use of proper equipment. Tight connections between cables and connectors, use of impedance matched hardware throughout, and use of high-quality equipment with calibration reports where necessary are all good preventative measures against VSWR. VSWR can be measured with high-accuracy instrumentation such as SWR meters, but this measurement is beyond the scope of this text and the job tasks of a network administrator.

Solutions to VSWR

To prevent the negative effects of VSWR, it is imperative that all cables, connectors, and devices have impedances that match as closely as possible to each other. Never use 75-Ohm cable with 50-Ohm devices, for example. Most of today's wireless LAN devices have an impedance of 50 Ohms, but it is still recommended that you check each device before implementation, just to be sure. Every device from the transmitter to the antenna must have impedances matching as closely as possible, including cables, connectors, antennas, amplifiers, attenuators, the transmitter output circuit, and the receiver input circuit.

Principles of Antennas

It is not our intention to teach antenna theory in this book, but rather to explain some very basic antenna principals that directly relate to use of wireless LANs. It is not necessary for a wireless LAN administrator to thoroughly understand antenna design in order to administer the network. A couple of key points that are important to understand about antennas are:

- Antennas convert electrical energy into RF waves in the case of a transmitting antenna, or RF waves into electrical energy in the case of a receiving antenna.

- The physical dimensions of an antenna, such as its length, are directly related to the frequency at which the antenna can propagate waves or receive propagated waves.

Some essential points of understanding in administering license-free wireless LANs are line of sight, the effects of the Fresnel (pronounced "fra-NEL") Zone, and antenna gain through focused beamwidths. These points will be discussed in this section.

Line of Sight (LOS)

With visible light, visual LOS (also called simply 'LOS') is defined as the apparently straight line from the object in sight (the transmitter) to the observer's eye (the receiver). The LOS is an *apparently* straight line because light waves are subject to changes in direction due to refraction, diffraction, and reflection in the same way as RF frequencies. Figure 2.10 illustrates LOS. RF works very much the same way as visible light within wireless LAN frequencies with one major exception: RF LOS can also be affected by blockage of the Fresnel Zone.

FIGURE 2.10   Line of Sight

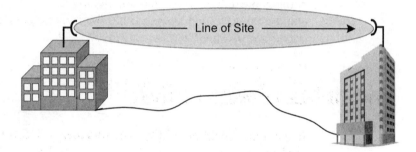

Imagine that you are looking through a two-foot long piece of pipe. Imagine further that an obstruction were blocking part of the inside of the pipe. Obviously, this obstruction would block your view of the objects at the other end of the pipe. This simple illustration shows how RF works when objects block the Fresnel Zone, except that, with the pipe scenario, you can still see the other end to some degree. With RF, that same limited ability to see translates into a broken or corrupted connection. RF LOS is important because RF doesn't behave in exactly the same manner as visible light.

Fresnel Zone

A consideration when planning or troubleshooting an RF link is the Fresnel Zone. The Fresnel Zone occupies a series of concentric ellipsoid-shaped areas around the LOS path, as can be seen in Figure 2.11. The Fresnel Zone is important to the integrity of the RF link because it defines an area around the LOS that can introduce RF signal interference if blocked. Objects in the Fresnel Zone such as trees, hilltops, and buildings can diffract or reflect the main signal away from the receiver, changing the RF LOS. These same objects can absorb or scatter the main RF signal, causing degradation or complete signal loss.

FIGURE 2.11 Fresnel Zone

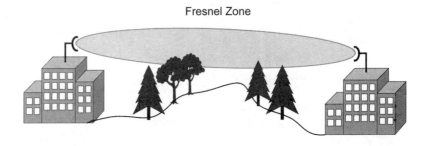

Fresnel Zone

The radius of the Fresnel Zone at its widest point can be calculated by the following formula,

$$r = 43.3 \times \sqrt{\tfrac{d}{4f}}$$

where d is the link distance in miles, f is the frequency in GHz, and the answer, r, is in feet. For example, suppose there is a 2.4000 GHz link 5 miles (8.35 km) in length. The resulting Fresnel Zone would have a radius of 31.25 feet (9.52 meters).

Fresnel Zone calculations are not part of the CWNA exam. The formula is provided to you for your administrative tasks.

Obstructions

Considering the importance of Fresnel Zone clearance, it is also important to quantify the degree to which the Fresnel Zone can be blocked. Since an RF signal, when partially blocked, will bend around the obstacle to some degree, some blockage of the Fresnel Zone can occur without significant link disruption. Typically, 20% - 40% Fresnel Zone blockage introduces little to no interference into the link. It is always suggested to err to the conservative side allowing no more than 20% blockage of the Fresnel Zone. Obviously, if trees or other growing objects are the source of the blockage, you might want to consider designing the link based on 0% blockage.

If the Fresnel Zone of a proposed RF link is more than 20% blocked, or if an active link becomes blocked by new construction or tree growth, raising the height of the antennas will usually alleviate the problem.

A question commonly asked about the Fresnel Zone when using indoor wireless LAN equipment such as PC cards and access points is how blockage of the Fresnel Zone affects indoor installations. In most indoor installations, RF signals pass through, reflect off, and refract around walls, furniture, and other obstructions. The Fresnel Zone is not encroached upon unless the signal is partially or fully blocked. This is sometimes the case, but is rarely noticed due to most wireless users being mobile. In a mobile environment, the Fresnel Zone is constantly changing so the user normally dismisses it thinking that the coverage is simply "bad" where they are located - giving no thought to why the coverage is bad.

Antenna Gain

An antenna element – without the amplifiers and filters typically associated with it – is a passive device. There is no conditioning, amplifying, or manipulating of the signal by the antenna element itself. The antenna can create the effect of amplification by virtue of its physical shape. Antenna amplification is the result of focusing the RF radiation into a tighter beam, just as the bulb of a flashlight can be focused into a tighter beam creating a seemingly brighter light source that sends the light further. The focusing of the radiation is measured by way of beamwidths, which are measured in degrees horizontal and vertical. For example, an omni-directional antenna has a 360-degree horizontal beamwidth. By limiting the 360-degree beamwidth into a more focused beam of, say, 30 degrees, at the same power, the RF waves will be radiated further. This is how patch, panel, and Yagi antennas (all of which are semi-directional antennas) are designed. Highly directional antennas take this theory a step further by very tightly focusing both horizontal and vertical beamwidths to maximize distance of the propagated wave at low power.

Intentional Radiator

As defined by the Federal Communication Commission (FCC), an intentional radiator is an RF device that is specifically designed to generate and radiate RF signals. In terms of hardware, an intentional radiator will include the RF device and all cabling and connectors up to, but not including, the antenna, as illustrated in Figure 2.12 below.

FIGURE 2.12 Intentional Radiator

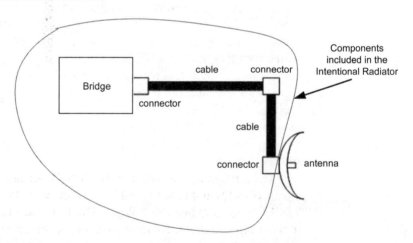

Any reference to "power output of the Intentional Radiator" refers to the power output at the end of the last cable or connector before the antenna. For example, consider a 30-milliwatt transmitter that loses 15 milliwatts of power in the cable and another 5 milliwatts from the connector at the antenna. The power at the intentional radiator would be 10 milliwatts. As an administrator, it is your responsibility to understand the FCC rules relating to Intentional Radiators and their power output. Understanding how power output is measured, how much power is allowed, and how to calculate these values are all covered in this book. FCC regulations concerning output power at the Intentional Radiator and EIRP are found in Part 47 CFR, Chapter 1, Section 15.247 dated October 1, 2000.

Equivalent Isotropically Radiated Power (EIRP)

EIRP is the power actually radiated by the antenna element, as shown in Figure 2.13. This concept is important because it is regulated by the FCC and because it is used in calculating whether or not a wireless link is viable. EIRP takes into account the gain of the antenna.

FIGURE 2.13   EIRP

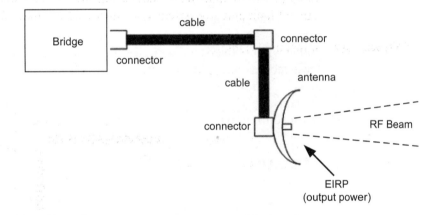

Suppose a transmitting station uses a 10-dBi antenna (which amplifies the signal 10-fold) and is fed by 100 milliwatts from the intentional radiator. The EIRP is 1000 mW, or 1 Watt. The FCC has rules defining both the power output at the intentional radiator and the antenna element.

 Failure to comply with FCC rules regarding power output can subject the administrator or the organization (or both) to legal action and fines.

Radio Frequency Mathematics

There are four important areas of power calculation in a wireless LAN. These areas are:

- Power at the transmitting device

- Loss and gain of connectivity devices between the transmitting device and the antenna - such as cables, connectors, amplifiers, attenuators, and splitters   *Transmission line.*

- Power at the last connector before the RF signal enters the antenna (Intentional Radiator)

- Power at the antenna element (EIRP)

These areas will be discussed in calculation examples in forthcoming sections.   Each of these areas will help to determine whether RF links are viable without overstepping power limitations set by the FCC.   Each of these factors must be taken into account when planning a wireless LAN, and all of these factors are related mathematically.   The following section explains the units of measurement that are used to calculate power output when configuring wireless LAN devices.

Units of Measure

There are a few standard units of measure that a wireless network administrator should become familiar with in order to be effective in implementing and troubleshooting wireless LANs. We will discuss them all in detail, giving examples of their usage. We will then put them to use in some sample math problems so that you have a solid grasp of what is required as part of the CWNA's job tasks.

Watts (W)

The basic unit of power is a watt. A watt is defined as one ampere (A) of current at one volt (V). As an example of what these units mean, think of a garden hose that has water flowing through it. The pressure on the water line would represent the voltage in an electrical circuit. The water flow would represent the amperes (current) flowing through the garden hose. Think of a watt as the result of a given amount of pressure and a given amount of water in the garden hose. One watt is equal to an Ampere multiplied times a Volt.

A typical 120-volt plug-in night-light is about 7 watts. On a clear night this 7 W light may be seen 50 miles (83 km) away in all directions, and, if we could somehow encode information, such as with Morse code, we would have a wireless link established. Remember, we are only interested in sending and receiving data, not illuminating the receiver with RF energy as we would illuminate a room with light. You can see that relatively little power is required to form an RF link of great distance. The FCC allows only 4 watts of power to be radiated from an antenna in a point-to-multipoint wireless LAN connection using unlicensed 2.4 GHz spread spectrum equipment. Four watts might not seem like much power, but it is enough to send a clear RF data signal for miles.

Milliwatt

When implementing wireless LANs, power levels as low as 1 milliwatt (1/1000 watt, abbreviated as "mW") can be used for a small area, and power levels on a single wireless LAN segment are rarely above 100 mW - enough to communicate up to a half mile (0.83 km) in optimum conditions. Access points generally have the ability to radiate 30-100 mW of power, depending on the manufacturer. It is only in the case of point-to-point outdoor connections between buildings that power levels above 100 mW would be used. Most of the power levels referred to by administrators will be in mW or dBm. These two units of measurement both represent an absolute amount of power and are both industry standard measurements.

Decibels

When a receiver is very sensitive to RF signals, it may be able to pick up signals as small as 0.000000001 Watts. Other than its obvious numerical meaning, this tiny number has little intuitive meaning to the layperson and will likely be ignored or misread. Decibels allow us to represent these numbers by making them more manageable and understandable. Decibels are based on a logarithmic relationship to the previously explained linear measurement of power: watts. Concerning RF, a logarithm is the exponent to which the number 10 must be raised to reach some given value.

If we are given the number 1000 and asked to find the logarithm (log), we find that log 1000 = 3 because $10^3 = 1000$. Notice that our logarithm, 3, is the exponent. An important thing to note about logarithms is that the logarithm of a negative number or of zero does not exist.

Log (-100) = undefined!

Log (0) = undefined!

On the linear watt scale we can plot points of absolute power. Absolute power measurement refers to the measurement of power in relation to some fixed reference. On most linear scales (watts, degrees Kelvin, miles per hour), the reference is fixed at zero, which usually describes the absence of the thing measured: zero watts = no power, zero degrees Kelvin = no thermal energy, zero MPH = no movement. On a logarithmic scale, the reference cannot be zero because the log of zero does not exist. Decibels are a relative measurement unit unlike the absolute measurement of milliwatts.

Gain and Loss Measurements

Power gain and loss are measured in decibels, not in watts, because gain and loss are relative concepts and a decibel is a relative measurement. Gain or loss in an RF system may be referred to by absolute power measurement (e.g. ten watts of power) or by a relative power measurement (e.g. half of its power). Losing half of the power in a system corresponds to losing 3 decibels. If a system loses half of its power (-3 dB), then loses half again (another -3 dB), then the total system loss is 3/4 of the original power - ½ first, then ¼ (½ of ½). Clearly, no absolute measurement of watts can quantify this asymmetrical loss in a meaningful way, but decibels do just that.

As a quick and easy reference, there are some numbers related to gain and loss that an administrator should be familiar with. These numbers are:

-3 dB = half the power in mW

+3 dB = double the power in mW
-10 dB = one tenth the power in mW
+10 dB = ten times the power in mW

We refer to these quick references as the 10's and 3's of RF math. When calculating power gain and loss, one can almost always divide an amount of gain or loss by 10 or 3 or both. These values give the administrator the ability to quickly and easily calculate RF loss and gain with a fair amount of accuracy without the use of a calculator. In the case where use of this method is not possible, there are conversion formulas, shown below, that can be used for these calculations.

The following is the general equation for converting mW to dBm:

$$P_{dbm} = 10\log_{PmW}$$

This equation can be manipulated to reverse the conversion, now converting dBm to mW:

$$Pmw = \log^{-1}\left(\frac{P_{dbm}}{10}\right)$$

*Note: $\log^{-1}$ denotes the inverse logarithm (inverse log)

You will not be tested on logarithmic functions using these formulas as part of the CWNA exam. These formulas are provided only for your reference in case they are needed during your administrative tasks. Calculators are not needed on the CWNA exam.

Another important point is that gains and losses are additive. If an access point were connected to a cable whose loss was -2 dB and then a connector whose loss was -1 dB, then these loss measurements would be additive and yield a total of -3 dB of loss. We will walk through some RF calculations in the coming sections to give you a better idea of how to relate these numbers to actual scenarios.

dBm

The reference point that relates the logarithmic dB scale to the linear watt scale is:

1 mW = 0 dBm

The *m* in dBm refers simply to the fact that the reference is 1 milliwatt (1 mW) and therefore a dBm measurement is a measurement of absolute power.

The relationship between the decibels scale and the watt scale can be estimated using the following rules of thumb:

+3 dB will double the watt value:

   (10 mW + 3dB ≈ 20 mW)

Likewise, -3 dB will halve the watt value:

   (100 mW - 3dB ≈ 50 mW)

+10 dB will increase the watt value by ten-fold:

   (10 mW + 10dB ≈ 100 mW)

Conversely, -10 dB will decrease the watt value to one tenth of that value:

   (300 mW - 10dB ≈ 30 mW)

These rules will allow a quick calculation of milliwatt power levels when given power levels, gains, and losses in dBm and dB. Figure 2.14 shows that the reference point is always the same, but power levels can move in either direction from the reference point depending on whether they represent a power gain or loss.

FIGURE 2.14 Power level chart

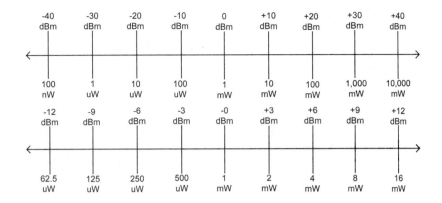

In the top chart of Figure 2.14, gains and losses of 10 dB are shown at each increment. Notice that a gain of +10 dB from the reference point of 1 mW moves the power to +10 dBm (10 mW). Conversely, notice that a loss of -10 dB moves the power to -10 dBm (100 microwatts). On the bottom chart, the same principal applies. These charts both represent the same thing, except that one is incremented in gains and losses of 3 dB and the other for gains and losses of 10 dB. They have been separated into two charts for ease of viewing. Using these charts, one can easily convert dBm and mW power levels.

Examples

+43 dBm divided into 10's and 3's would equal +10 +10 +10 +10 +3. From the reference point, the charts show you that you would multiply the milliwatt value (starting at the reference point) times a factor of 10 four times then times a factor of 2 one time yielding the following:

    1 mW x **10** = 10 mW
    10 mW x **10** = 100 mW
    100 mW x **10** = 1,000 mW
    1,000 mW x **10** = 10,000 mW
    10,000 mW x **2** = 20,000 mW = 20 watts

So, we now see that +43 dBm equals 20 watts of power. Another example that takes into consideration measurement negative from the reference point would be -26 dBm.

In this example, we see that -26 dBm equals -10 -10 -3 -3. From the reference point, the charts show you that you would divide the milliwatt value (starting at the reference point) by a factor of 10 twice and by a factor of 2 twice yielding the following:

1 mW / **10** = 100 uW
100 uW / **10** = 10 uW
10 uW / **2** = 5 uW
5 uW / **2** = 2.5 uW

So, we now see that -26 dBm equals 2.5 microwatts of power.

dBi

As discussed previously, gain and loss are measured in decibels. When quantifying the gain of an antenna, the decibel units are represented by dBi. The unit of measurement dBi refers only to the gain of an antenna. The "i" stands for "isotropic", which means that the change in power is referenced against an isotropic radiator. An isotropic radiator is a theoretical ideal transmitter that produces useful electromagnetic field output in all directions with equal intensity, and at 100-percent efficiency, in three-dimensional space. One example of an isotropic radiator is the sun. Think of dBi as being referenced against perfection. The dBi measurement is used in RF calculations in the same manner as dB. Units of dBi are relative.

Consider a 10 dBi antenna with 1 watt of power applied. What is the EIRP (output power at the antenna element)?

1 W + 10 dBi (a ten-fold increase) = 10 W

This calculation works in the same fashion as showing gain measured in dB. A gain of 10 dBi multiplies the input power of the antenna by a factor of ten. Antennas, unless they are malfunctioning, do not degrade the signal, so the dBi value is always positive. Like dB, dBi is a relative unit of measure and can be added to or subtracted from other decibel units. For example, if an RF signal is reduced by 3 dB as it runs through a copper cable, then is transmitted by an antenna with a gain of 5 dBi, the result is an overall gain of +2 dB.

Example

Given the RF circuit in Figure 2.15, determine the power at all marked points in milliwatts.

FIGURE 2.15   Sample wireless LAN configuration

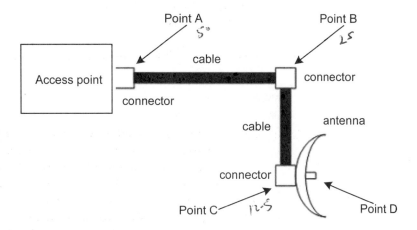

Access Point	Point A	Point B	Point C	Point D
100 mW	-3 dB	-3 dB	-3 dB	+12 dBi
= 100 mW	÷2	÷2	÷2	(x2 x2 x2x2)
= 100 mW	÷2	÷2	÷2	x16
= 50 mW		÷2	÷2	x16
= 25 mW			÷2	x16
= 12.5 mW				x16
= 200 mW				

You may from time to time encounter the unit *dBd*. dBd is defined as decibels referenced to a dipole antenna vice an isotropic antenna. Remember that dBi refers to an isotropic antenna. 0dBd = 2.14dBi.

Accurate Measurements

Although these techniques are helpful and expedient in some situations, there are times when rounded or even numbers may not be available. In these times, using the formula is the best method of doing RF calculations. Since the decibel is a unit of relative power measurement, a change in power level is implied. If the power level is given in dBm, then change in dB is simple to calculate:

Initial power = 20 dBm
Final power = 33 dBm
Change in power, ΔP = 33 – 20 = +13 dB, the value is positive, indicating an increase in power.

If the power levels are given in milliwatts, the process can become more complicated:

Initial power = 130 mW
Final power = 5.2 W
Change in power,

$$\Delta P = 10\log\left(\frac{P_f}{P_i}\right)$$

$$= 10\log\left(\frac{5.2W}{130mW}\right)$$

$$= 10\log 40$$

$$= 10 * 1.6$$

$$= 16dB$$

You will not be tested on logarithmic functions using these formulas as part of the CWNA exam, but your understanding of power calculations using the 10's and 3's will be tested. These formulas are provided only for your reference in case they are needed during your administrative tasks. Calculators are not needed on the CWNA exam.

Key Terms

Before taking the exam, you should be familiar with the following terms:

antenna

impedance

Line of sight

logarithm

Review Questions

1. When visual line of sight (LOS) is present, RF LOS will always be present.

    A. This statement is true

    B. This statement is false

    C. It depends on the configuration of the antennas

2. When RF LOS is present, visual LOS will always be present.

    A. This statement is true

    B. This statement is false

    C. It depends on the specific factors

3. What unit of measurement is used to quantify the power gain or loss of an RF signal? Choose all that apply.

    A. dBi

    B. dBm

    C. Watts

    D. dB

4. Using which of the following will reduce VSWR? Choose all that apply.

    A. Cables and connectors that all have an impedance of 50 Ohms

    B. Cables with a 50 Ohm impedance and connectors with 75 Ohm impedance

    C. Cables and connectors that all have an impedance of 75 Ohms

    D. Cables with 75 Ohm impedance and connectors with 50 Ohm impedance

5. In an RF circuit, what is the intentional radiator defined as?

   A. The output of the transmitting device

   B. The output of the last connector before the signal enters the antenna

   C. The output as measured after the antenna

   D. The output after the first length of cable attached to the transmitting device

6. *dBi* is a relative measurement of decibels to which one of the following?

   A. Internet

   B. Intentional radiator

   C. Isotropic radiator

   D. Isotropic radio

7. Which one of the following is considered impedance in an RF circuit?

   A. The inability to transmit RF signals

   B. The pressure that causes current flow

   C. Resistance to current flow, measured in Ohms

   D. The frequency on which an RF transmitter sends signals

8. In RF mathematics, 1 watt equals what measurement of dBm?

   A. 1

   B. 3

   C. 10

   D. 30

   E. 100

9. Which one of the following RF behaviors is defined as "the bending of a wave as it passes through a medium of different density"?

    A. Diffraction

    B. Reflection

    C. Refraction

    D. Distraction

10. A year ago, while working for your current organization, you installed a wireless link between two buildings. Recently you have received reports that the throughput of the link has decreased. After investigating the connection problems, you discover there is a tree within the Fresnel Zone of the link that is causing 25% blockage of the connection. Which of the following statements are true? Choose all that apply.

    A. The tree cannot be the problem, because only 25% of the connection is blocked

    B. The tree might be the problem, because up to 40% of the Fresnel Zone can be blocked without causing problems

    C. If the tree is the problem, raising the heights of both antennas will fix the problem

    D. If the tree is the problem, increasing the power at the transmitters at each end of the link will fix the problem

11. Given an access point with 100 mW of output power connected through a 50-foot cable with 3 dB of loss to an antenna with 10 dBi of gain, what is the EIRP at the antenna in mW?

    A. 100 mW

    B. 250 mW

    C. 500 mW

    D. 1 W

12. Given a wireless bridge with 200 mW of output power connected through a 100 foot cable with 6 dB of loss to an antenna with 9 dBi of gain, what is the EIRP at the antenna in dBm?

   A. 20 dBm

   B. 26 dBm

   C. 30 dBm

   D. 36 dBm

13. Given an access point with an output power of 100 mW connected through a cable with a loss of 2 dB to antenna with a gain of 11 dBi, what is the EIRP in mW?

   A. 200 mW

   B. 400 mW

   C. 800 mW

   D. 1 W

14. Given an access point with an output power of 20 dBm connected through a cable with a loss of 6 dB to an amplifier with a 10 dB gain, then through a cable with 3 dB of loss to an antenna with 6 dBi of gain, what is the EIRP in dBm?

   A. 18 dBm

   B. 23 dBm

   C. 25 dBm

   D. 27 dBm

15. What is the net gain or loss of a circuit if it is using two cables with 3 dB loss each, one amplifier with a 12 dB gain, 1 antenna with 9 dBi gain, and an attenuator with a loss of 5 dB?

    A. 5 dB

    B. 10 dB

    C. 15 dB

    D. 20 dB

16. Which of the following is a cause of VSWR?

    A. Mismatched impedances between wireless LAN connectors

    B. Too much power being radiated from the antenna element

    C. The incorrect type of antenna used to transmit a signal

    D. Use of the incorrect RF frequency band

17. Radio waves propagate (move) away from the source (the antenna) in what manner?

    A. In a straight line in all directions at once within the vertical and horizontal beamwidths

    B. In circles spiraling away from the antenna

    C. In spherical, concentric circles within the horizontal beamwidth

    D. Up and down across the area of coverage

18. Why is the Fresnel Zone important to the integrity of the RF link?

    A. The Fresnel Zone defines the area of coverage in a typical RF coverage cell

    B. The Fresnel Zone must always be 100% clear of any and all blockage for a wireless LAN to operate properly

    C. The Fresnel Zone defines an area around the LOS that can introduce RF signal interference if blocked

    D. The Fresnel Zone does not change with the length of the RF link

19. The FCC allows how many watts of power to be radiated from an antenna in a point-to-multipoint wireless LAN connection using unlicensed 2.4 GHz spread spectrum equipment?

    A. 1 watt

    B. 2 watts

    C. 3 watts

    D. 4 watts

20. In regards to gain and loss measurements in wireless LANs, the statement that gains and losses are additive is:

    A. Always true

    B. Always false

    C. Sometimes true

    D. Sometimes false

    E. It depends on the equipment manufacturer

Answers to Review Questions

1.   B. In order to have RF LOS, the Fresnel Zone must be clear. Having a clear visual line of sight between two points does not necessarily mean that your Fresnel Zone is clear. The radius of the Fresnel Zone can be calculated with a simple formula.

2.   C. Due to weather, smog, or distance, the person configuring the RF link may not be able to see the other end, yet because there is nothing in the Fresnel Zone interfering with the RF signal, the link works fine.

3.   A, D. Power gain or loss is a change in power, not an absolute amount of power. For this reason, dB and dBi are correct because they are measurements of a change in power.

4.   A, C. It's important in keeping VSWR to a minimum that all devices in an RF system be impedance-matched. This means that all devices in the system must be 50 ohms, 75 ohms, or whatever impedance is being used, just so that all devices match.

5.   B. The FCC defines the Intentional Radiator as the input power to the antenna. This definition means that the power output of the transmitter, plus all cabling, connectors, splitters, amplifiers, and attenuators before the antenna is included as part of Intentional Radiator.

6.   C. There's no such thing as the perfect antenna, yet that's exactly what an isotropic radiator is. An isotropic radiator radiates power evenly in all directions (a spherical pattern). Omni-directional antennas have a doughnut-shaped coverage pattern that has gain relative to an isotropic radiator due to the squeezing of the RF field. All antennas are referenced against this imaginary antenna for quantifiable measurement.

7.   C. Impedance (measured in Ohms) is a resistance to current flow in any electrical circuit. RF signals are high-frequency alternating current (AC) and experience loss due to resistance while in a copper conductor such as cabling.

8.   D. The mathematical reference point most commonly used with wireless LANs is 0 dBm = 1 mW. Using the simple calculation of adding 30 dB, we can quickly see that 1 watt = 30 dBm.

9.   C. Refraction of RF waves works similarly to visible light bending as it passes from air into water. Be careful not to confuse refraction and diffraction.

10. B, C. Raising the antennas on each end will fix the problem, but what happens in another year when the tree has grown again? This is only a short-term fix. Turning up the power will not always solve the problem since the problem may be retransmissions due to packet errors instead of decreased signal amplitude. Trimming the tree as a test, and then cutting it down if it is the problem is the solution to this problem. The tree could be the problem because any encroachment into the Fresnel Zone can cause signal degradation. Typically, 20-40% blockage of the Fresnel Zone does not present a problem, but as previously stated any blockage of the Fresnel Zone should be avoided if at all possible. In this case, it's quite possible that only 25% blockage could be a serious problem as there may be other factors to consider that we are unaware of.

11. C. 100 mW with a 3 dB loss results in 50 mW of output power remaining because a 3 dB loss cuts the power in half. A gain of 10 dBi will multiply the remaining power of 50 mW by a factor of 10 yielding 500 mW of output power at the antenna element (referred to as EIRP).

12. B. Converting 200 mW to dBm, we see that we start out with 23 dBm. From this point, it's a simple addition/subtraction problem. 23 dBm - 6 dB + 9 dBi = 26 dBm.

13. C. Starting with 100 mW of output power, and not being able to use the 10's and 3's, we have a more complex math problem. A trick here is to first realize that gains and losses are additive so a 2 dB loss and an 11 dBi gain equals 9 dB of change. Luckily, 9 dB is divisible by 3, so we have 100 x 2 x 2 x 2 = 800 mW of output power at the antenna (EIRP).

14. D. This question is a simple addition/subtraction problem from start to finish. 20 dBm - 6 dB + 10 dB - 3 dB + 6 dBi = 27 dBm. It starts and ends with absolute amounts of power, but adds and subtracts changes in power along the way.

15. B. Instead of the usual question that begins and ends with an absolute amount of power (measured in mW or dBm), this question is testing your understanding of the additive nature of power change. -3 dB –3 dB +12 dB +9 dBi – 5dB yields a combined power change of +10 dB.

16. A. Having mismatched impedances between any two devices in a system can cause VSWR at that point of connection. This concept applies to cables, connectors, the output circuit of the transmitter, the input circuit of the receiver, the antenna, and any other device in the system.

17. A. The angles of the horizontal and vertical beamwidth determine exactly what direction the RF waves will propagate from the antenna. Waves propagate within these angles in all directions simultaneously.

18. C. The Fresnel Zone is an area around the direct path between the transmitter and the receiver that must be mostly clear (60-80%) in order to avoid RF signal interference. Trees, buildings, and many other objects tend to get into the Fresnel Zone of long-distance RF links. It's important to try to keep the Fresnel Zone as clear as possible. There is a simple formula for calculating the radius of the Fresnel Zone.

19. D. The FCC defines EIRP as the output from the antenna. EIRP in a point-to-multipoint configuration (which includes any configuration using an omni-directional antenna) is limited to 4 watts by the FCC.

20. A. Gains and losses in a wireless LAN system using like units (dB & dBi) are always additive. Sometimes this means adding in negative numbers (losses) and sometimes the numbers are positive (gain). As you've seen in some of the practice questions in this section, gain and loss can be calculated by adding all gains and losses in a system.

Spread Spectrum Technology

CWNA Exam Objectives Covered:

❖ Identify some of the different uses for spread spectrum technologies:

- Wireless LANs

- Wireless PANs

- Wireless WANs

❖ Comprehend the differences between, and apply the different types of spread spectrum technologies:

- FHSS

- DSSS

❖ Identify and apply the concepts which make up the functionality of spread spectrum technology:

- Co-location

- Channels

- Dwell time

- Throughput

- Hop time

In order to administer and troubleshoot wireless LANs effectively, a good understanding of spread spectrum technology and its implementation is required. In this section, we will cover what spread spectrum technology is and how it is used according to FCC guidelines. We will differentiate and compare the two main spread spectrum technologies and discuss, in depth, how spread spectrum technology is implemented in wireless LANs.

Introducing Spread Spectrum

Spread spectrum is a communications technique characterized by wide bandwidth and low peak power. Spread spectrum communication uses various modulation techniques in wireless LANs and possesses many advantages over its precursor, narrow band communication. Spread spectrum signals are noise-like, hard to detect, and even harder to intercept or demodulate without the proper equipment. Jamming and interference have a lesser affect on a spread spectrum communication than on narrow band communications. For these reasons, spread spectrum has long been a favorite of the military. In order to discuss what spread spectrum is we must first establish a reference by discussing the concept of narrowband transmission.

Narrow Band Transmission

A narrowband transmission is a communications technology that uses only enough of the frequency spectrum to carry the data signal, and no more. It has always been the FCC's mission to conserve frequency usage as much as possible, handing out only what is absolutely necessary to get the job done. Spread spectrum is in opposition to that mission since it uses much wider frequency bands than is necessary to transmit the information. This brings us to the first requirement for a signal to be considered spread spectrum. A signal is a spread spectrum signal when *the bandwidth is much wider than what is required to send the information.*

Figure 3.1 illustrates the difference between narrowband and spread spectrum transmissions. Notice that one of the characteristics of narrow band is high peak power. More power is required to send a transmission when using a smaller frequency range. In order for narrow band signals to be received, they must stand out above the general level of noise, called the *noise floor*, by a significant amount. Because its band is so narrow, a high peak power ensures error-free reception of a narrow band signal.

FIGURE 3.1   Narrow band vs. spread spectrum on a frequency domain

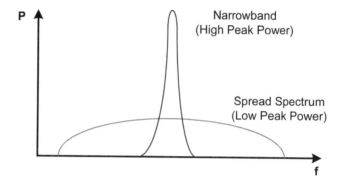

A compelling argument against narrowband transmission—other than the high peak power required to send it—is that narrow band signals can be jammed or experience interference very easily. Jamming is the intentional overpowering of a transmission using unwanted signals transmitted on the same band. Because its band is so narrow, other narrow band signals, including noise, can completely eliminate the information by overpowering a narrowband transmission, much like a passing train overpowers a quiet conversation.

Spread Spectrum Technology

Spread spectrum technology allows us to take the same amount of information that we previously would have sent using a narrow band carrier signal and spread it out over a much larger frequency range. For example, we may use 1 MHz at 10 Watts with narrow band, but 20 MHz at 100 mW with spread spectrum. By using a wider frequency spectrum, we reduce the probability that the data will be corrupted or jammed. A narrow band jamming attempt on a spread spectrum signal would likely be thwarted by virtue of only a small part of the information falling into the narrow band signal's frequency range. Most of the digital data would be received error-free. Today's spread spectrum RF radios can retransmit any small amount of data loss due to narrowband interference.

While the spread spectrum band is relatively wide, the peak power of the signal is quite low. This is the second requirement for a signal to be considered spread spectrum. For a signal to be considered spread spectrum, it must use low power. These two characteristics of spread spectrum (use of a wide band of frequencies and very low power) make it look to most receivers as if it were a noise signal. Noise is a wide band, low power signal, but the difference is that noise is unwanted. Furthermore, since most radio receivers will view the spread spectrum signal as noise, these receivers will not attempt to demodulate or interpret it, creating a slightly more secure communication.

Uses of Spread Spectrum

This inherent security is what interested the military in spread spectrum technology through the 1950s and 1960s. Because of its noise-like characteristics, spread spectrum signals could be sent under the noses of enemies using classic communication techniques. Security was all but guaranteed. Naturally, this perceived security of communication was only valid so long as no one else used the technology. If another group were to use the same technology, these spread spectrum communications could be discovered, if not intercepted and decoded.

In the 1980s, the FCC implemented a set of rules making spread spectrum technology available to the public and encouraging research and investigation into the commercialization of spread spectrum technology. Though at first glance it may seem that the military had lost its advantage, it had not. The bands used by the military are different from the bands used by the public. Also, the military uses very different modulation and encoding techniques to ensure that its spread spectrum communications are far more difficult to intercept than those of the general public.

Since the 1980s, when research began in earnest, spread spectrum technologies have been used in cordless phones, global positioning systems (GPS), digital cellular telephony (CDMA), personal communications system (PCS), and now wireless local area networks (wireless LANs). Amateur radio enthusiasts are now beginning to experiment with spread spectrum technologies for many of the reasons we've discussed.

In addition to wireless LANs (WLANs), wireless personal area networks (WPANs), wireless metropolitan area networks (WMANs), and wireless wide area networks (WWANs) are also taking advantage of spread spectrum technologies. WPANs use Bluetooth technology to take advantage of very low power requirements to allow wireless networking within a very short range. WWANs and WMANs can use highly directional, high gain antennas to establish long-distance, high-speed RF links with relatively low power.

Wireless Local Area Networks

Wireless LANs, WMANs, and WWANs use the same spread spectrum technologies in different ways. For example, a wireless LAN might be used within a building to provide connectivity for mobile users, or bridges might be used to provide building-to-building connectivity across a campus. These are specific uses of spread spectrum technology that fit within the description of a Local Area Network (LAN).

The most common uses of spread spectrum technology today lie in a combination of wireless 802.11 compliant LANs and 802.15 compliant Bluetooth devices. These two technologies have captured a tremendous market share, so it is ironic that the two function much differently, play within the same FCC rules, and yet interfere with each other greatly. Considerable research, time, and resources have gone into making these two technologies coexist peacefully.

Wireless Personal Area Networks

Bluetooth, the most popular of WPAN technologies is specified by the IEEE 802.15 standard. The FCC regulations regarding spread spectrum use are broad, allowing for differing types of spread spectrum implementations. Some forms of spread spectrum introduce the concept of frequency hopping, meaning that the transmitting and receiving systems hop from frequency to frequency within a frequency band transmitting data as they go. For example, Bluetooth hops approximately 1600 times per second while HomeRF technology (a wide band WLAN technology) hops approximately 50 times per second. Both of these technologies vary greatly from the standard 802.11 WLAN, which typically hops 5-10 times per second.

Each of these technologies has different uses in the marketplace, but all fall within the FCC regulations. For example, a typical 802.11 frequency hopping WLAN might be implemented as an enterprise wireless networking solution while HomeRF is only implemented in home environments due to lower output power restrictions by the FCC.

Wireless Metropolitan Area Networks

Other spread spectrum uses, such as wireless links that span an entire city using high-power point-to-point links to create a network, fall into the category known as Wireless Metropolitan Area Networks, or WMANs. Meshing many point-to-point wireless links to form a network across a very large geographical area is considered a WMAN, but still uses the same technologies as the WLAN.

The difference between a WLAN and a WMAN, if any, would be that in many cases, WMANs use licensed frequencies instead of the unlicensed frequencies typically used with WLANs. The reason for this difference is that the organization implementing the network will have control of the frequency range where the WMAN is being implemented and will not have to worry about the chance of someone else implementing an interfering network. The same factors apply to WWANs.

FCC Specifications

Though there are many different implementations of spread spectrum technology, only two types are specified by the FCC. The law specifies spread spectrum devices in Title 47, a collection of laws passed by congress under the heading "Telegraphs, Telephones, and Radiotelegraphs." These laws provide the basis for implementation and regulation by the FCC.

The FCC regulations can be found in the Codes of Federal Regulation (CFR), volume 47 (the regulations are found in the CFR volume with the same number as the Title), part 15. Wireless LAN devices described in these regulations are sometimes called "part 15 devices."

These FCC regulations describe two spread spectrum technologies: *direct sequence spread spectrum (DSSS)* and *frequency hopping spread spectrum (FHSS)*.

Frequency Hopping Spread Spectrum (FHSS)

Frequency hopping spread spectrum is a spread spectrum technique that uses frequency agility to spread the data over more than 83 MHz. Frequency agility refers to the radio's ability to change transmission frequency abruptly within the usable RF frequency band. In the case of frequency hopping wireless LANs, the usable portion of the 2.4 GHz ISM band is 83.5 MHz, per FCC regulation and the IEEE 802.11 standard.

How FHSS Works

In frequency hopping systems, the carrier changes frequency, or *hops*, according to a pseudorandom sequence. The pseudorandom sequence is a list of several frequencies to which the carrier will hop at specified time intervals before repeating the pattern. The transmitter uses this hop sequence to select its transmission frequencies. The carrier will remain at a certain frequency for a specified time (known as the *dwell time*), and then use a small amount of time to hop to the next frequency (*hop time*). When the list of frequencies has been exhausted, the transmitter will repeat the sequence.

Fig. 3.2 shows a frequency hopping system using a hop sequence of five frequencies over a 5 MHz band. In this example, the sequence is:

1. 2.449 GHz

2. 2.452 GHz

3. 2.448 GHz

4. 2.450 GHz

5. 2.451 GHz

FIGURE 3.2   Single frequency hopping system

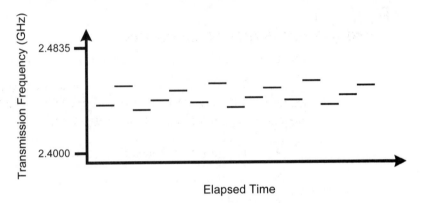

Once the radio has transmitted the information on the 2.451 GHz carrier, the radio will repeat the hop sequence, starting again at 2.449 GHz. The process of repeating the sequence will continue until the information is received completely.

The receiver radio is synchronized to the transmitting radio's hop sequence in order to receive on the proper frequency at the proper time. The signal is then demodulated and used by the receiving computer.

Effects of Narrow Band Interference

Frequency hopping is a method of sending data where the transmission and receiving systems hop along a repeatable pattern of frequencies together. As is the case with all spread spectrum technologies, frequency hopping systems are resistant—but not immune—to narrow band interference. In our example in Figure 3.2, if a signal were to interfere with our frequency hopping signal on, say, 2.451 GHz, only that portion of the spread spectrum signal would be lost. The rest of the spread spectrum signal would remain intact, and the lost data would be retransmitted.

In reality, an interfering narrow band signal may occupy several megahertz of bandwidth. Since a frequency hopping band is over 83 MHz wide, even this interfering signal will cause little degradation of the spread spectrum signal.

Frequency Hopping Systems

It is the job of the IEEE to create standards of operation within the confines of the regulations created by the FCC. The IEEE and OpenAir standards regarding FHSS systems describe:

- what frequency bands may be used
- hop sequences
- dwell times
- data rates

The IEEE 802.11 standard specifies data rates of 1 Mbps and 2 Mbps and OpenAir (a standard created by the now defunct Wireless LAN Interoperability Forum) specifies data rates of 800 kbps and 1.6 Mbps. In order for a frequency hopping system to be 802.11 or OpenAir compliant, it must operate in the 2.4 GHz ISM band (which is defined by the FCC as being from 2.4000 GHz to 2.5000 GHz). Both standards allow operation in the range of 2.4000 GHz to 2.4835 GHz.

Since the Wireless LAN Interoperability Forum (WLIF) is no longer supporting the OpenAir standard, IEEE compliant systems will be the main focus for FHSS systems in this book.

Channels

A frequency hopping system will operate using a specified hop pattern called a *channel*. Frequency hopping systems typically use the FCC's 26 standard hop patterns or a subset thereof. Some frequency hopping systems will allow custom hop patterns to be created, and others even allow synchronization between systems to completely eliminate collisions in a co-located environment.

FIGURE 3.3   Co-located frequency hopping systems

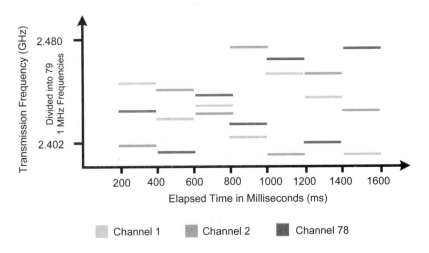

Channel 1   Channel 2   Channel 78

Though it is possible to have as many as 79 synchronized, co-located access points, with this many systems, each frequency hopping radio would require precise synchronization with all of the others in order not to interfere with (transmit on the same frequency as) another frequency hopping radio in the area. The cost of such a set of systems is prohibitive and is generally not considered an option. If synchronized radios are used, the expense tends to dictate 12 co-located systems as the maximum.

If non-synchronized radios are to be used, then 26 systems can be co-located in a wireless LAN; this number is considered to be the maximum in a medium-traffic wireless LAN. Increasing the traffic significantly or routinely transferring large files places the practical limit on the number of co-located systems at about 15. More than 15 co-located frequency-hopping systems in this environment will interfere to the extent that collisions will begin to reduce the aggregate throughput of the wireless LAN.

Dwell Time

When discussing frequency hopping systems, we are discussing systems that must transmit on a specified frequency for a time, and then hop to a different frequency to continue transmitting. When a frequency hopping system transmits on a frequency, it must do so for a specified amount of time. This time is called the *dwell time*. Once the dwell time has expired, the system will switch to a different frequency and begin to transmit again.

Suppose a frequency hopping system transmits on only two frequencies, 2.401 GHz and 2.402 GHz. The system will transmit on the 2.401 GHz frequency for the duration of the dwell time—100 milliseconds (ms), for example. After 100ms the radio must change its transmitter frequency to 2.402 GHz and send information at that frequency for 100ms. Since, in our example, the radio is only using 2.401 and 2.402 GHz, the radio will hop back to 2.401 GHz and begin the process over again.

Hop Time

When considering the hopping action of a frequency hopping radio, dwell time is only part of the story. When a frequency hopping radio jumps from frequency A to frequency B, it must change the transmit frequency in one of two ways. It either must switch to a different circuit tuned to the new frequency, or it must change some element of the current circuit in order to tune to the new frequency. In either case, the process of changing to the new frequency must be complete before transmission can resume, and this change takes time due to electrical latencies inherent in the circuitry. There is a small amount of time during this frequency change in which the radio is not transmitting called the *hop time*. The hop time is measured in microseconds (μs) and with relatively long dwell times of around 100-200 ms, the hop time is not significant. A typical 802.11 FHSS system hops between channels in 200-300 μs.

With very short dwell times of 500 – 600µs, like those being used in some frequency hopping systems such as Bluetooth, hop time can become very significant. If we look at the effect of hop time in terms of data throughput, we discover that the longer the hop time in relation to the dwell time, the slower the data rate of bits being transmitted.

This translates roughly to *longer dwell time = greater throughput*.

Dwell Time Limits

The FCC defines the maximum dwell time of a frequency hopping spread spectrum system at 400 ms per carrier frequency in any 30 second time period. For example, if a transmitter uses a frequency for 100 ms, then hops through the entire sequence of 75 hops (each hop having the same 100 ms dwell time) returning to the original frequency, it has expended slightly over 7.5 seconds in this hopping sequence. The reason it is not exactly 7.5 seconds is due to hop time. Hopping through the hop sequence four consecutive times would yield 400 ms on each of the carrier frequencies during this timeframe of just barely over 30 seconds (7.5 seconds x 4 passes through the hop sequence) which is allowable by FCC rules. Other examples of how a FHSS system might stay within the FCC rules would be a dwell time of 200 ms passing through the hop sequence only twice in 30 seconds or a dwell time of 400 ms passing through the hop sequence only once in 30 seconds. Any of these scenarios are perfectly fine for a manufacturer to implement. The major difference between each of these scenarios is how hop time affects throughput. Using a dwell time of 100 ms, 4 times as many hops must be made as when using a 400 ms dwell time. This additional hopping time decreases system throughput.

Normally, frequency hopping radios will not be programmed to operate at the legal limit; but instead, provide some room between the legal limit and the actual operating range in order to provide the operator with the flexibility of adjustment. By adjusting the dwell time, an administrator can optimize the FHSS network for areas where there is either considerable interference or very little interference. In an area where there is little interference, longer dwell time, and hence greater throughput, is desirable. Conversely, in an area where there is considerable interference and many retransmissions are likely due to corrupted data packets, shorter dwell times are desirable.

FCC Rules affecting FHSS

On August 21, 2000, the FCC changed the rules governing how FHSS can be implemented. The rule changes allowed frequency hopping systems to be more flexible and more robust. The rules are typically divided into "pre- 8/31/2000" rules and "post- 8/31/2000" rules, but the FCC allows for some decision-making on the part of the manufacturer or the implementer. If a manufacturer creates a frequency hopping system today, the manufacturer may use either the "pre- 8/31/2000" rules or the "post- 8/31/2000" rules, depending on his needs. If the manufacturer decides to use the "post- 8/31/2000" rules, then the manufacturer will be bound by all of these rules. Conversely, if using the "pre- 8/31/2000" rules, the manufacturer will be bound by that set of rules. A manufacturer cannot use some provisions from the "pre- 8/31/2000" rules and mix them with other provisions of the "post- 8/31/2000" rules.

Prior to 8/31/00, FHSS systems were mandated by the FCC (and the IEEE) to use at least 75 of the possible 79 carrier frequencies in a frequency hop set at a maximum output power of 1 Watt at the intentional radiator. Each carrier frequency is a multiple of 1 MHz between 2.402 GHz and 2.480 GHz. This rule states that the system must hop on 75 of the 79 frequencies before repeating the pattern.

This rule was amended on 8/31/00 to state that only 15 hops in a set were required, but other changes ensued as well. For example, the maximum output power of a system complying with these new rules is 125 mW and can have a maximum of 5 MHz of carrier frequency bandwidth. Remember, with an increase in bandwidth for the same information, less peak power is required. As further explanation of this rule change, though not exactly in the same wording used by the FCC regulation, the number of hops multiplied times the bandwidth of the carrier had to equal a total span of at least 75 MHz. For example, if 25 hops are used, a carrier frequency only 3 MHz wide is required, or if 15 hops are used, a carrier frequency 5 MHz wide (the maximum) must be used. It is important to note that systems may comply with either the pre- 8/31/00 rule or the post- 8/31/00 rule, but no mixing or matching of pieces of each rule is allowed.

 The IEEE did not change the 802.11 standard to reflect the post 8/31/00 rules. Rather, HomeRF is the only organization to adopt these changes into any sort of technical standard.

No overlapping frequencies are allowed under either rule. If the minimum 75 MHz of used bandwidth within the frequency spectrum were cut into pieces as wide as the carrier frequency bandwidth in use, they would have to sit side-by-side throughout the spectrum with no overlap. This regulation translates into 75 non-overlapping carrier frequencies under the pre- 8/31/00 rules and 15-74 non-overlapping carrier frequencies under the post- 8/31/00 rules.

The IEEE states in the 802.11 standard that FHSS systems will have at least 6 MHz of carrier frequency separation between hops. Therefore, a FHSS system transmitting on 2.410 GHz must hop to at least 2.404 if decreasing in frequency or 2.416 if increasing in frequency. This requirement was left unchanged by the IEEE after the FCC change on 8/31/00.

The pre- 8/31/00 FCC rules concerning FHSS systems allowed a maximum of 2 Mbps by today's technology. By increasing the maximum carrier bandwidth from 1 MHz to 5 MHz, the maximum data rate was increased to 10 Mbps.

Direct Sequence Spread Spectrum (DSSS)

Direct sequence spread spectrum is very widely known and the most used of the spread spectrum types, owing most of its popularity to its ease of implementation and high data rates. The majority of wireless LAN equipment on the market today uses DSSS technology. DSSS is a method of sending data in which the transmitting and receiving systems are both on a 22 MHz-wide set of frequencies. The wide channel enables devices to transmit more information at a higher data rate than current FHSS systems.

How DSSS Works

DSSS combines a data signal at the sending station with a higher data rate bit sequence, which is referred to as a *chipping code* or *processing gain*. A high processing gain increases the signal's resistance to interference. In the past, the FCC had specified a minimum liner processing gain of 10, while most commercial products actually operated under 20. The FCC made an important change on May 16, 2002 that removed all processing gain requirements. The IEEE 802.11 working group has set their minimum processing gain requirements at 11.

The process of direct sequence begins with a carrier being modulated with a code sequence. The number of "chips" in the code will determine how much spreading occurs, and the number of chips per bit and the speed of the code (in chips per second) will determine the data rate.

Direct Sequence Systems

In the 2.4 GHz ISM band, the IEEE specifies the use of DSSS at a data rate of 1 or 2 Mbps under the 802.11 standard. Under the 802.11b standard—sometimes called high-rate wireless—data rates of 5.5 and 11 Mbps are specified.

IEEE 802.11b devices operating at 5.5 or 11 Mbps are able to communicate with 802.11 devices operating at 1 or 2 Mbps because the 802.11b standard provides for backward compatibility. Users employing 802.11 devices do not need to upgrade their entire wireless LAN in order to use 802.11b devices on their network.

A recent addition to the list of devices using direct sequence technology is the IEEE 802.11a standard, which specifies units that can operate at up to 54 Mbps. Unfortunately for 802.11 and 802.11b device users, 802.11a is wholly incompatible with 802.11b because it does not use the 2.4 GHz band, but instead uses the 5 GHz UNII bands.

For a short while this was a problem because many users wanted to take advantage of the direct sequence technology delivering data rates of 54 Mbps, but did not want to incur the cost of a complete wireless LAN upgrade. So recently the IEEE 802.11g standard was approved to specify direct sequence systems operating in the 2.4 GHz ISM band that can deliver up to 54 Mbps data rate. The 802.11g technology became the first 54 Mbps technology that was backward compatible with 802.11 and 802.11b devices.

As of this writing, the first draft of the 802.11g standard has been approved as a future standard, but the specifications of this new standard are still in draft form. More information about 802.11g can be found at http://standards.ieee.org/cgi-bin/status?wireless.

Channels

Unlike frequency hopping systems that use hop sequences to define the channels, direct sequence systems use a more conventional definition of channels. Each channel is a contiguous band of frequencies 22 MHz wide, and 1 MHz carrier frequencies are used just as with FHSS. Channel 1, for instance, operates from 2.401 GHz to 2.423 GHz (2.412 GHz ± 11 MHz); channel 2 operates from 2.406 to 2.429 GHz (2.417 ± 11 MHz), and so forth. Figure 3.4 illustrates this point.

FIGURE 3.4   DSSS channel allocation and spectral relationship

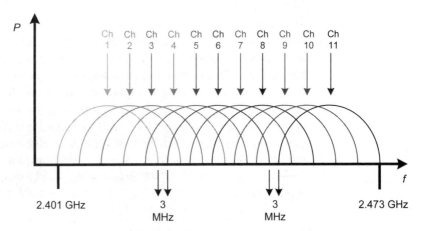

The chart in Figure 3.5 has a complete list of channels used in the United States and Europe. The 802.11b Standard specification specifies only 11 channels for non-licensed use in the United States. We can see that

channels 1 and 2 overlap by a significant amount. Each of the frequencies listed in this chart are considered center frequencies. From this center frequency, 11 MHz is added and subtracted to get the useable 22 MHz wide channel. It is easy to see that adjacent channels (channels directly next to each other) would overlap significantly.

FIGURE 3.5   DSSS channel frequency assignments

Channel ID	FCC Channel Frequencies GHz	ETSI Channel Frequencies GHz
1	2.412	N/A
2	2.417	N/A
3	2.422	2.422
4	2.427	2.427
5	2.432	2.432
6	2.437	2.437
7	2.442	2.442
8	2.447	2.447
9	2.452	2.452
10	2.457	2.457
11	2.462	2.462

To use DSSS systems with overlapping channels in the same physical space would cause interference between the systems. DSSS systems with overlapping channels should not be co-located because there will almost always be a drastic or complete reduction in throughput. Because the center frequencies are 5 MHz apart and the channels are 22 MHz wide, channels should be co-located only if the channel numbers are at least five apart: channels 1 and 6 do not overlap, channels 2 and 7 do not overlap, etc. There is a maximum of three co-located direct sequence systems possible because channels 1, 6 and 11 are the only theoretically non-overlapping channels. The 3 non-overlapping channels are illustrated in Figure 3.6

The word "theoretically" is used here because, as we will discus in Chapter 9 – Troubleshooting, channel 6 can in fact overlap (depending on the equipment used and distance between systems) with channels 1 and 11, causing degradation of the wireless LAN connection and speed.

FIGURE 3.6   DSSS non-overlapping channels

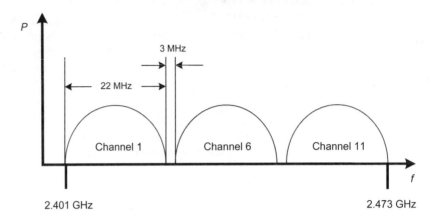

Effects of Narrow Band Interference

Like frequency hopping systems, direct sequence systems are also resistant to narrow band interference due to their spread spectrum characteristics. A DSSS signal is more susceptible to narrow band interference than FHSS because the DSSS band is much smaller (22 MHz wide instead of the 79 MHz wide band used by FHSS) and the information is transmitted along the entire band simultaneously instead of one frequency at a time. With FHSS, frequency agility and a wide frequency band ensures that the interference is only influential for a small amount of time, corrupting only a small portion of the data.

FCC Rules affecting DSSS

Just as with FHSS systems, the FCC has regulated that DSSS systems use a maximum of 1 watt of transmit power in point-to-multipoint configurations. The maximum output power is independent of the channel selection, meaning that, regardless of the channel used, the same power output maximum applies. This regulation applies to spread spectrum in both the 2.4 GHz ISM band and the upper 5 GHz UNII bands (discussed in Chapter 6).

Comparing FHSS and DSSS

Both FHSS and DSSS technologies have their advantages and disadvantages, and it is incumbent on the wireless LAN administrator to give each its due weight when deciding how to implement a wireless LAN. This section will cover some of the factors that should be discussed when determining which technology is appropriate for your organization, including:

- Narrowband interference
- Co-location
- Cost
- Equipment compatibility & availability
- Data rate & throughput
- Security
- Standards support

Narrowband Interference

The advantages of FHSS include a greater resistance to narrow band interference. DSSS systems may be affected by narrow band interference more than FHSS because of the use of 22 MHz wide contiguous bands instead of the 79 MHz used by FHSS. This fact may be a serious consideration if the proposed wireless LAN site is in an environment that has such interference present.

Cost

When implementing a wireless LAN, the advantages of DSSS may be more compelling than those of FHSS systems, particularly when driven by a tight budget. The cost of implementing a direct sequence system is far less than that of a frequency hopping system. DSSS equipment is widely available in today's marketplace, and its rapid adoption has helped in driving down the cost. Only a few short years ago, equipment was only affordable by enterprise customers. Today, very good quality 802.11b compliant PC cards can be purchased for under $100. FHSS cards complying with either the 802.11 or OpenAir standards typically run between $150 and $350 in today's market depending on the manufacturer and the standards to which the cards adhere.

Co-location

An advantage of FHSS over DSSS is the ability for many more frequency hopping systems to be co-located than direct sequence systems. Since frequency hopping systems are "frequency agile" and make use of 79 discrete channels, frequency hopping systems have a co-location advantage over direct sequence systems, which have a maximum co-location of 3 access points.

FIGURE 3.7   Co-location comparison

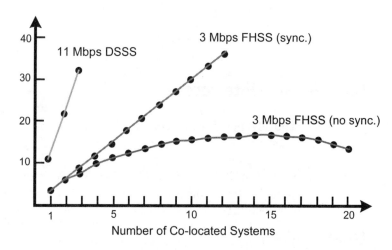

However, when calculating the hardware costs of an FHSS system to get the same throughput as a DSSS system, the advantage quickly disappears. Because DSSS can have 3 co-located access points, the maximum throughput for this configuration would be:

3 access points x 11 Mbps = 33 Mbps

At roughly 50% of rated bandwidth, the DSSS system throughput would be approximately:

33 Mbps / 2 = 16.5 Mbps

To achieve roughly the same rated system bandwidth using an IEEE 802.11 compliant FHSS system would require:

16 access points x 2 Mbps = 32 Mbps

At roughly 50% of rated bandwidth, the FHSS system throughput would be approximately:

32 Mbps / 2 = 16 Mbps

In this configuration, an FHSS system would require 13 additional access points to be purchased to get the same throughput as the DSSS system. Also, additional installation services for these units, cables, connectors, and antennas would all need to be purchased.

As you can see, there are advantages to co-location for each type of system. If the objectives are low cost and high throughput, clearly DSSS technology wins out. If keeping users segmented using different access points in a dense co-location environment is the objective, FHSS might be a viable alternative.

Equipment compatibility and availability

The Wi-Fi Alliance provides testing of 802.11b compliant DSSS wireless LAN equipment to ensure that such equipment will operate in the presence of and interoperate with other 802.11b DSSS devices. The interoperability standard that the Wi-Fi Alliance created and now uses is called Wireless Fidelity, or Wi-Fi™, and those devices that pass the tests for interoperability are "Wi-Fi compliant" devices. Devices so deemed are allowed to affix the Wi-Fi logo on the related marketing material and devices themselves showing that they have been tested and interoperate with other Wi-Fi compliant devices.

There are no such compatibility tests for equipment that uses FHSS. There are standards such as 802.11 and OpenAir, but no organization has stepped forward to do the same kind of compatibility testing for FHSS as the Wi-Fi Alliance does for DSSS.

Due to the immense popularity of 802.11b compliant radios, it is much easier to obtain these units. The demand seems only to be growing for the Wi-Fi compliant radios while the demand for FHSS radios has remained fairly steady, even decreasing to some degree over the past year.

Data rate & throughput

The latest frequency hopping systems are slower than the latest DSSS systems mostly because their data rate is only 2 Mbps. Though some FHSS systems operate at 3 Mbps or more, these systems are not 802.11 compliant and may not interoperate with other FHSS systems. FHSS and DSSS systems have a throughput (data actually sent) of only about half of the data rate. When testing the throughput of a new wireless LAN installation, achieving 5 – 6 Mbps on the 11 Mbps setting for DSSS or 1 Mbps on the 2 Mbps setting is common using DSSS.

HomeRF 2.0 uses wide band frequency hopping technology to achieve 10 Mbps data rates, which in turn achieve approximately 5 Mbps of actual throughput. The catch is that comparing HomeRF 2.0 to 802.11 or 802.11b systems is not really comparing apples to apples. The difference is HomeRF's limited power output (125 mW) as compared to that of 802.11 systems (1 watt).

When wireless frames are transmitted, there are pauses between data frames for control signals and other overhead tasks. With frequency hopping systems, this "interframe spacing" is longer than that used by direct sequence systems, causing a slow-down in the rate that data is actually sent (throughput). Additionally, when the frequency hopping system is in the process of changing the transmit frequency, no data is sent. This translates to more lost throughput, albeit only a minor amount. Some wireless LAN systems use proprietary physical layer protocols in order to increase throughput. These methods work, yielding throughputs as high as 80% of the data rate, but in so doing, sacrifice interoperability.

Security

It is widely touted—and is a myth—that frequency hopping systems are inherently more secure than direct sequence systems. The first fact that disproves this myth is that FHSS radios are only produced by a minimal number of manufacturers. Of this small list of manufacturers, all of them adhere to standards such as 802.11 or OpenAir in order to sell their products effectively. Second, each of these manufacturers uses a standard set of hop sequences, which generally comply with a pre-determined list, produced by the standards body (IEEE or WLIF). These 2 items together make breaking the code of hop sequences relatively simple.

Other reasons that make finding the hop sequence quite simple is that the channel number is broadcasted in the clear with each beacon. Also, the MAC address of the transmitting access point can be seen with each beacon (which indicates the manufacturer of the radio). Some manufacturers allow the administrator the flexibility of defining custom hopping patterns. However, even this custom capability is no level of security since fairly unsophisticated devices such as spectrum analyzers and a standard laptop computer can be used to track the hopping pattern of a FHSS radio in a matter of seconds.

Standards Support

As previously discussed, DSSS has gained wide acceptance due to low cost, high speed, the Wi-Fi Alliance's Wi-Fi interoperability standards, and many other factors. This market acceptance will only accelerate due to the industry moving toward newer, faster DSSS systems such as the new 802.11g and 802.11a compliant wireless LAN hardware. The Wi-Fi Alliance's recent announcement that the Wi-Fi standard would also cover 5 GHz DSSS systems operating in the UNII bands will help move the industry along even faster in the same direction it is already headed. The new standards for FHSS systems include HomeRF 2.0 and 802.15 (in support of WPANs such as Bluetooth), but none for advancing FHSS systems in the enterprise. All of these standards and technologies will be further discussed at in Chapter 6 (Organizations and Regulations).

Key Terms

Before taking the exam, you should be familiar with the following terms:

channel

chipping code

co-location

direct sequence

dwell time

frequency hopping

hop time

interoperability

narrow band

noise floor

processing gain

throughput

Review Questions

1. Increasing the dwell time for an FHSS system will increase the throughput.

    A. This statement is always true

    B. This statement is always false

    C. It depends on the manufacturer of the equipment

2. Which one of the following dwell times will result in the greatest throughput in a FHSS system and will still be within FCC regulations?

    A. 100 ms

    B. 200 ms

    C. 300 ms

    D. 400 ms

3. An 802.11b compliant wireless LAN configuration using DSSS can have a maximum of __ﾐ__ non-overlapping, co-located access points.

    A. 3

    B. 15

    C. 26

    D. 79

4. Consider the following two wireless LAN configurations:

   System 1. IEEE 802.11 compliant FHSS system, 6 co-located access points running at maximum data rate.

   System 2. IEEE 802.11b compliant DSSS system, 3 co-located access points running at 50% of maximum data rate.

   Which one of the following statements is true?

   A. System 1 will have more throughput

   B. System 2 will have more throughput

   C. System 1 and System 2 will have the same throughput

5. Channels on direct sequence systems for 802.11b equipment are ___ MHz wide.

   A. 5

   B. 20

   C. 22

   D. 83

6. Which of the following are advantages of 802.11b DSSS over 802.11 FHSS? Choose all that apply.

   A. Cost

   B. Throughput

   C. Security

   D. Resistance to narrowband interference

7. If having compatible equipment from different manufactures were an important factor when purchasing wireless LAN equipment, which of the following spread spectrum technologies would be the best choice?

   A. FHSS

   B. DSSS

8. The FCC has two sets of rules regarding FHSS that are known as before and after which of the following dates?

   A. 06/30/2000

   B. 08/31/1999

   C. 08/31/2000

   D. 08/31/2001

9. The latest published FCC rules regarding power output for FHSS states a maximum output of which one of the following?

   A. 100 mW

   B. 125 mW

   C. 200 mW

   D. 1 W

10. The FCC specifies how many channels in the 2.4 GHz ISM band that can be used for DSSS in the United States?

    A. 3

    B. 6

    C. 9

    D. 11

11. You have been hired on as a consultant to increase the capacity of an existing wireless LAN based on FHSS technology. After your research is completed you recommend that a replacement system based on DSSS would be better. Which of the following could be your arguments to defend your position? Choose all that apply.

    A. The DSSS devices will cost less and have more throughput

    B. The DSSS devices will cost more but have more throughput

    C. Additional new FHSS devices may not be compatible with the older devices

    D. DSSS is more secure than FHSS

12. The statement, "802.11b wireless LAN devices are backward compatible with 802.11 wireless LAN devices" is:

    A. Always true

    B. Always false

    C. Sometimes true

13. What is considered to be the maximum number of co-located FHSS access points in a wireless LAN, if non-synchronized radios are to be used?

    A. 3

    B. 16

    C. 20

    D. 26

14. In Frequency Hopping wireless LAN systems, the term *hopping* refers to which one of the following?

    A. Switching between throughput speeds from 11 Mbps to 5.5 Mbps

    B. What happens when the carrier frequency is changed

    C. The change that occurs as a result of the RF signal getting weaker

    D. Changing technologies from FHSS to DSSS

15. A DSSS channel is more susceptible to narrowband interference than a FHSS channel because of which of the following? Choose all that apply.

    A. The DSSS channel is much smaller (22 MHz wide instead of the 79 MHz wide band used by FHSS)

    B. The information is transmitted along the entire band simultaneously instead of one frequency at a time

    C. FHSS systems simply avoid the frequency on which the narrowband interference is located

    D. FHSS systems only use one frequency at a time, so the narrowband interference must be on the same exact frequency at the same time

16. The *noise floor* is defined by which one of the following?

    A. The general level of RF noise in the environment around the wireless LAN

    B. The noise that is generated as a result of foot traffic

    C. A fixed level of -100 dBm

    D. The level of noise at which a wireless LAN starts working

17. Which one of the following is *not* described by the IEEE and OpenAir standards regarding FHSS systems?

    A. What frequency bands may be used

    B. Hop sequences

    C. Allowable levels of interference

    D. Dwell times

    E. Data rates

18. An RF signal is considered spread spectrum when which of the following are true? Choose all that apply.

    A. The system sending the signal is using infrared technology

    B. The power required to send the information is significantly greater than is necessary

    C. The bandwidth used is much wider than what is required to send the information

    D. The bandwidth used is much less than what is used to send the information

19. Some 2.4 GHz FHSS systems operate at 3 Mbps or more. Which of the following is true regarding these systems?

    A. They are always IEEE 802.11 compliant

    B. They may not interoperate with other FHSS systems

    C. They are always OpenAir compliant

    D. They are backwards compatible with 900 MHz systems

20. How many different types of implementations of spread spectrum technology does the FCC specify for the 2.4 GHz ISM band?

    A. 1

    B. 2

    C. 3

    D. 4

Answers to Review Questions

1. A. The dwell time is the time spent by a transmitter on a certain frequency actually transmitting data. The longer a transmitter stays on a given frequency, the higher the throughput of the system will be. Hopping between frequencies takes time and takes away from the system throughput.

2. D. 400 ms is the legal limit on dwell time per the FCC. This dwell time is also the most advantageous for systems with the goal of maximized throughput.

3. A. Using Direct Sequence technology within the 2.4 GHz ISM allows only three non-overlapping channels within the 83.5 MHz allotted by the FCC. These channels are 1, 6, & 11.

4. B. Six IEEE 802.11 compliant access points, synchronized to have absolutely no collisions, would yield a maximum data rate of 12 Mbps because each system has a maximum data rate of 2 Mbps. Three 802.11b compliant access points on non-overlapping channels would yield a maximum data rate of 16.5 Mbps because each system has a data rate of 5.5 Mbps (half of the maximum 11 Mbps). Since throughput on each of these systems is approximately 50% of the data rate due to overhead with the CSMA/CA protocol, the 802.11b systems would yield greater throughput.

5. C. Channels on 802.11b compliant DSSS systems in the 2.4 GHz band are 22 MHz wide. This is in contrast to the OFDM channels used by the 802.11a standard using the 5 GHz UNII bands, which are each 20 MHz wide.

6. A, B. The 802.11b standard specifies rates up to 11 Mbps whereas the highest data rate specified by the 802.11 standard is 2 Mbps. Therefore, the DSSS technology specified in 802.11b is significantly faster than that of 802.11 FHSS. 802.11b compliant hardware is often as little as 1/3 of the price of 802.11 FHSS hardware offering a much better value to the average user. Security is implemented in both standards in the same fashion, and FHSS has better resistance to narrowband interference due to frequency diversity.

7. B. DSSS technologies have become amazingly popular with 802.11b Wi-Fi compliant devices. FHSS devices have taken a back

seat with 802.11 and OpenAir standards losing popularity in comparison to IEEE's 802.11b and the Wi-Fi Alliance's Wi-Fi standards. Wi-Fi has become the de-facto standard in DSSS wireless LAN equipment interoperability.

8. C. On 8/31/00, the FCC changed the rules regarding use of FHSS systems. Systems manufactured to meet the new rules of 8/31/00 are referred to as using Wide Band Frequency Hopping. These changes in rules are explained in detail in the FHSS section.

9. B. With the FCC rules regarding FHSS equipment, a manufacturer could either implement a piece of equipment to meet the old rules or the new rules. Under the old rules, the maximum power output was 1 watt, but under the new rules, due to a significant increase in carrier bandwidth, the power limit was changed to 125 mW.

10. D. There are 14 channels specified for use by the FCC and IEEE for spread spectrum technologies in the 2.4 GHz ISM band. Of these, only 11 may be used in the United States.

11. A, C. Implementations of DSSS hardware meeting the 802.11b standard are both fast and inexpensive. One problem that might be encountered with FHSS systems is compatibility. There are two standards manufacturers can choose to use for creating their hardware - 802.11 and OpenAir - but both are losing popularity. They are incompatible standards and there is no organization performing OpenAir and 802.11 FHSS testing for interoperability. Buying two OpenAir FHSS systems is no guarantee of interoperability.

12. C. The 802.11b standard supports DSSS devices only whereas the 802.11 standard supports DSSS and FHSS. This being the case, an administrator could have a situation where there are 802.11 FHSS nodes and access points in place. Trying to add 802.11b devices into the network will not work for clients that are using FHSS PCMCIA cards. This would only work if the existing WLAN consists of 802.11 DSSS clients and access points.

13. D. When synchronized radios are used, a maximum of 12 radios in a system is currently available (no vendor currently has the ability to synchronize more than 12 radios). With unsynchronized radios, a recommended maximum of 15 radios should be used for the best performance, but up to 26 radios can be used before collisions hinder performance more than the throughput gain of adding another access point.

14. B. When a FHSS system hops, both the transmitter and receiver systems change the carrier frequency in a synchronized fashion.

15. A, B, D. Frequency hopping systems use the entire useable range of the 2.4 GHz ISM band with a range of 83.5 MHz whereas direct sequence systems use only a 22 MHz portion of the same frequency band. For this reason, the same narrowband signal will disrupt the DSSS system more. Additionally, if the narrowband signal is either intermittent or changes frequencies, the chance of it affecting FHSS is slim.

16. A. The noise floor is a mixture of all of the background RF radiation found in the environment surrounding the system in use. The noise floor is generally in the -100 dBm area, but can be much higher or much lower depending on the environment. RF signals must be higher than the noise floor to be detectible as a valid, useful signal by a receiver. Spread spectrum systems are much closer to the noise floor than are narrowband signals.

17. C. Both the OpenAir and 802.11 standards define all parameters necessary for functioning of the equipment. These specifications include dwell times, data rates, data rate fallback functionality, frequency hop patterns (channels), and the frequency bands to be used. This is not a comprehensive list.

18. C. Spread spectrum transmitters spread a data signal out over a wide band of frequencies using many symbols per bit for redundancy and using very low power.

19. B. FHSS systems that can transmit data at 3 Mbps may or may not have the ability to slow their data rate to 2 or 1 Mbps, which is specified by the 802.11 standard. These systems could comply with the IEEE standard if they could transmit at 2 & 1 Mbps or the OpenAir standard if they could transmit at 1.6 Mbps and 800 kbps. While they are transmitting at other than these speeds, they are NOT

compliant with either standard.

20. B. The FCC specifies use of two types of spread spectrum technology in the 2.4 GHz ISM band. These types are Frequency Hopping and Direct Sequence.

Wireless LAN Infrastructure Devices

CWNA Exam Objectives Covered:

❖ Identify the purpose of the following infrastructure devices and explain how to install, configure, and manage them:

- Access Points

- Bridges

- Workgroup Bridges

❖ Identify the purpose of the following wireless LAN client devices and explain how to install, configure, and manage them:

- PCMCIA Cards

- Serial and Ethernet Converters

- USB Devices

- PCI/ISA Devices

❖ Identify the purpose of the following wireless LAN gateway devices and explain how to install, configure, and manage them:

- Residential Gateways

- Enterprise Gateways

This chapter of the book may be the most important section of the book for you, the CWNA candidate, to have access to at least some wireless LAN hardware. As mentioned in previous chapters, you can purchase a basic home or SOHO wireless network for under $400, including an access point, wireless PC Cards, and possibly a USB client. Although with this type of equipment you won't get hands-on experience with every piece of hardware covered in this chapter, you will have a good idea of how the devices communicate and otherwise behave using RF technology.

This chapter covers the different categories of wireless network infrastructure equipment and some of the variations within each category. From reading this chapter alone, you should be noticeably more versed in the actual implementation of wireless LANs, simply by being aware of all the different kinds of wireless LAN equipment that you have at your disposal when you begin to create or add to a wireless network. These hardware items are the physical building blocks for any wireless LAN.

In general, we will cover each type of hardware in this section in a similar manner according to the following topics:

- Definition and role of the hardware on the network
- Common options that might be included with the hardware
- How to install and configure the hardware

The goal of this section of the book is to make you aware of all the types of hardware that are available for the many varying wireless LAN configurations that you will encounter as a wireless LAN administrator. Antennas and wireless LAN accessories are covered in Chapter 5.

Access Points

Second only to the basic wireless PC card, the access point, or "AP", is probably the most common wireless LAN device with which you will work as a wireless LAN administrator. As its name suggests, the access point provides clients with a point of access into a network. An access point is a half-duplex device with intelligence equivalent to that of a sophisticated Ethernet switch. Figure 4.1 shows an example of an access point, while Figure 4.2 illustrates where an access point is used on a wireless LAN.

FIGURE 4.1   A sample access point

FIGURE 4.2   An access point installed on a network

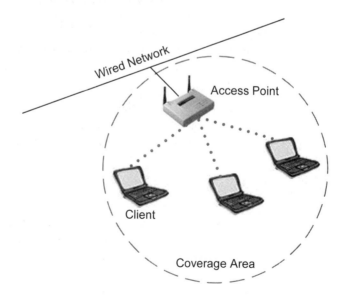

Access Point Modes

Access points communicate with their wireless clients, with the wired network, and with other access points. There are three modes in which an access point can be configured:

- Root Mode
- Repeater Mode
- Bridge Mode

Each of these modes is described below.

Root Mode

Root Mode is used when the access point is connected to a wired backbone through its wired (usually Ethernet) interface. Most access points that support modes other than root mode come configured in root mode by default. When an access point is connected to the wired segment through its Ethernet port, it will normally be configured for root mode. When in root mode, access points that are connected to the same wired distribution system can talk to each other over the wired segment. Access points talk to each other to coordinate roaming functionality such as reassociation. Wireless clients can communicate with other wireless clients that are located in different cells through their respective access points across the wired segment, as shown in Figure 4.3.

FIGURE 4.3   An access point in root mode

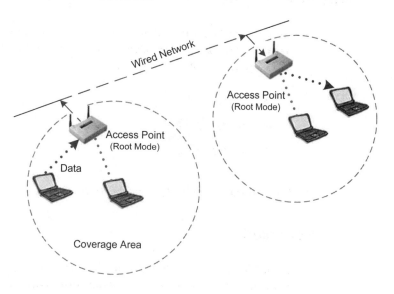

Bridge Mode

In bridge mode, access points act exactly like wireless bridges, which will be discussed later in this chapter. In fact, they become wireless bridges while configured in this manner. Only a small number of access points on the market have bridge functionality, which typically adds significant cost to the equipment. We will explain shortly how wireless bridges function, but you can see from Figure 4.4 that clients do not associate to bridges, but rather, bridges are used to link two or more wired segments together wirelessly.

FIGURE 4.4   An access point in bridge mode

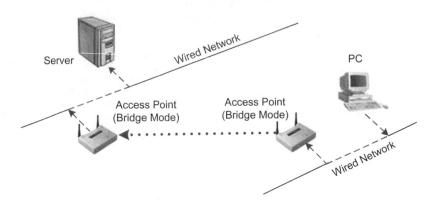

Repeater Mode

In repeater mode, access points have the ability to provide a wireless upstream link into the wired network rather than the normal wired link. As you can see in Figure 4.5, one access point serves as the root access point and the other serves as a wireless repeater. The access point in repeater mode connects to clients as an access point and connects to the upstream root access point as a client itself. Using an access point in repeater mode is not suggested unless absolutely necessary because cells around each access point in this scenario must overlap by a minimum of 50%. This configuration drastically reduces the range at which clients can connect to the repeater access point. Additionally, the repeater access point is communicating with the clients as well as the upstream access point over the wireless link, reducing throughput on the wireless segment. Users attached to the repeater access point will likely experience low throughput and high latencies in this scenario. It is typical for the wired Ethernet port to be disabled while in repeater mode.

FIGURE 4.5   An access point in repeater mode

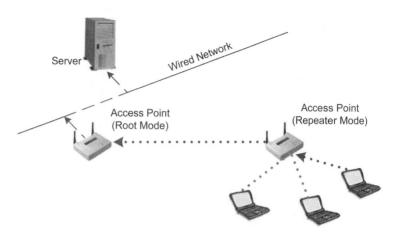

Common Options

An access point is considered a portal because it allows client connectivity from an 802.11 network to 802.3 or 802.5 networks. Access points are available with many different hardware and software options. The most common of these options are:

- Fixed or Detachable Antennas

- Advanced Filtering Capabilities

- Removable (Modular) Radio Cards

- Variable Output Power

- Varied Types of Wired Connectivity

Fixed or Detachable Antennas

Depending on your organization or client's needs, you will need to choose between having an access point with fixed (meaning non-removable) antennas or detachable antennas. An access point with detachable antennas gives you the ability to attach a different antenna to the access point using whatever length of cable you require. For example, if you needed to mount the access point inside, and give outdoor users access to the network, you could attach a cable and an outdoor antenna directly to the access point and mount only the antenna outside.

Access points may be shipped with or without diversity antennas. Wireless LAN antenna diversity is the use of multiple antennas with multiple inputs on a single receiver in order to sample signals arriving through each antenna. The point of sampling two antennas is to pick the input signal of whichever antenna has the best reception. The two antennas might have different signal reception because of a phenomenon called multipath, which will be discussed in detail in Chapter 9.

Advanced Filtering Capabilities

MAC or protocol filtering functionality may be included on an access point. Filtering is typically used to screen out intruders on your wireless LAN. As a basic security provision (covered in Chapter 10 - Security), an access point can be configured to filter out devices that are not listed in the access point's MAC filter list, which the administrator controls.

Protocol filtering allows the administrator to decide and control which protocols should be used across the wireless link. For example, if an administrator only wishes to provide http access across the wireless link so that users can browse the web and check their web-based email, then setting an http protocol filter would prevent all other types of protocol access to that segment of the network.

Removable (Modular) Radio Cards

Some manufacturers allow you to add and remove radios to and from built-in PCMCIA slots on the access point. Some access points may have two PCMCIA slots for special functionality. Having two radio slots in an access point allows one radio card to act as an access point while the other radio card is acting as a bridge (in most cases a wireless backbone). Another somewhat dissimilar use is to use each radio card as an independent access point. Having each card act as an independent access point allows an administrator to accommodate twice as many users in the same physical space without the purchase of a second access point, further reducing costs. When the access point is configured in this manner, each radio card should be configured on a non-overlapping channel, ideally channels 1 and 11, respectively.

Variable Output Power

Variable output power allows the administrator to control the power (in milliwatts) that the access point uses to send its data. Controlling the power output may become necessary in some situations where distant nodes cannot locate the access point. It also may simply be a luxury that allows you to control the area of coverage for the access point. As the power output is increased on the access point, clients will be able to move farther away from the access point without losing connectivity. This feature can also aid in security by allowing for proper sizing of RF cells so that intruders cannot connect to the network from outside the building's walls.

The alternative to the variable output power feature is use of fixed output access points. With a fixed output from the access point, creative measures such as amplifiers, attenuators, long cables, or high-gain antennas may have to be implemented. Controlling output power both from the access point and from the antenna is also important regarding operation within FCC guidelines. We will discuss use of these items in Chapter 5, Antennas and Accessories.

Varied Types of Wired Connectivity

Connectivity options for an access point can include a link for 10baseTx, 10/100baseTx, 100baseTx, 100baseFx, token ring, or others. Because an access point is typically the device through which clients communicate with the wired network backbone, the administrator must understand how to properly connect the access point into the wired network. Proper network design and connectivity will help prevent the access point from being a bottleneck and will result in far fewer problems due to malfunctioning equipment.

Consider using a standard, off-the-shelf access point for use in an enterprise wireless LAN. If, in this case, the access point were to be located 150 meters from the nearest wiring closet, running a category 5 (Cat5) Ethernet cable to the access point probably will not work. This scenario would be a problem because Ethernet over Cat5 cable is only specified to 100 meters. In this case, purchasing an access point that had a 100baseFx connector and running fiber from the wiring closet to the access point mounting location ahead of time would allow this configuration to function properly, and more easily.

Configuration and Management

The method or methods used to configure and manage access points will vary with each manufacturer. Most brands offer at least console, telnet, USB, or a built-in web server for browser access, and some access points will have custom configuration and management software. The manufacturer configures the access point with an IP address during the initial configuration. If the administrator needs to reset the device to factory defaults, there will usually be a hardware reset button on the outside of the unit for this purpose.

Features found in access points vary. However, one thing is constant: the more features the access point has, the more the access point will cost. For example, some SOHO access points will have WEP, MAC filters, and even a built-in web server. If features such as viewing the association table, 802.1x/EAP support, VPN support, routing functionality, Inter-access point protocol, and RADIUS support are required, expect to pay several times as much for an enterprise-level access point.

Even features that are standard on Wi-Fi compliant access points sometimes vary in their implementation. For example, two different brands of a SOHO access point may offer MAC filters, but only one of them might offer MAC filtering where you can explicitly permit *and* explicitly deny stations, rather than only one or the other. Some access points support full-duplex 10/100 wired connectivity whereas others offer only 10baseT half duplex connectivity on the wired side.

Understanding what features to expect on a SOHO, mid-range, and enterprise-level access points is an important part of being a wireless network administrator. Below is a list of features to look for in SOHO and enterprise categories. This listing is by no means comprehensive because manufacturers release new features frequently at each level. This list is meant to provide an idea of where to start in looking for an appropriate access point. These lists build upon each other beginning with the SOHO level access point, meaning that every higher level includes the features of the layer below it.

Small Office, Home Office (SOHO)

- MAC filters
- WEP (64- or 128-bit)
- USB or console configuration interface
- Simple built-in web server configuration interface
- Simple custom configuration application

Enterprise

- Advanced custom configuration application
- Advanced built-in web server configuration interface
- Telnet access
- SNMP management
- 802.1x/EAP
- RADIUS client
- VPN client and server
- Routing (static/dynamic)
- Repeater functions
- Bridging functions

Using the manufacturer's manuals and quick start guides will provide more specific information for each brand. Some of these functions, such as those having to do with security like RADIUS and VPN support, will be discussed in later sections. Some of these functions are included as part of the pre-requisites to reading this book, such as telnet, USB, and web-servers. Other topics, such as static and dynamic routing, are beyond the scope of this book.

As a wireless LAN administrator, you should know your environment, look for products that fit your deployment and security needs, and then compare features among 3 or 4 vendors that make products for that particular market segment. This evaluation process will undoubtedly take a substantial amount of time, but time spent learning about the different products on the market is useful. The best possible resource for learning about each of the competing brands in a particular market is each manufacturer's website.

When choosing an access point, be sure to take into account manufacturer support, in addition to features and price.

Mounting

Some things to keep in mind when mounting access points are:

- Use heavy duty zip ties to mount access points to columns or beams.
- Do not cover access point lights when mounting access point with zip ties.
- Mount access points upside down so that indicator lights can be seen from the floor
- Label access points
- When column mounting, it's possible to use a 2x4 beam as a base for the access point. Mount the 2x4 to the column and then mount the access point to the 2x4.
- When beam mounting, one may use zip ties directly or perhaps a 2x4 mounted to the beam with beam clamps with the access point mounted to it. Do not forget to mount the antenna the same way as is specified in the site survey
- Some access points come with slide mount holes and others may have a separate mounting kit or frame with which to mount them. Some do not, by design, allow for mounting.

Figure 4.6 shows some examples of mounting access points.

FIGURE 4.6   Mounting access points

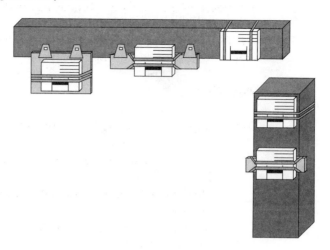

Wireless Bridges

A wireless bridge provides connectivity between two wired LAN segments, and is used in point-to-point or point-to-multipoint configurations. A wireless bridge is a half-duplex device capable of layer 2 wireless connectivity only. Figure 4.7 shows an example of a wireless bridge, while Figure 4.8 illustrates where a wireless bridge is used on a wireless LAN.

FIGURE 4.7   A sample wireless bridge

FIGURE 4.8   A point-to-point wireless bridge link

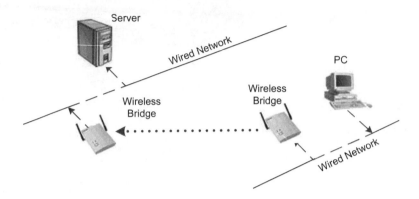

Wireless Bridge Modes

Wireless bridges communicate with other wireless bridges in one of four modes:

- Root Mode
- Non-root Mode
- Access Point Mode
- Repeater Mode

Each of these modes is described below.

Root Mode

One bridge in each group of bridges must be set as the root bridge. A root bridge can only communicate with non-root bridges and other client devices and cannot associate with another root bridge. Figure 4.9 illustrates a root bridge communicating with non-root bridges.

FIGURE 4.9   A root bridge communicating with non-root bridges

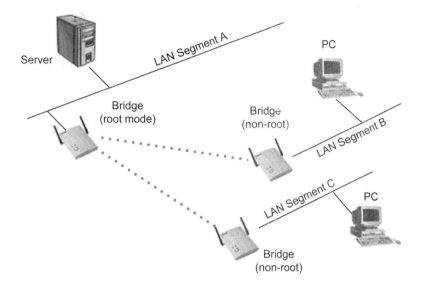

Non-root Mode

Wireless bridges in non-root mode attach, wirelessly, to wireless bridges that are in root mode. Some manufacturers' wireless bridges support *client* connectivity to non-root mode bridges while the bridge is in *access point* mode. This mode is actually a special mode where the bridge is acting as both an access point and as a bridge simultaneously. Client devices associate to access points (or bridges in access point mode) and bridges talk to bridges.

When using the Spanning Tree Protocol, all non-root bridges must have connectivity to the root bridge.

Access Point Mode

Some manufacturers give the administrator the ability to have clients connect to bridges, which is actually just giving the bridge access point functionality. In some cases, the bridge has an "access point" mode that converts the bridge into an access point entirely.

Repeater Mode

Wireless bridges can also be configured as repeaters, as shown in Figure 4.10. In repeater configuration, a bridge will be positioned between two other bridges for the purpose of extending the length of the wireless bridged segment. While using a wireless bridge in this configuration has the advantage of extending the link, it has the disadvantage of decreased throughput due to having to repeat all frames using the same half duplex radio. Repeater bridges are non-root bridges, and many times the wired port will be disabled while the bridge is in repeater mode.

FIGURE 4.10   A wireless bridge in repeater mode

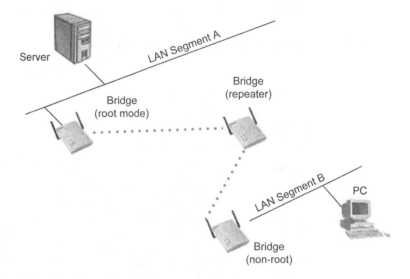

Common Options

The hardware and software options of a wireless bridge are similar to those of an access point, and for many of the same purposes:

- Fixed or Detachable Antennas
- Advanced Filtering Capabilities
- Removable (Modular) Radio Cards

- Variable Output Power
- Varied Types of Wired Connectivity

Fixed or Detachable Antennas

Wireless bridge antennas may be fixed or detachable and may come with or without diversity. Many times, diversity is not considered when configuring a wireless bridge because both bridges (one at each end of the link) will be static, and the environment around the wireless bridges tends not to change very often. For these reasons, multipath is typically not as much of a concern as it is with access points and mobile users.

Detachable antennas are a particularly nice feature with wireless bridges because they provide the ability to mount the bridge indoors and run a cable outdoors to connect to the antenna. In almost all cases, semi-directional or directional antennas are used with wireless bridges. The alternative to connecting a detachable antenna to a wireless bridge and mounting the bridge indoors is mounting the wireless bridge outdoors in a NEMA-compliant weatherproof enclosure.

In 1926, the Electric Power Club and the Associated Manufacturers of Electrical Supplies merged their operations to form the National Electrical Manufacturers Association (NEMA). Even though its roots go back more than 75 years, from that day to the present, NEMA has always focused on standardization of electrical equipment, advocacy on behalf of the industry, and economic analysis. Among other things, NEMA specifies standards for enclosures that are used in every industry for protecting the contents of the enclosure from the negative effects of adverse weather conditions.

Advanced Filtering Capabilities

MAC or protocol filters may be built into a wireless bridge. As a basic security provision, the administrator may configure a wireless bridge to allow or disallow network access to particular devices based on their MAC address.

Most wireless bridges offer protocol filtering. Protocol filtering is the use of layer 3-7 protocol filters allowing or disallowing specific packets or datagrams based on their layer 3 protocols, layer 4 port, or even layer 7 application. Protocol filters are useful for limiting use of the wireless LAN. For example, an administrator may prevent a group of users from using bandwidth-intensive applications based on the port or protocol used by the application.

Removable (Modular) Radio Cards

Having the ability to form a wireless backbone using one of the two radio card slots found in some bridges reduces the number of devices from four to two when providing client connectivity and bridging functionality. Typically these functions would require an access point and a bridge on both ends of the link. Some wireless bridges perform these same functions using a single radio. While still performing the same tasks, this configuration allows for much less throughput than if separate sets of radios are used for the access point and bridging functions.

Variable Output Power

Variable Output Power feature allows the administrator to control the power (in milliwatts) that the bridge uses to send its RF signal. This functionality is especially useful when performing an outdoor site survey because it allows the site surveyor the flexibility of controlling the output power without adding and subtracting amplifiers, attenuators, and lengths of cable from the circuit during testing. Used in conjunction with amplifiers, variable output in the bridge can be useful on long-distance links in reducing the amount of time it takes to fine-tune the output power such that the power is high enough to create a viable link and low enough to stay within FCC regulations.

Varied Types of Wired Connectivity

Connectivity options for a wireless bridge can include 10baseTx, 10/100baseTx, 100baseTx, or 100baseFx. Always attempt to establish a full-duplex connection to the wired segment in order to maximize the throughput of the wireless bridge. It is important when preparing to purchase a wireless bridge to take note of certain issues, such as the distance from the nearest wiring closet, for the purpose of specifying wired connectivity options for wireless bridges.

Configuration and Management

Wireless bridges have much the same configuration accessibility as do access points: console, telnet, HTTP, SNMP, or custom configuration and management software.   Many bridges support Power over Ethernet (PoE) as well (discussed in Chapter 5).   Once wireless bridges are implemented, throughput checks should be done regularly to confirm that the link has not degraded because a piece of the equipment was moved or the antenna shifted.

Wireless bridges usually come with a factory default IP address and can be accessed via the methods mentioned above for initial configuration. There is almost always a hardware reset button on the outside of the unit for resetting the unit back to factory defaults.

Wireless Workgroup Bridges

Similar to and often confused with wireless bridges are wireless *workgroup* bridges (WGB). The biggest difference between a bridge and a workgroup bridge is that the workgroup bridge is a *client* device. A wireless workgroup bridge is capable of aggregating multiple wired LAN client devices into one collective wireless LAN client.

In the association table on an access point, a workgroup bridge will appear in the table as a single client device. The MAC addresses of devices behind the workgroup bridge will not be seen on the access point. Workgroup bridges are especially useful in environments with mobile classrooms, mobile offices, or even remote campus buildings where a small group of users need access into the main network. Bridges can be used for this type of functionality, but if an access point rather than a bridge is in place at the central site, then using a workgroup bridge prevents the administrator from having to buy an additional bridge for the central site. Figure 4.11 shows an example of a wireless workgroup bridge, while Figure 4.12 illustrates where it is used on a wireless LAN.

In an indoor environment in which a group of users is physically separated from the main body of network users, a workgroup bridge can be ideal for connecting the entire group back into the main network wirelessly. Additionally, workgroup bridges may have protocol filtering capabilities allowing the administrator to control traffic across the wireless link.

FIGURE 4.11   A sample wireless workgroup bridge

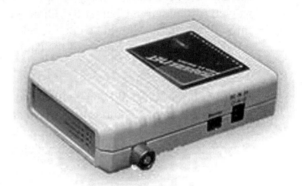

FIGURE 4.12   A wireless workgroup bridge installed on a network

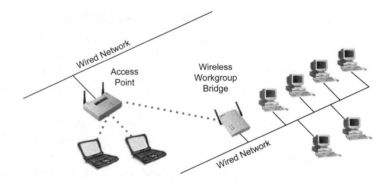

Common Options

Because the wireless workgroup bridge is a type of bridge, many of the options that you will find in a bridge – MAC and protocol filtering, fixed or detachable antennas, variable power output, and varied types of wired connectivity – are also found in a workgroup bridge. There is a limit to the number of stations that may use the workgroup bridge from the wired segment. This number ranges between 8 and 128 depending on the manufacturer. Use of more than about 30 clients over the wireless segment is likely to cause throughput to drop to a point at which users might feel that the wireless link is simply too slow to adequately perform their job tasks.

Configuration and Management

The methods used to access, configure, and manage a wireless workgroup bridge are similar to those of a wireless bridge: console, telnet, HTTP, SNMP support, or custom configuration and management software. Workgroup bridges are configured for a default IP address from the manufacturer, but can be changed either by accessing the unit via console port, web browser, telnet, or custom software application. The administrator can reset the device to factory defaults by using the hardware reset button on the device.

Wireless LAN Client Devices

The term "client devices" will, for purposes of this discussion, cover several wireless LAN devices that an access point recognizes as a client on a network. These devices include:

- PCMCIA & Compact Flash Cards
- Ethernet & Serial Converters
- USB Adapters
- PCI & ISA Adapters

Wireless LAN clients are end-user nodes such as desktop, laptop, or PDA computers that need wireless connectivity into the wireless network infrastructure. The wireless LAN client devices listed above provide connectivity for wireless LAN clients. It is important to understand that manufacturers only make radio cards in two physical formats, and those are PCMCIA and Compact Flash (CF). All radio cards are built (by the manufacturers) into these card formats and then connected to adapters such as PCI, ISA, USB, etc.

PCMCIA & Compact Flash Cards

The most common component on any wireless network is the PCMCIA card. More commonly known as "PC cards", these devices are used in notebook (laptop) computers and PDAs. The PC card is the component that provides the connection between a client device and the network. The PC card serves as a modular radio in access points, bridges, workgroup bridges, USB adapters, PCI & ISA adapters, and even print servers. Figure 4.13 shows an example of a PCMCIA card.

FIGURE 4.13 A sample PCMCIA card

Antennas on PC cards vary with each manufacturer. You might notice that several manufacturers use the same antenna while others use radically different models. Some are small and flat such as the one shown in figure 4.13, while others are detachable and connected to the PC card via a short cable. Some PC cards are shipped with multiple antennas and even accessories for mounting detachable antennas to the laptop or desktop case with Velcro.

There are two major manufacturers of radio chipsets that make up the heart of the very popular 802.11b PC and CF cards: Agere Systems (formerly Lucent Technologies) and Intersil. Atheros is the first to mass-produce chip sets for the 802.11a standard that uses the 5 GHz UNII frequency bands. These manufacturers sell their chipsets to the PC and CF radio card manufacturers (the wireless LAN hardware manufacturing companies) who use the radios in their product lines.

Compact Flash Cards, more commonly known as "CF cards", are very similar to wireless PC cards in that they have the same functionality, but CF cards are much smaller and typically used in PDAs. Wireless CF cards draw very little power and are about the size of a matchbook.

Wireless Ethernet & Serial Converters

Ethernet and serial converters are used with any device having Ethernet or legacy 9-pin serial ports for the purpose of converting those network connections into wireless LAN connections. When you use a wireless Ethernet converter, you are externally connecting a wireless LAN radio to that device with a category 5 (Cat5) cable. A common use of wireless Ethernet converters is connection of an Ethernet-based print server to a wireless network.

Serial devices are considered legacy devices and are rarely used with personal computers. Serial converters are typically used on old equipment that uses legacy serial for network connectivity such as terminals, telemetry equipment, and serial printers. Many times manufacturers will sell a client device that includes both a serial and Ethernet converter in the same enclosure.

These Ethernet and serial converter devices do not normally include the PC card radio. Instead, the PC card must be purchased separately and installed in the PCMCIA slot in the converter enclosure. Ethernet converters in particular allow administrators to convert a large number of wired nodes to wireless in a short period of time.

Configuration of Ethernet and serial converters varies. In most cases, console access is provided via a 9-pin legacy serial port. Figure 4.14 shows an example of an Ethernet and serial converter.

FIGURE 4.14   A sample Ethernet and serial converter

USB Adapters

USB clients are becoming very popular due to their simple connectivity. USB client devices support plug–n–play, and require no additional power other than what is delivered through the USB port on the computer. Some USB clients utilize modular, easily removable radio cards and others have a fixed internal card that cannot be removed without opening the case. When purchasing a USB client device, be sure you understand whether or not the USB adapter includes the PC card radio. In cases of a USB adapter that requires a PC card, it is recommended, although not always required, that you use the same vendor's equipment for both the adapter and the PC card. Figure 4.15 shows an example of a USB client.

FIGURE 4.15   A sample USB client

PCI & ISA Adapters

Wireless PCI and ISA are installed inside a desktop or server computer. Wireless PCI devices are plug–n–play compatible, but may also only come as an "empty" PCI card and require a PC card to be inserted into the PCMCIA slot once the PCI card is installed into the computer. Wireless ISA cards will likely not be plug-n-play compatible and will require manual configuration both via a software utility and in the operating system. Since the operating system cannot configure ISA devices that aren't plug-n-play compatible, the administrator must make sure the adapter's setting and those of the operating system match. Manufacturers typically have separate drivers for the PCI or ISA adapters and the PC card that will be inserted into each. As with USB adapters, it is recommended that you use the same vendor's equipment for the PCI/ISA adapters and the PC card. Figure 4.16 shows an example of a PCI adapter with a PC card inserted.

FIGURE 4.16   A sample PCI Adapter

Configuration and Management

There are two steps to installing wireless LAN client devices:

1. Install the drivers

2. Install manufacturer's wireless utilities

Driver Installation

The drivers included for cards are installed the same way drivers for any other type of PC hardware would be. Most devices (other than ISA adapters) are plug-n-play compatible, which means that when the client device is first installed, the user will be prompted to insert the CD or disks containing the driver software into the machine. Specific steps for device installation will vary by manufacturer. Be sure to follow the instruction manuals for your specific brand of hardware.

 When purchasing client devices, make sure the drivers are included for the specific operating system in which you will be installing the hardware.

Serial & Ethernet converters require no special drivers to work; however, wireless LAN client utilities can still be installed and utilized.

Manufacturer Utilities

Some manufacturers offer a full suite of utilities and others simply provide the user with the most basic means of connectivity. A robust set of utilities might include:

- Site Survey tools (Covered in Chapter 11, Site Survey Fundamentals)
- Spectrum Analyzer
- Power and speed monitoring tools
- Profile configuration utilities
- Link status monitor with link testing functionality

Site survey tools can include many different items that allow the user to find networks, identify MAC addresses of access points, quantify signal strengths and signal-to-noise ratios, and see interfering access points all at the same time during a site survey.

Spectrum analyzer software has many practical uses including finding interference sources and overlapping wireless LAN channels in the immediate area around your wireless LAN.

Power output and speed configuration utilities and monitors are useful for knowing what a wireless link is capable of doing at any particular time. For example, if a user were planning on transferring a large amount of data from a server to a laptop, the user may not want to start the transfer until the wireless connection to the network is 11 Mbps instead of 1 Mbps. Knowing the location of the point at which throughput increases/decreases is valuable for increasing user productivity.

Profile configuration utilities ease administration tasks considerably when changing from one wireless network to another. Instead of manually having to reconfigure all of a wireless client's settings each time you change networks, you may configure profiles for each wireless network during the initial configuration of the client device to save time later.

Link status monitor utilities allow the user to view packet errors, successful transmissions, connection speed, link viability, and many other valuable parameters. There is usually a utility for doing real-time link connectivity tests so that, for example, an administrator would be able to see how stable a wireless link is while in the presence of heavy RF interference or signal blockage.

Common Functionality

Manufacturers' utilities vary greatly in their functionality, but share a common set of configurable parameters. Each of these parameters is discussed in detail in this book.

- Infrastructure mode / Ad Hoc mode
- SSID (a.k.a. Network Name)
- Channel (if in ad hoc mode)
- WEP Keys
- Authentication type (Open System, Shared Key)

Wireless Residential Gateways

A wireless residential gateway is a device designed to connect a small number of wireless nodes to a single device for Layer 2 (wired and wireless) and Layer 3 connectivity to the Internet or to another network. Manufacturers have begun combining the roles of access points and gateways into a single device. Wireless residential gateways usually include a built-in hub or switch as well as a fully configurable, Wi-Fi compliant access point. The WAN port on a wireless residential gateway is the Internet-facing Ethernet port that may be connected to the Internet through one of the following:

- Cable modem
- xDSL modem
- Analog modem
- Satellite modem

Figure 4.17 shows an example of a wireless residential gateway, while Figure 4.18 illustrates where a wireless residential gateway is used on a wireless LAN.

FIGURE 4.17   A sample wireless residential gateway

FIGURE 4.18   A wireless residential gateway installed on a network

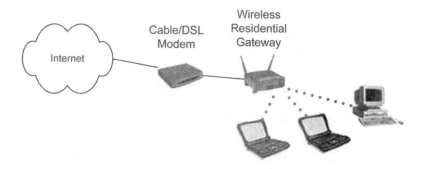

Common Options

Because wireless residential gateways are becoming increasingly popular in homes of telecommuters and in small businesses, manufacturers have begun adding more features to these devices to aid in productivity and security. Common options that most wireless residential gateways include are:

- Point-to-Point Protocol over Ethernet (PPPoE)
- Network Address Translation (NAT)
- Port Address Translation (PAT)
- Ethernet switching
- Virtual Servers
- Print Serving
- Fail-over routing
- Virtual Private Networks (VPNs)
- Dynamic Host Configuration Protocol (DHCP) Server and Client
- Configurable Firewall

This diverse array of functionality allows home and small office users to afford an all-in-one single device solution that is easily configurable and meets most business needs. Residential gateways have been around for quite some time, but recently, with the extreme popularity of 802.11b compliant wireless devices, wireless was added as a feature. Wireless residential gateways have all of the expected SOHO-class access point configuration selections such as WEP, MAC filters, channel selection, and SSID.

Configuration and Management

Configuring and installing wireless residential gateways generally consists of browsing to the built-in HTTP server via one of the built-in Ethernet ports and changing the user-configurable settings to meet your particular needs. This configuration may include changing ISP, LAN, or VPN settings. Configuration and monitoring are done in similar fashion through the browser interface. Some wireless residential gateways units support console, telnet, and USB connectivity for management and configuration. The text-based menus typically provided by the console port and telnet sessions are less user-friendly than the browser interface, but adequate for configuration. Statistics that can be monitored may include items such as up-time, dynamic IP addresses, VPN connectivity, and associated clients. These settings are usually well marked or explained for the non-technical home or home office user.

 When you choose to install a wireless residential gateway at your home or business, be aware that your ISP will not provide technical support for getting your unit connected to the Internet unless they specifically state that they will. ISPs will usually only support the hardware that you have purchased from them or that they have installed. This lack of service can be especially frustrating to the non-technical user who must configure the correct IP addresses and settings in the gateway unit to get Internet access. Your best source of support for installing these devices is the manual provided with the device or someone who has already successfully installed similar units and can provide free guidance. Wireless residential gateways are so common now that many individuals that consider themselves non-technical have gained significant experience installing and configuring them.

Enterprise Wireless Gateways

An enterprise wireless gateway is a device that can provide specialized authentication and connectivity for wireless clients. Enterprise wireless gateways are appropriate for large-scale wireless LAN environments providing a multitude of manageable wireless LAN services such as rate limiting, Quality of Service (QoS), and profile management.

It is important that an enterprise wireless gateway device needs to have a powerful CPU and fast Ethernet interfaces because it may be supporting many access points, all of which send traffic to and through the enterprise wireless gateway. Enterprise wireless gateway units usually support a variety of WLAN and WPAN technologies such as 802.11 standard devices, Bluetooth, HomeRF, and more. Enterprise wireless gateways support SNMP and allow enterprise-wide simultaneous upgrades of user profiles. These devices can be configured for hot fail-over (when installed in pairs), support of RADIUS, LDAP, Windows NT authentication databases, and data encryption using industry-standard VPN tunnel types. Figure 4.19 shows an example of an enterprise wireless gateway, while Figure 4.20 illustrates where it is used on a wireless LAN.

FIGURE 4.19   A sample enterprise wireless gateway

FIGURE 4.20 An enterprise wireless gateway installed on a network

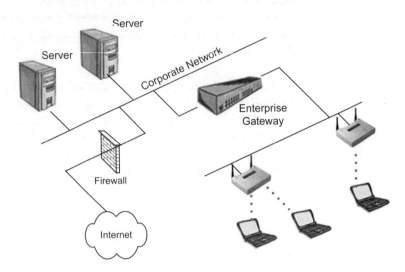

Authentication technologies incorporated into enterprise wireless gateways are often built into the more advanced levels of access points. For example, VPN and 802.1x/EAP connectivity are supported in many brands of enterprise level access points.

Enterprise wireless gateways do have features, such as Role-Based Access Control (RBAC), that are not found in any access points. RBAC allows an administrator to assign a certain level of wireless network access to a particular job position in the company. If the person doing that job is replaced, the new person automatically gains the same network rights as the replaced person. Having the ability to limit a wireless user's access to corporate resources, as part of the "role", can be a useful security feature.

Class of service is typically supported, and an administrator can assign levels of service to a particular user or role. For example, a guest account might be able to use only 500 kbps on the wireless network whereas an administrator might be allowed 2 Mbps connectivity.

In some cases, Mobile IP is supported by the enterprise wireless gateway, allowing a user to roam across a layer 3 boundary. User roaming may even be defined as part of an enterprise wireless gateway policy, allowing the user to roam only where the administrator allows. Some enterprise wireless gateways support packet queuing and prioritization, user tracking, and even time/date controls to specify when users may access the wireless network.

MAC spoofing prevention and complete session logging are also supported and aid greatly in securing the wireless LAN. There are many more features that vary significantly between manufacturers. Enterprise wireless gateways are so comprehensive that we highly recommend that the administrator take the manufacturer's training class before making a purchase so that the deployment of the enterprise wireless gateway will go more smoothly.

Consultants finding themselves in a situation of having to provide a security solution for a wireless LAN deployment with many access points that do not support advanced security features might find enterprise wireless gateways to be a good solution. Enterprise wireless gateways are expensive, but considering the number of management and security solutions they provide, usually worth the expense.

Configuration and Management

Enterprise wireless gateways are installed in the main data path on the wired LAN segment just past the access point(s) as seen in Figure 4.19. Enterprise wireless gateways are configured through console ports (using CLI), telnet, internal HTTP or HTTPS servers, etc. Centralized management of only a few devices is one big advantage of using enterprise wireless gateways. An administrator, from a single console, can easily manage a large wireless deployment using only a few central devices instead of a very large number of access points.

Enterprise wireless gateways are normally upgraded through use of TFTP in the same fashion as many switches and routers on the market today. Configuration backups can often be automated so that the administrator won't have to spend additional management time backing up or recovering from lost configuration files. Enterprise wireless gateways are mostly manufactured as rack-mountable 1U or 2U devices that can fit into your existing data center design.

Key Terms

Before taking the exam, you should be familiar with the following terms:

bridge mode

configurable firewall

converters

detachable antenna

Dynamic Host Configuration Protocol (DHCP) Server and Client

Ethernet switching

fail-over routing

modular cards

Network Address Translation (NAT)

Point-to-Point Protocol over Ethernet (PPPoE)

Port Address Translation (PAT)

portal

print serving

profiles

repeater mode

root mode

SNMP

wired connectivity

variable output

USB

Virtual Private Networks (VPNs)

virtual servers

Review Questions

1. Why would it not be a good idea to have a number of access points in repeater mode in series? Choose all that apply.

    A. Throughput would be reduced to unacceptable levels

    B. The access points would all be required to be physically connected to the network

    C. Users attached to the repeater access point will likely experience high latencies

    D. Legacy serial devices would not be able to communicate with the root access point

2. You are installing a wireless LAN in a factory, and the laptop client computers have no USB support. Which one of the following client devices could be used as a stand-alone client connection to the wireless LAN?

    A. ISA adapter

    B. PCI adapter

    C. PCMCIA card

    D. Ethernet converter

3. You need to connect two wired networks together that currently share no network connectivity between them. Using only access points to connect the networks, what mode would the access points need to be placed in?

    A. Root mode

    B. Repeater mode

    C. Bridging mode

4.   When an access point connects to another access point wirelessly for the purpose of extending the wireless segments to client out of range of the access point connected to the wired segment, the access point not connected to the wired LAN segment is in _____ mode.

   A.   Root

   B.   Repeater

   C.   Bridge

5.   Wireless bridges are used for which of the following functions? Choose all that apply.

   A.   Connecting mobile users to the wired LAN

   B.   Point-to-multipoint configurations

   C.   Building-to-building connectivity

   D.   Wireless security

6.   Properly aligning two wireless bridges will optimize their throughput. This statement is:

   A.   Always true

   B.   Always false

   C.   Depends on the manufacturer

7.   Your friend owns a small business, and asks you what he could buy to provide low-cost wireless Internet access for his 5 salespeople in the office. Which one of the following devices would be an appropriate solution?

   A.   Access point

   B.   Wireless workgroup bridge

   C.   Enterprise wireless gateway

   D.   Wireless residential gateway

8. A company has hired you to recommend wireless LAN equipment that will allow them to place limits on the bandwidth used by each of their wireless users. Which one of the following devices would you recommend?

    A. Access point

    B. Wireless workgroup bridge

    C. Enterprise wireless gateway

    D. Wireless residential gateway

9. In a situation in which you need to allow outdoor users to connect to your network via a wireless LAN, which one of the following features would allow you to use an indoor access point with an outdoor antenna?

    A. Antenna diversity

    B. Detachable antennas

    C. Plug and play support

    D. Modular radio cards

10. Which of the following wireless client devices would not be a plug–n-play device?

    A. USB Client

    B. PCMCIA Card

    C. ISA Card

    D. Compact Flash Card

11. Your client has a number of sales people that are located in a remote office building. Each sales person has both a PC and a laptop. The client wants to purchase a hardware solution that will permit each sales person to have wireless network connectivity for his or her PC and laptop. Only the PC or the laptop needs network access at any given time, and both have USB support. Which of the following solutions would work? Choose all that apply.

    A. 1 PCMCIA card

    B. 1 PCMCIA card, 1 PCI adapter

    C. 1 PCMCIA card, 1 USB adapter

    D. 1 PCMCIA card, 1 CF card

12. You have configured an access point in a small office and are concerned about hackers intruding on your wireless network. What settings will you adjust (from the manufacturer's default settings) on the unit to address this potential problem? Choose all that apply.

    A. Detachable antennas

    B. MAC Filtering

    C. Radio card position

    D. Output power

    E. WEP configuration

13. Which of the following are common security options that most wireless residential gateways include? Choose all that apply.

    A. PPPoE – Point-to-Point Protocol over Ethernet

    B. Virtual Servers

    C. Routing

    D. PAT – Port Address Translation

    E. VPN Client or VPN Client Passthrough

14. Which of the following are wired connectivity options that a wireless bridge can include? Choose all that apply.

    A. 10baseTx

    B. 10baseFL

    C. 10/100baseTx

    D. 1000baseSX

    E. 100baseFx

15. A workgroup bridge is a(n) _____ device.

    A. Client

    B. Infrastructure

    C. Gateway

    D. Antenna

16. Which one of the following is not a hardware or software option on a wireless bridge?

    A. Fixed or detachable antennas

    B. Advanced filtering capabilities

    C. Removable (modular) radio cards

    D. Full duplex radio links

    E. Varied Types of Wired Connectivity

17. Ethernet and serial converters are used with devices having which of the following physical connectivity? Choose all that apply.

    A. 9-pin serial ports

    B. Ethernet ports

    C. USB Ports

    D. Parallel Ports

18. Why is an access point considered a portal?

    A. An access point allows client connectivity from an 802.11 network to either 802.3 or 802.5 networks

    B. An access point always connects users to the Internet

    C. An access point connects clients to one another

    D. An access point is a gateway to another collision domain

19. The statement that *an access point is a half duplex wireless device* is which one of the following?

    A. Always true

    B. Always false

    C. Dependent on the maker of the access point

20. A USB adapter is used with which type of wireless LAN device?

    A. Gateway

    B. Access point

    C. Bridge

    D. Client

    E. Converter

Answers to Review Questions

1. A, C. When an access point is used in repeater mode, throughput of the wireless connection to clients is significantly reduced due to the access point having to listen to the clients *and* retransmit every frame upstream over the same wireless segment. Additionally, repeaters can cause very high latencies for data transmissions, which may make some transmissions impossible to perform such as real-time audio or video.

2. C. PCI cards and Ethernet converters use PCMCIA cards for connectivity into the wireless LAN. In this scenario, only PCMCIA cards themselves are standalone wireless LAN connectivity devices.

3. C. Access points, when serving in root or repeater mode, allow only client connectivity. In this scenario, wireless bridges should be used, but in their absence, many wireless access points support a bridging mode where the access points can effectively be a wireless bridge connecting two wired segments together wirelessly. Although an access point in repeater mode can talk to another access point, it does so as a client and on behalf of other clients, and multiple wired segments cannot be connected using access points in this manner.

4. B. The purpose behind repeater mode is to extend the wireless segment to users who cannot see the access point connected to the wired LAN. Many times repeater mode is used because an additional access point could not be connected to the wired infrastructure in a particular area of a facility.

5. B, C. There are two basic configurations using wireless bridges: point-to-point and point-to-multipoint. Building-to-building bridging can take on either of these configurations. Clients cannot connect to wireless bridges, and wireless bridges are not security devices.

6. A. If highly directional antennas are misaligned only slightly, it can result in a loss of throughput in the wireless link. For this reason, administrators often use semi-directional antennas in order to simplify the task of alignment and to minimize the chance of misalignment caused by things such as wind loading.

7. D. Wireless residential gateways, which are sometimes referred to as SOHO devices, provide the necessary connectivity for both wired and wireless clients in a small network environment. Additionally, these gateways provide needed upstream Internet connectivity and internal functionality, such as DHCP, that eases administrative overhead.

8. C. Some wireless enterprise gateways support role-based access control (RBAC) where profiles can be attached to user accounts allowing specific types of access functionality, such as rate limiting, on a per-user basis.

9. B. Access points and bridges are typically mounted inside the building unless placed in a weatherproof enclosure. It is often more economical to place access points and bridges indoors, requiring that the antenna be detachable. Mounting the antenna outdoors and running a long cable between the antenna and access point allow the administrator to protect the access point against weather and theft.

10. C. Wireless ISA devices do not support plug-n-play functionality, and therefore require manual configuration. Legacy 9-pin serial wireless client devices likewise do not support plug-n-play configuration. PCI, PCMCIA, CF, and USB devices support plug-n-play.

11. B, C. With a PCI card, the desktop computer would be able to accept the PCMCIA card. The PCMCIA card can be inserted directly into the laptop computer. Likewise the USB adapter can be connected to either computer, and the PCMCIA card can be inserted into the PCMCIA adapter.

12. B, D, E. If output power is only high enough to allow company personnel to attach to the network, but not passers-by, then the network is likely more secure. Setting WEP keys and MAC filters before deployment is a very good idea for small wireless networks.

13. B, D, E. Port Address Translation is a many-to-one configuration variance of Network Address Translation. Using private IP addresses in the corporate environment and using public IP addresses on the Internet connection allows a degree of security for corporate users. Likewise, VPN client or VPN client passthrough functionality allows SOHO users to connect to a corporate VPN server over the Internet using a secure tunnel. Virtual servers must be manually configured by the administrator to direct packets to a particular server. This type of manual control allows the administrator to keep the internal servers secure.

14. A, C, E. 10baseTx, 10/100baseTx, and 100baseFx are common wired Ethernet ports on access points, bridges, and even workgroup bridges. Cat5 or short-haul fiber is used to connect these devices to the wired distribution system. 10baseFL is basically obsolete, and using gigabit Ethernet connectivity such as 1000baseSx would increase costs of the infrastructure device but add no further speed to the network. Since access points and bridges only have a maximum of 100 Mbps on the fastest available wireless LAN system (802.11a devices in proprietary mode), there is no need to have a connection on the wired segment faster than 100 Mbps.

15. A. Workgroup bridges are client devices capable of advanced filtering and connecting a group of wired users on a wired network segment to another wired segment over a wireless link as a single, collective client.

16. D. All wireless LAN radios are half duplex. Because radios can either transmit or receive on a particular frequency, but not both simultaneously, full-duplex communications are not possible on a wireless LAN without using multiple radios and multiple frequencies at one time. Wireless LAN radio manufacturers do not build their radios to be full duplex capable because of the very high cost of doing so.

17. A, B. Ethernet converters are used to connect wired stations to the wireless network via standard wired Ethernet ports that are already installed in the computer. Serial converters are used to connect stations that have no network connectivity or have legacy serial network connectivity to the wireless network via the standard 9-pin serial (COM) port.

18. A. A portal is a device that connects dissimilar media types such as

802.11 wireless and 802.3 Ethernet, or maybe even 802.5 Token Ring.

19. A. All wireless LAN radios are half duplex. The same radios used for client connectivity are used for access points, bridges, and workgroup bridges.

20. D. A USB adapter connects a computer's USB port to a wireless network using a standard PCMCIA radio (whether internally fixed or externally modular).

Antennas and Accessories

CWNA Exam Objectives Covered:

❖ Identify the basic attributes, purpose, and function of the following types of antennas

- Omni-directional/dipole

- Semi-directional

- Highly-directional

❖ Describe the proper locations and methods for installing antennas

❖ Explain the concepts of polarization, gain, beamwidth, and free-space path loss as they apply to implementing solutions that require antennas

❖ Identify the purpose of the following wireless LAN accessories and explain how to install, configure, and manage them

- Power over Ethernet devices

- Amplifiers

- Attenuators

- Lightning arrestors

- RF connectors and cables

- RF splitters

In This Chapter

RF Antennas

Power over Ethernet

Accessories

In the previous chapter, we discussed the many different pieces of wireless LAN equipment that are available on the market today for creating simple and complex wireless LANs. In this chapter, we will discuss a basic element of the devices that make access points, bridges, pc cards and other wireless devices communicate: antennas.

Antennas are most often used to increase the range of wireless LAN systems, but proper antenna selection can also enhance the security of your wireless LAN. A properly chosen and positioned antenna can reduce the signal leaking out of your workspace, and make signal interception extremely difficult. In this chapter, we will explain the radiation patterns of different antenna designs, and how the positioning of the user's antenna makes a difference in signal reception.

There are three general categories into which all wireless LAN antennas fall: omni-directional, semi-directional, and highly-directional. We will discuss the attributes of each of these groups in-depth, as well as the proper methods for installing each kind of antenna. We will also explain polarization, coverage patterns, appropriate uses, and address the many different items that are used to connect antennas to other wireless LAN hardware.

Up to now, we have discussed RF theory and some of the major categories of wireless LAN devices that an administrator will use on a daily basis. This knowledge is a good foundation, but is of little value without a solid working knowledge of antennas, which are the devices that actually send and receive the RF signals.

This chapter will also cover wireless LAN accessories such as:

- RF Amplifiers
- RF Attenuators
- Lightning Arrestors
- RF Connectors
- RF Cables
- RF Splitters
- Pigtails

Knowledge of these devices' uses, specifications, and effects on RF signal strength is essential to being able to build a functional wireless LAN.

Power over Ethernet (PoE) has become an important factor in today's wireless networks spawning new product lines and new standards. PoE technology will be discussed along with the different types of PoE equipment that can be used to deliver power to a PoE-enabled device.

RF Antennas

An RF antenna is a device used to convert high frequency (RF) signals on a transmission line (a cable or waveguide) into propagated waves in the air. The electrical fields emitted from antennas are called *beams* or *lobes*. There are three generic categories of RF antennas:

- Omni-directional
- Semi-directional
- Highly-directional

Each category has multiple types of antennas, each having different RF characteristics and appropriate uses. As the gain of an antenna goes up, the coverage area narrows so that high-gain antennas offer longer coverage areas than low-gain antennas at the same input power level. There are many types of antenna mounts, each suited to fit a particular need. After studying this section, you will understand which antenna and mount best meets your needs and why.

Omni-directional (Dipole) Antennas

The most common wireless LAN antenna is the dipole antenna. Simple to design, the dipole antenna is standard equipment on most access points. The dipole is an omni-directional antenna, because it radiates its energy equally in all directions around its axis. Directional antennas concentrate their energy into a cone, known as a "beam." The dipole has a radiating element just one inch long that performs an equivalent function to the "rabbit ears" antennas on television sets. The dipole antennas used with wireless LANs are much smaller because wireless LAN frequencies are in the 2.4 GHz microwave spectrum instead of the 100 MHz TV spectrum.

As the frequency gets higher, the wavelength and the antennas become smaller.

Figure 5.1 shows that the dipole's radiant energy is concentrated into a region that looks like a doughnut, with the dipole vertically through the "hole" of the "doughnut." The signal from an omni-directional antenna radiates in a 360-degree horizontal beam. If an antenna radiates in all directions equally (forming a sphere), it is called an isotropic radiator. The sun is a good example of an isotropic radiator. We cannot make an isotropic radiator, which is the theoretical reference for antennas, but rather, practical antennas all have some type of gain over that of an isotropic radiator. The higher the gain, the more we horizontally squeeze our doughnut until it starts looking like a pancake, as is the case with very high gain antennas.

FIGURE 5.1   Dipole Doughnut

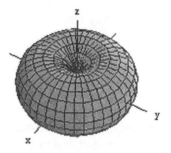

The dipole radiates equally in all directions around its axis, but does not radiate along the length of the wire itself - hence the doughnut pattern. Notice the side view of a dipole radiator as it radiates waves in Figure 5.2. This figure also illustrates that dipole antennas form a "figure 8" in their radiation pattern if viewed standing beside a perpendicular antenna.

FIGURE 5.2   Dipole side-view

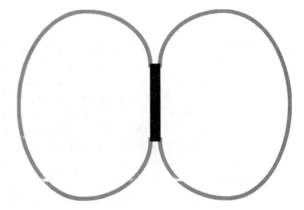

If a dipole antenna is placed in the center of a single floor of a multistory building, most of its energy will be radiated along that floor, with some significant fraction sent to the floors above and below the access point. Figure 5.3 shows examples of some different types of omni-directional antennas. Figure 5.4 shows a two-dimensional example of the top view and side view of a dipole antenna.

FIGURE 5.3   Sample omni-directional antennas

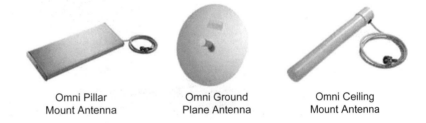

Omni Pillar
Mount Antenna

Omni Ground
Plane Antenna

Omni Ceiling
Mount Antenna

FIGURE 5.4 Coverage area of an omni-directional antenna

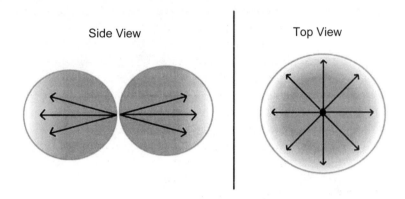

Side View   Top View

High-gain omni-directional antennas offer more horizontal coverage area, but the vertical coverage area is reduced, as can be seen in Figure 5.5. This characteristic can be an important consideration when mounting a high-gain omni antenna indoors on the ceiling. If the ceiling is too high, the coverage area may not reach the floor, where the users are located.

FIGURE 5.5 Coverage area of a high-gain omni-directional antenna

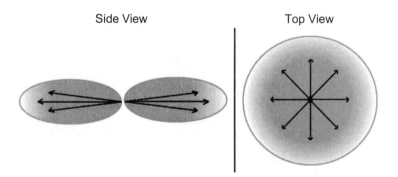

Side View   Top View

Usage

Omni-directional antennas are used when coverage in all directions around the horizontal axis of the antenna is required. Omni-directional antennas are most effective where large coverage areas are needed around a central point. For example, placing an omni-directional antenna in the middle of a large, open room would provide good coverage. Omni-directional antennas are commonly used for *point-to-multipoint* designs with a star topology (See Figure 5.6). Used outdoors, an omni-directional antenna should be placed on top of a structure (such as a building) in the middle of the coverage area. For example, on a college campus the antenna might be placed in the center of the campus for the greatest coverage area. When used indoors, the antenna should be placed in the middle of the building or desired coverage area, near the ceiling, for optimum coverage. Omni-directional antennas emit a large coverage area in a circular pattern and are suitable for warehouses or tradeshows where coverage is usually from one corner of the building to the other.

FIGURE 5.6   Point-to-multipoint link

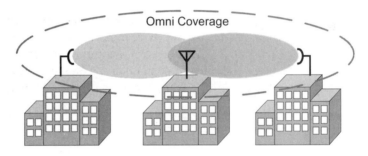

Semi-directional Antennas

Semi-directional antennas come in many different styles and shapes. Some semi-directional antennas types frequently used with wireless LANs are Patch, Panel, and Yagi (pronounced "YAH-gee") antennas. All of these antennas are generally flat and designed for wall mounting. Each type has different coverage characteristics. Figure 5.7 shows some examples of semi-directional antennas.

FIGURE 5.7 Sample semi-directional antennas

Yagi Antenna   Patch Antenna   Panel Antenna

These antennas direct the energy from the transmitter significantly more in one particular direction rather than the uniform, circular pattern that is common with the omni-directional antenna. Semi-directional antennas often radiate in a hemispherical or cylindrical coverage pattern as can be seen in Figure 5.8.

FIGURE 5.8 Coverage area of a semi-directional antenna

Directional Patch Antenna | Directional Yagi Antenna

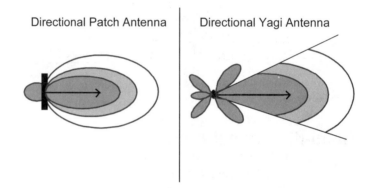

Usage

Semi-directional antennas are ideally suited for short and medium range bridging. For example, two office buildings that are across the street from one another and need to share a network connection would be a good scenario in which to implement semi-directional antennas. In a large indoor space, if the transmitter must be located in the corner or at the end of a building, a corridor, or a large room, a semi-directional antenna would be a good choice to provide the proper coverage. Yagi antennas are most often used on short to medium length building-to-building bridging up to 2 miles (3.3 km). Patch and panel antennas are more typically used on short range building-to-building and in-building directional links. Figure 5.9 illustrates a link between two buildings using semi-directional antennas.

FIGURE 5.9   Point-to-point link using semi-directional antennas

Many times, during an indoor site survey, engineers will constantly be thinking of how to best locate *omni*-directional antennas. In some cases, semi-directional antennas provide such long-range coverage that they may eliminate the need for multiple access points in a building. For example, in a long hallway, several access points with omni antennas may be used or perhaps only one or two access points with properly placed semi-directional antennas - saving the customer a significant amount of money. In some cases, semi-directional antennas have back and side lobes that, if used effectively, may further reduce the need for additional access points. Specifically, Yagi antennas are appropriate for signal coverage down pathways or aisles in warehouses, rail yards, retail stores, or manufacturing facilities.

Highly-directional Antennas

As their name would suggest, highly-directional antennas emit the most narrow signal beam of any antenna type and have the greatest gain of these three groups of antennas. Highly-directional antennas are typically concave, dish-shaped devices, as can be seen in Figures 5.10 and 5.11. These antennas are ideal for long distance, point-to-point wireless links. Some models are referred to as *parabolic dishes* because they resemble small satellite dishes. Others are called *grid* antennas due to their perforated design for resistance to wind loading.

FIGURE 5.10 Sample of a highly-directional parabolic dish antenna

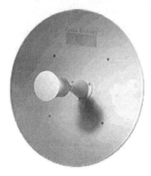

FIGURE 5.11 Sample of a highly-directional grid antenna

Figure 5.12 illustrates the radiation pattern of a high-gain antenna.

FIGURE 5.12 Radiation pattern of a highly-directional antenna

Usage

High-gain antennas do not have a coverage area that client devices can use. These antennas are used for point-to-point communication links, and can transmit at distances up to 25 miles (42 km). Potential uses of highly directional antennas might be to connect two buildings that are miles away from each other and have no line of sight obstructions between them. Additionally, these antennas can be aimed directly at each other within a building in order to "blast" through an obstruction. This setup would be used in order to get network connectivity to places that cannot be wired and where normal wireless networks will not work.

 Highly directional antennas have a very narrow beamwidth and must be accurately aimed at each other.

RF Antenna Concepts

There are several concepts that are essential knowledge when implementing solutions that require RF antennas. Among those that will be described are:

- Polarization

- Gain

- Beamwidth

- Free Space Path Loss

The above list is by no means a comprehensive list of all RF antenna concepts, but rather a set of must-have fundamentals that allow an administrator to understand how wireless LAN equipment functions over the wireless medium. A solid understanding of basic antenna functionality is the key to moving forward in learning more advanced RF concepts.

Knowing where to place antennas, how to position them, how much power they are radiating, the distance that radiated power is likely to travel, and how much of that power can be picked up by receivers is, many times, the most complex part of an administrator's job.

Polarization

A radio wave is actually made of up two fields, one electric and one magnetic. These two fields are on planes perpendicular to each other, as shown in figure 5.13.

FIGURE 5.13   E-planes and H-planes

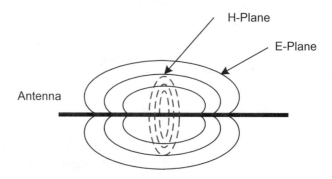

The sum of the two fields is called the electro-magnetic field. Energy is transferred back and forth from one field to the other, in the process known as "oscillation." The plane that is parallel with the antenna element is referred to as the "E-plane" whereas the plane that is perpendicular to the antenna element is referred to as the "H-plane." We are interested primarily in the electric field since its position and direction with reference to the Earth's surface (the ground) determines wave polarization.

Polarization is the physical orientation of the antenna in a horizontal or vertical position. The electric field is parallel to the radiating elements (the antenna element is the metal part of the antenna that is doing the radiating) so, if the antenna is vertical, then the polarization is vertical.

- *Horizontal polarization* - the electric field is parallel to the ground
- *Vertical polarization* - the electric field is perpendicular to the ground

Vertical polarization, which is typically used in wireless LANs, is perpendicular to the Earth's plane. Notice the dual antennas sticking up vertically from most any access point - these antennas are vertically polarized in that position. Horizontal polarization is parallel to the Earth. Figure 5.14 illustrates the effects polarization can have when antennas are not aligned correctly. Antennas that are not polarized in the same way are not able to communicate with each other effectively.

FIGURE 5.14   Polarization

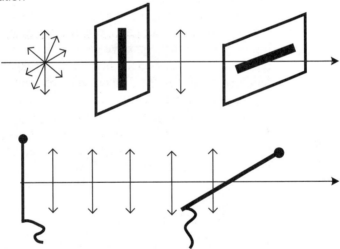

Practical Use

The designers of the antennas for PCMCIA cards face a real problem. It is not easy to form antennas onto the small circuit board inside the plastic cover that sticks off the end of the PCMCIA card. Rarely do antennas built into PCMCIA cards provide adequate coverage, especially when the client is roaming. The polarization of PCMCIA cards and that of access points is sometimes not the same, which is why turning your laptop in different directions generally improves reception. PDAs, which usually have a vertically oriented PCMCIA card, normally exhibit good reception. External, detachable antennas mounted with Velcro to the laptop computer vertically almost always show great improvement over the snap-on antennas included with most PCMCIA cards. In areas where there are a high number of PCMCIA card users, it is often recommended to orient access point antennas horizontally for better reception.

Gain

Antenna gain is specified in dBi, which means decibels referenced to an isotropic radiator. An isotropic radiator is a sphere that radiates power equally in all directions simultaneously. We haven't the ability to make an isotropic radiator, but instead we can make omni-directional antennas such as a dipole that radiates power in a 360-degree horizontal fashion, but not 360 degrees vertically. RF signal radiation in this fashion gives us a doughnut pattern. The more we horizontally squeeze this doughnut, the flatter it becomes, forming more of a pancake shape when the gain is very high. Antennas have passive gain, which means they do not increase the power that is input into them, but rather shape the radiation field to lengthen or shorten the distance the propagated wave will travel. The higher the antenna gain, the farther the wave will travel, concentrating its output wave more tightly so that more of the power is delivered to the destination (the receiving antenna) at long distances. As was shown in Figure 5.5, the coverage has been squeezed vertically so that the coverage pattern is elongated, reaching further.

Beamwidth

As we've discussed previously, narrowing, or focusing antenna beams increases the antenna's gain (measured in dBi). An antenna's beamwidth means just what it sounds like: the "width" of the RF signal beam that the antenna transmits. Figure 5.15 illustrates the term beamwidth.

FIGURE 5.15   Beamwidth of an antenna

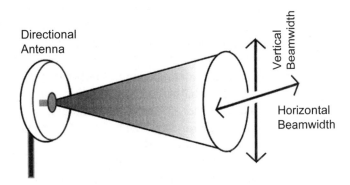

There are two vectors to consider when discussing an antenna's beamwidths: the vertical and the horizontal. The vertical beamwidth is measured in degrees and is perpendicular to the Earth's surface. The horizontal beamwidth is measured in degrees and is parallel to the Earth's surface. Beamwidth is important for you to know because each type of antenna has different beamwidth specifications. The chart below can be used as a quick reference guide for beamwidths.

Antenna Type	Horizontal Beamwidth (in degrees)	Vertical Beamwidth (in degrees)
Omni-directional	360	Ranges from 7-80
Patch/Panel	Ranges from 30-180	Ranges from 6-90
Yagi	Ranges from 30-78	Ranges from 14-64
Parabolic Dish	Ranges from 4-25	Ranges from 4-21

Selecting an antenna with appropriately wide or narrow beamwidths is essential in having the desired RF coverage pattern. For example, imagine a long hallway in a hospital. There are rooms on both sides of the hallway, and instead of using several access points with omni antennas, you have decided to use a single access point with a semi-directional antenna such as a patch antenna.

The access point and patch antenna are placed at one end of the hallway facing down the hallway. For complete coverage on the floors directly above and below this floor a patch antenna could be chosen with a significantly large vertical beamwidth such as 60-90 degrees. After some testing, you may find that your selection of a patch antenna with 80 degrees vertical beamwidth does the job well.

Now the horizontal beamwidth needed must be decided on. Due to the length of the hallway, testing may reveal a high-gain patch antenna must be used in order to have adequate signal coverage at the opposite end. Having this high gain, the patch antenna's horizontal beamwidths are significantly narrowed such that the rooms on each side of the hallway do not have adequate coverage. Additionally, the high-gain antenna doesn't have a large enough vertical beamwidth to cover the floors immediately above and below. In this case, you might decide to use two patch antennas - one at each end of the hallway facing each other. They would both be low gain with wide horizontal and vertical beamwidths such that the rooms on each side of the hallway are covered along with the floors above and below. Due to the low gain, the antennas may each only cover a portion (maybe half) of the length of the hallway.

As you can see from this example, appropriate selection of beamwidths to have the right coverage pattern is essential and may likely determine how much hardware (such as access points) needs to be purchased for an installation.

Free Space Path Loss

Free Space Path Loss (or just Path Loss) refers to the loss incurred by an RF signal due largely to "signal dispersion" which is a natural broadening of the wave front. The wider the wave front, the less power can be induced into the receiving antenna. As the transmitted signal propagates, its power level decreases at a rate inversely proportional to the distance traveled and proportional to the wavelength of the signal. The power level becomes a very important factor when considering link viability.

The Path Loss equation is one of the foundations of link budget calculations. Path Loss represents the single greatest source of loss in a wireless system. Below is the formula for Path Loss.

$$PathLoss = 20LOG_{10} \left[\frac{4 \Pi d}{\lambda} \right] \{dB\}$$

You will not be tested on the Path Loss formula in the CWNA exam, but it is provided for your administrative reference.

The 6dB Rule

Close inspection of the Path Loss equation yields a relationship that is useful in dealing with link budget issues. Each 6 dB increase in EIRP equates to a doubling of range. Conversely, a 6 dB reduction in EIRP translates into a cutting of the range in half. Below is a chart that gives you a rough estimate of the Path Loss for given distances between transmitter and receiver at 2.4 GHz.

Distance	Loss (in dB)
100 meters	80.23
200 meters	86.25
500 meters	94.21
1,000 meters	100.23
2,000 meters	106.25
5,000 meters	114.21
10,000 meters	120.23

This chart above is provided for your reference, and is not tested on the CWNA exam.

Antenna Installation

It is very important to have proper installation of the antennas in a wireless LAN. An improper installation can lead to damage or destruction of your equipment and can also lead to personal injury. Equally as important as personal safety is good performance of the wireless LAN system, which is achieved through proper placement, mounting, orientation, and alignment. In this section we will cover:

- Placement
- Mounting
- Appropriate Use
- Orientation
- Alignment
- Safety
- Maintenance

Placement

Mount omni-directional antennas attached to access points near the middle of the desired coverage area whenever possible. Place the antenna as high as possible to increase coverage area, being careful that users located somewhat below the antenna still have reception, particularly when using high-gain omni antennas. Outdoor antennas should be mounted above obstructions such as trees and buildings such that no objects encroach on the Fresnel Zone.

Mounting

Once you have calculated the necessary output power, gain, and distance that you need to transmit your RF signal, and have chosen the appropriate antenna for the job, you must mount the antenna. There are several options for mounting antennas both indoors and outdoors, some of which are shown in Figure 5.16.

FIGURE 5.16   Mounting antennas

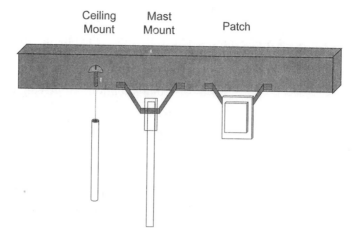

Antenna Mounting Options

- ceiling mount - typically hung from crossbars of drop ceilings
- wall mount - forces the signal away from a perpendicular surface
- pillar mount - mounts flush to a perpendicular surface
- ground plane - sits flat on the ground
- mast mount - the antenna mounts to a pole
- articulating mount - movable mast mount
- chimney mount - various hardware to allow antenna mounting to a chimney
- tripod-mast - the antenna sits atop a tripod

There is no perfect answer for where to mount your particular antenna. You will learn in Chapter 11 (Site Surveying Fundamentals) that the recommended placement and mounting of antennas will be part of a proper site survey. There is no substitute for on- the-job training, which is where you are likely to learn how to mount wireless LAN antennas using various types of mounting hardware. Each type of mount will come with instructions from the manufacturer on how to install and secure it.

There are many different variations of each mount type because manufacturers each have their own way of designing the mounting kit.

Some things to keep in mind when mounting antennas are:

- Many times the brackets shipped with the antenna may not work for a particular situation. Modifying brackets or building custom brackets may be necessary.

- Do not hang an antenna by its cable and make sure the mounting is solid and secure. The cable can break and cable sway can produce a moving cell.

- Exactly how the antenna is to be mounted should be specified for each antenna in the site survey report

Mounting Aesthetics

Antennas are usually unsightly and should be hidden. Some manufacturers make ceiling panel antennas. When aesthetics are important, patch or panel antennas might be used rather than omni antennas. If possible, antennas should be hidden to avoid damage by children and also by adults who purposefully seek to damage the gear.

Appropriate Use

Use indoor antennas inside of buildings and outdoor antennas outside of buildings unless the indoor area is significantly large to warrant use of an outdoor antenna. Outdoor antennas are most often sealed to prevent water from entering the antenna element area and made of plastics able to withstand extreme heat and cold. Indoor antennas are not made for outdoor use and generally cannot withstand the elements.

Orientation

Antenna orientation determines polarization, which was discussed previously as having a significant impact on signal reception. If an antenna is oriented with the electrical field parallel to the Earth's surface, then the clients (if the antenna is mounted to an access point) should also have this same orientation for maximum reception. The reverse is also true with both having the electrical field oriented perpendicular to the Earth's surface. The throughput of a bridge link will be drastically reduced if each end of the link does not have the same antenna orientation.

Alignment

Antenna alignment is sometimes critical and other times not. Some antennas have very wide horizontal and vertical beamwidths allowing the administrator to aim two antennas in a building-to-building bridging environment in each other's general direction and get almost perfect reception. Alignment is more important when implementing long-distance bridging links using highly-directional antennas. Wireless bridges come with alignment software that aids the administrator in optimizing antenna alignment for best reception, which reduces lost packets and high retry counts while maximizing signal strength. When using access points with omni-directional or semi-directional antennas, proper alignment usually is a matter of covering the appropriate area such that wireless clients can connect in places where connectivity is required.

Safety

RF antennas, like other electrical devices, can be dangerous to implement and operate. The following guidelines should be observed whenever you or one of your associates is installing or otherwise working with RF antennas.

Follow the Manual

Carefully follow instructions provided with all antennas. Following all provided instructions will prevent damage to the antenna and personal injury. Most of the safety precautions found in antenna manufacturers' manuals are common sense.

Do not touch when power is applied

Never touch a high-gain antenna to any part of your body or point it toward your body while it is transmitting. The FCC allows very high amounts of RF power to be transmitted in the license free bands when configuring a point-to-point link. Putting any part of your body in front of a 2.4 GHz highly-directional antenna that is transmitting at high power would be the equivalent to putting your body in a microwave oven.

Professional Installers

For most elevated antenna installations, consider using a professional installer. Professional climbers and installers are trained in proper climbing safety, and will be able to better install and secure your wireless LAN antenna if it is to be mounted in on a pole, tower, or other type of elevated construction.

Metal Obstructions

Keep antennas away from metal obstructions such as heating and air-conditioning ducts, large ceiling trusses, building superstructures, and major power cabling runs. These types of metal obstructions create a significant amount of multipath. And, since these types of metal obstructions reflect a large portion of the RF signal, if the signal is being broadcasted at high power, the reflected signal could be dangerous to bystanders.

Power Lines

Antenna towers should be a safe distance from overhead power lines. The recommended safe distance is twice the antenna height. Since wireless LAN antennas are generally small, this recommended practice does not usually apply. It is not a good idea to have wireless LAN antennas near significant power sources because an electrical short between the power source and the wireless LAN could be dangerous to personnel working on the wireless LAN and would likely destroy the wireless LAN equipment.

Grounding Rods

Use special grounding rods and follow the National Electrical Code and local Electrical codes for proper outdoor antenna and tower grounding. Grounding rods should generally have less than 5 ohms to Earth ground. The recommended resistance is 2 ohms or less. Grounding rods can prevent damage to the wireless LAN equipment and might even save the life of anyone climbing on the tower if the tower is struck by lightning.

Maintenance

To prevent moisture entry into antenna cable, seal all external cable connectors using commercial products such as coax compatible electrical tape or Coax-Seal. Moisture that has entered connectors and cabling is very difficult to remove. It is usually more economical to replace the cable and connectors than to remove the moisture. Connectors and cables with any amount of water will likely make the RF signal erratic and can cause significant signal degradation because the presence of water will change the cable's impedance, and hence the VSWR.

When installing outdoor RF cabling, make sure to mount connectors facing downward and use drip loops in the cabling so that water will be directed away from points where moisture is likely to enter connections. Check seals periodically. Sealant materials can sometimes dry rot when exposed to the sun for long periods of time and may need replacing from time to time.

Power over Ethernet (PoE) Devices

Power over Ethernet (PoE) is a method of delivering DC voltage to an access point, wireless bridge, or wireless workgroup bridge over the Cat5 Ethernet cable for the purpose of powering the unit. PoE is used when AC power receptacles are not available where wireless LAN infrastructure devices are to be installed. The Ethernet cable is used to carry both the power and the data to the units.

Consider a warehouse where the access points need to be installed in the ceiling of the building. The labor costs that would be incurred to install electrical outlets throughout the ceiling of the building to power the access points would be considerable. Hiring an electrician to do this type of work would be very expensive and time consuming. Remember that Ethernet cables can only carry data reliably for 100 meters and, for any distance more than 100 meters, PoE is not a viable solution. Figure 5.17 illustrates how a PoE device would provide power to an access point.

FIGURE 5.17   PoE installation

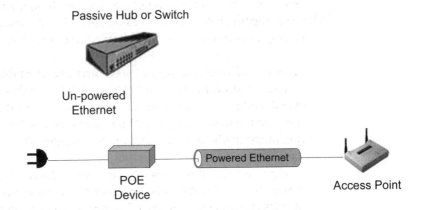

Many times the best places to install access points or bridges for RF connectivity will have no AC power source. Therefore, PoE can be a great help in implementing a well-designed wireless network. Some manufacturers allow for *only* PoE to power up their devices, not standard AC power.

Common PoE Options

PoE devices are available in several types.

- Single-port DC voltage injectors
- Multi-port DC voltage injectors
- Ethernet switches designed to inject DC voltage on each port on a given pair of pins

Although configuration and management is generally not necessary for a PoE device, there are some caveats to be aware of if and when you begin to implement PoE.

First, there is no industry standard on implementation of PoE. This means that the manufacturers of PoE equipment have not worked together and agreed on how this equipment should interface with other devices. If you are using a wireless device such as an access point and will be powering it using PoE, it is recommended that you purchase the PoE device from the same manufacturer as the access point. This recommendation holds true for any device when considering powering with PoE.

Second, and similar in nature to the first caveat, is that the output voltage required to power a wireless LAN device differs from manufacturer to manufacturer. This caveat is another reason to use the same vendor's equipment when using PoE. When in doubt, ask the manufacturer or the vendor from whom the equipment was purchased.

Finally, the unused pins used to carry the current over Ethernet are not standardized. One manufacturer may carry power on pins 4 and 5, while another carries power on pins 7 and 8. If you connect a cable carrying power on pins 4 and 5 to an access point that does not accept power on those pins, the access point will not power up.

Single-port DC Voltage Injectors

Access points and bridges that specify mandatory use of PoE include single-port DC voltage injectors for the purpose of powering the unit. See Figure 5.18 below for an example of a single-port DC voltage injector. These single-port injectors are acceptable when used with a small number of wireless infrastructure devices, but quickly become a burden, cluttering wiring closets, when building medium or large wireless networks.

FIGURE 5.18 A single-port PoE injector

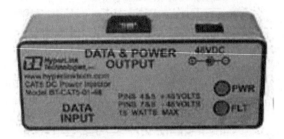

Multi-port DC Voltage Injectors

Several manufacturers offer multi-port injectors including 4, 6, or 12-port
models. These models may be more economical or convenient for
installations where many devices are to be powered through the Cat5
cable originating in a single wiring closet or from a single switch. Multi-
port DC voltage injectors typically operate in exactly the same manner as
their single-port counterparts. See Figure 5.19 for an example of a multi-
port PoE injector. A multi-port DC voltage injector looks like an Ethernet
switch with twice as many ports. A multi-port DC voltage injector is a
pass-through device to which you connect the Ethernet switch (or hub) to
the input port, and then connect the PoE client device to the output
device, both via Cat5 cable. The PoE injector connects to an AC power
source in the wiring closet. These multi-port injectors are appropriate for
medium-sized wireless network installations where up to 50 access points
are required, but in large enterprise rollouts, even the most dense multi-
port DC voltage injectors combined with Ethernet hubs or switches can
become cluttered when installed in a wiring closet.

FIGURE 5.19   A multi-port PoE injector

Active Ethernet Switches

The next step up for large enterprise installations of access points is the implementation of active Ethernet switches. These devices incorporate DC voltage injection into the Ethernet switch itself allowing for large numbers of PoE devices without any additional hardware in the network. See Figure 5.20 for an example of an Active Ethernet switch. Wiring closets will not have any additional hardware other than the Ethernet switches that would already be there for a non-PoE network. Several manufacturers make these switches in many different configurations (number of ports). In many Active Ethernet switches, the switch can auto-sense PoE client devices on the network. If the switch does not detect a PoE device on the line, the DC voltage is switched off for that port.

FIGURE 5.20   An Active Ethernet switch

As you can see from the picture, an Active Ethernet switch looks no different from an ordinary Ethernet switch. The only difference is the added internal functionality of supplying DC voltage to each port.

PoE Compatibility

Devices that are not "PoE Compatible" can be converted to Power-over-Ethernet by way of a DC "picker" or "tap". These are sometimes called Active Ethernet "splitters". This device picks-off the DC voltage that has been injected into the CAT5 cable by the injector and makes it available to the equipment through the regular DC power jack.

In order to use Power-over-Ethernet one of the two following device combinations are needed:

(Injector) + (PoE compatible device)

or

(Injector) + (non-PoE compatible device) + (Picker)

FIGURE 5.21   PoE using an injector

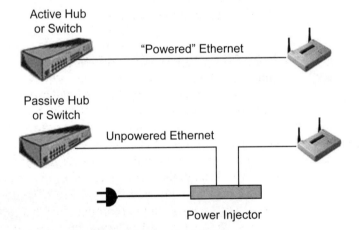

Types of Injectors

There are 2 basic types of Injectors available: *passive* and *fault protected*. Each type is typically available in a variety of voltage levels and number of ports.

Passive injectors place a DC voltage onto a CAT5 cable. These devices provide no short-circuit or over-current protection.

Fault protected injectors provide continuous fault monitoring and protection to detect short circuits and over-current conditions in the CAT5 cable.

Types of Picker / Taps

Two basic types of pickers and taps are available: *passive* and *regulated*. A passive tap simply takes the voltage from the Cat5 cable and directs it to the equipment for direct connection. Therefore, if the injector injects 48 VDC (Volts of Direct Current), then 48 VDC will be produced at the output of the passive tap.

A regulated tap takes the voltage on the Cat5 cable and converts it to another voltage. Several regulated voltages are available (5 VDC, 6 VDC, & 12 VDC) allowing a wide variety of non-PoE equipment to be powered through the Cat5 cable.

Voltage and Pinout Standards

Although the IEEE is working on standards such as 802.3af for PoE, a definitive standard has yet to be introduced. At present, different equipment vendors use different PoE voltages and Cat5 pin configurations to provide the DC power. Therefore, it is important to select the appropriate PoE devices for each piece of equipment you plan to power through the Cat5 cable. The IEEE has standardized on the use of 48 VDC as the injected PoE voltage. The use of this higher voltage reduces the current flowing through the Cat5 cable and therefore increases the load and increases the Cat5 cable length limitations. Where the maximum cable length has not been a major consideration, some vendors have chosen 24 VDC and even 12 VDC as their injected voltage.

Fault Protection

The primary purpose of fault protection is to protect the cable, the equipment, and the power supply in the event of a fault or short-circuit. During normal operation, a fault may never occur in the Cat5 cable. However, there are many ways a fault might be introduced into the Cat5 cable, including the following examples:

- The attached device may be totally incompatible with PoE and may have some non-standard or defective connection that short-circuits the PoE conductors. At present, most non-PoE devices have no connection on the PoE pins.

- Incorrectly wired Cat5 cabling. Cut or crushed Cat5 cable, in which the insulation on one or more of the conductors have come in contact with each other or another conducting material.

During any fault condition, the fault-protection circuit shuts off the DC voltage injected onto the cable. Fault protection circuit operation varies from model to model. Some models continuously monitor the cable and restore power automatically once the fault is removed. Some models must be manually reset by pressing a reset button or cycling power.

Wireless LAN Accessories

When the time comes to connect all of your wireless LAN devices together, you will need to purchase the appropriate cables and accessories that will maximize your throughput, minimize your signal loss, and, most importantly, allow you to make the connections correctly. This section will discuss the different types of accessories and where they fit into a wireless LAN design. The following types of accessories are discussed in this section:

- RF Amplifiers
- RF Attenuators
- Lightning Arrestors
- RF Connectors
- RF Cables
- RF Splitters

Each of these devices is important to building a successful wireless LAN. Some items are used more than others, and some items are mandatory whereas others are optional. It is likely that an administrator will have to install and use all of these items multiple times while implementing and managing a wireless LAN.

RF Amplifiers

As its name suggests, an RF amplifier is used to amplify, or increase the amplitude of, an RF signal. This positive increase in power is called GAIN and is measured in +dB. An amplifier will be used when compensating for the loss incurred by the RF signal, either due to the distance between antennas or the length of cable from a wireless infrastructure device to its antenna. Most RF amplifiers used with wireless LANs are powered using DC voltage fed onto the RF cable with a DC injector near the RF signal source (such as the access point or bridge).

Sometimes this DC voltage used to power RF amplifiers is called "phantom voltage" because the RF amplifier seems to magically power up. This DC injector is powered using AC voltage from a wall outlet, so it might be located in a wiring closet. In this scenario, the RF cable carries both the high frequency RF signal and the DC voltage necessary to power the in-line amplifier, which, in turn, boosts the RF signal amplitude. Figure 5.22 below depicts both an RF amplifier and a DC power injector.

FIGURE 5.22   A sample of a fixed-gain RF amplifier

Copyright Young Design, Inc. 2002, YDI.com

RF amplifiers come in two types: unidirectional and bi-directional. Unidirectional amplifiers compensate for the signal loss incurred over long RF cables by increasing the signal level before it is injected into the transmitting antenna. Bi-directional amplifiers boost the effective sensitivity of the receiving antenna by amplifying the received signal before it is fed into the access point, bridge, or client device. Bi-directional amplifiers should be placed as close to the antenna as possible so as to effectively compensate for cable loss between the antenna and the receiver (access point or bridge) for received signals. Most amplifiers used with wireless LANs are bi-directional and are preferred for use because they can be used to boost and cleanup weak signals coming into the antenna before the signal is passed onto the receiving device.

Common Options

Before you ever get to a point of deciding which amplifier to purchase, you should already know the amplifier specification requirements. Once you know the impedance (ohms), gain (dB), frequency response (range in GHz), VSWR, input (mW or dBm), and output (mW or dBm) specifications, you are ready to select an RF amplifier.

Frequency response is likely the first specification you will decide upon. If a wireless LAN uses the 5 GHz frequency spectrum, an amplifier that works only in the 2.4 GHz frequency spectrum will not work. Determine how much gain, input, and output power is required by performing the necessary RF math calculations. The amplifier should match impedances with all of the other wireless LAN hardware between the transmitter and the antenna. Generally, wireless LAN components have an impedance of 50 ohms; however, it is always a good idea to check the impedance of every component on a wireless LAN.

The amplifier must be connected into the network, so an amplifier should be chosen with the same kinds of connectors as the cables and/or antennas to which the amplifier will be connected. Typically, RF amplifiers will have either SMA or N-Type connectors. SMA and N-Type connectors perform well and are widely used.

Make sure that the amplifier you purchase comes with a calibration report and certificate. Although it is not feasible to disassemble your wireless LAN and send amplifiers in for calibration, an initial calibration report will at least let you know whether or not it started out working within the manufacturer's specifications.

Configuration & Management

RF amplifiers used with wireless LANs are installed in series with the main signal path as seen below in Figure 5.23. Amplifiers are typically mounted to a solid surface using screws through the amplifier's flange plates.

FIGURE 5.23   RF amplifier placement in the wireless LAN system

Access Point   Amplifier

⚠ Variable amplifiers are not recommended because the settings could inadvertently be changed, resulting in damage to the antenna or other downstream equipment or a violation of FCC rules governing output power in the ISM or UNII bands or certified systems. Fixed, linear RF amplifiers are recommended, and the RF calculations should be done ahead of time to make sure the RF signal strength will meet your application's needs and will be within FCC guidelines. These calculations are usually performed by the manufacturer that sells the amplifier as part of an FCC certified system.

Special Stipulations

The FCC's CFR 15.204 states that EVERY system used in the ISM and UNII bands must be certified as a complete system and given a certification number by the FCC. This certification will be accompanied by a certificate that will list the pieces of equipment and their FCC identifiers that are permitted for use with that specific wireless LAN system. All pieces of the wireless LAN setup that are used must be listed in the certificate. Understanding this requirement becomes especially crucial when dealing with amplifiers. A "system" is defined as the transmitting device, the cabling, connectors, amplifiers, attenuators, splitters, and the antenna. Manufacturers obtain FCC approval or "certification" of their hardware such that an end-user may purchase any of their radio devices and antennas and use them as a system without contacting the FCC for testing and certification. When additional devices such as amplifiers are added into the system, the manufacturer's certification no longer applies and a user must obtain his own certification of his system. This might cost as much as $12,000 per system. An answer to this problem might be to purchase an FCC certified system from a reputable vendor that meets the requirements of the wireless network.

CFR 15.204 does not allow an amplifier to be marketed or sold when not part of a "certified" system. The FCC maintains a database of certified systems and companies holding these certifications. This database can be searched at the following web address: http://gullfoss2.fcc.gov/cgi-bin/ws.exe/prod/oet/forms/reports/Search_Form.hts?form=Generic_Search. A typical system certification is shown in Figure 5.24.

FIGURE 5.24   FCC certification example

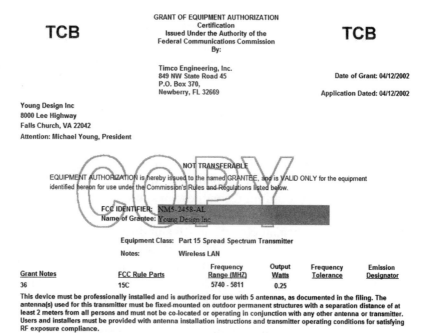

GRANT OF EQUIPMENT AUTHORIZATION
Certification
Issued Under the Authority of the
Federal Communications Commission
By:

TCB   **TCB**

Timco Engineering, Inc.
849 NW State Road 45
P.O. Box 370,
Newberry, FL 32669

Date of Grant: 04/12/2002

Application Dated: 04/12/2002

Young Design Inc
8000 Lee Highway
Falls Church, VA 22042
Attention: Michael Young, President

NOT TRANSFERABLE

EQUIPMENT AUTHORIZATION is hereby issued to the named GRANTEE, and is VALID ONLY for the equipment
identified hereon for use under the Commission's Rules and Regulations listed below.

FCC IDENTIFIER: NM5-2458-AL
Name of Grantee: Young Design Inc

Equipment Class: Part 15 Spread Spectrum Transmitter

Notes: Wireless LAN

Grant Notes	FCC Rule Parts	Frequency Range (MHZ)	Output Watts	Frequency Tolerance	Emission Designator
36	15C	5740 - 5811	0.25		

This device must be professionally installed and is authorized for use with 5 antennas, as documented in the filing. The
antenna(s) used for this transmitter must be fixed-mounted on outdoor permanent structures with a separation distance of at
least 2 meters from all persons and must not be co-located or operating in conjunction with any other antenna or transmitter.
Users and installers must be provided with antenna installation instructions and transmitter operating conditions for satisfying
RF exposure compliance.

36:   Certain antennas used with this equipment require a minimum cable length, or have output power limitations as
documented in the application.

This website is meticulously maintained by the FCC, and is always
current. Typical updates are a minimum of weekly. The end-user is
liable for violations of FCC rules while they use the equipment. FCC
violations may result in fines of $27,500 - $1,200,000 per violation. The
FCC usually typically allows a violator a brief (e.g. 10 days) time to
correct the problem and report to the FCC how the violation was repaired.
It is not uncommon for the FCC to audit a Wireless ISP looking for
certified system infractions.

Many manufacturers do not produce amplifiers to be used with their
systems. For this reason, there are companies that produce amplifiers (but
not wireless LAN hardware) that obtain FCC certification of an entire
wireless LAN system using their amplifiers and another vendor's wireless
LAN hardware together. Be careful in what type of amplifiers you buy in
that some amplifiers cause the FCC to only certify systems as being able
to use DSSS channels 2-10 or 3-9 instead of 1-11 like an un-amplified

system. This is due to how the RF signal is amplified and bleeds over into licensed RF frequency spectrum outside of the ISM or UNII bands.

The FCC's CFR 15.203 says that installers are responsible to make sure that intentional radiators are used with authorized antennas. Antennas may be made such that they can be repaired, but not attached to non-certified matching intentional radiators.

One common question that we would like to address regarding CFR 15.204 is that one manufacturer's antennas may not be used with another manufacturer's intentional radiator (bridge, PC Card, or access point for example) without FCC certification as a system. This ruling directly affects those individuals that would connect a Pringles can antenna to a PC Card for the purpose of war driving.

When purchasing an RF amplifier for use as part of a wireless LAN, ask for a copy of the FCC certification documenting use of the amplifier BEFORE you purchase. There are two classes of changes that can be made to an FCC certification. First is a class I change. This type of change can be made by the manufacturer who may document a change that has no negative affect on RF propagation or signal density (increasing interference with other systems in your immediate environment) by noting on the FCC certificate and then writing a brief synopsis on what the change involved and why it had no negative affect. A class II change is a change that does negatively affect RF propagation or signal density and requires that the FCC recertify the system.

RF Attenuators

An RF attenuator is a device that causes precisely measured loss (in –dB) in an RF signal. While an amplifier will increase the RF signal, an attenuator will decrease it. Why would you need or want to *decrease* your RF signal? Consider the case where an access point has a fixed output of 100mW, and the only antenna available is an omni-directional antenna with +20 dBi gain. Using this equipment together would violate FCC rules for power output, so an attenuator could be added to decrease the RF signal down to 30mW before it entered the antenna. This configuration would put the power output within FCC parameters. Figure 5.25 shows examples of fixed-loss RF attenuators with BNC connectors (left) and SMA connectors (right). Figure 5.26 shows an example of an RF step attenuator.

FIGURE 5.25   A sample of a fixed-loss RF attenuator

FIGURE 5.26   A sample of a RF step attenuator (variable loss)

Common Options

RF attenuators are available as either fixed-loss or variable-loss. Like variable amplifiers, variable attenuators allow the administrator to configure the amount of loss that is caused in the RF signal with precision. Variable RF attenuators are not used in wireless LAN systems due to the FCC's regulations on certified systems. They are typically used in site surveys in order to determine antenna gain, necessity of amplifiers, etc.

 Variable attenuators are not recommended because the settings could inadvertently be changed, resulting in damage to the antenna or receiving equipment. Fixed RF attenuators are recommended where the RF calculations are done ahead of time to assure the signals are within FCC guidelines. Once the necessary attenuation is calculated, the appropriate fixed-loss attenuator can be purchased.

FIGURE 5.27 RF Attenuator placement in a wireless LAN

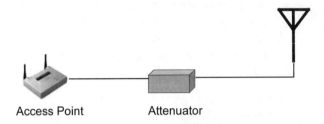

Access Point   Attenuator

In choosing what kind of attenuator is required, consider the similar items as when choosing an RF amplifier (see above). The type of attenuator (fixed or variable loss), impedance, ratings (input power, loss, and frequency response), and connector types should all be part of the decision-making process.

 All attenuators should come with a calibration report and certificate. It may not be feasible to disassemble your wireless LAN in order to calibrate an attenuator annually so making sure that the attenuator meets the manufacturer's specifications prior to installation is a good idea.

Configuration and Management

Figure 5.27 above shows the proper placement in a wireless LAN for an RF attenuator, which is directly in series with the main signal path. Fixed, coaxial attenuators are connected directly between any two connection points between the transmitter and the antenna. For example, a fixed, coaxial attenuator might be connected directly on the output of an access point, at the input to the antenna, or anywhere between these two points if multiple RF cables are used.

Configuration of RF attenuators is not required unless a variable attenuator is being used, in which case the amount of attenuation required is configured according to your RF calculations. Configuration instructions for any particular attenuator will be included in the manufacturer's user manual. To reiterate, you will likely not see the FCC certify a system that has a variable attenuator.

Lightning Arrestors

A lightning arrestor is used to shunt into the ground transient current that is caused by lightning. Lightning arrestors are used for protecting wireless LAN hardware such as access points, bridges, and workgroup bridges that are attached to a coaxial transmission line. Coaxial transmission lines are susceptible to surges from nearby lightning strikes.

 One common misconception about lightning arrestors is that they are installed to protect against a direct lightning strike. If a bolt of lightning strikes your wireless LAN antenna with the best lightning arrestor on the market installed, your antenna will be destroyed and your wireless LAN will probably be damaged as well. A lightning arrestor is not meant to withstand a direct lightning strike, nor protect your network from such a strike.

A lightning arrestor can generally shunt (redirect) surges of up to 5000 Amperes at up to 50 Volts. Lightning arrestors (depending on type) function as follows:

1. Lightning strikes a nearby object

2. Transient currents are induced into the antenna or the RF transmission line

3. The lightning arrestor senses these currents and immediately ionizes the gases held internally to cause a short (a path of almost no resistance) directly to earth ground

Figure 5.28 shows some types of lightning arrestors. The one shown on the right shunts transient currents to ground by way of the physical characteristics of the lightning arrestor itself while allowing the appropriate RF signals to pass.

FIGURE 5.28 Sample lightning arrestors

Copyright Young Design, Inc. 2002, YDI.com

Figure 5.29 shows how a lightning arrestor is installed on a wireless LAN. When objects are struck by lightning an electric field is built around that object for just an instant. When the lightning ceases to induce electricity into the object, the field collapses. When the field collapses, it induces high amounts of current into nearby objects, which, in this case, would be your wireless LAN antenna or coaxial transmission line. Lightning is discharged as a direct current (DC) pulse, but then causes an alternating current (AC) component to be formed resonating as high as 1 GHz. However, most of the power is dissipated from DC to 10 MHz.

FIGURE 5.29 A lightning arrestor installed on a network

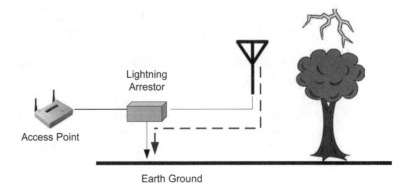

Common Options

There are few options on a lightning arrestor, and the cost will be $50 - $150 for any brand. However, there are some attributes that should be considered for any lightning arrestor that is purchased:

- It should meet the IEEE standard of <8 µS

- Reusable

- Gas tube breakdown voltage

- Connector types

- Frequency response

- Impedance

- Insertion loss

- VSWR rating

- Warranty

IEEE Standards

Most lightning arrestors are able to trigger a short to Earth ground in under 2 microseconds (µS), but the IEEE specifies that this process should happen in no more than 8 µS. It is very important that the lightning arrestor you choose at least meet the IEEE standard.

Reusable Units

Some lightning arrestors are reusable after a lightning strike, and some are not. It is more cost effective to own an arrestor that can be used a number of times. Some reusable models have replaceable gas discharge tube elements that are cheaper to replace than the entire lightning arrestor. Other models may have physical characteristics that allow the lightning arrestor to do its job properly multiple times with no replaceable parts.

Voltage Breakdown

Some lightning arrestors support the passing of DC voltage for use in powering RF amplifiers and others do not. A lightning arrestor should be able to pass the DC voltage used in powering RF amplifiers if you plan on placing an RF amplifier closer to the antenna than the lightning arrestor. The gas tube breakdown voltage (the voltage at which the arrestor begins shorting current to ground) should be higher than the voltage required to operate in-line RF amplifiers. It is suggested that you place lightning arrestors as the last component on the RF transmission line before the antenna so that the lightning arrestor can protect amplifiers and attenuators along with your bridge or access point.

Connector Types

Make sure the connector types of the lightning arrestor you choose match those on the cable you are planning to use on your wireless LAN. If they do not match, then adapter connectors will have to be used, inserting more loss into the RF circuit than is necessary.

Frequency Response

The frequency response specification of the lightning arrestor should be at least as high as the highest frequency used in a wireless LAN. For example, if you are using only a 2.4 GHz wireless LAN, a lightning arrestor that is specified for use at up to 3 GHz is best.

Impedance

The impedance of the arrestor should match all of the other devices in the circuit between the transmitter and the antenna. Impedance is usually 50 ohms in most wireless LANs.

Insertion Loss

The insertion loss should be significantly low (perhaps around 0.1 dB) so as not to cause high RF signal amplitude loss as the signal passes through the arrestor.

VSWR Rating

The VSWR rating of a good quality lightning arrestor will be around 1.1:1, but some may be as high as 1.5:1. The lower the ratio of the device, the better, since reflected voltage degrades the main RF signal.

Warranty

Regardless of the quality of a lightning arrestor, the unit can malfunction. Seek out a manufacturer that offers a good warranty on their lightning arrestors. Some manufacturers offer a highly desirable "No Matter What" type of warranty.

Configuration & Maintenance

No configuration is necessary for a lightning arrestor. Lightning arrestors are installed in series with the main RF signal path, and the grounding connection should be attached to an Earth ground with a measurable resistance of 5 ohms or less. It is recommended that you test an Earth ground connection with an appropriate Earth ground resistance tester before deciding that the installation of the lightning arrestor is satisfactory. Make it a point, along with other periodic maintenance tasks, to check the Earth ground resistance and the gas discharge tube regularly.

RF Splitters

An RF Splitter is a device that has a single input connector and multiple output connectors. An RF Splitter is used for the purpose of splitting a single signal into multiple independent RF signals. Use of splitters in everyday implementations of wireless LANs is not recommended. Sometimes two 120-degree panel antennas or two 90-degree panel antennas may be combined with a splitter and equal-length cables when the antennas are pointing in opposite directions. This configuration will produce a bi-directional coverage area, which may be ideal for covering the area along a river or major highway. Back-to-back 90 degree panels may be separated by as little as 10 inches or as much as 40 inches on either side of the mast or tower. Each panel in this configuration may have a mechanical down tilt. The resultant gain in each of the main radiation lobes is reduced by 3 - 4 dB in these configurations.

When installing an RF splitter, the input connector should always face the source of the RF signal. The output connectors (sometimes called "taps") are connected facing the destination of the RF signal (the antenna). Figure 5.30 shows two examples of RF splitters. Figure 5.31 illustrates how an RF splitter would be used in a wireless LAN installation.

Splitters may be used to keep track of power output on a wireless LAN link. By hooking a power meter to one output of the splitter and the RF antenna to the other, an administrator can actively monitor the output at any given time. In this scenario, the power meter, the antenna, and the splitter must all have equal impedance. Although not a common practice, removing the power meter from one output of the splitter and replacing it with a 50 ohm dummy load would allow the administrator to move the power meter from one connection point to another throughout the wireless LAN while making output power measurements.

Power splitters are yet another device that can be used as part of a wireless LAN. Keep in mind that the splitter MUST be part of a certified system if used in your wireless LAN.

FIGURE 5.30   Sample RF Splitters

FIGURE 5.31   A RF Splitter installed on a network

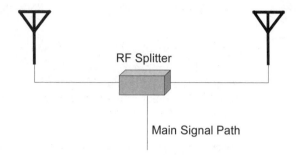

Choosing an RF Splitter

Below is a checklist of things to consider when choosing an RF splitter.

- Insertion loss
- Frequency response
- Impedance
- VSWR rating
- High isolation impedance
- Power ratings
- Connector types
- Calibration report
- Mounting
- DC voltage passing

Insertion Loss

Low insertion loss (loss incurred by just introducing the item into the circuit) is necessary because simply putting the splitter in the RF circuit can cause a significant RF signal amplitude decrease. Insertion loss of 0.5 dB or less is considered good for an RF splitter.

Do not confuse insertion loss with the loss of amplitude incurred between the input connector and any output connector (called "through loss"). The number of connectors on an RF splitter will determine the number of ways (speaking in terms of power division) that the RF amplitude will be split. A two-way splitter should have 3-4 dB loss between the input connector and either output connector. Loss higher than this can be attributed either to insertion loss (which is added to through loss when measured) or to inaccuracies in the splitter's ability to divide the power between output connectors.

Frequency Response

The frequency response specification of the splitter should be at least as high as the highest frequency used in the wireless LAN. For example, if you were using only a 2.4 GHz wireless LAN, a splitter that is specified for use at up to 3 GHz would be best.

Impedance

The impedance of the splitter, which is usually 50 ohms in most wireless LANs, should match all of the other devices in the circuit between the transmitter and the antenna.

VSWR Rating

As with many other RF devices, VSWR ratings should be as close to 1:1 as possible. Typical VSWR ratings on RF splitters are < 1.5:1. Low VSWR ratings on splitters are much more critical than on many other devices in an RF system, because reflected RF power in a splitter may be reflected in multiple directions inside the splitter, affecting both the splitter input signal and all splitter output signals.

High Isolation Impedance

High isolation impedance between ports on an RF splitter is important for several reasons. First, a load on one output port should not affect the output power on another output port of the splitter. Second, a signal arriving into the output port of a splitter (such as the received RF signal) should be directed to the input port rather than to another output port. These requirements are accomplished through high impedance between output connectors. Typical isolation (resistance causing separation) is 20 dB or more between ports.

Power Ratings

Splitters are rated for power input maximums, which means that you are limited in the amount of power that you can run feed into your splitter. Exceeding the manufacturer's power rating will result in damage to the RF splitter.

Connector Types

RF splitters will generally have N-type or SMA connectors. It is very important to purchase a splitter with the same connector types as the cable being used. Doing so cuts down on adapter connectors, which reduce RF signal amplitude. This knowledge is especially important when using splitters, since splitters already cut the signal amplitude in an RF system.

Calibration Report

All RF splitters should come with a calibration report that shows insertion loss, frequency response, through loss at each connector, etc. Having splitters calibrated once per year is not feasible so it is essential that the administrator know before initial installation whether or not the splitter meets the manufacturer's specifications. Continued calibration requires taking the wireless LAN off line for an extended period of time, and may not be practical in many situations.

Mounting

Mounting an RF splitter is usually a matter of putting screws through the flange plates into whatever surface on which the splitter will be mounted. Some models come with pole-mounting hardware using "U" bolts, mounting plates, and standard-sized nuts. Depending on the manufacturer, the splitter might be weatherproof, meaning it can be mounted outside on a pole without fear of water causing problems. When this is the case, be sure to seal cable connections and use drip loops.

DC Voltage Passing

Some RF splitters have the option of passing the required DC voltage to all output ports in parallel. This feature is helpful when there are RF amplifiers, which power internal circuitry with DC voltage originating from a DC voltage injector in a wiring closet, located on the output of each splitter port.

RF Connectors

RF connectors are specific types of connection devices used to connect cables to devices or devices to devices. Traditionally, N, F, SMA, BNC, & TNC connectors (or derivatives) have been used for RF connectors on wireless LANs.

In 1994, the FCC and DOC (now Industry Canada) ruled that connectors for use with wireless LAN devices should be proprietary between manufacturers. For this reason, many variations on each connector type exist such as:

- N-type
- Reverse polarity N-type
- Reverse threaded N-type

Figure 5.32 illustrates the N and SMA type connectors.

FIGURE 5.32   Sample N-type and SMA connectors

The N Connector   The SMA Connector

Choosing an RF Connector

There are five things that should be considered when purchasing and installing any RF connector, and they are similar in nature to the criteria for choosing RF amplifiers and attenuators.

1. The RF connector should match the impedance of all other wireless LAN components (generally 50 ohms). This is normally not a problem since even when you purchase like connectors with different impedances, they will not properly fit together because of center-pin sizing.

2. Know how much insertion loss each connector inserted into the signal path causes. The amount of loss caused will factor into your calculations for signal strength required and distance allowed.

3. Know the upper frequency limit (frequency response) specified for the particular connectors. This point will be very important as 5 Ghz wireless LANs become more and more common. Some connectors are rated only as high as 3 GHz, which is fine for use with 2.4 GHz wireless LANs, but will not work for 5 GHz wireless LANs. Some connectors are rated only up to 1 GHz and will not work with wireless LANs at all, other than legacy 900 MHz wireless LANs.

4. Beware of bad quality connectors. First, always consider purchasing from a reputable company. Second, purchase only high-quality connectors made by name-brand manufacturers. This kind of purchasing particularity will help eliminate many problems with sporadic RF signals, VSWR, and bad connections.

5. Make sure you know both the type of connector (N, F, SMA, etc.) that you need and the sex of the connector. Connectors come in male and female. Male connectors have a center pin, and female connectors have a center receptacle.

RF Cables

In the same manner that you must choose the proper cables for your 10 Gbps wired infrastructure backbone, you must choose the proper cables for connecting an antenna to an access point or wireless bridge. Below are some criteria to be considered in choosing the proper cables for your wireless network.

- Cables introduce loss into a wireless LAN, so make sure the shortest cable length necessary is used.

- Plan to purchase pre-cut lengths of cable with pre-installed connectors. Doing so minimizes the possibility of bad connections between the connector and the cable. Professional manufacturing practices are almost always superior to cables manufactured by untrained individuals.

- Look for the lowest loss cable available at your particular price range (the lower the loss, the more expensive the cable). Cables are typically rated for loss in dB/100-feet. The table in Figure 5.33 illustrates the loss that is introduced by adding cables to a wireless LAN.

- Purchase cable that has the same impedance as all of your other wireless LAN components (generally 50 ohms).

- The frequency response of the cable should be considered as a primary decision factor in your purchase. With 2.4 GHz wireless LANs, a cable with a rating of at least 2.5 GHz should be used. With 5 GHz wireless LANs, a cable with a rating of at least 6 GHz should be used.

- One might have to use an extension cable when an access point and its remote antenna are far apart (such as in an outdoor installation). In this case, be aware that connectors drop ~0.25 dB and cable loss can be very significant (depending on cable type used). Use of longer Cat5 cable can sometimes remedy the situation by allowing the access point to be moved closer to the antenna. RG-58 cable should never be used for extension cables due to bad frequency response. LMR, Heliax, or other appropriate high-frequency cable should be used for extensions.

If the FCC performs an inspection on your wireless LAN (which they are authorized to do at any time), they will make note of the manufacturer, model number, length, and type of connectors on your RF cable. These pieces of information should be documented in your system's FCC certificate.

FIGURE 5.33   Coaxial cable attenuation ratings (in dB/100 feet at X MHz)

LMR CABLE	30	50	150	220	450	900	1500	1800	2000	2500
100A	3.9	5.1	8.9	10.9	15.8	22.8	30.1	33.2	35.2	39.8
195	2.0	2.6	4.4	5.4	7.8	11.1	14.5	16.0	16.9	19.0
200	1.8	2.3	4.0	4.8	7.0	9.9	12.9	14.2	15.0	16.9
240	1.3	1.7	3.0	3.7	5.3	7.6	9.9	10.9	11.5	12.9
300	1.1	1.4	2.4	2.9	4.2	6.1	7.9	8.7	9.2	10.4
400	0.7	0.9	1.5	1.9	2.7	3.9	5.1	5.7	6.0	6.8
400UF	0.8	1.1	1.7	2.2	3.1	4.5	5.9	6.6	6.9	7.8
500	0.54	.70	1.2	1.5	2.2	3.1	4.1	4.6	4.8	5.5
600	0.42	.55	1.0	1.2	1.7	2.5	3.3	3.7	3.9	4.4
600UF	0.48	.63	1.15	1.4	2.0	2.9	3.8	4.3	4.5	5.1
900	0.29	0.37	0.66	0.80	1.17	1.70	2.24	2.48	2.63	2.98
1200	0.21	0.27	0.48	0.59	0.89	1.3	1.7	1.9	2.0	2.3
1700	0.15	0.19	0.35	0.43	0.63	0.94	1.3	1.4	1.5	1.7

There are three major manufacturers of RF cable used with wireless LANs. Those are Andrew, Times Microwave, and Belden. Andrew's Heliax cable, Times Microwave's LMR, and Belden's RF-series are all popular in the wireless LAN industry. LMR cable has become somewhat of an industry standard in the same way Xerox became known for copiers. Sometimes the term "LMR" is used in place of "RF cable" in the same way "Xerox" is used in place of "copy."

RF "Pigtail" Adapter Cable

Pigtail adapter cables are used to connect cables that have industry-standard connectors to manufacturer's wireless LAN equipment. Pigtails are used to adapt proprietary connectors to industry standard connectors like N-type and SMA connectors. One end of the pigtail cable is the proprietary connector while the other end is the industry-standard connector. Figure 5.34 shows an example of a pigtail cable.

FIGURE 5.34   Sample RF Pigtail adapter

The DOC and FCC (United States Federal Communications Commission) ruling of June 23, 1994, stated that connectors manufactured after June 23, 1994 must be manufactured as proprietary antenna connectors. The 1994 rule was intended to discourage use of amplifiers, high-gain antennas, or other means of increasing RF radiation significantly. The rules are further intended to discourage "home brew" systems which are installed by inexperienced users and which - either accidentally or intentionally - do not comply with FCC regulations for use in the ISM band.

Since this rule was enacted, consumers have had to obtain proprietary connectors from manufacturers to connect to an industry standard connector. Third party manufacturers have begun custom making these adapter cables (called "pigtails") and selling them inexpensively on the open market. Keep in mind that the FCC's CFR 15.204 does NOT allow "home brew" systems of any kind. All systems must be certified, and a system is defined as an intentional radiator, an antenna, and everything between. Those individuals using security utilities such as Netstumbler with a Pringles can (or similar) antennas are in violation of this FCC regulation. This is mentioned both to answer the commonly asked question and as an example of how this regulation is interpreted by the FCC. Any pigtails or antennas used with a wireless LAN in the ISM or UNII bands must be part of a certified system and documented as such by the FCC.

Frequency Converter

Frequency converters are used for converting one frequency range to another for the purpose of decongesting a frequency band. Suppose many companies that were located in the same multi-tenant office building had wireless LANs (which is common). Each of these companies wants building-to-building wireless connectivity with a building next door because each of these companies has an office in the adjacent building. It is easy to see that only 3 companies will be able to use wireless LAN building-to-building bridging due to a limited number of non-overlapping channels. In this case, a frequency converter may be deployed that will use existing 2.4 GHz wireless equipment, but will convert the frequencies to a less congested band (such as the 5.8 GHz upper UNII band) for this wireless bridge segment.

FIGURE 5.35   Sample frequency converter

Copyright Young Design, Inc. 2002, YDI.com

Proper antennas and cables must be used when using a frequency converter due to both antennas and cables having limited frequency response, but it can be a very economical solution in a congested area. The alternative would be to replace all wireless LAN hardware with new 5 GHz hardware. Figure 5.36 shows how a frequency converter would be installed in a wireless LAN configuration.

FIGURE 5.36 Using a frequency converter

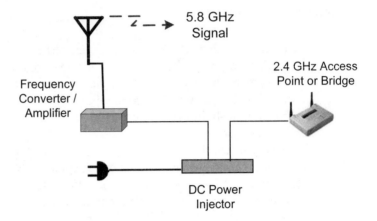

Bandwidth Control Units

Wireless LANs are a shared medium with very low throughput in comparison with today's wired LAN technologies. For this reason, bandwidth on wireless LANs must be conserved and protected - especially in outdoor environments such as would be found with wireless Internet service providers (WISPs). Bandwidth should be controlled in such a manner that each user has a reliable and consistent connectivity experience and gets what they are paying for. With indoor wireless LAN installations, it is not as common to use a Bandwidth Control Unit (BCU) because many users are expecting to have the same experience as they had on the wired LAN. This simply isn't feasible considering the extreme bandwidth differences. However, administrators strive to give indoor LAN users as much bandwidth as possible by not overloading access points. In a wireless LAN, the BCU is placed between the access point or bridge and the network, as shown in Figure 5.37.

FIGURE 5.37   Using a bandwidth control unit

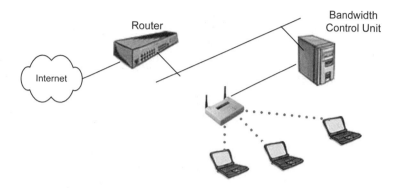

BCUs typically work by filtering on MAC addresses in order to drop each user into a pre-assigned queue. Each queue has particular properties such as upstream and downstream bandwidth. Multiple users might be put into the same queue. This allows for precise bandwidth control and accounting per user. BCUs are managed through various software packages, such as the one shown in Figure 5.38.

FIGURE 5.38   Manager application for a BCU

TS Queue	Status	Assignment	Utilization %	Pkts Sent	Bytes Sent	Pkts Discard
Queue 1	320/128	1	50	2,762	2,112,044	21
Queue 2	320	1	1	288,693	118,436,003	1,023
Queue 3	320	1	0	927	103,326	0
Queue 4	320	1	0	2,861	306,041	0
Queue 5	320	1	0	59	8,855	0
Queue 6	320	1	0	14,217	8,735,724	0

Test Kits

There are many types of test kits on the market. One of the most valuable types of test kits in the wireless LAN industry is one used for testing cables and connectors. The kit might consist of an RF signal generator and a through-line power meter. The signal generator can be hooked directly to the power meter to get a baseline measurement. When putting cables and connectors between the signal generator and the power meter, it can be determined if they meet the manufacturer's specifications and if they are intermittent. The connectors on cables can become worn and loose making a bad or intermittently bad connection. They can also take on water, which would be highly detrimental to their RF characteristics. It is important to test cables and connectors before deployment and periodically as possible thereafter.

FIGURE 5.39   Sample test kit

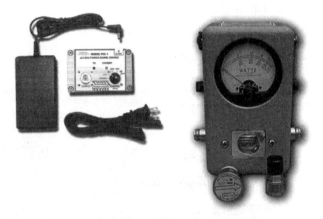

Key Terms

Before taking the exam, you should be familiar with the following terms:

azimuth

beam

beamwidth

bi-directional amplifier

coverage area

horizontal beamwidth

lobe

narrowing

n-type

pigtails

point-to-multipoint

point-to-point

radiation pattern

SMA-type

transient current

unidirectional amplifier

unused pair

vertical beamwidth

Review Questions

1. In a small warehouse installation, you must provide the greatest coverage area possible for the users inside the warehouse. The warehouse is free from tall obstructions such as shelving, but has a high ceiling. You have decided to use a low-gain omni-directional antenna to achieve your goal. For the best coverage area, where should the antenna be installed?

   A. In the center of the building on the roof

   B. In the center of the building on the ceiling

   C. In one of the corners of the building

   D. On one of the walls of the building

2. When purchasing RF connectors, which of the following should be considered when making your decision? Choose all that apply.

   A. Impedance

   B. Insertion loss

   C. Gain

   D. Maximum frequency allowed

3. You have been hired as a consultant to install a wireless LAN that will connect only two buildings that are 1.5 miles (2.5 km) apart at 11 Mbps. Which one of the following antennas would you use?

   A. Omni-directional

   B. High-gain Dipole

   C. High-gain Yagi

   D. Parabolic dish

4. You have been hired as a consultant to install a wireless LAN that will connect two buildings that are 10 miles (16.7 km) apart. In this particular area, wind gusts are a problem. Which one of the following antennas would you use?

    A. High-gain Grid

    B. High-gain Dipole

    C. High-gain Yagi

    D. Parabolic dish

5. You have been hired as a consultant to install a wireless LAN that will connect four buildings that are 100 meters apart. Which of the following antennas could you use? Choose all that apply.

    A. 4 dipole antennas

    B. 4 patch antennas

    C. 1 dipole and 3 patch antennas

    D. 2 parabolic dish antennas and 2 Yagi antennas

    E. 4 panel antennas

6. A wireless LAN installation has a 50-meter cable running between the access point and a highly-directional antenna. The output signal being sent and received is very weak at each end of the link. What device could you add to the configuration that would fix the problem?

    A. Uni-directional amplifier

    B. Bi-directional amplifier

    C. Uni-directional attenuator

    D. Bi-directional attenuator

7. The RF signal amplitude loss that occurs because of the natural broadening of the RF wave front is referred to as which one of the following?

   A. Fresnel zone loss

   B. Coverage area loss

   C. Radiation pattern loss

   D. Free space path loss

8. PoE could be used in which one of the following scenarios?

   A. To power an antenna that is less than 100 meters away from an access point

   B. To power an antenna that is more than 100 meters away from an access point

   C. To power an access point that is less than 100 meters away from a wiring closet

   D. To power an access point that is more than 100 meters away from a wiring closet

9. You are performing an outdoor installation of an omni-directional antenna. Which of the following will you need to do to ensure proper installation? Choose all that apply.

   A. Check that RF LOS exists with the other antennas in the installation

   B. Check that visual LOS exists with the other antennas in the installation

   C. Install a lightning arrestor to protect against transient currents

   D. Seal all the cable connections in the series to prevent water damage

10. Which of the following are true about PoE devices from different manufacturers? Choose all that apply.

    A. They always use the same unused pairs for sending current

    B. They are guaranteed to interoperate with devices from other vendors

    C. They use the same output voltage

    D. They may cause damage to devices from other vendors

11. You have purchased a semi-directional antenna from Vendor A, and an access point from Vendor B that have been certified as a system by the FCC through a third party. What type of cables or connectors must be used as part of this system in order to connect the access point to the antenna?

    A. An RF cable with industry standard connectors and a pigtail cable with appropriate connectors

    B. An RF cable with connectors matching the access point and a pigtail cable with appropriate connectors for the antenna and RF cable connection

    C. An RF cable with N connectors and a pigtail with N connectors on both sides

    D. An RF cable with SMA connectors and a pigtail with N connectors on both sides

12. An antenna's beamwidth refers to which one of the following?

    A. The width of the RF signal beam that the antenna transmits

    B. The width of the antenna main element

    C. The width of the mounting beam on which the antenna is mounted

    D. The width of the beam of the RF signal relative to the Earth's surface

13. When should an omni-directional antenna be used?

    A. When coverage in all horizontal directions from the antenna is required

    B. When coverage in a specific direction is required

    C. When coverage is required over more than 7 miles (11.7 km) in a specific direction

    D. Indoors only, for short-range coverage of non-roaming wireless LAN clients

14. Which of the following are names of semi-directional antenna types? Choose all that apply.

    A. Yagi

    B. Omni

    C. Patch

    D. Panel

    E. Point-to-point

15. The coverage area of a Yagi antenna is ONLY in the direction that the antenna is pointing. This statement is:

    A. Always true

    B. Always false

    C. Sometimes true, depending on the antenna manufacturer

    D. Depends on how the antenna itself is installed

16. Polarization is defined as which one of the following?

    A. The direction of the RF antenna in relation to the north and south poles

    B. The magnetic force behind the antenna element

    C. The power sources of an antenna that cause the antenna to transmit signal in more than one direction

    D. The physical orientation of the antenna in a horizontal or vertical position

17. Which one of the following is an accurate description of an access point with vertically polarized antennas?

    A.   Both antennas are standing perpendicular to the Earth's surface

    B.   Both antennas are standing parallel to the Earth's surface

    C.   One antenna is parallel to the Earth's surface and the other is perpendicular to the Earth's surface

18. What is the unit of measurement for gain as related to an RF antenna?

    A.   Decibels

    B.   Watts

    C.   dBi

    D.   dBm

    E.   dB

19. Which one of the following defines Free Space Path Loss?

    A.   The loss incurred by an RF signal whose path has crossed a large free space

    B.   What occurs as an RF signal is deflected off of its intended path into free space

    C.   The loss incurred by an RF signal due largely to "signal dispersion" which is a natural broadening of the wave front

    D.   The weakening of the RF signal propagation due to an infinite amount of free space

20. Which of the following are variations of the "N-type" connector?

    A.   Standard N-type

    B.   Reverse threaded N-type

    C.   Reverse polarity N-type

    D.   Dual head N-type

Answers to Review Questions

1. B. In an open area where maximum user coverage is required, using a low-gain omni antenna makes practical and economic sense. Warehouses typically have high ceilings, so use of a high-gain omni might not be effective for users below the antenna. Mounting the antenna near the center of the intended coverage area in an out-of-the-way place like the ceiling is most effective.

2. A, B, D. Making sure the connector you choose has the right impedance for your system, has a low insertion loss, and supports frequencies at least as high as the circuit with which you'll be using it are critical. There is a vast range of quality in connector choices where seemingly the same connector might cost $1.00 from one manufacturer and $20.00 from another. Typically, the more expensive manufacturer has made their connector to exacting standards and fully guarantees their product.

3. C. Yagi antennas are most often used on short to medium length building-to-building bridging up to 2 miles (3.3 km). Patch and panel antennas are more typically used on short range building-to-building and in-building directional links and Parabolic Dish antennas are more often used on very long distance links such as 2-25 miles (3-42 km). Omni-directional and dipole antennas are the same thing and are mostly used indoors. If omni antennas are used outdoors, the required coverage area is often relatively small.

4. A. While both parabolic dish and grid antennas will perform the function of connecting building miles apart, the grid antenna is designed for maximum resistance to wind loading by being perforated to let the wind pass through it. A parabolic dish in this scenario would likely cause intermittent service for the wireless link due to wind loading.

5. A, C. In this very short-range scenario, 4 omni-directional antennas such as dipoles could be used. The better scenario for security reasons is to use a single omni-directional antenna and three semi-directional antennas using only as much power at each antenna as necessary. This configuration forms a star topology, which is commonly used in such point-to-multipoint scenarios.

6. B. By adding a bi-directional amplifier to this scenario, the signal

produced by the access point will be amplified before the antenna transmits the signal. Even though the received signal is the same amplitude as before, the bi-directional amplifier boosts the signal before it enters the access point so that the signal is above the amplitude threshold of the access point.

7. D. Free Space Path Loss or just "Path Loss" is the reason that the amplitude of the RF signal at the receiver is significantly less than what was transmitted. Path Loss is a result of both the natural broadening of the wave front and the size of the receiving aperture.

8. C. Power over Ethernet is used for getting DC power to an access point from a power injector. Access points located further than 100 meters from a wiring closet (where the injector will be located) will not have the luxury of PoE because the DC power is sent over the same cable as the data. Since Cat5 cable can only extend to 100 meters and still be used for reliable data transmission, PoE should not be used on cable lengths over 100 meters.

9. A, C, D. RF line of sight is critical for the proper functioning of any wireless LAN link. Not having line of sight means that throughput will be reduced, possibly significantly. Installing lightning arrestors, sealing connectors that are outside the building, proper grounding, and lightning rods may all be significant parts of an outdoor installation. Visual line of sight is not necessary in order to have a good RF connection. Fog, smog, rain, snow, or long distances might for good RF LOS and no Visual LOS.

10. D. Since no standard yet exists for PoE, manufacturers implement PoE in various ways. Various voltages and polarities are used as well as different sets of unused pins in the Cat5 cable. Be careful not to damage your wireless LAN equipment by using PoE equipment from one vendor and wireless LAN equipment from another. PoE is sometimes called Power-over-LAN as well.

11. B. A pigtail cable is used to adapt two different kinds of connectors. Typically one of the connectors is an industry standard type such as an N type or SMA, but not necessarily. Having the RF cable's connector match the access point's connector saves from having to purchase separate adapter connectors, which would insert more loss into the circuit. The pigtail cable will be attached to the RF cable and the antenna.

12. A. Beamwidth refers to the angle of transmission (for both horizontal and vertical) from an antenna. For example, a patch antenna might have a 45-degree vertical beamwidth and a 65-degree horizontal beamwidth whereas a dipole antenna might have a 40-degree vertical beamwidth and would have a 360-degree horizontal beamwidth.

13. A. Omni-directional antennas radiate in a 360-degree field around the element, providing complete coverage in the shape of a doughnut horizontally around the antenna.

14. A, C, D. Yagi, Patch, and Panel antennas are common types of semi-directional antennas that loosely focus their radiation pattern in general direction.

15. B. Yagi antennas always have a back lobe and sometimes have significant side lobes as well. The size of these lobes depends on the gain and design of the antenna. Whether or not the side and rear lobes are used effectively is irrelevant to this question. The lobes are there regardless of whether or not they are used. Sometimes these lobes can even interfere with other systems when care is not taken to aim them properly or to block them with obstacles.

16. D. Since the electric field around the antenna is parallel with the radiating element, and the electric field defines the polarization, the orientation of the antenna determines whether the antenna is vertically or horizontally polarized.

17. A. If the access point is sitting on a flat platform and if its antennas are oriented such that they are vertical (perpendicular to the Earth's surface), then it is vertically polarized. Both of the diversity antennas commonly found on access points should be oriented in the same fashion. It is not uncommon to get better reception with horizontally polarized antennas when using PCMCIA cards in laptop computer. It all depends on the mounting and positioning of the access point and the relative location of the laptop computers.

18. C. The unit of measure "dBi" means an amount of gain relative to an isotropic radiator. Isotropic radiators are spheres that radiate RF in all directions simultaneously such as the sun. We are unable to make such an isotropic radiator, so any amount of horizontal squeezing of this sphere is considered gain over the distance that the isotropic radiator would have radiated the signal. Decibels, or "dB", are the

unit of measure used to measure gain or loss of an RF signal while in a copper conductor or waveguide.

19. C. When thinking of Path Loss, consider blowing a bubble with chewing gum. As the bubble gets larger, the amount of gum at any point on the surface gets thinner. If a one-inch square section of this bubble were taken while the bubble is small, more gum would be gathered than if the same amount of gum were taken when the bubble is much larger. This natural broadening of the wavefront thins the amount of power that a receiver can gather. The one-inch section of gum represents how much power the receiving aperture (antenna element) can receive.

20. A, B, C. Due to the Canadian Department of Communications and FCC regulations implemented in 1994, manufacturers had to produce proprietary connectors for their wireless LAN equipment. Because of this fact, many different variations on connector types have been created. A good example is the N-type connector. There are standard, reverse threaded, and reverse polarity N-type connectors on the market today. There's no such thing as a dual head N-type connector.

Wireless LAN Organizations And Standards

CWNA Exam Objectives Covered:

❖ Identify, apply, and comprehend the differences between the following wireless LAN standards:

- 802.11
- 802.11b
- 802.11a
- 802.11g
- Bluetooth
- Infrared
- HomeRF

❖ Understand the roles of the following organizations in providing direction and accountability within the wireless LAN industry:

- FCC
- IEEE
- The Wi-Fi Alliance
- WLANA
- IrDA
- ETSI

In This Chapter

FCC

IEEE

Wireless LAN
Organizations

Competing
Technologies

Most computer-related hardware and technologies are based on some standards, and wireless LANs are no exception. There are organizations that define and support the standards that allow hardware from different manufacturers to function together seamlessly. In this chapter we will discuss the FCC's role in defining and enforcing the laws governing wireless communication and the IEEE's role in creating standards that allow wireless devices to work together. We will also cover the different frequency bands on which wireless LANs operate, and examine the 802.11 family of standards. We will discuss some of the major organizations in the wireless LAN marketplace as well as the roles they fill in the industry. Finally, we will cover some of the emerging technologies and standards and discuss their impact on the wireless LAN industry.

By understanding the laws and the standards that govern and guide wireless LAN technology, you will be able to ensure that any wireless system you implement will be interoperable and comply with the law. Furthermore, familiarity with these statutes and standards, as well as the organizations that create them, will greatly enhance your ability to research and find the latest information about wireless LANs.

Federal Communications Commission

The Federal Communications Commission (FCC) is an independent United States government agency, directly responsible to Congress. The FCC was established by the Communications Act of 1934 and is charged with regulating interstate and international communications by radio, television, wire, satellite, and cable. The FCC's jurisdiction covers not only the 50 states and the District of Columbia, but also all U.S. possessions such as Puerto Rico, Guam, and The Virgin Islands.

The FCC makes the laws within which wireless LAN devices must operate. The FCC mandates where on the radio frequency spectrum wireless LANs can operate and at what power, using which transmission technologies, and how and where various pieces of wireless LAN hardware may be used.

The website for the FCC is www.fcc.gov

ISM and UNII Bands

The FCC establishes rules limiting which frequencies wireless LANs can use and the output power on each of those frequency bands. The FCC has specified that wireless LANs can use the Industrial, Scientific, and Medical (ISM) bands, which are license free. The ISM bands are located starting at 902 MHz, 2.4 GHz, and 5.8 GHz and vary in width from about 26 MHz to 150 MHz.

In addition to the ISM bands, the FCC specifies three Unlicensed National Information Infrastructure (UNII) bands. Each one of these UNII bands is in the 5 GHz range and is 100 MHz wide. Figure 6.1 illustrates the ISM and UNII bands available.

FIGURE 6.1   ISM and UNII Spectra

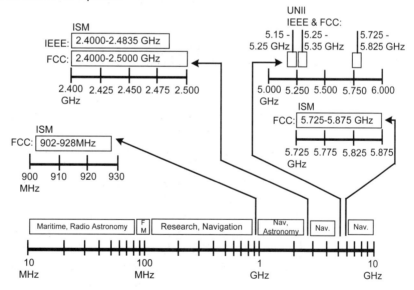

Advantages and Disadvantages of License-Free Bands

When implementing any wireless system on a license-free band, there is no requirement to petition the FCC for bandwidth and power needs. Limits on the power of transmission exist, but there is no procedure for receiving permission to transmit at such power. Furthermore, there are no licensing requirements and, thus, no cost associated with licensing. The license-free nature of the ISM and UNII bands is very important because it allows entities like small businesses and households to implement wireless systems and fosters the growth of the wireless LAN market.

Such freedom from licensing carries with it a major disadvantage to license-free band users. The same license-free band you use (or intend to use) is also license-free to others. Suppose you install a wireless LAN segment on your home network. If your neighbor also installs a wireless LAN segment in his home, his system may interfere with yours, and vise versa. Furthermore, if he uses a higher-power system, his wireless LAN may disable yours by "whiting out" your wireless traffic. The two competing systems don't necessarily have to be on the same channel, or even be the same spread spectrum technology.

Industrial Scientific Medical (ISM) Bands

There are three license-free ISM bands. They are the 900 MHz, 2.4 GHz, and 5.8 GHz bands. Of these, the FCC has specified that wireless LANs may use the 900 MHz and 2.4 GHz bands.

900 MHz ISM Band

The 900 MHz ISM band is defined as the range of frequencies from 902 MHz to 928 MHz. This band may be additionally (and correctly) defined as 915 MHz ± 13 MHz. Though the 900 MHz ISM band was once used by wireless LANs, it has been largely abandoned in favor of the higher frequency bands, which have wider bandwidths and allow more throughput. Some of the wireless devices that still use the 900 MHz band are wireless home phones and wireless camera systems. Organizations that use 900 MHz wireless LANs find out the hard way that obsolete equipment is expensive to replace should any piece of their hardware malfunctions. A single 900 MHz radio card may cost as much as $800 and might only be able to transmit at speeds up to 1 Mbps. In comparison, an 802.11b compliant wireless card will support speeds up to 11 Mbps and sell for roughly $100. Finding support or replacements for these older 900 MHz units is almost impossible.

2.4 GHz ISM Band

This band is used by all 802.11, 802.11b, and 802.11g-compliant devices and is by far the most populated space of the three bands presented in this chapter. The 2.4 GHz ISM band is bound by 2.4000 GHz and 2.5000 GHz (2.4500 GHz ± 50 MHz), as defined by the FCC. Of the 100 MHz between 2.4000 and 2.5000 GHz, only the frequencies 2.4000 – 2.4835 GHz are actually used by wireless LAN devices. The principal reason for this limitation is that the FCC has specified power output only for this range of frequencies within the 2.4 GHz ISM band.

5.8 GHz ISM Band

This band is also frequently called the 5 GHz ISM Band. The 5.8 GHz ISM is bound by 5.725 GHz and 5.875 GHz, which yields a 150 MHz bandwidth. This band of frequencies is *not* specified for use by wireless LAN devices, so it tends to present some confusion. The 5.8 GHz ISM band overlaps part of another license-free band, the Upper UNII band, causing the 5.8 GHz ISM band to be confused with the 5 GHz Upper UNII band, which *is* used with wireless LANs.

Unlicensed National Information Infrastructure Bands

The 5 GHz UNII bands are made up of three separate 100 MHz-wide bands, which are used by 802.11a-compliant devices. The three bands are known as the lower, middle, and upper bands. Within each of these three bands, there are four non-overlapping OFDM channels, each separated by 5 MHz. The FCC mandates that the lower band be used indoors, the middle band be used indoors or outdoors, and the upper band be allocated for outdoor use. Since access points are mostly mounted indoors, the 5 GHz UNII bands would allow for 8 non-overlapping access points indoors using both the lower and middle UNII bands.

Lower Band

The lower band is bound by 5.15 GHz and 5.25 GHz and is specified by the FCC to have a maximum output power of 50 mW. When implementing 802.11a compliant devices, the IEEE has specified 40 mW (80%) as the maximum output power for 802.11a-compliant radios, reserving the lower band for indoor operation only.

 It is important to realize that it is possible for a radio to transmit at 50 mW and operate within the limits of the law, but still not be compliant with the 802.11a standards. It is also important to distinguish between what the law allows for and what the standard specifies. In some rare installation scenarios, you may be required to work outside the specifications of the standards in order to accomplish a business goal.

Middle Band

The middle UNII band is bound by 5.25 GHz and 5.35 GHz and is specified at 250 mW of output power by the FCC. The power output specified by IEEE for the middle UNII band is 200 mW. This power limit allows operation of devices either indoors or outdoors and is commonly used for short outdoor hops between closely spaced buildings. In the case of a home installation, such a configuration might include an RF link between the house and the garage, or the house and a neighbor's house. Due to reasonable power output and flexible indoor/outdoor use restrictions, products manufactured to work in the middle UNII band could enjoy wide acceptance in the future.

Upper Band

The upper UNII band is reserved for outdoor links and is limited by the FCC to 1 Watt (1000 mW) of output power. This band occupies the range of frequencies between 5.725 GHz and 5.825 GHz, and is often confused with the 5.8 GHz ISM band. The IEEE specifies the maximum output power for this band as 800 mW, which is plenty of power for almost any outdoor implementation, except for large campuses or long-distance RF links.

Power Output Rules

The FCC enforces certain rules regarding the power radiated by the antenna element, depending on whether the implementation is a point-to-multipoint or a point-to-point implementation. The term used for the power radiated by the antenna is *Equivalent Isotropically Radiated Power* (EIRP).

Point-to-Multipoint (PtMP)

PtMP links have a central point of connection and two or more non-central connection points. PtMP links are typically configured in a star topology. The central connection point may or may not have an omnidirectional antenna (an omnidirectional antenna produces a 360 degree horizontal beam). It is important to note that when an omnidirectional antenna is used, the FCC automatically considers the link a PtMP link. Regarding the setup of a PtMP link, the FCC limits the EIRP to 4 Watts in both the 2.4 GHz ISM band and upper 5 GHz UNII band. Furthermore, the power limit set for the intentional radiator (the device transmitting the RF signal) in each of these bands is 1 Watt. If the transmitting wireless LAN devices are adjustable with respect to their output power, then the system can be customized to the needs of the user.

Suppose a radio transmitting at 1 Watt (+30 dBm) is connected directly to a 12 dBi omnidirectional antenna. The total output power at the antenna is about 16 Watts, which is well above the 4 Watt limit. The FCC stipulates that *for each 3 dBi above the antenna's initial 6 dBi of gain, the power at the intentional radiator must be reduced by 3 dB below the initial +30 dBm*. For our example, since the antenna gain is 12 dBi, the power at the intentional radiator must be reduced by 6 dB. This reduction will result in an intentional radiator power of +24 dBm (30 dBm – 6 dB), or 250 mW and an EIRP of 36 dBm (24 dBm + 12 dBi), or 4 Watts. Clearly this rule can become confusing, but the end result must be that the power at the intentional radiator must never be more than 1 Watt (see Figure 6.2), and the EIRP must never be above 4 Watts for a PtMP connection.

FIGURE 6.2   Point-to-Multipoint Power Limit Table

Power at Antenna (dBm)	Antenna Gain (dBi)	EIRP (dBm)	EIRP (watts)
30	6	36	4
27	9	36	4
24	12	36	4
21	15	36	4
18	18	36	4
15	21	36	4
12	24	36	4

The specific information contained in Figure 6.2 is not covered on the CWNA exam. The information is provided as a resource for your administrative tasks.

When using an omnidirectional antenna, the rules for point-to-multipoint links must be followed, regardless of whether the actual implementation is point-to-point or point-to-multipoint.

Point-to-Point (PtP)

PtP links include a single directional transmitting antenna and a single directional receiving antenna. These connections will typically include building-to-building or similar links and must abide by special rules. When installing a 2.4 GHz PtP link, the 4 Watt power limit all but disappears in favor of a sliding power limit. Regarding a PtP link, the FCC mandates that *for every 3 dBi above the initial 6 dBi of antenna gain, the power at the intentional radiator must be reduced by 1 dB from the initial +30 dBm.*

Consider our previous example, using the same values: 1 Watt (+30 dBm) at the intentional radiator and a 12 dBi antenna (in this case the antenna will be a directional antenna). The total output power is still 16 Watts. In this example, since the antenna gain is 12 dBi, the power at the intentional radiator must be reduced by 2 dB, as opposed to a 6 dB reduction in the previous example. This reduction will result in an intentional radiator power of 28 dBm (30 dBm – 2 dB), or about 630 mW and an EIRP of 40 dBm (28 dBm + 12 dBi), or 10 Watts. In the case of PtP links, the power at the intentional radiator is still limited to 1 Watt, but the limit of the EIRP *increases* with the gain of the antenna (Figure 6.3). It is very important to clearly distinguish between the rules that govern PtP and PtMP wireless links.

FIGURE 6.3   Point-to-Point Power Limit Table

Power at Antenna (dBm)	Max Antenna Gain (dBi)	EIRP (dBm)	EIRP (watts)
30	6	36	4
29	9	38	6.3
28	12	40	10
27	15	42	16
26	18	44	25
25	21	46	39.8
24	24	48	63
23	27	50	100
22	30	52	158

The specific information contained in Figure 6.3 is not covered on the CWNA exam. The information is provided as a resource for your administrative tasks.

The FCC has a different rule for PtP links in the upper UNII band. Fixed point-to-point UNII devices operating in the 5.725 - 5.825 GHz band may employ transmitting antennas with directional gain up to 23 dBi without any corresponding reduction in the transmitter peak output power. For fixed, point-to-point UNII transmitters that employ a directional antenna gain greater than 23 dBi, a 1 dB reduction in peak transmitter power for each 1 dBi of antenna gain in excess of 23 dBi is required. Notice that by having an output power maximum of +30 dBm at the intentional radiator, and having a maximum of 23 dBi antenna gain before any reduction in transmitter output power is required, this allows these 5 GHz UNII systems to have an output of 200 Watts EIRP.

Institute of Electrical and Electronics Engineers

The Institute of Electrical and Electronics Engineers (*IEEE*) is the key standards maker for most things related to information technology in the United States. The IEEE creates its standards within the laws created by the FCC. The IEEE specifies many technology standards such as Public Key Cryptography (IEEE 1363), FireWire (IEEE 1394), Ethernet (IEEE 802.3), and Wireless LANs (IEEE 802.11).

The website for the IEEE is www.ieee.org

It is part of the mission of the IEEE to develop standards for wireless LAN operation within the framework of the FCC rules and regulations. Following are the four main IEEE standards for wireless LANs that are either in use or in draft form:

- 802.11
- 802.11b
- 802.11a
- 802.11g

IEEE 802.11

The 802.11 standard was the first standard describing the operation of wireless LANs. This standard contained all of the available transmission technologies including Direct Sequence Spread Spectrum (DSSS), Frequency Hopping Spread Spectrum (FHSS), and infrared.

Infrared's wireless LAN market share is quite small and the technology is very limited by its functionality. Due to the lack of popularity of infrared technology in the wireless LAN marketplace, IR will be mentioned, but not covered in detail in this book.

The IEEE 802.11 standard describes DSSS systems that operate at 1 Mbps and 2 Mbps only. If a DSSS system operates at other data rates as well, such as 1 Mbps, 2 Mbps, and 11 Mbps, then it can still be an 802.11-compliant system. If, however, the system is operating at any rate other than 1 or 2 Mbps, then, even though the system is 802.11-compliant because of its ability to work at 1 & 2 Mbps, it is not operating in an 802.11-compliant mode and cannot be expected to communicate with other 802.11-compliant devices.

IEEE 802.11 is one of two standards that describe the operation of frequency hopping wireless LAN systems. If a wireless LAN administrator encounters a frequency hopping system, then it is likely to be either an 802.11-compliant or OpenAir compliant system (discussed below). The 802.11 standard describes use of FHSS systems at 1 and 2 Mbps. There are many FHSS systems on the market that extend this functionality by offering proprietary modes that operate at 3-10 Mbps, but just as with DSSS, if the system is operating at speeds other than 1 & 2 Mbps, it cannot be expected to automatically communicate with other 802.11-compliant devices.

802.11 compliant products operate strictly in the 2.4 GHz ISM band between 2.4000 and 2.4835 GHz. Infrared, also covered by 802.11, is light-based technology and does not fall into the 2.4 GHz ISM band.

IEEE 802.11b

Though the 802.11 standard was successful in allowing DSSS as well as FHSS systems to interoperate, the technology has outgrown the standard. Soon after the approval and implementation of 802.11, DSSS wireless LANs were exchanging data at up to 11 Mbps. But, without a standard to guide the operation of such devices, there came to be problems with interoperability and implementation. The manufacturers ironed out most of the implementation problems, so the job of IEEE was relatively easy: create a standard that complied with the general operation of wireless LANs then on the market. It is not uncommon for the standards to follow the technology in this way, particularly when the technology evolves quickly.

IEEE 802.11b, referred to as "High-Rate" and Wi-Fi™, specifies direct sequencing (DSSS) systems that operate at 1, 2, 5.5 and 11 Mbps. The 802.11b standard does *not* describe any FHSS systems, and 802.11b-compliant devices are also 802.11-compliant by default, meaning they are backward compatible and support both 2 and 1 Mbps data rates. Backward compatibility is very important because it allows a wireless LAN to be upgraded without the cost of replacing the core hardware. This low-cost feature, together with the high data rate, has made the 802.11b-compliant hardware very popular.

The high data rate of 802.11b-compliant devices is the result of using a different coding technique. Though the system is still a direct sequencing system, the way the chips are coded (CCK rather than Barker Code) along with the way the information is modulated (DQPSK at 2, 5.5, & 11 Mbps and DBPSK at 1 Mbps) allows for a greater amount of data to be transferred in the same time frame. 802.11b compliant products operate only in the 2.4 GHz ISM band between 2.4000 and 2.4835 GHz. Modulation and coding are further discussed in Chapter 8 (MAC & Physical Layers).

IEEE 802.11a

The IEEE 802.11a standard describes wireless LAN device operation in the 5 GHz UNII bands. Operation in the UNII bands automatically makes 802.11a devices incompatible with all other devices complying with the other 802.11 series of standards. The reason for this incompatibility is simple: systems using 5 GHz frequencies will not communicate with systems using 2.4 GHz frequencies.

Using the UNII bands, most devices are able to achieve data rates of 6, 9, 12, 18, 24, 36, 48, and 54 Mbps. Some of the devices employing the UNII bands have achieved data rates of 108 Mbps by using proprietary technology, such as *rate doubling*. The highest rates of some of these devices are the result of newer technologies not specified by the 802.11a standard. IEEE 802.11a specifies data rates of only 6, 12, and 24 Mbps. A wireless LAN device must support at least these data rates in the UNII bands in order to be 802.11a-compliant. The maximum data rate specified by the 802.11a standard is 54 Mbps. Figure 6.4 outlines the various power limits for 802.11a devices in several countries.

FIGURE 6.4   802.11a Power Output Limits in Various Countries

Country Band	USA/CAN	Europe	France	Spain	Japan
5.15- 5.25	50mW	200mW	200mW	200mW	200mW
5.25- 5.35	250mW	200mW	200mW	200mW	
5.725- 5.825	1W				

The 802.11a standard specifies the use of the OFDM (Orthogonal Frequency Division Multiplexing) technology. OFDM is the secret behind how 802.11a gets up to 54 Mbps data rates. OFDM creates eight non-overlapping channels 20 MHz wide across the two lower bands of the 5 GHz UNII band (four channels in each of the two lower bands). Each of these eight channels is subdivided into 52 subcarriers, each approximately 300 KHz wide (as shown in Figure 6.5). Each subcarrier is transmitted in parallel, meaning that they are sent and receive simultaneously. A receiving station then processes these 52 incoming signals, each one representing a fraction of the total data transmitted, and makes up the complete transmission.

FIGURE 6.5   OFDM and 802.11a

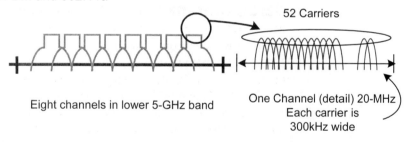

52 Carriers

Eight channels in lower 5-GHz band

One Channel (detail) 20-MHz
Each carrier is
300kHz wide

Due to the large amount of information being transmitted at such high rates, some means of error correction was required to prevent data loss. As such, Forward Error Correction (FEC) was added to IEEE 802.11a. FEC essentially sends two copies of the information in each transmission, a primary and secondary. If the primary transmission is damaged en route, the receiving station can recreate the lost data by running the secondary transmission through a set of algorithms. The performance impact is fairly negligible due to the high data rate.

IEEE 802.11g

802.11g provides the same maximum speed of 802.11a, coupled with backwards compatibility for 802.11b devices. This backwards compatibility will make upgrading wireless LANs simple and inexpensive. Since 802.11g technology is new, 802.11g devices are not yet available as of this writing.

IEEE 802.11g specifies operation in the 2.4 GHz ISM band. To achieve the higher data rates found in 802.11a, 802.11g compliant devices utilize Orthogonal Frequency Division Multiplexing (OFDM) modulation technology. These devices can automatically switch to DQPSK modulation in order to communicate with the slower 802.11b- and 802.11-compatable devices. With all of the apparent advantages, 802.11g's use of the crowded 2.4 GHz band could prove to be a disadvantage.

As of this writing, the 802.11g standard has been approved as a standard, but the specifications of this standard are still in draft form. Final specifications for 802.11g are expected in late 2002 or early 2003.

IEEE Standards Summary

Figure 6.6 provides a quick summary of the major points of the 802.11, 802.11a, 802.11b and 802.11g standards.

FIGURE 6.6   Summary of IEEE Wireless LAN Standards

	802.11	**802.11a**	**802.11b**	**802.11g**
Frequency	2.4 GHz	5 GHz	2.4 GHz	2.4 GHz
Data Rate(s)	1, 2 Mbps	5, 9, 12, 18, 24, 36, 48, 54 Mbps	1, 2, 5.5, 11 Mbps	6, 9, 12, 15, 24, 36, 48, 54 Mbps
Modulation	FHSS, DSSS	OFDM	DSSS	OFDM
Effective Data Throughput	1.2 Mbps	32 Mbps	5 Mbps	32 Mbps
Advertised Range	300 feet	225 feet	300 feet	300 feet
Encryption Available?	Yes	Yes	Yes	Yes
Encryption Type	40-bit RC4	40-bit, 104-bit RC4	40-bit, 104-bit RC4	40-bit, 104-bit RC4
Provides Authentication?	No	No	No	No
Network Support	Ethernet (IEEE 802.3)	Ethernet (IEEE 802.3)	Ethernet (IEEE 802.3)	Ethernet (IEEE 802.3)

Major Organizations

Whereas the FCC and the IEEE are responsible for defining the laws and standards as they apply to wireless LANs in the United States, there are several other organizations, both in the U.S. and in other countries, which contribute to growth and education in the wireless LAN marketplace. In this section, we will look at three of these organizations:

- The Wi-Fi Alliance
- European Telecommunications Standards Institute (ETSI)
- Wireless LAN Association (WLANA)

Wi-Fi Alliance

The Wi-Fi Alliance promotes and tests for wireless LAN interoperability of 802.11b devices and 802.11a devices. The Wi-Fi Alliance's mission is *to certify interoperability of Wi-Fi™ (IEEE 802.11) products and to promote Wi-Fi as the global wireless LAN standard across all market segments.* As an administrator, you must resolve conflicts among wireless LAN devices that result from interference, incompatibility, or other problems.

When a product meets the interoperability requirements as described in the Wi-Fi Alliance's test matrix, the Wi-Fi Alliance grants the product a certification of interoperability, which allows the vendor to use the Wi-Fi logo on advertising and packaging for the certified product. The Wi-Fi seal of approval assures the end user of interoperability with other wireless LAN devices that also bear the Wi-Fi logo.

Among the Wi-Fi Alliance's list of interoperability checks is the use of 40-bit WEP keys. Note that 40- and 64-bit keys are the same thing. A 40-bit "secret" key is concatenated with a 24-bit Initialization Vector (IV) to reach the 64-bits. In the same manner, 104- and 128-bit keys are the same. The Wi-Fi Alliance does not specify interoperability of 128-bit keys; hence, no compatibility is to be expected between vendors displaying the Wi-Fi seal when using 128-bit WEP keys. Nevertheless, many 128-bit systems from different vendors are interoperable.

There are many other factors besides use of 40-bit WEP keys that are required to meet the Wi-Fi Alliance's Wi-Fi criteria. These factors include support of fragmentation, PSP mode, SSID probe requests, and others. Some of these topics will be discussed in later chapters.

In October 2002, the Wi-Fi Alliance announced that a new standards based solution to counteract the weaknesses in WEP would be included in all Wi-Fi products starting in early 2003. WPA (Wi-Fi Protected Access) will include both TKIP and 802.1*x* with EAP authentication--as part of all Wi-Fi certified devices starting in early 2003. This is an interim solution that is aimed at providing protection now without the need to wait for the forthcoming IEEE 802.11i standard. WPA is an extremely valuable solution that will immediately bring increased security to home and business wireless networks from the get-go by protecting against the vulnerabilities inherent with WEP. In an enterprise environment, WPA can work together with a RADIUS server to ensure mutual authentication for all wireless users. Look for WPA products for new wireless network implementations.

The website for the Wi-Fi Alliance is www.wi-fi.com

European Telecommunications Standards Institute

The European Telecommunications Standards Institute (ETSI) is chartered with producing communications standards for Europe in the same way that the IEEE is for the United States. The standards ETSI has established, HiPerLAN/2 for example, directly compete against standards created by the IEEE such as 802.11a. There has been much discussion about IEEE and ETSI unifying on certain wireless technologies, but nothing has materialized as of this writing. This effort is referred to as the "5UP" initiative for "5 GHz Unified Protocol." The IEEE's attempt at interoperability with ETSI's HiperLAN/2 standard is the new forthcoming 802.11h standard.

ETSI's original HiPerLAN standard for wireless, dubbed HiperLAN/1, supported rates of up to 24 Mbps using DSSS technology with a range of approximately 150 feet (45.7 meters). HiperLAN/1 used the lower and middle UNII bands, as do HiperLAN/2, 802.11a, and the new 802.11h standard. The new HiperLAN/2 standard supports rates of up to 54 Mbps and uses all three of the UNII bands.

ETSI's HiperLAN/2 standard has interchangeable convergence layers, support for QoS, and supports DES and 3DES encryption. The supported convergence layers are ATM, Ethernet, PPP, FireWire, and 3G. Supported QoS awareness includes 802.1p, RSVP, and DiffServ-FC.

The website for ETSI is www.etsi.org

Wireless LAN Association

The Wireless LAN Association's mission is to educate and raise consumer awareness regarding the use and availability of wireless LANs and to promote the wireless LAN industry in general. The Wireless LAN Association (*WLANA*) is an educational resource for those seeking to learn more about wireless LANs. WLANA can also help if you are looking for a specific wireless LAN product or service.

WLANA has many partners within the industry that contribute content to the WLANA directory of information. It is this directory, along with the many white papers and case studies that WLANA provides, that offer you valuable information for making your own decisions about wireless LAN implementation.

 The website for WLANA is www.wlana.org

Competing Technologies

There are several technologies that compete with the 802.11 family of standards. As business needs change, and technologies improve, there will continue to be new standards created to support the marketplace as well as new inventions that drive enterprise spending. Other wireless LAN technologies and standards that are in use today include:

- HomeRF
- Bluetooth
- Infrared
- OpenAir

HomeRF

HomeRF operates in the 2.4 GHz band and uses frequency hopping technology. HomeRF devices hop at about 50 hops per second—about 5 to 20 times faster than most 802.11-compliant FHSS devices. The new version of HomeRF, HomeRF 2.0 uses the new "wide band" frequency hopping rules approved by the FCC, and is the first to do so. This is to say that the IEEE has not adopted the wide-band frequency hopping rules into the 802.11 series of standards. Recall that these rules, implemented after 08/31/00, include:

- Maximum of 5 MHz wide carrier frequencies

- Minimum of 15 hops in a sequence

- Maximum of 125 mW of output power

Because HomeRF allows an increase over the former 1 MHz wide carrier frequencies, and flexibility in implementing less than the previously required 75 hops, one might think that wide band frequency hopping would be quite popular among corporations and vendors alike. This, however, is not the case. As advantageous as the resulting 10 Mbps data rate is, it does not overshadow the disadvantage of 125 mW of output power, which limits use of wide band frequency hopping devices to an approximate range of 150 - 300 feet (46 - 92 meters). This outcome limits the use of wideband frequency hopping devices primarily to SOHO environments.

HomeRF units use the Shared Wireless Access Protocol (SWAP) protocol, which is a combination of CSMA (used in local area networks) and TDMA (used in cellular phones) protocols. SWAP is a hybrid of the 802.11 and DECT standards and was developed by the HomeRF working group. HomeRF devices are the only devices currently on the market that follow the wideband frequency hopping rules. HomeRF devices are considered more secure than 802.11 products using WEP because of the 32-bit initialization vector (IV) HomeRF uses (in contrast to 802.11's 24-bit IV). Additionally, HomeRF has specified how the IV is to be chosen during encryption, whereas 802.11 does not, leaving 802.11 open for attack due to weak implementations.

Some particularly interesting features of HomeRF 2.0 are:

- ~50 hops per second
- Uses 2.4 GHz ISM band
- Meets FCC regulations for spread spectrum technologies

- 10 Mbps data rate with fallback to 5 Mbps, 1.6 Mbps and 0.8 Mbps
- Backwards compatible with OpenAir standard
- Simultaneous host/client and peer/peer topology
- Built-in security measures against eavesdropping and denial of service
- Support for prioritized streaming media sessions and toll-quality two-way voice connections
- Enhanced roaming capabilities
- Can support up to 25 nodes in HomeRF 2.0, 10 nodes in HomeRF 1.0

 The website for HomeRF is www.homerf.org

Bluetooth

Bluetooth is another frequency hopping technology that operates in the 2.4 GHz ISM band. The hop rate of Bluetooth devices is about 1600 hops per second (about 625μs dwell time), so it has considerably more overhead than 802.11-compliant frequency hopping systems. The high hop rate also gives the technology greater resistance to spurious narrow band noise. Bluetooth systems are not designed for high throughput, but rather for simple use, low power, and short range (WPANs). The new IEEE 802.15 draft for WPANs includes specifications for Bluetooth.

A major disadvantage of using Bluetooth technology is that it tends to completely disrupt other 2.4 GHz networks. The high hop rate of Bluetooth over the entire usable 2.4 GHz band makes the Bluetooth signal appear to all other systems as *all-band noise*, or *all-band interference*. Bluetooth also affects other FHSS systems. All-band interference, as the name implies, disrupts the signal over its entire range of useable frequencies, rendering the main signal useless. Curiously, the counter-interference (interference provided by the wireless LAN interfering with Bluetooth) does not impact the Bluetooth devices as severely as Bluetooth impacts the 802.11 compliant wireless LAN. It is now common for placards to be mounted in wireless LAN areas that read "No Bluetooth" in eye-catching print.

Bluetooth devices operate in three power classes: 1 mW, 2.5 mW, and 100 mW. Currently there are few if any implementations of Class 3 (100 mW) Bluetooth devices, so range data is not readily available; however, Class 2 (2.5 mW) Bluetooth devices have a maximum range of 33 feet (10 meters). Naturally, if extended ranged is desired, the use of directional antennas is a possible solution, though most Bluetooth devices are mobile devices.

The website for the Bluetooth Special Interest Group (SIG) is www.bluetooth.com

Infrared Data Association (IrDA)

IrDA is not a standard like Bluetooth, HomeRF, and the 802.11 series of standards; rather, IrDA is an organization. Founded in June of 1993, IrDA is a member-funded organization whose charter is "to create an interoperable, low-cost, low-power, half-duplex, serial data interconnection standard that supports a walk-up point-to-point user model that is adaptable to a wide range of computer devices." Infrared data transmission is known by most for its use in calculators, printers, some building-to-building and in-room computer networks, and now in handheld computers.

Infrared

Infrared (IR) is a light-based transmission technology and is not spread spectrum—spread spectrum technologies all use RF radiation. IR devices can achieve a maximum data rate of 4 Mbps at close range, but as a light-based technology, other sources of IR light can interfere with IR transmissions. The typical data rate of an IR device is about 115 kbps, which is good for exchanging data between handheld devices. An important advantage of IR networks is that they do not interfere with spread spectrum RF networks. For this reason, the two are complementary and can easily be used together.

Security

The security of IR devices is inherently excellent for two main reasons. First, IR cannot travel though walls at such a low power (2 mW maximum) and second, a hacker or eavesdropper must directly intercept the beam in order to gain access to the information being transferred. Single room networks that need wireless connectivity must be assured of security benefit from IR networks. With PDAs and laptop computers, IR is used for point-to-point connectivity at very short range so security would be almost irrelevant in these instances.

Stability

Though IR will not pass through walls, it will bounce off walls and ceilings, which aids in single room networking. Infrared is not disrupted by electromagnetic signals, which promotes the stability of an IR system. Broadcast IR devices are available and can be mounted on the ceiling. An IR broadcast device (which is analogous to an RF antenna) will transmit the IR carrier and information in all directions so that these signals can be picked up by nearby IR clients. For power consumption reasons, broadcast IR is normally implemented indoors. Point-to-point IR transmitters can be used outdoors, and have a maximum range of about 3280 feet (1 km), but this range may be shortened by the presence of sunlight. Sunlight is approximately 60% infrared light, which severely dilutes broadcast IR signals. On sunny days when transferring data between laptop computers or PDAs, the two devices may have to be held closer together for good IR data transfer.

 The website for IrDA is www.irda.org

Wireless LAN Interoperability Forum (WLIF)

The OpenAir standard was a standard created by the Wireless LAN Interoperability Forum (now defunct), for which many wireless LAN systems were created to comply as an alternative to 802.11. OpenAir specified two speeds - 800 kbps and 1.6 Mbps. OpenAir and 802.11

systems are not compatible and will not interoperate. Since there are currently several product lines still available that comply with the OpenAir standard, it is important that the wireless LAN administrator know that OpenAir exists; however, OpenAir is quickly losing support among vendors and no new products are being made that comply with this standard. OpenAir was the first attempt at interoperability and standardization among wireless LANs. OpenAir focused on FHSS devices operating at only two speeds.

The website for WLIF has been removed

Key Terms

Before taking the exam, you should be familiar with the following terms:

infrared

ISM bands

UNII bands

Review Questions

1. What data rates does the 802.11 standard specify when using DSSS?

    A.   1 Mbps only

    B.   2 Mbps only

    C.   4 Mbps only

    D.   1 & 2 Mbps

    E.   1, 2, & 4 Mbps

2. The three UNII bands used for wireless LANs are each how wide?

    A.   100 MHz

    B.   102 MHz

    C.   110 MHz

    D.   120 MHz

3. The FCC specifies rules for wireless LANs regarding which of the following? Choose all that apply.

    A.   Power output

    B.   Frequencies

    C.   Modulation

    D.   Data rates

4.   Which of the following is NOT one of the ISM bands used with wireless LANs? Choose all that apply.

   A.   900 MHz

   B.   2.4 GHz

   C.   4.5 GHz

   D.   5.8 GHz

5.   The 802.11b standard specifies which of the following data rates using DSSS technology?

   A.   1 & 2 Mbps

   B.   5.5 & 11 Mbps

   C.   1, 2, & 11 Mbps

   D.   1, 2, 5.5, & 11 Mbps

6.   The 802.11b standard specifies which of the following spread spectrum technologies?

   A.   FHSS

   B.   DSSS

   C.   Infrared

   D.   Key hopping

7.   Which of the following standards specifies use of FHSS technology?

   A.   802.11

   B.   802.11b

   C.   802.11a

   D.   802.11g

   E.   OpenAir

8. What is the FCC limit on EIRP for a point-to-multipoint link?

    A. 1 Watt

    B. 2 Watts

    C. 3 Watts

    D. 4 Watts

9. Why are 802.11a devices incompatible with all other 802.11 family devices?

    A. 802.11a devices operate at a maximum of 54 Mbps

    B. 802.11a devices operate in the 5 GHz ISM band

    C. 802.11a devices operate in the 5 GHz UNII bands

    D. 802.11a devices use Barker Code modulation

10. Which of the following statements are true? Choose all that apply.

    A. The IEEE is government regulated

    B. The FCC is a government agency

    C. The IEEE sets the allowable RF power outputs in the United States

    D. The FCC specifies connectivity speeds for the 802.11 standard

11. What does the Wi-Fi™ seal of approval indicate?

    A. A vendor's hardware has a Wi-Fi Alliance chipset in it

    B. A vendor's hardware has been proven interoperable with other vendor's hardware

    C. A wireless LAN meets the IEEE 802.11 standard

    D. A wireless LAN meets FCC regulations

12. Which organization creates the regulations that wireless LANs must abide by?

    A.   IEEE

    B.   FCC

    C.   The Wi-Fi Alliance

    D.   WLANA

13. You have been hired to take over the administration of a wireless LAN on a small college campus. The campus uses one omni-directional antenna to connect 6 buildings. One day an inspector with the FCC tells you that the power output at the element of your antenna is too high and violating FCC laws. What is the maximum power output at which you can set the EIRP to comply with the law?

    A.   125 mW

    B.   1 W

    C.   2 W

    D.   4W

14. The FCC's jurisdiction covers which of the following? Choose all that apply.

    A.   The 50 United States only

    B.   The 50 United States and the District of Columbia

    C.   The 50 United States, the District of Columbia, and all U.S. possessions such as Puerto Rico, Guam, and the Virgin Islands

    D.   All of Europe

15. Which one of the following is a disadvantage of a license-free radio frequency band?

    A.   No licensing fees or paperwork

    B.   Regulation by the FCC in the US

    C.   Possible random interference with other networks

    D.   Lower cost of equipment

16. "ISM" stands for which one of the following?

    A.   International Scientific Measurement

    B.   International Standards Makers

    C.   Industrial Standard Machine

    D.   Industrial, Scientific, and Medical

17. Which of the following does NOT specify use of equipment that uses the 2.4 GHz ISM band?

    A.   802.11

    B.   802.11a

    C.   802.11b

    D.   802.11g

    E.   802.1x

18. Which one of the following defines the acronym "UNII"?

    A.   Unlicensed National Information Invention

    B.   Unlicensed National Information Infrastructure

    C.   Unlicensed Nominal Information Infrastructure

    D.   Unlicensed National Innovation Infrastructure

19. Which one of the following is the key standards maker for most information technology arenas in the United States?

    A. The Wi-Fi Alliance

    B. FCC

    C. IEEE

    D. WLANA

    E. IrDA

20. Which one of the following was the FIRST IEEE standard describing the operation of wireless LANs?

    A. 802.11

    B. 802.11a

    C. 802.11b

    D. 802.11g

Answers to Review Questions

1. D. The 802.11 standard specifies data rates for FHSS, DSSS, and infrared technologies. The two speeds specified by the 802.11 standard are 1 Mbps and 2 Mbps. Speeds for DSSS were thereafter amended with the 802.11b standard to add both 5.5 & 11 Mbps speeds.

2. A. Each of the three 5 GHz UNII bands are exactly 100 MHz wide. The lower band ranges from 5.15 - 5.25 GHz. The middle band ranges from 5.25 - 5.35 GHz. The upper band ranges from 5.725 - 5.825 GHz.

3. A, B. The FCC mandates which frequencies may be used for what purposes. They specify which frequency bands will be licensed or unlicensed, and they specify the maximum output power within each frequency band.

4. C, D. There are three ISM bands specified by the FCC. The first is the 902 - 928 MHz band. The second is the 2.4000 - 2.5000 GHz band, and the third is the 5.825 - 5.875 GHz band. Of these, only the first two bands are specified for use by Wireless LAN equipment. There is no 4.5 GHz band.

5. D. Although the most significant changes from the original 802.11 standard was the additional data rates of 5.5 & 11 Mbps, the 1 & 2 Mbps data rates are still specified in 802.11b for backwards compatibility with the 802.11 standard.

6. B. The 802.11b standard only specifies use of DSSS technology. The original 802.11 standard specified use of DSSS, FHSS, and infrared technologies.

7. A, E. Both the original 802.11 and the OpenAir standards specified use of FHSS technology. The most significant difference between these two standards is the supported speeds. OpenAir specifies 800 kbps and 1.6 Mbps whereas 802.11 specifies 1 Mbps and 2 Mbps.

8. D. For point-to-multipoint links, the FCC specifies 1 watt at the intentional radiator and 4 watts EIRP (measured at the antenna element). For point-to-point links, there are specific, more complicated rules to follow to understand the maximum output power allowed.

9. C. Since 802.11a devices use the three 5 GHz UNII bands, they cannot communicate with other wireless LAN devices operating in accordance with the 802.11, 802.11b, and 802.11g standards. These standards use the 2.4 GHz ISM band instead of the 5 GHz UNII bands.

10. B. The FCC is a government agency responsible for regulating frequency spectra within the United States. As a part of that responsibility, the FCC regulates the unlicensed bands used by wireless LANs.

11. B. The Wireless Fidelity (a.k.a. Wi-Fi) seal indicates that a vendor's hardware has undergone extensive testing to assure interoperability with other devices manufactured to meet the 802.11b standard. In order to be interoperable with other 802.11b equipment, the equipment under test would most likely have to meet the same 802.11b standards.

12. B. The FCC creates the regulations (laws) to which wireless LAN equipment must adhere. The IEEE creates standards for the purpose of interoperability within the industry. The Wi-Fi Alliance creates the tests and certification program to assure interoperability within the industry using specific standards. WLANA is responsible for promoting and educating the wireless LAN industry.

13. D. The FCC mandates a 4 watt maximum EIRP in a point-to-multipoint circuit. One important part of this rule is the understanding that any time an omni-directional antenna is used, the circuit is automatically considered point-to-multipoint.

14. C. Clicking on the "About the FCC" link on the homepage of the FCC (www.fcc.gov) yields this information in the first paragraph.

15. C. It is said that the biggest advantage of using wireless LANs is that they are license free. It is also said that the biggest disadvantage to using wireless LANs is that they are license free. Sometimes the fact that nearby license-free networks interfere with yours seems to outweigh the implementation ease and cost factors of the frequency spectrum being license free.

16. D. The FCC created the ISM bands with specific industry uses in mind: Industrial, Scientific, and Medical related uses. However, since the availability of the ISM bands, license-free wireless LAN gear has enjoyed broad popularity and diverse use.

17. B, E. The 802.1x standard is centered on port-based access control. This standard can be used to enhance the security of wireless systems, but is not a wireless LAN standard itself. The 802.11a standard specifies use of the 5 GHz UNII bands.

18. B. There are three UNII bands, all specified for use by various 802.11a compliant devices. These three UNII bands are 100 MHz wide and each have different maximum output power limits and usage requirements.

19. C. The IEEE creates standards for most every type of connectivity, whether wired or wireless. The IEEE's role in keeping each information technology industry working within certain standards is quite important to rapid advancement of the industry.

20. A. The original 802.11 standard was started in 1990 and finished in 1997. It underwent several revisions after 1997, the final being the 1999 revision. Since the 1999 version of 802.11, there have been several new 802.11-based standards published by the IEEE such as 802.11b and 802.11a. Several more drafts related to wireless LANs are currently on their way to becoming standards such as 802.11i, 802.11g, and 802.11f.

802.11 Network Architecture

CWNA Exam Objectives Covered:

❖ Identify and apply the processes involved in authentication and association:

- Authentication
- Association
- Open System authentication
- Shared Key authentication
- Secret keys & certificates
- AAA Support

❖ Recognize the following concepts associated with wireless LAN Service Sets:

- BSS
- ESS
- IBSS
- SSID
- Infrastructure Mode
- Ad hoc Mode
- Roaming

❖ Understand the implications of the following power management features of wireless LANs:

- PSP Mode
- CAM
- Beacons
- TIM
- ATIM
- ATIM Windows

This chapter covers some of the key concepts found in the 802.11 network architecture. Most of the topics in this chapter are defined directly in the 802.11 standard, and are required for implementation of 802.11-compliant hardware. In this chapter, we're going to examine the process by which clients connect to an access point, the terms used for organizing wireless LANs, and how power management is accomplished in wireless LAN client devices.

Without a solid understanding of the principals covered in this chapter, it would be quite difficult to design, administer, or troubleshoot a wireless LAN. This chapter holds some of the most elementary steps of both wireless LAN design and administration. As you administer wireless LANs, the understanding of these concepts will allow you to more intelligently manage your day-to-day operations.

Locating a Wireless LAN

When you install, configure, and finally start up a wireless LAN client device such as a USB client or PCMCIA card, the client will automatically "listen" to see if there is a wireless LAN within range. The client is also discovering if it can associate with that wireless LAN. This process of listening is called *scanning*. Scanning occurs before any other process, since scanning is how the client *finds* the network.

There are two kinds of scanning: passive scanning and active scanning. In finding an access point, client stations follow a trail of breadcrumbs left by the access point. These breadcrumbs are called service set identifiers (SSID) and beacons. These tools serve as a means for a client station to find any and all access points.

Service Set Identifier

The service set identifier (SSID) is a unique, case sensitive, alphanumeric value from 2-32 characters long used by wireless LANs as a network name. This naming handle is used for segmenting networks, as a rudimentary security measure, and in the process of joining a network. The SSID value is sent in beacons, probe requests, probe responses, and other types of frames. A client station must be configured for the correct SSID in order to join a network. The administrator configures the SSID (sometimes called the ESSID) in each access point. Some clients have the ability to use any SSID value instead of only one manually specified by the administrator. If clients are to roam seamlessly among a group of access points, the clients and all access points must be configured with matching SSIDs. The most important point about an SSID is that it must match EXACTLY between access points and clients. Do not confuse the SSID (ESSID) with the BSSID. The Basic Service Set Identifier is a 6-byte hex number identifying the access point where the frame originated or was relayed, whereas the SSID and ESSID are interchangeable terms denoting the network name or identifier.

Beacons

Beacons (short for *beacon management frame*) are short frames that are sent from the access point to stations (infrastructure mode) or station-to-station (ad hoc mode) in order to organize and synchronize wireless communication on the wireless LAN. Beacons serve several functions, including the following.

Time Synchronization

Beacons synchronize clients by way of a time-stamp at the exact moment of transmission. When the client receives the beacon, it changes its own clock to reflect the clock of the access point. Once this change is made, the two clocks are synchronized. Synchronizing the clocks of communicating units will ensure that all time-sensitive functions, such as hopping in FHSS systems, are performed without error. The beacon also contains the beacon interval, which informs stations how often to expect the beacon.

FH or DS Parameter Sets

Beacons contain information specifically geared to the spread spectrum technology the system is using. For example, in a FHSS system, hop and dwell time parameters and hop sequence are included in the beacon. In a DSSS system, the beacon contains channel information.

SSID Information

Stations look in beacons for the SSID of the network they wish to join. When this information is found, the station looks at the MAC address of where the beacon originated and sends an authentication request in hopes of associating with that access point. If a station is set to accept any SSID, then the station will attempt to join the network through the first access point that sends a beacon or the one with the strongest signal strength if there are multiple access points.

Traffic Indication Map (TIM)

The TIM is used an as indicator of which sleeping stations have packets queued at the access point. This information is passed in each beacon to all associated stations. While sleeping, synchronized stations power up their receivers, listen for the beacon, check the TIM to see if they are listed, then, if they are not listed, they power down their receivers and continue sleeping.

Supported Rates

With wireless networks, there are many supported speeds depending on the standard of the hardware in use. For example, an 802.11b compliant device supports 11, 5.5, 2, & 1 Mbps speeds. This capability information is passed in the beacons to inform the stations what speeds are supported on the access point.

There is more information passed within beacons, but this list covers everything that could be considered important from an administrator's point of view.

Passive Scanning

Passive scanning is the process of listening for beacons on each channel for a specific period of time after the station is initialized. These beacons are sent by access points (infrastructure mode) or client stations (ad hoc mode), and the scanning station catalogs characteristics about the access points or stations based on these beacons. The station searching for a network listens for beacons until it hears a beacon listing the SSID of the network it wishes to join. The station then attempts to join the network through the access point that sent the beacon. Passive scanning is illustrated in Figure 7.1.

In configurations where there are multiple access points, the SSID of the network the station wishes to join may be broadcast by more than one of these access points. In this situation, the station will attempt to join the network through the access point with the strongest signal strength and the lowest bit error rate.

FIGURE 7.1   Passive Scanning

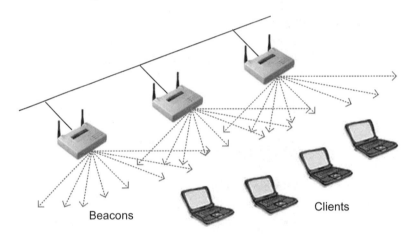

Beacons   Clients

Stations continue passive scanning even after associating to an access point. Passive scanning saves time reconnecting to the network if the client is disconnected (disassociated) from the access point to which the client is currently connected. By maintaining a list of available access points and their characteristics (channel, signal strength, SSID, etc), the station can quickly locate the best access point should its current connection be broken for any reason.

Stations will roam from one access point to another after the radio signal from the access point where the station is connected gets to a certain low level of signal strength. Roaming is implemented so that the station can stay connected to the network. Stations use the information obtained through passive scanning for locating the next best access point (or ad hoc network) to use for connectivity back into the network. For this reason, overlap between access point cells is usually specified at approximately 20-30%. This overlap allows stations to seamlessly roam between access points while disconnecting and reconnecting without the user's knowledge.

Because the sensitivity threshold on some radios does not work properly, sometimes an administrator will see a radio stay attached to an access point until the signal is broken due to extremely low signal strength instead of roaming to another access point that has a better signal. This situation is a known problem with some hardware and should be reported to the manufacturer if you are experiencing this problem.

Active Scanning

Active scanning involves the sending of a probe request frame from a wireless station. Stations send this probe frame when they are actively seeking a network to join. The probe frame will contain either the SSID of the network they wish to join or a broadcast SSID. If a probe request is sent specifying an SSID, then only access points that are servicing that SSID will respond with a probe response frame. If a probe request frame is sent with a broadcast SSID, then all access points within reach will respond with a probe response frame, as can be seen in Figure 7.2.

The point of probing in this manner is to locate access points through which the station can attach to the network. Once an access point with the proper SSID is found, the station initiates the authentication and association steps of joining the network through that access point.

FIGURE 7.2   Active Scanning

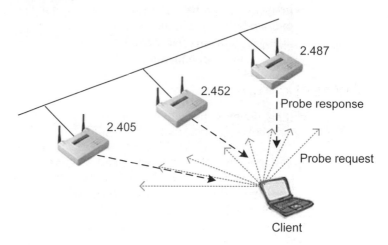

The information passed from the access point to the station in probe response frames is almost identical to that of beacons. Probe response frames differ from beacons only in that they are not time-stamped and they do not include a Traffic Indication Map (TIM).

The signal strength of the probe response frames that the PC Card receives back helps determine the access point with which the PC card will attempt to associate. The station generally chooses the access point with the strongest signal strength and lowest bit error rate (BER). The BER is a ratio of corrupted packets to good packets typically determined by the Signal-to-Noise Ratio of the signal. If the peak of an RF signal is somewhere near the noise floor, then the receiver may confuse the data signal with noise.

Authentication & Association

The process of connecting to a wireless LAN consists of two separate sub-processes. These sub-processes always occur in the same order, and are called *authentication* and *association*. For example, when we speak of a wireless PC card connecting to a wireless LAN, we say that the PC card has been authenticated by and has associated with a certain access point. Keep in mind that when we speak of association, we are speaking of Layer 2 connectivity, and authentication pertains directly to the radio

PC card, not to the user. Understanding the steps involved in getting a client connected to an access point is crucial to security, troubleshooting, and management of the wireless LAN.

Authentication

The first step in connecting to a wireless LAN is authentication. Authentication is the process through which a wireless node (PC Card, USB Client, etc.) has its identity verified by the network (usually the access point) to which the node is attempting to connect. This verification occurs when the access point to which the client is connecting verifies that the client is who it says it is. To put it another way, the access point responds to a client requesting to connect by verifying the client's identity before any connection happens. Sometimes the authentication process is null, meaning that, although both the client and access point have to proceed through this step in order to associate, there's really no special identity required for association. This is the case when most brand new access points and PC cards are installed in their default configuration. We will discuss two types of authentication processes later in this chapter.

The client begins the authentication process by sending an authentication request frame to the access point (in infrastructure mode). The access point will either accept or deny this request, thereafter notifying the station of its decision with an authentication response frame. The authentication process can be accomplished at the access point, or the access point might pass along this responsibility to an upstream authentication server such as RADIUS. The RADIUS server would perform the authentication based on a list of criteria, and then return its results to the access point so that the access point could return the results to the client station.

Association

Once a wireless client has been authenticated, the client then associates with the access point. *Associated* is the state at which a client is allowed to pass data through an access point. If your PC card is associated to an access point, you are connected to that access point, and hence, the network.

The process of becoming associated is as follows. When a client wishes to connect, the client sends an authentication request to the access point and receives back an authentication response. After authentication is completed, the station sends an association request frame to the access point who replies to the client with an association response frame either allowing or disallowing association.

States of Authentication & Association

The complete process of authentication and association has three distinct states:

1. Unauthenticated and unassociated

2. Authenticated and unassociated

3. Authenticated and associated

Unauthenticated and Unassociated

In this initial state, the wireless node is completely disconnected from the network and unable to pass frames through the access point. Access points keep a table of client connection statuses known as the association table. It's important to note that different vendors refer to the unauthenticated and unassociated state in their access points' association table differently. This table will typically show "unauthenticated" for any client that has not completed the authentication process or has attempted authentication and failed.

Authenticated and Unassociated

In this second state, the wireless client has passed the authentication process, but is not yet associated with the access point. The client is not yet allowed to send or receive data through the access point. The access point's association table will typically show "authenticated." Because clients pass the authentication stage and immediately proceed into the association stage very quickly (milliseconds), rarely do you see the "authenticated" step on the access point. It is far more likely that you will see "unauthenticated" or "associated" - which brings us to the last stage.

Authenticated and Associated

In this final state, your wireless node is completely connected to the network and able to send and receive data through the access point to which the node is connected (associated). Figure 7.3 illustrates a client associating with an access point. You will likely see "associated" in the access point's association table denoting that this client is fully connected and authorized to pass traffic through the access point. As you can deduce from the description of each of these three states, advanced wireless network security measures would be implemented at the point at which the client is attempting to authenticate.

FIGURE 7.3   Association

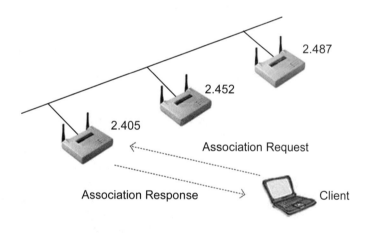

It's important to note that mobile wireless clients can authenticate to more than one access point at a time, but may only associate with one access point. This pre-authentication makes for faster and smoother roaming when the client moves from the coverage area of one AP to another. You can verify clients pre-authenticating by checking the Association Table of your Access Points.

Authentication Methods

The IEEE 802.11 standard specifies two methods of authentication: *Open System authentication* and *Shared Key authentication*. The simpler and also the more secure of the two methods is Open System authentication. For a client to become authenticated, the client must walk through a series of steps with the access point. This series of steps varies depending on the authentication process used. Below, we will discuss each authentication process specified by the 802.11 standard, how they work, and why they are used.

Open System Authentication

Open System authentication is a method of null authentication and is specified by the IEEE 802.11 as the default setting in wireless LAN equipment. Using this method of authentication, a station can associate with any access point that uses Open System authentication based only on having the right service set identifier (SSID). The SSIDs must match on both the access point and client before a client is allowed to complete the authentication process. Uses of the SSID relating to security will be discussed in Chapter 10 (Security). The Open System authentication process is used effectively in both secure and non-secure environments.

Open System Authentication Process

The Open System authentication process occurs as follows:

1. The wireless client makes a request to associate to the access point

2. The access point authenticates the client and sends a positive response and the client becomes associated (connected)

These steps can be seen in Figure 7.4.

FIGURE 7.4   Open System Authentication Process

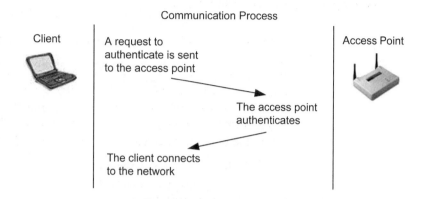

Open System authentication is a very simple process. As the wireless LAN administrator, you have the option of using WEP (wired equivalent privacy) encryption with Open System authentication. If WEP is used with the Open System authentication process, there is still no verification of the WEP key on each side of the connection during authentication. Rather, the WEP key is used only for encrypting data once the client is authenticated and associated.

Open System authentication is used in several scenarios, but there are two main reasons to use it. First, Open System authentication is considered the more secure of the two available authentication methods for reasons explained below. Second, Open System authentication is simple to configure because it requires no configuration at all. All 802.11-compliant wireless LAN hardware is configured to use Open System authentication by default, making it easy to get started building and connecting your wireless LAN right out of the box.

Shared Key Authentication

Shared Key authentication is a method of authentication that requires use of WEP. WEP encryption uses keys that are entered (usually by the administrator) into both the client and the access point. These keys must match on both sides for WEP to work properly. Shared Key authentication uses WEP keys in two fashions, as we will describe here.

Shared Key Authentication Process

The authentication process using Shared Key authentication occurs as follows.

1. A client requests association to an access point – this step is the same as that of Open System authentication.

2. The access point issues a challenge to the client – this challenge is randomly generated plain text, which is sent from the access point to the client in the clear.

3. The client responds to the challenge – the client responds by encrypting the challenge text using the client's WEP key and sending it back to the access point.

4. The access point responds to the client's response – The access point decrypts the client's encrypted response to verify that the challenge text is encrypted using a matching WEP key. Through this process, the access point determines whether or not the client has the correct WEP key. If the client's WEP key is correct, the access point will respond positively and authenticate the client. If the client's WEP key is not correct, the access point will respond negatively, and not authenticate the client, leaving the client unauthenticated and unassociated.

This process is shown in Figure 7.5.

FIGURE 7.5   Shared Key Authentication Process

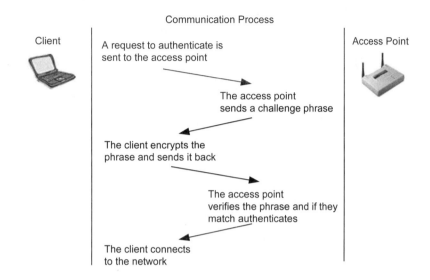

It would seem that the Shared Key authentication process is more secure than that of Open System authentication, but as you will soon see, it is not. Rather, Shared Key authentication opens the door for would-be hackers. It is important to understand both ways that WEP is used. The WEP key can be used during the Shared Key authentication process to verify a client's identity, but it can also be used for encryption of the data payload send by the client through the access point. This type of WEP use is further discussed in Chapter 10 (Security).

Authentication Security

Shared Key authentication is not considered secure because the access point transmits the challenge text in the clear and receives the same challenge text encrypted with the WEP key. This scenario allows a hacker using a network analyzer to see both the plaintext challenge and the encrypted challenge. Having both of these values, a hacker could use a simple cracking program to derive the WEP key. Once the WEP key is obtained, the hacker could decrypt encrypted traffic. It is for this reason that Open System authentication is considered more secure than Shared Key authentication.

It is important for the wireless network administrator to understand that neither Open System nor Shared Key authentication types are secure, and for this reason a wireless LAN security solution, above and beyond what the 802.11 standard specifies, is important and necessary.

Shared Secrets & Certificates

Shared secrets are strings of numbers or text that are commonly referred to as the WEP key. Certificates are another method of user identification used with wireless networks. Just as with WEP keys, certificates (which are authentication documents) are placed on the client machine ahead of time. This placement is done so that when the user wishes to authenticate to the wireless network, the authentication mechanism is already in place on the client station. Both of these methods have historically been implemented in a manual fashion, but there are applications available today that allow automation of this process.

Emerging Wireless Security Solutions

There are many new authentication security solutions and protocols on the market today, including VPN and 802.1x using Extensible Authentication Protocol (EAP). Many of these security solutions involve passing authentication through to authentication servers upstream from the access point while keeping the client waiting during the authentication phase. Windows XP has native support for 802.11, 802.1x, and EAP. Cisco and other wireless LAN manufacturers also support these standards. For this reason, it is easy to see that the 802.1x and EAP authentication solution could be a common solution in the wireless LAN security market.

802.1x and EAP

The 802.1x (port-based network access control) standard is relatively new, and devices that support it have the ability to allow a connection into the network at layer 2 only if user authentication is successful. This protocol works well for access points that need the ability to keep users disconnected if they are not supposed to be on the network. EAP is a layer 2 protocol that is a flexible replacement for PAP or CHAP under PPP that works over local area networks. EAP allows plug-ins at either end of a link through which many methods of authentication can be used. In the past, PAP and/or CHAP have been used for user authentication, and both support using passwords. The need for a stronger, more flexible alternative is clear with wireless networks since more varied implementations abound with wireless than with wired networks.

Typically, user authentication is accomplished using a Remote Authentication Dial-In User Service (RADIUS) server and some type of user database (Native RADIUS, NDS, Active Directory, LDAP, etc.). The process of authenticating using EAP is shown in Figure 7.6. The new 802.11i standard includes support for 802.1x, EAP, AAA, mutual authentication, and key generation, none of which were included in the original 802.11 standard. *"AAA"* is an acronym for *authentication* (identifying who you are), *authorization* (attributes to allow you to perform certain tasks on the network), and *accounting* (shows what you've done and where you've been on the network).

In the 802.1x standard model, network authentication consists of three pieces: the supplicant, the authenticator, and the authentication server.

FIGURE 7.6   802.1x and EAP

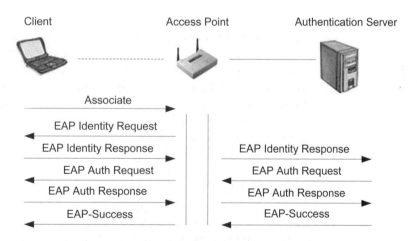

Because wireless LAN security is essential – and EAP authentication types provide the means of securing the wireless LAN connection – vendors are rapidly developing and adding EAP authentication types to their wireless LAN access points. Knowing the type of EAP being used is important in understanding the characteristics of the authentication method such as passwords, key generation, mutual authentication, and protocol. Some of the commonly deployed EAP authentication types include:

EAP-MD-5 Challenge. The earliest EAP authentication type, this essentially duplicates CHAP password protection on a wireless LAN. EAP-MD5 represents a kind of base-level EAP support among 802.1x devices.

EAP-Cisco Wireless. Also called *LEAP* (Lightweight Extensible Authentication Protocol), this EAP authentication type is used primarily in Cisco wireless LAN access points. LEAP provides security during credential exchange, encrypts data transmission using dynamically generated WEP keys, and supports mutual authentication.

EAP-TLS (Transport Layer Security). EAP-TLS provides for certificate-based, mutual authentication of the client and the network. EAP-TLS relies on client-side and server-side certificates to perform authentication, using dynamically generated user- and session-based WEP keys distributed to secure the connection. Windows XP includes an EAP-TLS client, and EAP-TLS is also supported by Windows 2000.

EAP-TTLS. Funk Software and Certicom have jointly developed *EAP-TTLS* (Tunneled Transport Layer Security). EAP-TTLS is an extension of EAP-TLS, which provides for certificate-based, mutual authentication of the client and network. Unlike EAP-TLS, however, EAP-TTLS requires only server-side certificates, eliminating the need to configure certificates for each wireless LAN client.

In addition, EAP-TTLS supports legacy password protocols, so you can deploy it against your existing authentication system (such as Active Directory or NDS). EAP-TTLS securely tunnels client authentication within TLS records, ensuring that the user remains anonymous to eavesdroppers on the wireless link. Dynamically generated user- and session-based WEP keys are distributed to secure the connection.

PEAP (Protected EAP). Cisco and Microsoft have developed *PEAP*, which is a direct competitor with EAP-TTLS. It uses tunneled server-side certificates and username/password credentials for client to authenticate to a server. *PEAP* is supported in Windows XP with Service Pack 1 and is also supported by Cisco's ACU version 5.05 and higher. *PEAP* supports mutual authentication as well, which adds increased security.

EAP-SRP (Secure Remote Password). SRP is a secure, password-based authentication and key-exchange protocol. It solves the problem of authenticating clients to servers securely in cases where the user of the client software must memorize a small secret (like a password) and carries no other secret information. The server carries a verifier for each user, which allows the server to authenticate the client. However, if the verifier were compromised, the attacker would not be allowed to impersonate the client. In addition, SRP exchanges a cryptographically strong secret as a byproduct of successful authentication, which enables the two parties to communicate securely.

EAP-SIM (GSM). EAP-SIM is a mechanism for Mobile IP network access authentication and registration key generation using the GSM Subscriber Identity Module (SIM). The rationale for using the GSM SIM with Mobile IP is to leverage the existing GSM authorization infrastructure with the existing user base and the existing SIM card distribution channels. By using the SIM key exchange, no other preconfigured security association besides the SIM card is required on the mobile node. The idea is not to use the GSM radio access technology, but to use GSM SIM authorization with Mobile IP over any link layer, for example on Wireless LAN access networks.

It is likely that this list of EAP authentication types will grow as more and more vendors enter the wireless LAN security market, and until the market chooses a standard.

 The different types of EAP authentication are not covered on the CWNA exam, but understanding what EAP is and how it is used in general is a key element in being effective as a wireless network administrator.

VPN Solutions

VPN technology provides the means to securely transmit data between two network devices over an unsecure data transport medium. It is commonly used to link remote computers or networks to a corporate server via the Internet. However, VPN is also a solution for protecting data on a wireless network. VPN works by creating a tunnel on top of a protocol such as IP. Traffic inside the tunnel is encrypted, and totally isolated as can be seen in Figures 7.7 and 7.8. VPN technology provides three levels of security: user authentication, encryption, and data authentication.

- User authentication ensures that only authorized users (over a specific device) are able to connect, send, and receive data over the wireless network.

- Encryption offers additional protection as it ensures that even if transmissions are intercepted, they cannot be decoded without significant time and effort.

- Data authentication ensures the integrity of data on the wireless network, guaranteeing that all traffic is from authenticated devices only.

FIGURE 7.7   Access point with an integrated VPN server

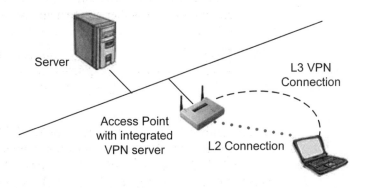

FIGURE 7.8   Access point with an external VPN server

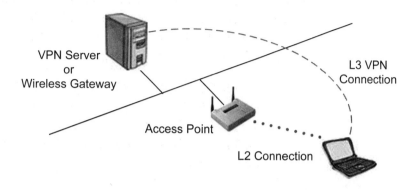

Applying VPN technology to secure a wireless network requires a different approach than when it is used on wired networks for the following reasons.

- The inherent repeater function of wireless access points automatically forwards traffic between wireless LAN stations that communicate together and that appear on the same wireless network.

- The range of the wireless network will likely extend beyond the physical boundaries of an office or home, giving intruders the means to compromise the network.

The ease and scalability with which wireless LAN solutions can be deployed makes them ideal solutions for many different environments. As a result, implementation of VPN security will vary based on the needs of each type of environment. For example, a hacker with a wireless protocol analyzer, if he obtained the WEP key, could decode packets in real time. With a VPN solution, the packets would not only be encrypted, but also tunneled. This extra layer of security provides many benefits at the access level.

An important note here is that not all VPNs let wireless users roam between subnets or networks without "breaking" the secure tunnel, and not all VPNs will permit transport and applications connections to remain established during roaming. Another stumbling block is the operating system – what operating system or systems do the mobile clients have to be running in order to get the protections of a wireless VPN.

Service Sets

A *service set* is a term used to describe the basic components of a fully operational wireless LAN. In other words, there are three ways to configure a wireless LAN, and each way requires a different set of hardware. The three ways to configure a wireless LAN are:

- Basic service set
- Extended service set
- Independent basic service set

Basic Service Set (BSS)

When one access point is connected to a wired network and a set of wireless stations, the network configuration is referred to as a basic service set (BSS). A basic service set consists of only one access point and one or more wireless clients, as shown in Figure 7.9. A basic service set uses *infrastructure mode* - a mode that requires use of an access point and in which all of the wireless traffic traverses the access point. No direct client-to-client transmissions are allowed.

FIGURE 7.9   Basic Service Set

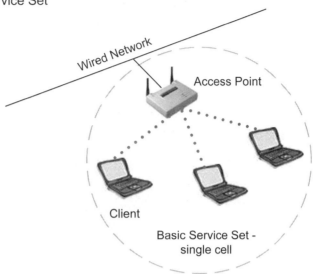

Each wireless client must use the access point to communicate with any other wireless client or any wired host on the network. The BSS covers a single cell, or RF area, around the access point with varying data rate zones (concentric circles) of differing data speeds, measured in Mbps. The data speeds in these concentric circles will depend on the technology being utilized. If the BSS were made up of 802.11b equipment, then the concentric circles would have data speeds of 11, 5.5, 2, and 1 Mbps. The data rates get smaller as the circles get farther away from the access point. A BSS has one unique SSID.

Extended Service Set (ESS)

An extended service set is defined as two or more basic service sets connected by a common distribution system, as shown in Figure 7.10. The distribution system can be either wired, wireless, LAN, WAN, or any other method of network connectivity. An ESS must have at least 2 access points operating in infrastructure mode. Similar to a BSS, all packets in an ESS must go through one of the access points.

FIGURE 7.10   Extended Service Set

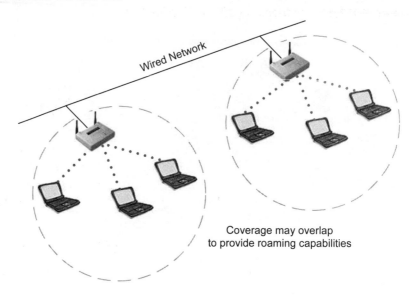

Coverage may overlap
to provide roaming capabilities

Other characteristics of extended service sets, according to the 802.11 standard, are that an ESS covers multiple cells, allows – but does not require – roaming capabilities, and does not require the same SSID in both basic service sets.

Independent Basic Service Set (IBSS)

An independent basic service set is also known as an *ad hoc* network. An IBSS has no access point or any other access to a distribution system, but covers one single cell and has one SSID, as shown in Figure 7.11. The clients in an IBSS alternate the responsibility of sending beacons since there is no access point to perform this task.

FIGURE 7.11   Independent Basic Service Set

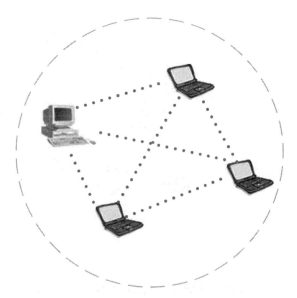

In order to transmit data *outside* an IBSS, one of the clients in the IBSS must be acting as a gateway, or router, using a software solution for this purpose. In an IBSS, clients make direct connections to each other when transmitting data, and for this reason, an IBSS is often referred to as a *peer-to-peer* network.

Roaming

Roaming is the process or ability of a wireless client to move seamlessly from one cell (or BSS) to another without losing network connectivity. Access points hand the client off from one to another in a way that is invisible to the client, ensuring unbroken connectivity. Figure 7.12 illustrates a client roaming from one BSS to another BSS.

When any area in the building is within reception range of more than one access point, the cells' coverage overlaps. Overlapping coverage areas are an important attribute of the wireless LAN setup, because it enables seamless roaming between overlapping cells. Roaming allows mobile users with portable stations to move freely between overlapping cells, constantly maintaining their network connection.

FIGURE 7.12   Roaming in an ESS

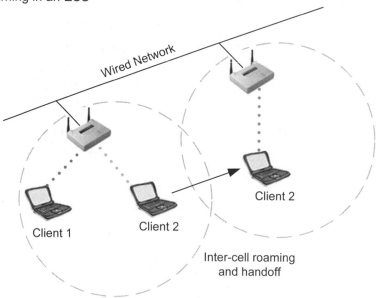

When roaming is seamless, a work session can be maintained while moving from one cell to another. Multiple access points can provide wireless roaming coverage for an entire building or campus.

When the coverage area of two or more access points overlap, the stations in the overlapping area can establish the best possible connection with one of the access points while continuously searching for the best access point. In order to minimize packet loss during switchover, the "old" and "new" access points communicate to coordinate the roaming process. This function is similar to a cellular phones' handover, with two main differences:

- On a packet-based LAN system, the transition from cell to cell may be performed between packet transmissions, as opposed to telephony where the transition may occur during a phone conversation.

- On a voice system, a temporary disconnection may not affect the conversation, while in a packet-based environment it significantly reduces performance because the upper layer protocols then retransmit the data.

Standards

The 802.11 standard does not define how roaming should be performed, but does define the basic building blocks. These building blocks include active & passive scanning and a reassociation process. The reassociation process occurs when a wireless station roams from one access point to another, becoming associated with the new access point.

The 802.11 standard allows a client to roam among multiple access points operating on the same or separate channels. For example, every 100 ms, an access point might transmit a beacon signal that includes a time stamp for client synchronization, a traffic indication map, an indication of supported data rates, and other parameters. Roaming clients use the beacon to gauge the strength of their existing connection to the access point. If the connection is weak, the roaming station can attempt to associate itself with a new access point.

To meet the needs of mobile radio communications, the 802.11b standard must be tolerant of connections being dropped and re-established. The standard attempts to ensure minimum disruption to data delivery, and provides some features for caching and forwarding messages between BSSs.

Particular implementations of some higher layer protocols such as TCP/IP may be less tolerant. For example, in a network where DHCP is used to assign IP addresses, a roaming node may lose its connection when it moves across cell boundaries. The node will then have to re-establish the connection when it enters the next BSS or cell. Software solutions are available to address this particular problem.

One such solution is Mobile IP. Mobile IP is an Internet Engineering Task Force (IETF) Request for Comment (RFC) (#2002) that was documented for the purpose of explaining how to best have mobile users stay connected to the Internet while moving between connection points. This is accomplished by use of home agents and foreign agents. These two work together to assure that traffic destined to a mobile node reaches the node no matter where it is connected. A home agent or foreign agent can be a computer, a router, or other similar device that is capable of running the Mobile IP protocol. There are some caveats in many Mobile

IP solutions that should be briefly addressed in this text so that the user understands what to look for in a Mobile IP solution.

First, Mobile IP does not allow mobile devices and mobility agents on the network to share state information about each session that a mobile device has established. This means that applications can't persist during periods when the mobile device cannot be reached. When the mobile devices reattaches to the network, there may be a need to clean up broken application sessions, log in again, re-authenticate, restart applications, and re-enter lost data (again a productivity loss, not to mention a usability failure). Second, "session persistence" means more than forwarding packets to a user's new location. If you don't have transport and application session persistence, the solution breaks down. Why? When a transport protocol cannot communicate to its peer, the underlying protocols, like TCP, assume that the disruption of service is due to network congestion. When this occurs, these protocols back off, reducing performance and eventually terminating the connection. The only way to solve this problem is to have mobile nodes deployed with a software solution that acts on behalf of the mobile device when it is unreachable.

The 802.11b standard leaves much of the detailed functioning of what it calls the distribution system to manufacturers. This decision was a deliberate decision on the part of the standard designers, because they were most concerned with making the standard entirely independent of any other existing network standards. As a practical matter, an overwhelming majority of 802.11b wireless LANs using ESS topologies are connected to Ethernet LANs and make heavy use of TCP/IP. Wireless LAN vendors have stepped into the gap to offer proprietary methods of facilitating roaming between nodes in an ESS.

 When a station roams from an old access point to a new access point, the new access point is responsible for ensuring that any bridges between the two access points are properly notified of the station's new location. The manner in which this is accomplished is not specified. The only requirement is that some method is implemented which ensures that packets will flow properly to the station's new access point. The new IEEE 802.11f draft addresses the issue of standardizing roaming with the introduction of the Inter Access Point Protocol (IAPP).

Connectivity

The 802.11 MAC layer is responsible for how a client associates with an access point. When an 802.11 client enters the range of one or more access points, the client chooses an access point to associate with (also called joining a BSS) based on signal strength and observed packet error rates.

Once associated with the access point, the station periodically surveys all 802.11 channels in order to assess whether a different access point would provide better performance characteristics. If the client determines that there is a stronger signal from a different access point, the client re-associates with the new access point, tuning to the radio channel to which that access point is set. The station will not attempt to roam until it drops below a manufacturer-defined signal strength threshold.

Reassociation

Reassociation usually occurs because the wireless station has physically moved away from the original access point, causing the signal to weaken. In other cases, reassociation occurs due to a change in radio characteristics in the building, or due simply to high network traffic on the original access point. In the latter case, this function is known as *load balancing*, since its primary function is to distribute the total wireless LAN load most efficiently across the available wireless infrastructure.

Association and reassociation differ only slightly in their use. Association request frames are used when joining a network for the first time. Reassociation request frames are used when roaming between access points so that the new access point knows to negotiate transfer of buffered frames from the old access point and to let the distribution system know that the client has moved. Reassociation is illustrated in Figure 7.13.

FIGURE 7.13   Roaming with reassociation

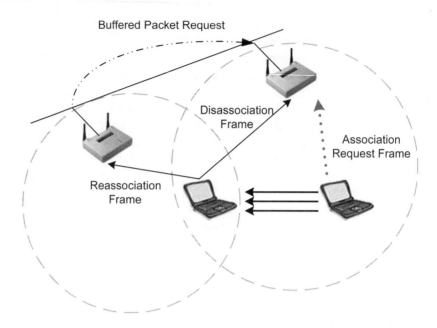

This process of dynamically associating and re-associating with access points allows network managers to set up wireless LANs with very broad coverage by creating a series of overlapping 802.11 cells throughout a building or across a campus.   To be successful, the IT manager ideally will employ *channel reuse*, taking care to configure each access point on an 802.11 DSSS channel that does not overlap with a channel used by a neighboring access point. While there are 14 partially overlapping channels specified in 802.11 DSSS (11 channels can be used within the U.S.), there are only 3 channels that do not overlap at all, and these are the best to use for multi-cell coverage. If two access points are in range of one another and are set to the same or partially overlapping channels, they may cause some interference for one another, thus lowering the total available bandwidth in the area of overlap.

VPN Use

Wireless VPN solutions are typically implemented in two fashions. First, a centralized VPN server is implemented upstream from the access points. This VPN server could be a proprietary hardware solution or a server with a VPN application running on it. Both serve the same purpose and provide the same type of security and connectivity. Having this VPN server (also acting as a gateway and firewall) between the wireless user and the core network provides a level of security similar to wired VPNs.

The second approach is a distributed set of VPN servers. Some manufacturers implement a VPN server into their access points. This type of solution would provide security for small office and medium-sized organizations without use of an external authentication mechanism like RADIUS. For scalability, these same access point/VPN servers typically support RADIUS.

Tunnels are built from the client station to the VPN server, as illustrated in Figure 7.14. When a user roams, the client is roaming between access points across layer 2 boundaries. This process is seamless to the layer 3 connectivity. However, if a tunnel is built to the access point or centralized VPN server and a layer 3 boundary is crossed, a mechanism of some kind must be provided for keeping the tunnel alive when the boundary is crossed.

FIGURE 7.14   Roaming within VPN tunnels

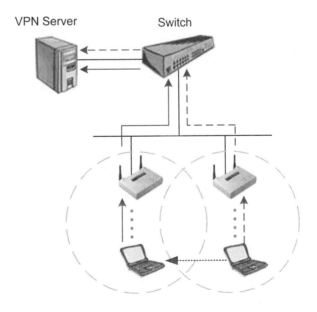

Layer 2 & 3 Boundaries

A constraint of existing technology is that wired networks are often segmented for manageability. Enterprises with multiple buildings, such as hospitals or large businesses, often implement a LAN in each building and then connect these LANs with routers or switch-routers. This is layer 3 segmentation has two major advantages. First, it contains broadcasts effectively, and second it allows access control between segments on the network. This type of segmentation can also be done at layer 2 using VLANs on switches. VLANs are often seen implemented floor-by-floor in multi-floor office buildings or for each remote building in a campus for the same reasons. Segmenting at layer 2 in this fashion segments the networks completely as if multiple networks were being implemented. When using routers such as seen in figure 7.15, users must have a method of roaming across router boundaries without losing their layer 3 connection. The layer 2 connection is still maintained by the access points, but since the IP subnet has changed while roaming, the connection to servers, for example, will be broken. Without subnet-roaming capability (such as with using a Mobile IP solution or using DHCP), wireless LAN access points must all be connected to a single subnet (a.k.a. "a flat network"). This work-around can be done at a loss of network management flexibility, but customers may be willing to incur this cost if they perceive that the value of the end system is high enough.

FIGURE 7.15   Roaming across Layer 3 boundaries

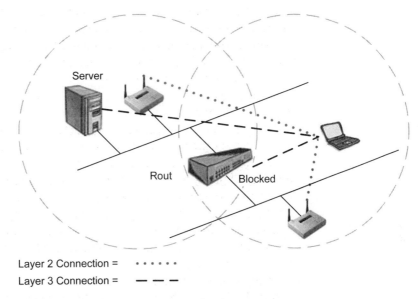

Layer 2 Connection = • • • • • •

Layer 3 Connection = — — —

Many network environments (e.g., multi-building campuses, multi-floored high rises, or older or historical buildings) cannot embrace a single subnet solution as a practical option. This wired architecture is at odds with current wireless LAN technology. Access points can't hand off a session when a remote device moves across router boundaries because crossing routers changes the client device's IP address. The wired system no longer knows where to send the message. When a mobile device reattaches to the network, all application end points are lost and users are forced to log in again, re-authenticate, relocate themselves in their applications, and recreate lost data. The same type of problem is incurred when using VLANs. Switches see users as roaming across VLAN boundaries.

FIGURE 7.16 Roaming Across VLANs

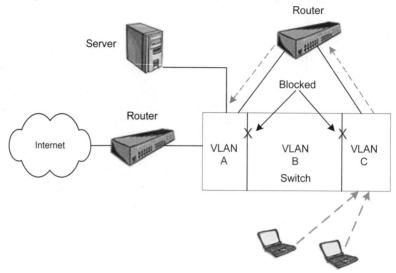

A hardware solution to this problem is to deploy all access points on a single VLAN using a flat IP subnet for all access points so that there is no change of IP address for roaming users and a Mobile IP solution isn't required. Users are then routed as a group back into the corporate network using a firewall, a router, a gateway device, etc. This solution can be difficult to implement in many instances, but is generally accepted as the "standard" methodology. There are many more instances where an enterprise must forego use of a wireless LAN altogether because such a solution just isn't practical.

Even with all access points on a single subnet, mobile users can still encounter coverage problems. If a user moves out of range, into a coverage hole, or simply suspends the device to prolong battery life, all application end points are lost and users in these situations again are also forced to log in again and find their way back to where they left off.

There are several layer 3 solutions on the market as of this writing. One such solution is an access point that has a built in VPN server and performs full routing, including routing protocols such as RIP. Another solution is implemented on a series of servers using the Mobile IP standard (RFC 2002). Many of the software solutions are implemented in somewhat the same manner.

Load Balancing

Congested areas with many users and heavy traffic load per unit may require a multi-cell structure. In a multi-cell structure, several co-located access points "illuminate" the same area creating a common coverage area, which increases aggregate throughput. Stations inside the common coverage area automatically associate with the access point that is less loaded and provides the best signal quality.

As illustrated in Figure 7.17, the stations are equally divided between the access points in order to equally share the load between all access points. Efficiency is maximized because all access points are working at the same low-level load. Load balancing is also known as load sharing and is configured on both the stations and the access point in most cases.

FIGURE 7.17   Load balancing

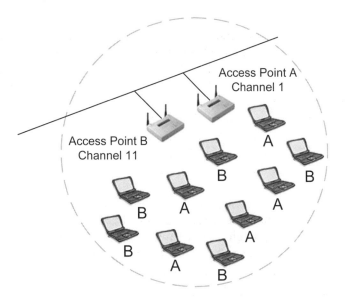

Power Management Features

Wireless clients operate in one of two power management modes specified by the IEEE 802.11 standard. These power management modes are active mode, which is commonly called *continuous aware mode* (CAM) and power save, which is commonly called *power save polling* (PSP) mode. Conserving power using a power-saving mode is especially important to mobile users whose laptops or PDAs run on batteries. Extending the life of these batteries allows the user to stay up and running longer without a recharge. Wireless LAN cards can draw a significant amount of power from the battery while in CAM, which is why power saving features are included in the 802.11 standard.

Continuous Aware Mode

Continuous aware mode is the setting during which the wireless client uses full power, does not "sleep," and is constantly in regular communication with the access point. Any computers that stay plugged into an AC power outlet continuously such as a desktop or server should be set for CAM. Under these circumstances, there is no reason to have the PC card conserve power.

Power Save Polling

Using power save polling (PSP) mode allows a wireless client to "sleep." By sleep, we mean that the client actually powers down for a very short amount of time, perhaps a small fraction of a second. This sleep is enough time to save a significant amount of power on the wireless client. In turn, the power saved by the wireless client enables a laptop computer user, for example, to work for a longer period of time on batteries, making that user more productive.

When using PSP, the wireless client behaves differently within basic service sets and independent basic service sets. The one similarity in behavior from a BSS to an IBSS is the sending and receiving of beacons.

The processes that operate during PSP mode, in both BSS and IBSS, are described below. Keep in mind that these processes occur many times per second. That fact allows your wireless LAN to maintain its connectivity, but also causes a certain amount of additional overhead. An administrator should consider this overhead when planning for the needs of the users on the wireless LAN.

PSP Mode in a Basic Service Set

When using PSP mode in a BSS, stations first send a frame to the access point to inform the access point that they are going to sleep, (temporarily powering down). The access point then records the sleeping stations as asleep. The access point buffers any frames that are intended for the sleeping stations. Traffic for those clients who are asleep continues arriving at the access point, but the access point cannot send traffic to a sleeping client. Therefore, packets get queued in a buffer marked for the sleeping client.

The access point is constantly sending beacons at a regular interval. Clients, since they are time-synchronized with the access point, know exactly when to receive the beacon. Clients that are sleeping will power up their receivers to listen for beacons, which contain the traffic indication map (TIM). If a station sees itself listed in the TIM, it powers up, and sends a frame to the access point notifying the access point that it is now awake and ready to receive the buffered data packets. Once the client has received its packets from the access point, the client sends a message to the access point informing it that the client is going back to 'sleep'. Then the process repeats itself over and over again. This process creates some overhead that would not be present if PSP mode were not being utilized. The steps of this process are shown in Figure 7.18.

FIGURE 7.18 PSP Mode in a BSS

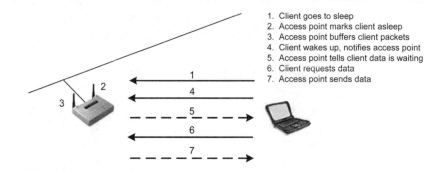

1. Client goes to sleep
2. Access point marks client asleep
3. Access point buffers client packets
4. Client wakes up, notifies access point
5. Access point tells client data is waiting
6. Client requests data
7. Access point sends data

PSP in an Independent Basic Service Set

The power saving communication process in an IBSS is very different than when power saving mode is used in a BSS. An IBSS does not contain an access point, so there is no device to buffer packets. Therefore, every station must buffer packets destined from itself to every other station in the Ad Hoc network. Stations alternate the sending of beacons on an IBSS network using varied methods, each dependent on the manufacturer.

When stations are using power saving mode, there is a period of time called an ATIM window, during which each station is fully awake and ready to receive data frames. A*d hoc traffic indication messages (ATIM)* are unicast frames used by stations to notify other stations that there is data destined to them and that they should stay awake long enough to receive it. ATIMs and beacons are both sent during the ATIM window. The process followed by stations in order to pass traffic between peers is:

- Stations are mandated by the standard to be awake for all beacons. They may never sleep more than one beacon period. Due to this fact, all stations will wake up before the ATIM window begins.

- The ATIM window begins, the designated station sends a beacon, and then stations send ATIM frames notifying other stations of buffered traffic destined to them.

- Stations receiving ATIM frames during the ATIM window stay awake to receive data frames. If no ATIM frames are received, stations may go back to sleep until the next beacon is due to begin at the beginning of the next ATIM window.

- The ATIM window closes, and stations begin transmitting data frames to each other. After receiving data frames, stations must remain awake until after the following ATIM window – unless they receive ATIM frames during the ATIM window notifying them to stay awake.

This PSP process for an IBSS is illustrated in Figure 7.19.

FIGURE 7.19 PSP Mode in an IBSS

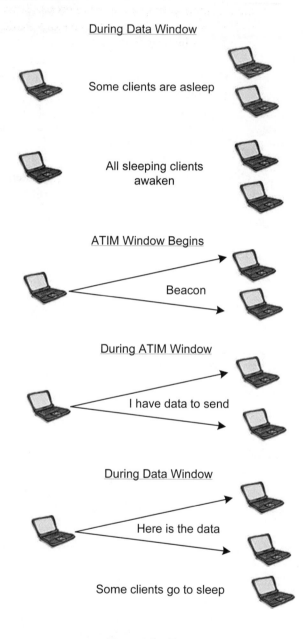

During Data Window

Some clients are asleep

All sleeping clients awaken

ATIM Window Begins

Beacon

During ATIM Window

I have data to send

During Data Window

Here is the data

Some clients go to sleep

Repeat the Process

As a wireless LAN administrator, you need to know what affect power management features will have on performance, battery life, broadcast traffic on your LAN, etc. In the example described above, the effects could be significant.

Key Terms

Before taking the exam, you should be familiar with the following terms:

AAA support

channel reuse

load balancing

multicell coverage

reassociation

Review Questions

1. A client that can transmit data over a wireless network is considered to be which of the following? Choose all that apply.

    A.   Unauthenticated

    B.   Unassociated

    C.   Authenticated

    D.   Associated

2. Which one of the following supports Authentication, Authorization, and Accounting (AAA)?

    A.   Open System authentication

    B.   Shared Key authentication

    C.   Open System and Shared Key authentication

    D.   802.11

    E.   None of the above

3. A basic service set has how many access points?

    A.   None

    B.   1

    C.   2

    D.   Unlimited

4. Shared Key authentication is more secure than Open System authentication.

    A.   This statement is always true

    B.   This statement is always false

    C.   It depends on whether or not WEP is utilized

5. A traffic indication map (TIM) is populated with station information when using which one of the following power management features in a basic or extended service set?

   A. Continuous aware mode

   B. Continuous power mode

   C. Power save polling mode

   D. Power aware polling mode

6. An ad hoc traffic indication message (ATIM) is sent when using which one of the following power management features in an independent basic service set?

   A. Continuous aware mode

   B. Continuous power mode

   C. Power save polling mode

   D. Power aware polling mode

7. An independent basic service set is also commonly referred to as which one of the following?

   A. Ad hoc mode

   B. Infrastructure mode

   C. Network mode

   D. Power save polling mode

8. The 802.11 standard specifies which of the following authentication processes? Choose all that apply.

    A. Open System authentication

    B. 802.1x/EAP

    C. Shared Key authentication

    D. RADIUS

9. Using power save polling mode (PSP) in a wireless LAN will result in which of the following? Choose all that apply.

    A. Increased throughput on the network due to less overhead traffic

    B. Decreased throughput on the network due to more overhead traffic

    C. Network traffic is not effected by using PSP

    D. Longer battery life on the clients that use PSP

10. In an ad hoc network, every client station buffers packets.

    A. This statement is always true

    B. This statement is always false

    C. It depends on whether one station is acting as a gateway

11. Which of the following are functions of the beacon frame?

    A. Load balancing all clients across multiple access points

    B. Broadcasting the SSID so that clients can connect to the access point

    C. Synchronizing the time between the access point and clients

    D. Allowing client authentication with the access point when using Shared Key authentication

12. What is passive scanning used for in a wireless LAN?

    A. Allows clients to authenticate with an access point

    B. Allows clients to actively search for any access points within range

    C. Reduces the time it takes clients to locate and associate to access points when roaming

    D. Helps determine which bridge the client will connect to

13. What does the acronym "SSID" stand for?

    A. Security Set Identifier

    B. Service Set Information Directory

    C. Service Set Identifier

    D. Security Service Information Dependency

14. The process of authentication and association has how many distinct states?

    A. 1

    B. 2

    C. 3

    D. 4

    E. 5

15. Why is Shared Key authentication considered a security risk?

    A. The access point transmits the challenge text in the clear and receives the same challenge text encrypted with the WEP key

    B. The keys are shared via broadcast with all network nodes

    C. A hacker could see the keys with a protocol analyzer

    D. The WEP keys used on all computers are the same

16. What is a basic service set?

    A.   The basic components of a wireless LAN

    B.   All clients in a wireless LAN that are being serviced by one access point

    C.   The area around an access point which can be serviced by the access point

    D.   One or more access points transmitting an RF signal

17. In a basic service set, or BSS, the access point must operate in which mode?

    A.   Repeater

    B.   Router

    C.   Bridge

    D.   Infrastructure

    E.   Gateway

18. An IBSS can also be called which of the following? Choose all that apply.

    A.   Peer-to-peer

    B.   Indifferent Basic Service Set

    C.   Ad hoc network

    D.   Internet Bindery Set Solution

19. Continuous Aware Mode, or CAM, should be configured on wireless LAN clients in which of the following situations?

    A. Portable laptop stations whose users need the ability to roam away from power sources

    B. Desktop stations that are rarely moved from their permanent location

    C. PDAs with limited battery life

    D. Laptop computers that can remain connected to a power source

20. Which of the following statements is true? Choose all that apply.

    A. Using power save polling (PSP) mode allows a wireless client to sleep

    B. Using power save polling (PSP) mode forces a wireless client to accept an access point's polling

    C. Using power save polling (PSP) mode allows a wireless client to accept packets while asleep

    D. Using power save polling (PSP) mode causes overhead in an ad hoc network

Answers to Review Questions

1.   C, D. A client station must be both authenticated (authorized) and associated (connected) before it is allowed to communicate with other nodes on the network. Authentication happens before association.

2.   E. The 802.11 standard does not support AAA. The 802.11 standard specifies both Shared Key and Open System authentication.

3.   B. A basic service set (BSS) may only have one access point. The cell around this single access point is where client stations may connect to the access point. The BSS typically connects into a wired LAN, but does not have to.

4.   B. While the process used by Shared Key authentication lends it to looking much more secure than Open System authentication, Shared Key opens the system up to attack with the vulnerability of passing both the plain text challenge and the encrypted challenge across the wireless segment. Since the WEP key is used both for authentication and data encryption, if the WEP key is compromised due to a weakness in the method of authenticating, then all encrypted data is compromised. For this reason, Open System authentication is considered more secure than shared key authentication.

5.   C. When a station is not sleeping, the access point has no need to buffer packets destined to that station. However, if a station is sleeping, there is a need for the access point to buffer its packets so that the packets are not lost. The TIM is used for the purpose of notifying stations using power save polling (PSP) mode that they have packets buffered at the access point. Client stations use power save poll frames to notify the access point to send the buffered packets.

6.   C. An ATIM is used for the purpose of notifying stations that are using power save poll (PSP) mode that there is data queued for them by other stations, awaiting delivery. After stations send the ATIMs to other stations, the ATIM window (the time during which ATIMs are sent) closes and the data is then delivered according to CSMA/CA medium access rules.

7.   A. The terms *ad hoc* and *IBSS* are interchangeable. Both indicate a

lack of an access point in a wireless LAN where stations are communicating directly with each other.

8. A, C. The 802.11 standard specifies use of only two processes of authentication. These processes are Shared Key authentication and Open System authentication. In order to comply with the 802.11 standard, the default setting on a system must be Open System authentication. The reason the IEEE specified Open System authentication as the default authentication method was to aid in ease of installation and configuration when receiving an access point or client station device from the manufacturer for the first time.

9. B, D. The advantage of using PSP mode is prolonged battery life on mobile stations. The drawback of using PSP is the additional overhead of PSP frames on the network. Of course, PSP frames are short and don't add very much overhead so overhead is likely not a big consideration in deciding on using PSP mode on stations.

10. A. In an ad hoc (IBSS) network, there is no access point to buffer packets for sleeping stations. Stations communicate directly with each other in an IBSS, creating the need for each station to buffer packets for each sleeping destination station for which it has packets buffered.

11. B, C. Sending time synchronization and SSID information are two of the main functions of the beacon management frame (often referred to simply as the *beacon*). There are many other important roles of the beacon including sending the TIM, supported communication rates, and FH/DS parameters.

12. C. By constantly monitoring beacons sent by all access points in its vicinity, a client station is able to keep abreast of which access point would be the best candidate for reassociation if its current link should fail. In knowing the best access point to attempt association with before the need arises, time is saved in reassociation, making roaming a more seamless process. Clients do not associate to bridges.

13. C. Although the SSID is often mistakenly quoted as "security set identifier", it actually stands for "service set identifier" denoting which service set a device is to participate in.

14. C. The authentication and association process has 3 distinct states that a client station moves through in becoming connected to the network. These are (1) unauthenticated & unassociated, (2) authentication & unassociated, and (3) authenticated & associated.

15. A. Because the plaintext challenge and the encrypted plaintext challenge are transmitted in the clear in sequence, a hacker could easily obtain both with a protocol analyzer. After obtaining these two pieces of information, some calculations could be performed on them to yield the WEP key, which could then be used for real-time decryption of data packets on the network.

16. B. A basic service set is a wireless LAN consisting of one access point wired to a distribution system servicing one or more wireless stations.

17. D. Basic service sets and extended service sets both use infrastructure mode on the access point and clients in order to communicate. Infrastructure mode specifies that all client communication must traverse the access point.

18. A, C. An ad hoc network is often referred to as a peer-to-peer network because, in this mode, stations communicate directly with each other as opposed to infrastructure mode where all communication must traverse the access point. The 802.11 standard uses the terminology "ad hoc", but peer-to-peer is a more common name for this type of network.

19. B, D. Stations that have a continuous power source other than batteries can use CAM instead of PSP to improve performance of both the station and the network.

20. A, D. PSP mode is a mode allowing wireless clients to sleep. Sleeping clients cannot receive packets so they are buffered at the access point. Any time PSP mode is used, it creates additional overhead on the wireless network segment. Polling is configured on a station, but is not related to PSP.

MAC and Physical Layers

CWNA Exam Objectives Covered:

❖ Understand and apply the following concepts surrounding wireless LAN Frames:

- The difference between wireless LAN and Ethernet frames

- Layer 3 Protocols supported by wireless LANs

❖ Specify the modes of operation involved in the movement of data traffic across wireless LANs:

- Distributed Coordination Function (DCF)

- Point Coordination Function (PCF)

- CSMA/CA vs. CSMA/CD

- Interframe spacing

- RTS/CTS

- Dynamic Rate Selection

- Modulation and coding

We mentioned earlier in this book how most of the technology in any wireless LAN is the same, but that manufacturers approach and utilize that technology differently. In this chapter we will discuss some of the MAC and Physical layer characteristics of wireless LANs that are common to all wireless LAN products, regardless of manufacturer. We will explain the difference between Ethernet and wireless LAN frames and how wireless LANs avoid collisions. We'll walk through how wireless LAN stations communicate with one another under normal circumstances, then how collision handling occurs in a wireless LAN.

It is important for you as a wireless LAN administrator to know this level of detail in order to be able to properly configure and administer an access point, as well as to be able to diagnose and solve problems that are common to wireless LANs.

How Wireless LANs Communicate

In order to understand how to configure and manage a wireless LAN, the administrator must understand communication parameters that are configurable on the equipment and how to implement those parameters. In order to estimate throughput across wireless LANs, one must understand the affects of these parameters and collision handling on system throughput. This section conveys a basic understanding of many configurable parameters and their affects on network performance.

Wireless LAN Frames vs. Ethernet Frames

Once a wireless client has joined a network, the client and the rest of the network will communicate by passing frames across the network, in almost the same manner as any other IEEE 802 network. To clear up a common misconception, wireless LANs do NOT use 802.3 Ethernet frames. The term *wireless Ethernet* is somewhat of a misnomer. Wireless LAN frames contain more information than common Ethernet frames do. The actual structure of a wireless LAN frame versus that of an Ethernet frame is beyond the scope of both the CWNA exam as well as a wireless LAN administrator's job.

There are three distinctly different types of wireless frames on the wireless LAN: control, management and data. Each of type of frame is constructed differently from the others and carries information related to its name. 802.3 Ethernet has a maximum frame size of 1518 bytes before fragmentation is required by the standard, but can be increased up to 9000 bytes (referred to as "Jumbo Frames"). Frames larger than 1518 bytes are normally fragmented to comply with the standard. Wireless LAN frames have a maximum frame size of 2346 bytes (of which 2312 bytes is available for the payload) before the 802.11 standard requires fragmentation. However, wireless frames are generally fragmented at 1518 bytes by the access point due to data traversing between wired Ethernet (802.3) and wireless (802.11) media. Wired frames have a maximum size of 1518 bytes (of which 1500 bytes is available for the payload), thus the reason why wireless frames are typically fragmented at 1518 bytes.

A subject seldom discussed is the preamble and header of a wireless frame. There are a few pieces of information that are important to know - especially if you are going to do any wireless protocol analysis. The preamble (a series of 1's and 0's used for bit synchronization at the beginning of each frame) is always sent at 1 Mbps to provide a common data rate that any receiver can interpret. There are two lengths of preamble (also called PLCP preamble) - long (128 bits) and short (56 bits). It is important that nodes at each end of a wireless link use the same preamble type. The 802.11b standard requires support of long preambles and provides an option for short preambles for the purpose of improving network efficiency when transmitting special types of traffic such as VoIP. After the preamble is sent, the header (also called PLCP header) is sent. For long preambles, the preamble and the header are both sent at 1 Mbps. For short preambles, the preamble is sent at 1 Mbps, and the header is sent at 2 Mbps. The Data Rate or "DR" field in the header specifies the rate at which the data will be transmitted. After sending the header, the transmitter can then change the data rate to whatever the header specifies. This same premise applies to beacons, which are also sent at 1 Mbps for the same reasons.

There are three different categories of frames generated within the confines of this overall frame format. These three frame categories and the types within each category are:

- Management Frames

  o Association request frame
  o Association response frame
  o Reassociation request frame
  o Reassociation response frame
  o Probe request frame
  o Probe response frame
  o Beacon frame
  o ATIM frame
  o Disassociation frame
  o Authentication frame
  o Deauthentication frame

- Control Frames

  o Request to send (RTS)
  o Clear to send (CTS)
  o Acknowledgement (ACK)
  o Power-Save Poll (PS Poll)
  o Contention-Free End (CF End)
  o CF End + CF Ack

- Data Frames

Certain types of frames (listed above) use certain fields within the overall frame type of a wireless frame. What a wireless LAN administrator needs to know is that wireless LANs support practically all Layer 3-7 protocols – IP, IPX, NetBEUI, AppleTalk, RIP, DNS, FTP, etc. The main differences from 802.3 Ethernet frames are implemented at the Media Access Control (MAC) sub layer of the Data Link layer and the entire Physical layer. Upper layer protocols are simply considered payload by the Layer 2 wireless frames.

Collision Handling

Since radio frequency is a shared medium, wireless LANs have to deal with the possibility of collisions just the same as traditional wired LANs do. The difference is that, on a wireless LAN, there is no means through which the sending station can determine that there has actually *been* a collision. It is impossible to detect a collision on a wireless LAN. For this reason, wireless LANs utilize the Carrier Sense Multiple Access / Collision *Avoidance* protocol, also known as CSMA/CA. CSMA/CA is somewhat similar to the protocol CSMA/CD, which is common on Ethernet networks.

The biggest difference between CSMA/CA and CSMA/CD is that CSMA/CA avoids collisions and uses positive acknowledgements (ACKs) instead of arbitrating use of the medium when collisions occur. The use of acknowledgements, or ACKs, works in a very simple manner. When a wireless station sends a packet, the receiving station sends back an ACK once that station actually receives the packet. If the sending station does not receive an ACK, the sending station assumes there was a collision and resends the data.

CSMA/CA, added to the large amount of control data used in wireless LANs, causes overhead that uses approximately 50% of the available bandwidth on a wireless LAN. This overhead, plus the additional overhead of protocols such as RTS/CTS that enhance collision avoidance, is responsible for the actual throughput of approximately 5.0 - 5.5 Mbps on a typical 802.11b wireless LAN rated at 11 Mbps. CSMA/CD also generates overhead, but only about 30% on an average use network. When an Ethernet network becomes congested, CSMA/CD can cause overhead of up to 70%, while a congested wireless network remains somewhat constant at around 50 - 55% throughput.

The CSMA/CA protocol avoids the probability of collisions among stations sharing the medium by using a *random back off time* if the station's physical or logical sensing mechanism indicates a busy medium. The period of time immediately following a busy medium is when the highest probability of collisions occurs, especially under high utilization. At this point in time, many stations may be waiting for the medium to become idle and will attempt to transmit at the same time. Once the medium is idle, a random back off time defers a station from transmitting a frame, minimizing the chance that stations will collide.

Fragmentation

Fragmentation of packets into shorter fragments adds protocol overhead and reduces protocol efficiency (decreases network throughput) when no errors are observed, but reduces the time spent on re-transmissions if errors occur. Larger packets have a higher probability of collisions on the network; hence, a method of varying packet fragment size is needed. The IEEE 802.11 standard provides support for fragmentation.

By decreasing the length of each packet, the probability of interference during packet transmission can be reduced, as illustrated in Figure 8.1. There is a tradeoff that must be made between the lower packet error rate that can be achieved by using shorter packets, and the increased overhead of more frames on the network due to fragmentation. Each fragment requires its own headers and ACK, so the adjustment of the fragmentation level is also an adjustment of the amount of overhead associated with each packet transmitted. Stations never fragment multicast and broadcast frames, but rather only unicast frames in order not to introduce unnecessary overhead into the network. Finding the optimal fragmentation setting to maximize the network throughput on an 802.11 network is an important part of administering a wireless LAN. Keep in mind that a 2346 byte frame is the largest frame that can traverse a wireless LAN segment without fragmentation, although most Access Points will fragment any frame larger than 1518 bytes before putting it on the wired segment.

FIGURE 8.1   Fragmentation

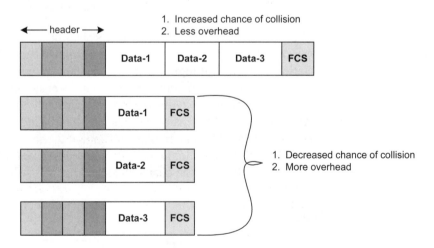

One way to use fragmentation to improve network throughput in times of heavy packet errors is to monitor the packet error rate on the network and adjust the fragmentation level manually. As a recommended practice, you should monitor the network at multiple times throughout a typical day to see what impact fragmentation adjustment will have at various times. Another method of adjustment is to configure the fragmentation threshold.

If your network is experiencing a high packet error rate (faulty packets), decrease the fragmentation threshold on the client stations and/or the access point (depending on which units allow these settings on your particular equipment). Start with the maximum value and gradually decrease the fragmentation threshold size until an improvement shows. If fragmentation is used, the network will experience a performance hit due to the overhead incurred with fragmentation. Sometimes this hit is acceptable in order to gain higher throughput due to a decrease in packet errors and subsequent retransmissions.

Fragment Bursting

As we previously discussed, the IEEE 802.11 standard allows frames to be fragmented into smaller pieces. Each fragment is uniquely numbered and is acknowledged by the recipient. In this way, the sending station cannot transmit the next fragment until the previous fragmented has been acknowledged. However, once the channel has been acquired via the RTS and CTS mechanism, multiple fragments can be sent in a row; this is called a fragment burst.

Typically, the NAV mechanism only keeps other stations from transmitting until the next ACK is sent. Fragment bursting allows an entire fragment burst to be sent without interference or interruption. Just as SIFS is used to allow stations to send an RTS, send a CTS or send an ACK, it can also be taken advantage of to send the next fragment in a group without the sending station needing to send another RTS again. Figure 8.2 shows fragment bursting by station A on a Wireless LAN.

FIGURE 8.2   Fragment Bursting

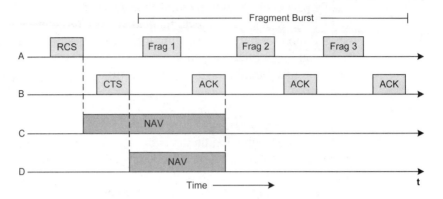

Fragmentation Dynamic Rate Shifting (DRS)

Adaptive (or Automatic) Rate Selection (ARS) and Dynamic Rate Shifting (DRS) are both terms used to describe the method of dynamic speed adjustment on wireless LAN clients. This speed adjustment occurs as distance increases between the client and the access point or as interference increases. It is imperative that a network administrator understands how this function works in order to plan for network throughput, cell sizes, power outputs of access points and stations, and security.

Modern spread spectrum systems are designed to make discrete jumps only to specified data rates, such as 1, 2, 5.5, and 11 Mbps. As distance increases between the access point and a station, the signal strength will decrease to a point where the current data rate cannot be maintained. When this signal strength decrease occurs, the transmitting unit will drop its data rate to the next lower specified data rate, say from 11 Mbps to 5.5 Mbps or from 2 Mbps to 1 Mbps. Figure 8.3 illustrates that, as the distance from the access point increases, the data rate decreases.

FIGURE 8.3   Dynamic Rate Shifting

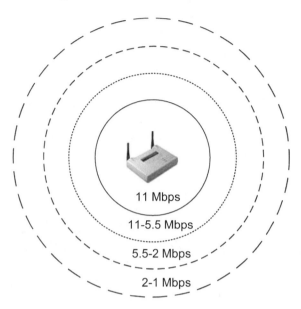

11 Mbps

11-5.5 Mbps

5.5-2 Mbps

2-1 Mbps

A wireless LAN system will never drop from 11 Mbps to 10 Mbps, for example, since 10 Mbps is not a specified data rate. The method of making such discrete jumps is typically called either ARS or DRS, depending on the manufacturer. Both FHSS and DSSS implement DRS, and the IEEE 802.11, IEEE 802.11b, HomeRF, and OpenAir standards require it.

Distributed Coordination Function

Distributed Coordination Function (DCF) is an access method specified in the 802.11 standard that allows all stations on a wireless LAN to contend for access on the shared transmission medium (RF) using the CSMA/CA protocol. In this case, the transmission medium is a portion of the radio frequency band that the wireless LAN is using to send data. Basic service sets (BSS), extended service sets (ESS), and independent basic service sets (IBSS) can all use DCF mode. The access points in these service sets act in the same manner as IEEE 802.3 based wired hubs to transmit their data, and DCF is the mode in which the access points send the data.

Point Coordination Function

Point Coordination Function (PCF) is a transmission mode allowing for contention-free frame transfers on a wireless LAN by making use of a polling mechanism. PCF has the advantage of guaranteeing a known amount of latency so that applications requiring QoS (voice or video for example) can be used. When using PCF, the access point on a wireless LAN performs the polling. For this reason, an ad hoc network cannot utilize PCF, because an ad hoc network has no access point to do the polling.

The PCF Process

First, a wireless station must tell the access point that the station is capable of answering a poll. Then the access point asks, or polls, each wireless station to see if that station needs to send a data frame across the network. PCF, through polling, generates a significant amount of overhead on a wireless LAN.

 When using PCF, only one access point should be on each non-overlapping channel to avoid much degraded performance due to co-channel interference.

DCF can be used without PCF, but PCF cannot be used without DCF. We will explain how these two modes co-exist as we discuss interframe spacing. DCF is scalable due to its contention-based design, whereas PCF, by design, limits the scalability of the wireless network by adding the additional overhead of polling frames.

Interframe Spacing

Interframe spacing doesn't sound like something an administrator would need to know; however, if you don't understand the types of interframe spacing, you cannot effectively grasp RTS/CTS, which helps you solve problems, or DCF and PCF, which are manually configured in the access point. Both of these functions are integral in the ongoing communications process of a wireless LAN. First, we will define each type of interframe space (IFS), and then we will explain how each type works on the wireless LAN.

As we learned when we discussed beacons, all stations on a wireless LAN are time-synchronized. All the stations on a wireless LAN are effectively 'ticking' time in sync with one another. Interframe spacing is the term we use to refer to standardized time spaces that are used on all 802.11 wireless LANs.

Three Types of Spacing

There are three main spacing intervals (interframe spaces): SIFS, DIFS, and PIFS. Each type of interframe space is used by a wireless LAN either to send certain types of messages across the network or to manage the intervals during which the stations contend for the transmission medium. Figure 8.4 illustrates the actual times that each interframe space takes for each type of 802.11 technology.

 There is a fourth interframe space called the Extended Interframe Space (EIFS), which is not covered on the CWNA exam. EIFS is a variable length space used as a waiting period when a frame transmission results in a bad reception of the frame due to an incorrect FCS value. EIFS is not a main focus of this section and an in-depth understanding of its functionality is not essential knowledge to a wireless network administrator.

FIGURE 8.4   Interframe spacing

IFS	DSSS	FHSS	Diffused Infrared
SIFS	10 uS	28 uS	7 uS
PIFS	30 uS	78 uS	15 uS
DIFS	50 uS	128 uS	23 uS

Interframe spaces are measured in microseconds and are used to defer a station's access to the medium and to provide various levels of priority. On a wireless network, everything is synchronized and all stations and access points use standard amounts of time (spaces) to perform various tasks. Each node knows these spaces and uses them appropriately. A set of standard spaces is specified for DSSS, FHSS, and Infrared as you can see from Figure 8.3. By using these spaces, each node knows when and if it is supposed to perform a certain action on the network.

Short Interframe Space (SIFS)

SIFS is the shortest fixed interframe space. SIFS are time spaces before and after which the following types of messages are sent. The list below is not an exhaustive list.

- RTS - Request-to-Send frame, used for reserving the medium by stations

- CTS - Clear-to-Send frame, used as a response by access points to the RTS frame generated by a station in order to ensure all stations have stopped transmitting

- ACK - Acknowledgement frame used for notifying sending stations that data arrived in readable format at the receiving station

SIFS provide the highest level of priority on a wireless LAN. The reason for SIFS having the highest priority is that stations constantly listen to the medium (carrier sense) awaiting a clear medium. Once the medium is clear, each station must wait a given amount of time (spacing) before proceeding with a transmission. The length of time a station must wait is determined by the function the station needs to perform. Each function on a wireless network falls into a spacing category. Tasks that are high priority fall into the SIFS category. If a station only has to wait a short period of time after the medium is clear to begin its transmissions, it would have priority over stations having to wait longer periods of time. SIFS is used for functions requiring a very short period of time, yet needing high priority in order to accomplish the goal.

Point Coordination Function Interframe Space (PIFS)

A PIFS interframe space is neither the shortest nor longest fixed interframe space, so it gets more priority than DIFS and less than SIFS. Access points use a PIFS interframe space *only* when the network is in point coordination function mode, which is manually configured by the administrator. PIFS are shorter in duration than DIFS (see Figure 8.4), so the access point will always win control of the medium before other contending stations in distributed coordination function (DCF) mode. PCF only works with DCF, not as a stand-alone operational mode so that, once the access point is finished polling, other stations can continue to contend for the transmission medium using DCF mode.

Distributed Coordination Function Interframe Space (DIFS)

DIFS is the longest fixed interframe space and is used by default on all 802.11-compliant stations that are using the distributed coordination function. Each station on the network using DCF mode is required to wait until DIFS has expired before any station can contend for the network. All stations operating according to DCF use DIFS for transmitting data frames and management frames. This spacing makes the transmission of these frames lower priority than PCF-based transmissions. Instead of all stations assuming the medium is clear and arbitrarily beginning transmissions simultaneously after DIFS (which would cause collisions), each station uses a random back off algorithm to determine how long to wait before sending its data.

The period of time directly following DIFS is referred to as the contention period (CP). All stations in DCF mode use the random back off algorithm during the contention period. During the random back off process, a station chooses a random number and multiplies it by the slot time to get the length of time to wait. The stations count down these slot times one by one, performing a clear channel assessment (CCA) after each slot time to see if the medium is busy. Whichever station's random back off time expires first, that station does a CCA, and provided the medium is clear and its Network Allocation Vector (NAV) is a value of zero, it begins transmission.

Once the first station has begun transmissions, all other stations sense that the medium is busy, and remember the remaining amount of their random back off time from the previous CP. This remaining amount of time is used in lieu of picking another random number during the next CP. This process assures fair access to the medium among all stations.

Once the random back off period is over, the transmitting station sends its data and receives back the ACK from the receiving station. This entire process then repeats. It stands to reason that most stations will chose different random numbers, eliminating most collisions. However, it is important to remember that collisions do happen on wireless LANs, but they cannot directly be detected. Collisions are assumed by the fact that the ACK is not received back from the destination station.

Slot Times

A slot time, which is pre-programmed into the radio in the same fashion as the SIFS, PIFS, and DIFS timeframes, is a standard period of time on a wireless network. Slot times are used within the CP in the same way a clock's second hand is used. A wireless node ticks slot times just like a clock ticks seconds. These slot times are determined by the wireless LAN technology being utilized.

- FHSS Slot Time = 50uS
- DSSS Slot Time = 20uS
- Infrared Slot Time = 8uS

Notice the following:

PIFS = SIFS + 1 Slot Time
DIFS = PIFS + 1 Slot Time

Also notice that FHSS has noticeably longer slot times, DIFS times, and PIFS times than DSSS. These longer times contribute to FHSS overhead, which decreases throughput.

The Communications Process

When you consider the PIFS process described above, it may seem as though the access point would *always* have control over the medium, since the access point does not have to wait for DIFS, but the stations do. This would be true, except for the existence of what is called a *superframe*. A superframe is a period of time, and it consists of two parts:

1. Contention Free Period (CFP) (which includes the beacon)

2. Contention Period (CP)

A diagram of the superframe is shown in Figure 8.5. The purpose of the superframe is to allow peaceful and fair co-existence between PCF and DCF mode clients on the network, allowing QoS for some, but not for others.

FIGURE 8.5   The Superframe

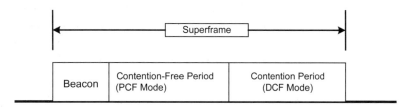

Again, remember that PIFS, and hence the superframe, only occurs when

1. The network is in point coordination function mode

2. The access point has been configured to do polling

3. The wireless clients have been configured to announce to the access point that they are pollable

Therefore, if we start from a hypothetical beginning point on a network that has the access point configured for PCF mode, and then some of the clients are configured for polling, the process is as follows.

1. The CFP begins, and the access point broadcasts a beacon.

2. During the contention free period, the access point polls stations to see if any station needs to send data.

3. If a station needs to send data, it sends one frame to the access point in response to the access point's poll

4. If a station does not need to send data, it returns a null frame to the access point in response to the access point's poll or simply ignores the poll

5. Polling continues throughout the contention free period

6. Once the contention free period (CFP) ends and the contention period (CP) begins (denoted by the AP sending a CF-End frame), the access point no longer polls stations. During the contention period, stations and the access point use DCF mode to contend for the medium.

7. The superframe ends with the end of the CP, and a new one begins with the following CFP.

Think of the CFP as using a "controlled access policy" and the CP as using a "random access policy." During the CFP, the access point is in complete control of all functions on the wireless network, whereas during the CP, stations arbitrate and randomly gain control over the medium. The access point, in PCF mode, does not have to wait for the DIFS to expire, but rather uses the PIFS, which is shorter than the DIFS, in order to capture the medium before any client using DCF mode does. Since the access point captures the medium and begins polling transmissions during the CFP, the DCF clients sense the medium as being busy and wait to transmit. After the CFP, the CP begins, during which all stations using DCF mode may contend for the medium and the access point switches to DCF mode. As stated above, the first part of the CFP is the beacon. Every beacon sent by the AP during the CFP has the NAV set to a sufficient amount of time to complete the CFP. This is the primary mechanism for keeping DCF mode clients quiet during the CFP.

Figure 8.6 illustrates a short timeline for a wireless LAN using DCF and PCF modes. Note that the DIFS and CP are hypothetical in this drawing since they can't happen due to the access point seizing the medium.

FIGURE 8.6   DCF/PCF mode timeline

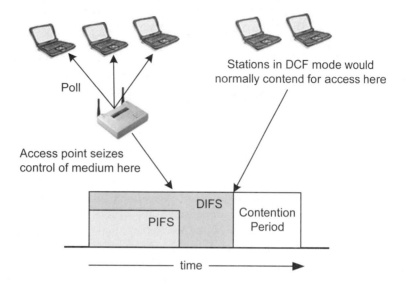

The process is somewhat simpler when a wireless LAN is only in DCF mode, because there is no polling and, hence, no superframe. This process is as follows:

1. Stations wait for DIFS to expire

2. During the CP, which immediately follows DIFS, stations calculate their random back off time based on a random number multiplied by a slot time

3. Stations tick down their random time with each passing slot time, checking the medium (CCA) at the end of each slot time. The station with the shortest time gains control of the medium first.

4. A station sends its data.

5. The receiving station receives the data and waits a SIFS before returning an ACK back to the station that transmitted the data.

6. The transmitting station receives the ACK and the process starts over from the beginning with a new DIFS.

Figure 8.7 illustrates a timeline for a DCF mode wireless LAN. Keep in mind that this timeline is a few milliseconds long. The whole process happens many times every second.

FIGURE 8.7 DCF timeline

Request to Send/Clear to Send (RTS/CTS)

There are two carrier sense mechanisms used on wireless networks. The first is *physical carrier sense*. Physical carrier sense functions by checking the signal strength, called the Received Signal Strength Indicator (RSSI), on the RF carrier signal to see if there is a station currently transmitting. The second is *virtual carrier sense*. Virtual carrier sense works by using a field called the Network Allocation Vector (NAV), which acts as a timer on the station. If a station wishes to broadcast its intention to use the network, the station sends a frame to the destination station, which will set the NAV field on all stations hearing the frame to the time necessary for the station to complete its transmission, plus the returning ACK frame. In this way, any station can reserve use of the network for specified periods of time. Virtual carrier sense is implemented with the RTS/CTS protocol.

The RTS/CTS protocol is an extension of the CSMA/CA protocol. As the wireless LAN administrator, you can take advantage of using this protocol to solve problems like Hidden Node (discussed in Chapter 9, Troubleshooting). Using RTS/CTS allows stations to broadcast their intent to send data across the network.

As you can imagine by the brief description above, RTS/CTS will cause significant network overhead. For this reason RTS/CTS is turned OFF by default on a wireless LAN. If you are experiencing an unusual amount of collisions on your wireless LAN (evidenced by high latency and low throughput) using RTS/CTS can actually increase the traffic flow on the network by decreasing the number of collisions. Use of RTS/CTS should not be done haphazardly. RTS/CTS should be configured after careful study of the network's collisions, throughput, latency, etc.

Some manufacturers do not allow administrators to change a station's RTS/CTS settings (and many other settings) unless they obtain the special password from the manufacturer. By default, an administrator is locked out of those features of the station's driver software. Normally, getting this password will not be easy. These manufacturers require the administrator to take their 1-2 day product seminar before they will allow the administrator to fill out a series of paperwork to obtain the necessary password(s).

Figure 8.8 illustrates the 4-way handshake process used for RTS/CTS. In short, the transmitting station broadcasts the RTS, followed by the CTS reply from the receiving station, both of which go through the access point. Next, the transmitting station sends its data payload through the access point to the receiving station, which immediately replies with an acknowledgement frame, or ACK. This process is used for every frame that is sent across the wireless network.

FIGURE 8.8   RTS/CTS handshaking

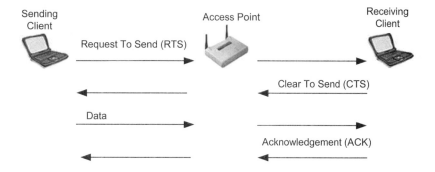

Configuring RTS/CTS

There are three settings on most access points and nodes for RTS/CTS:

- Off
- On
- On with Threshold

When RTS/CTS is turned on, every packet that goes through the wireless network is announced and cleared between the transmitting and receiving nodes prior to transmission, creating a significant amount of overhead and significantly less throughput. Generally, RTS/CTS should only be used in diagnosing network problems and when only very large packets are flowing across a congested wireless network, which is rare.

However, the "on with threshold" setting allows the administrator to control which packets (over a certain size - called the threshold) are announced and cleared to send by the stations. Since collisions affect larger packets more than smaller ones, you can set the RTS/CTS threshold to work only when a node wishes to send packets over a certain size. This setting allows you to customize the RTS/CTS setting to your network data traffic and optimize the throughput of your wireless LAN while preventing problems like Hidden Node.

Figure 8.9 depicts a DCF network using the RTS/CTS protocol to transmit data. Notice that the RTS and CTS transmissions are spaced by SIFS. The NAV is set with RTS on all nodes, and then reset on all nodes by the immediately following CTS.

FIGURE 8.9   RTS/CTS data transmission in DCF mode

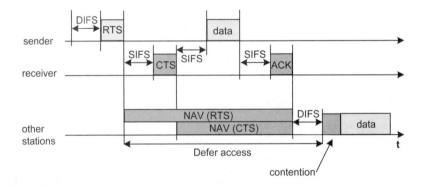

Modulation

Modulation, which is a Physical Layer function, is a process in which the radio transceiver prepares the digital signal within the NIC for transmission over the airwaves. Modulation is the process of adding data to a carrier by altering the amplitude, frequency, or phase of the carrier in a controlled manner. Knowing the many different kinds of modulations used with wireless LANs is helpful when trying to build a compatible network piece-by-piece.

FIGURE 8.10   Modulation and Spreading Code Types for 802.11 & 802.11b

		Spreading Code	Modulation Technology	Data Rate
2.4 GHz DSSS		Barker Code	DBPSK	1 Mbps
		Barker Code	DQPSK	2 Mbps
		CCK	DQPSK	5.5 Mbps
		CCK	DQPSK	11 Mbps
2.4 GHz FHSS		Barker Code	2GFSK	1 Mbps
		Barker Code	4GFSK	2 Mbps

Figure 8.10 shows the details of modulation and spreading code types used with Frequency Hopping and Direct Sequence wireless LANs in the 2.4 GHz ISM band. Differential Binary Phase Shift Keying (DBPSK), Differential Quadrature Phase Shift Keying (DQPSK), and Gaussian Frequency Shift Keying (GFSK) are the types of modulation used by 802.11 and 802.11b products on the market today. Barker Code and Complimentary Code Keying (CCK) are the types of spreading codes used in 802.11 and 802.11b wireless LANs. Bluetooth and HomeRF are both FHSS technologies that use GFSK modulation technology in the 2.4 GHz ISM band.

As higher transmission speeds are specified (such as when a system is using DRS), modulation techniques change in order to provide more data throughput. For example, 802.11g and 802.11a compliant wireless LAN equipment specify use of orthogonal frequency division multiplexing (OFDM), allowing speeds of up to 54 Mbps, which is a significant improvement over the 11 Mbps specified by 802.11b. Figure 8.11 shows the modulation types used for 802.11a networks.

FIGURE 8.11   Modulation types and data rates for 802.11a

Coding Technique	Modulation Technology	Data Rate
OFDM	DBPSK	6 Mbps
OFDM	DBPSK	9 Mbps
OFDM	DQPSK	12 Mbps
OFDM	DQPSK	18 Mbps
OFDM	16QAM	24 Mbps
OFDM	16QAM	36 Mbps
OFDM	64QAM	48 Mbps
OFDM	64QAM	54 Mbps

Orthogonal frequency division multiplexing (OFDM) is a communications technique that divides a communications channel into a number of equally spaced frequency bands. A subcarrier carrying a portion of the user information is transmitted in each band. Each subcarrier is orthogonal (independent of each other) with every other subcarrier, differentiating OFDM from the commonly used frequency division multiplexing (FDM). The 802.11g standard provides backwards compatibility by supporting CCK coding and even supports packet binary convolution coding (PBCC) as an option. Figure 8.12 shows the modulation types used for 802.11g networks.

FIGURE 8.12   Modulation types and data rates for 802.11g

Required Transmission Method	Optional Transmission Method	Data Rate
Barker		1 Mbps
Barker		2 Mbps
CCK	PBCC	5.5 Mbps
OFDM	CCK-OFDM	6 Mbps
OFDM	OFDM, CCK-OFDM	9 Mbps
CCK	PBCC	11 Mbps
OFDM	CCK-OFDM	12 Mbps
OFDM	OFDM, CCK-OFDM	18 Mbps
OFDM	PBCC	22 Mbps
OFDM	CCK-OFDM	24 Mbps
OFDM	PBCC	33 Mbps
OFDM	OFDM, CCK-OFDM	36 Mbps
OFDM	OFDM, CCK-OFDM	48 Mbps
OFDM	OFDM, CCK-OFDM	54 Mbps

Key Terms

Before taking the exam, you should be familiar with the following terms:

ACK

beacons

bit error rate

contention free period

contention period

DIFS

PIFS

polling

probe frame

SIFS

superframe

Review Questions

1. Which of the following service sets can use distributed coordination function (DCF) mode? Choose all that apply.

   A. BSS

   B. IBSS

   C. ESS

   D. IESS

2. Which of the following service sets can use point coordination function (PCF) mode? Choose all that apply.

   A. BSS

   B. IBSS

   C. ESS

   D. IESS

3. You have a large number of users on one access point and collisions are becoming a problem, causing reduced throughput. Some of the users are developers that do a significant amount of large file transfers during the day. Which RTS/CTS setting would best fix this problem?

   A. On

   B. Off

   C. On with threshold

4. Which one of the following is an advantage to using point coordination function (PCF) mode over distributed coordination mode (DCF)?

   A. PCF has a lower overhead than using DCF

   B. PCF can be used in and IBSS while DCF cannot

   C. PCF uses CSMA/CA while DCF does not

   D. PCF provides a given level of QoS

5. After a client station sends a data packet to another client station, the receiving station replies with an acknowledgement after which interframe space?

   A. IFS

   B. SIFS

   C. PIFS

   D. DIFS

6. Why is the CSMA/CA protocol used in order to avoid collisions in a wireless LAN?

   A. PCF mode requires use of a polling mechanism

   B. The overhead of sending acknowledgements is high

   C. All clients must acknowledge packets received while they're asleep

   D. It is not possible to detect collisions on a wireless LAN

7. End stations will broadcast a _____ when actively scanning for access points on the network.

    A. Beacon management frame

    B. Superframe

    C. Probe request frame

    D. Request to send

8. PIFS are only used during the communications of a wireless LAN when which of the following have occurred?

    A. The network is in point coordination function mode

    B. The access point has been configured to use RTS/CTS

    C. The access point has been configured to use CSMA/CD

    D. The network is configured for fragmentation

9. You have just finished installing your first wireless LAN with 802.11b equipment rated at 11 Mbps. After testing the throughput of the clients, you find your actual throughput is only 5.5 Mbps. What is the likely cause of this throughput?

    A. Wireless LANs use RTS/CTS by default

    B. Wireless LANs use the CSMA/CA protocol

    C. Use of PCF is reducing network throughput

    D. DRS has caused all of the clients to decrease their data rates

10. You have just finished installing your first wireless LAN with 802.11b equipment rated at 11 Mbps. After testing the throughput of the clients you find your actual throughput is only 5.5 Mbps. What can you change to get 11Mbps throughput?

    A. Turn off RTS/CTS

    B. Move all of the clients closer to the access point

    C. Turn up the power on the access point

    D. Purchase another access point and co-locate both together

11. 802.11b devices use what type of modulation at 11 Mbps?

    A. DBPSK

    B. DPSK

    C. DQPSK

    D. CCK

12. 802.11a devices use what type of modulation at 24 Mbps?

    A. DBPSK

    B. 16QAM

    C. OFDM

    D. CCK

13. If the sending station on a wireless LAN does not receive an ACK, the sending station assumes which one of the following?

    A. The receiving station is sleeping

    B. The receiving station is a hidden node

    C. There was a collision

    D. That RTS/CTS is turned on

14. Modulation is which of one of the following?

    A. The process by which digital data is modified to become RF data

    B. The process of adding data to a carrier by altering the amplitude, frequency, or phase of the carrier in a controlled manner

    C. The process of propagating an RF signal through the airwaves

    D. The means by which RF signals are received and processed by RF antennas

15. Which one of the following is not part of a superframe?

    A. Beacon

    B. Beacon Free Period

    C. Contention Free Period

    D. Contention Period

16. A superframe is used when which of the following is true? Choose all that apply

    A. The access point has been configured for point coordination function mode

    B. When beacons are disabled in the access point

    C. The wireless clients have been configured to announce to the access point that they are pollable

    D. The access point has been configured for distributed coordination function mode

17. What is the purpose of the superframe?

    A. To increase the throughput of all wireless LANs

    B. To ensure QoS for all voice and video applications running on wireless LANs

    C. To ensure that PCF- and DCF-mode clients do not communicate within the same wireless LAN

    D. To allow fair co-existence between PCF- and DCF- mode clients on the network

18. The acronym CCA stands for which one of the following?

    A. Close Client Association

    B. Clear Current Authentication

    C. Clear Channel Assessment

    D. Clean Channel Association

    E. Calculate Clear Assessment

19. The Network Allocation Vector (NAV) acts as:

    A. A timer on the station

    B. A navigational feature for RF signal propagation

    C. A location discovery tool for wireless LANs

    D. A tool for allocating the bandwidth of a wireless LAN

20. Using RTS/CTS allows wireless stations to do which of the following?

    A. Broadcast their intent to send data across the network to the receiving station

    B. Send their packets across the network at the maximum rated speed of the network

    C. Eliminate hidden nodes on the network

    D. Diagnose and reduce high overhead between stations

Answers to Review Questions

1. A, B, C. There is no such thing as an IESS service set type. The rest can all use DCF mode.

2. A, C. There is no such thing as an IESS service set type. Any time there is an access point present in the wireless LAN (which rules out IBSS networks), you can use PCF mode (provided the access point supports it). IBSS networks have no access points, and clients communicate directly with each other. There is no access point to perform polling.

3. C. By turning on RTS/CTS with the threshold set to a given packet size, the heavy bursts of traffic during the day would cause minimal disruption for other users in a congested WLAN. The threshold setting is used for occasions such as this with great success.

4. D. While PCF mode is not the answer to every QoS need, it does provide a given level of QoS by providing predictable latencies in the wireless LAN.

5. B. A short interframe space (SIFS) is used between the data packet receipt and the acknowledgement reply. SIFS are used before and after many frame types on wireless networks such as RTS, CTS, ACK, PSP frames, etc.

6. D. It is impossible to detect collisions on a wireless LAN. For this reason, the CSMA/CA protocol, the RTS/CTS protocol, and positive acknowledgements are used in order to reduce the possibility of collisions on the wireless LAN.

7. C. When a client station is actively seeking access points with which to associate, it sends probe request frames. All access points hearing the probe request frame respond with probe response frames. Probe response frames contain almost identical information to beacon management frames.

8. A. An access point using point coordination function mode uses PIFS interframe spaces in order to capture use of the medium before stations that are using DCF mode. PIFS is shorter than DIFS and therefore gives the access point priority over stations competing for use of the medium using DIFS.

9. B. Wireless LANs use the CSMA/CA protocol in order to avoid collisions on the network. The CSMA/CA protocol introduces approximately 50% overhead into the network reducing throughput to approximately half of the data rate.

10. D. The typical maximum throughput of an 802.11b access point is approximately 5.5 Mbps. This is due to protocols like CSMA/CA and RTS/CTS being used. In order to increase the throughput beyond this point, additional access points can be co-located (up to 3 in an area) using non-overlapping channels. Each access point is capable of the same 5.5 Mbps.

11. C. In many cases, manufacturers state that 802.11b devices use CCK modulation at 11 Mbps, but they do not. CCK is not a modulation type, but rather a coding technique. The modulation type used at 11 Mbps is DQPSK.

12. B. For every two steps in data rate using 802.11a, the modulation type is changed. Many manufacturers mistakenly list OFDM as the modulation type for all 802.11a devices, but this is incorrect. OFDM is not a modulation type, but rather a communications technique that can use various types of modulation.

13. C. Transmitting stations not receiving ACKs from receiving stations assume that there was a collision and begin resending the data.

14. B. There must be a means by which relevant data is imprinted or impressed upon RF frequencies to allow transmission of the data from one point to another. This process is referred to as modulation, and there are many modulation types. In this book, we address six kinds of modulation used with wireless LANs.

15. B. The superframe is a time period during which contention-free and contention-based clients can co-exist without disrupting each other. This time period consists of three periods - the contention-free period (CFP), which is for stations in PCF mode being polled by the access point, the contention period (CP), which is for stations in DCF mode, and the beacon.

16. A, C. Superframes are used when the access point is using PCF mode and polling stations that are configured to be polled. When all stations and the access point are using DCF mode, there is no contention-free period and, thus, no need for a superframe.

17. D. In allowing peaceful co-existence between DCF- and PCF-mode clients on the network, the superframe allows some nodes to have QoS and others to have the ability to contend for network access to maximize throughput.

18. C. A clear channel assessment is a function requested by the MAC layer and performed at the Physical layer where the physical layer senses the RF amplitude level on a particular frequency. If the amplitude is below a given threshold, the medium is considered to be clear and ready for frames to be transmitted. This is called a positive CCA. If the amplitude is above that same threshold, then the medium is considered busy. This is considered a negative CCA.

19. A. The NAV field is used on a station as a timer. When using the RTS/CTS protocol, RTS and CTS packets set the NAV on stations hearing them to an amount of time that they must wait before trying to access the medium.

20. A. The RTS/CTS protocol is a method of remedying problems caused by the hidden node problem on wireless LANs. While using RTS/CTS cannot eliminate hidden nodes, stations broadcasting their intention to transmit packets on the network can drastically reduce the problems hidden nodes cause with collisions on the network.

Troubleshooting Wireless LAN Installations

CWNA Exam Objectives Covered:

❖ Identify, understand and correct or compensate for the following wireless LAN implementation challenges:

- Multipath
- Hidden Node
- Near/Far
- RF Interference
- All-band interference
- System throughput
- Co-location throughput
- Weather

Just as traditional wired networks have challenges during implementation, wireless LANs have their own set of challenges, mainly dealing with the behavior of RF signals. In this chapter, we will discuss the more common obstacles to successful implementation of a wireless LAN, and how to troubleshoot them. There are different methods of discovering when these challenges exist, and each of the challenges discussed has its remedies and workarounds.

The challenges to implementing any wireless LAN discussed herein are considered by many to be "textbook" problems that can occur within any wireless LAN installation, and, therefore, can be avoided by careful planning and simply being aware that these problems can and will occur.

Multipath

If you will recall from Chapter 2, RF Fundamentals, there are two types of line of sight (LOS). First, there is *visual* LOS, which is what the human eye sees. Visual LOS is your first and most basic LOS test. If you can see the RF receiver from the installation point of the RF transmitter, then you have *visual* line of sight. Second, and different from visual LOS, is RF line of sight. RF LOS is what your RF device can "see".

The general behavior of an RF signal is to grow wider as it is transmitted farther. Because of this type of behavior, the RF signal will encounter objects in its path that will reflect, diffract, or otherwise interfere with the signal. When an RF wave is reflected off an object (water, tin roof, other metal object, etc.) while moving towards its receiver, multiple wave fronts are created (one for each reflection point). There are now waves moving in many directions, and many of these reflected waves are still headed toward the receiver. This behavior is where we get the term *multipath,* as shown in Figure 9.1. Multipath is defined as the composition of a primary signal plus duplicate or echoed wave fronts caused by reflections of waves off objects between the transmitter and receiver. The delay between the instant that the main signal arrives and the instant that the last reflected signal arrives is known as *delay spread.*

FIGURE 9.1   Multipath

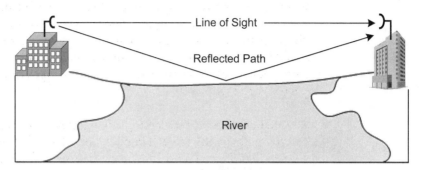

Effects of Multipath

Multipath can cause several different conditions, all of which can affect the transmission of the RF signal differently. These conditions include:

- Decreased Signal Amplitude (downfade)
- Corruption
- Nulling
- Increased Signal Amplitude (upfade)

Decreased Signal Amplitude

When an RF wave arrives at the receiver, many reflected waves may arrive at the same time from different directions. The combination of these waves' amplitudes is additive to the main RF wave. Reflected waves, if out-of-phase with the main wave, can cause decreased signal amplitude at the receiver, as illustrated in Figure 9.2. This occurrence is commonly referred to as *downfade* and should be taken into consideration when conducting a sight survey and selecting appropriate antennas.

FIGURE 9.2   Downfade

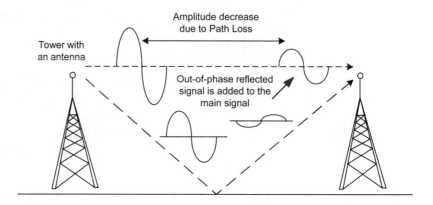

Corruption

Corrupted signals (waves) due to multipath can occur as a result of the same phenomena that cause decreased amplitude, but to a greater degree. When reflected waves arrive at the receiver out-of-phase with the main wave, as illustrated in Figure 9.3, they can cause the wave to be greatly reduced in amplitude instead of only slightly reduced. The amplitude reduction is such that the receiver is sensitive enough to detect most of the information being carried on the wave, but not all.

FIGURE 9.3   RF Signal Corruption

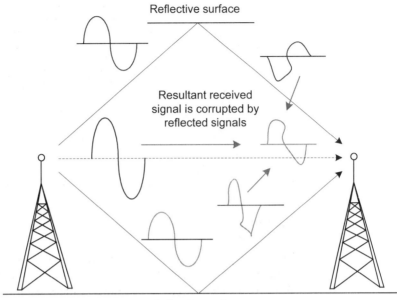

In such cases, the signal to noise ratio (SNR) is generally very low, where the signal itself is very close to the noise floor. The receiver is unable to clearly decipher between the information signal and noise, causing the data that is received to be only part (if any) of the transmitted data. This corruption of data will require the transmitter to resend the data, increasing overhead and decreasing throughput in the wireless LAN.

Nulling

The condition known as nulling occurs when one or more reflected waves arrive at the receiver out-of-phase with the main wave with such amplitude that the main wave's amplitude is cancelled. As illustrated in Figure 9.4, when reflected waves arrive out-of-phase with the main wave at the receiver, the condition can cancel or "null" the entire set of RF waves, including the main wave.

FIGURE 9.4   RF Signal Nulling

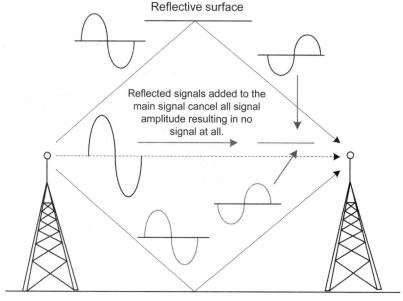

When nulling occurs, retransmission of the data will not solve the problem. The transmitter, receiver, or reflective objects must be moved. Sometimes more than one of these must be relocated to compensate for the nulling effects on the RF wave.

Increased Signal Amplitude

Multipath conditions can also cause a signal's amplitude to be increased from what it would have been without reflected waves present. *Upfade* is the term used to describe when multipath causes an RF signal to gain strength. Upfade, as illustrated in Figure 9.5, occurs due to reflected signals arriving at the receiver in-phase with the main signal. Similar to a decreased signal, all of these waves are additive to the main signal. *Under no circumstance can multipath cause the signal that reaches the receiver to be stronger than the transmitted signal when the signal left the transmitting device.* If multipath occurs in such a way as to be additive to the main signal, the total signal that reaches the receiver will be stronger than the signal would have otherwise been without multipath present.

FIGURE 9.5   Upfade

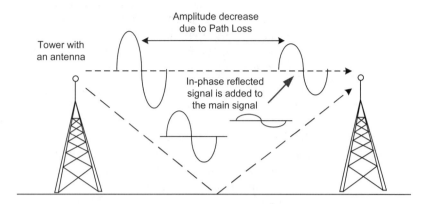

It is important to understand that a received RF signal can never be as large as the signal that was transmitted due to the significance of free space path loss (usually called *path loss*). Path loss is the effect of a signal losing amplitude due to expansion as the signal travels through open space.

Think of path loss as someone blowing a bubble with bubble gum. As the gum expands, the gum at any point becomes thinner. If someone were to reach out and grab a 1-inch square piece of this bubble, the amount of gum they would actually get would be less and less as the bubble expanded. If a person grabbed a piece of the bubble while it was still small (close to the person's mouth, which is the transmitter) the person would get a significant amount of gum. If the person waited to get that same size piece until the bubble were large (further from the transmitter), the piece would be only a very small amount of gum. This illustration shows that path loss is affected by two factors: first, the distance between transmitter and receiver, and second, the size of the receiving aperture (the size of the piece of gum that was grabbed).

Troubleshooting Multipath

An in-phase or out-of-phase RF wave cannot be seen, so we must look for the effects of multipath in order to detect its occurrence. When doing a link budget calculation, in order to find out just how much power output you will need to have a successful link between sites, you might calculate an output power level that should work, but doesn't. Such an occurrence is one way to determine that multipath is occurring.

Another common method of finding multipath is to look for RF coverage holes in a site survey (discussed in Chapter 11). These holes are created both by lack of coverage and by multipath reflections that cancel the main signal. Understanding the sources of multipath is crucial to eliminating its effects.

Multipath is caused by reflected RF waves, so obstacles that more easily reflect RF waves, such as metal blinds, bodies of water, and metal roofs, should be removed from or avoided in the signal path if possible. This procedure may include moving the transmitting and receiving antennas. Multipath is likely the most common "textbook" wireless LAN problem. Administrators and installers deal with multipath daily. Even wireless LAN users - because they are mobile - experience problems with multipath. Users may roam into an area with high multipath, not knowing why their RF signal has been so significantly degraded.

Solutions for Multipath

Antenna diversity was devised for the purpose of compensating for multipath. Antenna diversity means using multiple antennas, inputs, and receivers in order to compensate for the conditions that cause multipath. There are four types of *receiving* diversity, one of which is predominantly used in wireless LANs. The type of *transmission* diversity used by wireless LANs is also described below.

- Antenna Diversity - not active
  - Multiple antennas on single input
  - Rarely used
- Switching Diversity
  - Multiple antennas on multiple receivers
  - Switches receivers based on signal strength
- Antenna Switching Diversity – active
  - **Used by most WLAN manufacturers**
  - Multiple antennas on multiple inputs - single receiver
  - Signal is *received* through only one antenna at a time
- Phase Diversity
  - Patented proprietary technology
  - Adjusts phase of antenna to the phase of the signal in order to maintain signal quality
- Transmission Diversity
  - **Used by most WLAN manufacturers**
  - *Transmits* out of the antenna last used for reception
  - Can alternate antennas for transmission retries
  - A unit can either transmit or receive, but not both simultaneously

Figure 9.6 illustrates an access point with multiple antennas to compensate for multipath.

FIGURE 9.6   Antenna Diversity

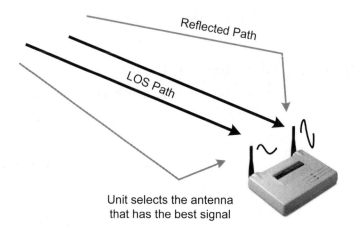

Unit selects the antenna
that has the best signal

Antenna diversity is made up of the following characteristics that work together to compensate for the effects of multipath:

1. Antenna diversity uses multiple antennas on multiple inputs to bring a signal to a single receiver.

2. The incoming RF signal is received through one antenna at a time. The receiving radio is constantly sampling the incoming signals from both antennas to determine which signal is of a higher quality. The receiving radio then chooses to accept the higher quality signal.

3. The radio transmits its next signal out of the antenna that was last used to receive an incoming signal because the received signal was a higher quality signal than from the other antenna. If the radio must retransmit a signal, it will alternate antennas until a successful transmission is made.

4. Finally, each antenna can be used to transmit or receive, but not both at the same time. Only one antenna may be used at a time, and that antenna may only transmit or receive, but not both, at any given instant.

Most access points in today's wireless LANs are built with dual antennas for exactly this purpose: to compensate for the degrading effects of multipath on signal quality and throughput.

Hidden Node

Multiple access protocols that enable networked computing devices to share a medium, such as Ethernet, are well developed and understood. However the nature of the wireless medium makes traditional methods of sharing a common connection more difficult.

Collision detection has caused many problems in wired networking, and even more so for wireless networks. Collisions occur when two or more nodes sharing a communication medium transmit data simultaneously. The two signals corrupt each other and the result is a group of unreadable packet fragments. Collisions have always been a problem for computer networks, and the simplest protocols often do not overcome this problem. More complex protocols such as CSMA/CD and CSMA/CA check the channel before transmitting data. CSMA/CD is the protocol used with Ethernet and involves checking the voltage on the wire before transmitting. However, the process is considerably more difficult for wireless systems since collisions are undetectable. A condition known as the hidden node problem has been identified in wireless systems and is caused by problems in transmission detection.

Hidden node is a situation encountered with wireless LANs in which at least one node is unable to hear (detect) one or more of the other nodes connected to the wireless LAN. In this situation, a node can see the access point, but cannot see that there are other clients also connected to the same access point due to some obstacle or a large amount of distance between the nodes. This situation causes a problem in medium access sharing, causing collisions between node transmissions. These collisions can result in significantly degraded throughput in the wireless LAN, as illustrated in Figure 9.7.

FIGURE 9.7   Hidden Node

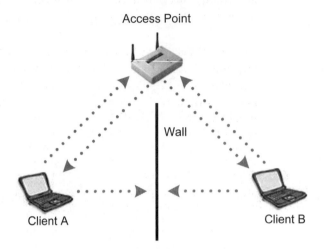

Figure 9.7 illustrates a brick wall with an access point sitting on top. On each side of the wall is a wireless station. These wireless stations cannot hear each other's transmissions, but both can hear the transmissions of the access point. If station A is transmitting a frame to the access point, and station B cannot hear this transmission, station B assumes that the medium is clear and can begin a transmission of its own to the access point. The access point will, at this point, be receiving transmissions that have originated at two points and there will be a collision. The collision will cause retransmissions by both stations A & B, and again, since they cannot hear each other, they will transmit at will thinking the medium is clear. There will likely be another collision. This problem is exacerbated with many active nodes on the wireless LAN that cannot hear one another.

Troubleshooting Hidden Node

The primary symptom of a hidden node is degraded throughput over the wireless LAN. Many times you will discover that you have a hidden node by hearing the complaints of users connected to the wireless LAN detecting an unusual sluggishness of the network. Throughput may be decreased by up to 40% because of a hidden node problem. Since wireless LANs use the CSMA/CA protocol, they already have an approximate overhead of 50%, but, during a hidden node problem, it is possible to lose almost half of the remaining throughput on the system.

Because the nature of a wireless LAN increases mobility, you may encounter a hidden node at any time, despite a flawless design of your wireless LAN. If a user moves his computer to a conference room, another office, or into a data room, the new location of that node can potentially be hidden from the rest of the nodes connected to your wireless LAN.

 To proactively troubleshoot a hidden node, you must test for degraded throughput and also find as many potential locations for a hidden node as possible during the initial and any subsequent site surveys.

Solutions for Hidden Node

Once you have done the troubleshooting and discovered that there is a hidden node problem, the problem node(s) must be located. Finding the node(s) will include a manual search for nodes that might be out of reach of the main cluster of nodes. This process is usually trial and error at best. Once these nodes are located, there are several remedies and workarounds for the problem.

- Use RTS/CTS
- Increase power to the nodes
- Remove obstacles
- Move the node

Use RTS/CTS

The RTS/CTS protocol is not necessarily a solution to the hidden node problem. Instead, it is a method of reducing the negative impact that hidden nodes have on the network. Hidden nodes cause excessive collisions, which have a severely detrimental impact on network throughput. The RTS/CTS (request-to-send/clear-to-send) protocol involves sending a small packet (RTS) to the intended recipient to prompt it to send back a packet (CTS) clearing the medium for data transmission before sending the data payload. This process informs any nearby stations that data is about to be sent, having them delay transmissions (and thereby avoiding collisions). Both the RTS and the CTS contain the length of the impending data transmission so that stations overhearing either the RTS or CTS frames know how long the transmission will take and when they can start to transmit again.

There are three settings for RTS/CTS on most access points and clients: *On*, *Off*, and *On with Threshold*. The network administrator must manually configure RTS/CTS settings. The *Off* setting is the default in order to reduce unnecessary network overhead caused by the RTS/CTS protocol. The threshold refers directly to the packet size that will trigger use of the RTS/CTS protocol. Since hidden nodes cause collisions, and collisions mainly affect larger packets, you may be able to overcome the hidden node problem by using the packet size threshold setting for RTS/CTS. What this setting essentially does is tell the access point to transmit all packets that are greater in size than "x" (your setting) using RTS/CTS and to transmit all other packets without RTS/CTS. If the hidden node is only having a minor impact on network throughput, then activating RTS/CTS might have a detrimental effect on throughput.

Try using RTS/CTS in the "On" mode as a test to see if your throughput is positively affected. If RTS/CTS increases throughput, then you have most likely confirmed the hidden node problem. You will encounter some additional overhead when using RTS/CTS, but your overall throughput should increase over what it was when the hidden node problem occurred.

Increase Power to the Nodes

Increasing the power (measured in milliwatts) of the nodes can solve the hidden node problem by allowing the cell around each node to increase in size, encompassing all of the other nodes. This configuration enables the non-hidden nodes to detect, or hear, the hidden node. If the non-hidden nodes can hear the hidden node, the hidden node is no longer hidden. Because wireless LANs use the CSMA/CA protocol, nodes will wait their turn before communicating with the access point.

Remove Obstacles

Increasing the power on your mobile nodes may not work if, for example, the reason one node is hidden is that there is a cement or steel wall preventing communication with other nodes. It is doubtful that you would be able to remove such an obstacle, but removal of the obstacle is another method of remedy for the hidden node problem. Keep these types of obstacles in mind when performing a site survey.

Move the Node

Another method of solving the hidden node problem is moving the nodes so that they can all hear each other. If you have found that the hidden node problem is the result of a user moving his computer to an area that is hidden from the other wireless nodes, you may have to force that user to move again. The alternative to forcing users to move is extending your wireless LAN to add proper coverage to the hidden area, perhaps using additional access points.

Near/Far

The near/far problem in wireless LAN implementation results from the scenario in which there exists multiple client nodes that are (a) very near to the access point and (b) have high power settings; and then at least one client that is (a) much farther away from the access point than the aforementioned client nodes, and (b) is using much less transmitting power than the other client nodes. The result of this type of situation is that the client(s) that are farther away from the access point and using less power simply cannot be heard over the traffic from the closer, high-powered clients, as illustrated in Figure 9.8.

FIGURE 9.8   Near/Far

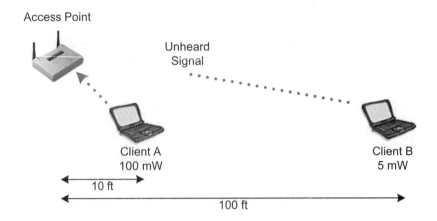

Near/far is similar in nature to a crowd of people all screaming at one time into a microphone, and one person whispering from 50 feet (15.2 meters) away from that same microphone. The voice of the person 50 feet (15.2 meters) away is not going to reach the microphone over the noise of the crowd shouting near the microphone. Even if the microphone is sensitive enough to pick up the whisper under silent conditions, the high-powered close-range conversations have effectively raised the noise floor to a point where low-amplitude inputs are not heard.

Getting back to wireless LANs, the node that is being drowned out is well within the normal range of the access point, but it simply cannot be heard over the signals of the other clients. What this means to you as an administrator is that you must be aware of the possibility of the near/far problem during site surveys and understand how to overcome the problem through proper wireless LAN design and troubleshooting techniques.

Troubleshooting Near/Far

Troubleshooting the near/far problem is normally as simple as taking a good look at the network design, locations of stations on the wireless network, and transmission output power of each node. These steps will give the administrator clues as to what is likely going on with the stations having connectivity problems. Since near/far prevents a node from communicating, the administrator should check to see if the station has drivers loaded properly for the wireless radio card and has associated with the access point (shown in the association table of the access point).

The next step in troubleshooting near/far is use of a wireless protocol analyzer. A wireless protocol analyzer will pick up transmissions from all stations it hears. One simple method of finding nodes whose signals are not being heard by the access point is to move around the network looking for stations with a faint signal in relation to the access point and nodes near the access point. Using this method, it should not be too time-consuming to locate such a node, depending on the size of the network and the complexity of the building structure. Locating this node and comparing its signal strength to that of nodes near the access point can solve the near/far problem fairly quickly.

Solutions for Near/Far

Although the near/far problem can be debilitating for those clients whose RF signals get drowned out, near/far is a relatively easy problem to overcome in most situations. It is imperative to understand that the CSMA/CA protocol solves much of the near/far problem with no intervention of the administrator. If a node can hear another node transmitting, it will stop its own transmissions, complying with shared medium access rules of CSMA/CA. However, if for any reason the near/far problem still exists in the network, below is a list of remedies that are easily implemented and can overcome the near/far problem.

- Increase power to remote node (the one that is being drowned out)

- Decrease power of local nodes (the close, loud ones)

- Move the remote node closer to the access point

One other solution is moving the access point to which the remote node is associated. However, this solution should be viewed as a last resort, since moving an access point will likely disrupt more clients than it would help. Furthermore, the need to move an access point likely reveals a flawed site survey or network design, which is a much bigger problem.

System Throughput

Throughput on a wireless LAN is based on many factors. For instance, the amount and type of interference may impact the amount of data that can be successfully transmitted. If additional security solutions are implemented, such as Wired Equivalent Privacy (WEP—discussed in depth in Chapter 10, Wireless LAN Security), then the additional overhead of encrypting and decrypting data will also cause a decrease in throughput. Using VPN tunnels will add additional overhead to a wireless LAN system in the same manner as will turning on WEP.

Greater distances between the transmitter and receiver will cause the throughput to decrease because an increase in the number of errors (bit error rate) will create a need for retransmissions. Modern spread spectrum systems are configured to make discrete jumps to specified data rates (1, 2, 5.5, and 11 Mbps). If 11 Mbps cannot be maintained, for example, then the device will drop to 5.5 Mbps. Since the throughput is about 50% of the data rate on a wireless LAN system, changing the data rate will have a significant impact on the throughput.

Hardware limitations will also dictate the data rate. If an IEEE 802.11 device is communicating with an IEEE 802.11b device, the data rate can be no more than 2 Mbps, despite the 802.11b device's ability to communicate at 11 Mbps. Correspondingly, the actual throughput will be less still—about 50%, or 1 Mbps. With wireless LAN hardware, another consideration must be taken into account: the amount of CPU power given to the access point. Having a slow CPU that cannot handle the full 11 Mbps data rate with128-bit WEP enabled will affect throughput.

The type of spread spectrum technology used, FHSS or DSSS, will make a difference in throughput for two specific reasons. First, the data rates for FHSS and DSSS systems are quite different. FHSS systems are typically in compliance with either the OpenAir standard and can transmit at 800 kbps or 1.6 Mbps, or the IEEE 802.11 standard, which allows them to transmit at 1 Mbps or 2 Mbps. Currently, DSSS systems comply with either the IEEE 802.11 standard or the 802.11b standard, supporting data rates of 1, 2, 5.5, & 11 Mbps. The second reason that the type of spread spectrum technology will affect throughput is that FHSS incurs the additional overhead of hop time.

Other factors limiting the throughput of a wireless LAN include proprietary data-link layer protocols, the use of fragmentation (which requires the re-assembly of packets), and packet size. Larger packets will result in greater throughput (assuming a good RF link) because the ratio of data to overhead is better.

RTS/CTS, a protocol used on some wireless LAN implementations and which is similar to the way that some serial links communicate, will create significant overhead because of the amount of handshaking that takes place during the transfer.

The number of users attempting to access the medium simultaneously will have an impact. An increase in simultaneous users will decrease the throughput each station receives from the access point.

Using PCF mode on an access point, thereby invoking polling on the wireless network, will decrease throughput. Polling causes lower throughput by introducing the extra overhead of a polling mechanism and mandatory responses from wireless stations even when no data needs to be sent by those stations.

Co-location Throughput (Theory vs. Reality)

Co-location is a common wireless LAN implementation technique that is used to provide more bandwidth and throughput to wireless users in a given area. RF theory, combined with FCC regulations, allows wireless LAN users in the United States three non-overlapping RF channels (1, 6, and 11). These 3 channels can be used to co-locate multiple (3) access points within the same physical area using 802.11b equipment, as can be seen in Figure 9.9.

FIGURE 9.9   Co-location Throughput

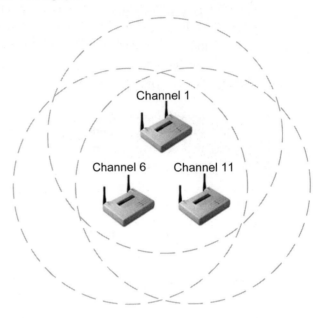

When co-locating multiple access points, it is highly recommended that you:

1. Use the same Spread Spectrum technology (either Direct Sequence or Frequency Hopping, but not both) for all access points

2. Use the same vendor for all access points

 Several vendors' access point configurations allow you to load balance, either automatically or manually. If this feature is available, it is recommended to use it.

The portion of the 2.4 GHz ISM band that is useable for wireless LANs consists of 83.5 MHz. DSSS channels are 22 MHz wide, and there are 11 channels specified for use in the United States. These channels are specifically designated ranges of frequencies within the ISM band. According to the center frequency and width given to each of these channels by the FCC, only three non-overlapping channels can exist in this band. Co-location of access points using non-overlapping channels in the same physical space has advantages in implementing wireless LANs, so we will first explain what *should* happen when you co-locate these access points properly, and then we will explain what *will* happen.

Theory: What Should Happen

For purposes of simplicity in this explanation, we will assume that all access points being used in this scenario are 802.11b-compliant, 11Mbps access points. When using only one access point in a simple wireless LAN, you should experience actual throughput of somewhere between 4.5 Mbps and 5.5 Mbps. You will never see the full 11 Mbps of rated bandwidth due to the half-duplex nature of the RF radios and overhead requirements for wireless LAN protocols such as CSMA/CA.

The RF theory of 3 non-overlapping channels should allow you to setup one access point on channel 1, one access point on channel 6, and one access point on channel 11 without any overlap in these access points' RF band usages. Therefore, you should see normal throughput of approximately 5 Mbps on all co-located access points, with no adjacent-channel interference. Adjacent-channel interference would cause degradation of throughput on one or both of the other access points.

Reality: What Does Happen

What actually happens is that channel 1 and channel 6 actually *do* have a small amount of overlap, as do channel 6 and channel 11. Figure 9.10 illustrates this overlap. The reason for this overlap is typically that both access points are transmitting at approximately the same high output power and are located relatively close to each other. So, instead of getting normal half-duplex throughput on all access points, a detrimental effect is seen on all three. Throughput can decrease to 4 Mbps or less on all three access points or may be unevenly distributed where the access points might have 3, 4, and 5 Mbps respectively.

FIGURE 9.10   DSSS channel overlap

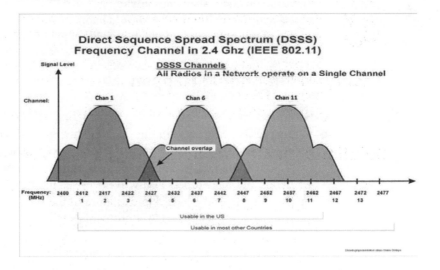

The portion of the theory that holds true is that adjacent channels (1, 2, 3, 4, and 5, for example) have significant overlap, to the point that using an access point on channel 1 and another on channel 3, for example, results in even lower throughput (2Mbps or less) on the two access points. In this case, in particular, a partial overlapping of channels occurs. It is typically seen that a full overlap results in better throughput for the two systems than does a partial overlap between systems.

All this discussion is not to say that you simply *cannot* co-locate three access points using channels 1, 6, and 11. Rather, it is to point out that when you do so, you should not expect the theory to hold completely true. You will experience degraded throughput that is significantly less than the normally expected rate of approximately 5 Mbps per access point unless care is taken to turn down the output power and spread the access points across a broader amount of physical space.

If you do co-locate three access points in this manner, it is recommended that you implement the co-location using the same manufacturer's hardware for all three access points. It has been noted in many lab scenarios that using differing vendors' equipment for co-location has a negative effect on throughput of one or more of the access points. This negative effect could be simply due to differing output power and proximity between access points, but could be related to many other factors as well.

Solutions for Co-location Throughput Problems

As a wireless LAN installer or administrator, you really have two choices when considering access point co-location. You can accept the degraded throughput, or you can attempt a workaround. Accepting the fact that your users will not have 5 Mbps of actual throughput to the network backbone on each access point may be an acceptable scenario. First, however, you must make sure that the users connecting to the network in this situation can still be productive and that they do not actually require the full 5 Mbps of throughput. The last thing you want to be responsible for as a wireless LAN administrator is a network that does not allow the users to do their jobs or achieve the connections that they require. An administrator's second option in this case is to attempt a workaround. Below, we describe some of the alternatives to co-location problems.

Use Two Access Points

One option, which is the easiest, is to use channels 1 and 11 with only 2 access points, as illustrated in Figure 9.11. Using only these two channels will ensure that you have no overlap between channels regardless of proximity between systems, and therefore, no detrimental effect on the throughput of each access point. By way of comparison, two access points operating at the maximum capacity of 5.5 Mbps (about the best that you can expect by any access point), give you a total capacity of 11 Mbps of aggregate throughput, whereas three access points operating at approximately 4 Mbps each (degraded from the maximum due to actual channel overlap) on average yields only 12 Mbps of aggregate throughput. For an additional 1 Mbps of throughput, an administrator would have to spend the extra money to buy another access point, the time and labor to install it, and the continued burden of managing it.

FIGURE 9.11 Using two access points instead of three

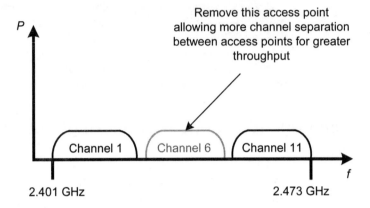

In certain instances, the extra 1 Mbps of bandwidth might still be advantageous, but in a small environment, it might not be practical. Don't forget that this scenario applies only to access points located in the same physical space serving the same client base, but using different, non-overlapping channels. This configuration does not apply to channel reuse, where cells on different non-overlapping channels are alternately spread throughout an area to avoid co-channel interference.

Use 802.11a Equipment

As a second option, you could use 802.11a compliant equipment operating in the 5 GHz UNII bands. The 5 GHz UNII bands, which are each wider than the 2.4 GHz ISM band, have three usable bands, and each band allows for four non-overlapping channels. By using a mixture of 802.11b and 802.11a equipment, more systems can be co-located in the same space without fear of interference between systems. With two (or three) co-located 802.11b systems and up to 8 co-located 802.11a systems, there is the potential for an incredible amount of throughput in the same physical space. The reason that we specify 8 instead of 12 co-located access points with 802.11a is that only the lower and middle bands (with 4 non-overlapping channels each) are specified for indoor use. Therefore, indoors, where most access points are placed, there's normally only the potential for up to 8 access points using 802.11a compliant devices.

Issues with 802.11a Equipment

802.11a equipment is now available from only a few vendors, and is more expensive than equipment that uses the 2.4 GHz frequency band. However, the 5 GHz band has the advantage of many more non-overlapping channels than the 2.4 GHz band (8 vs. 3), allowing you to implement many more co-located access points.

You must keep in mind that while the 2.4 GHz band allows for less expensive gear, the 2.4 GHz band is much more crowded, which means you are more likely to encounter interference from other nearby wireless LANs. Remember that 802.11a devices and 802.11b devices are incompatible. These devices do not see, hear, or communicate with one another because they utilize different frequency bands and different modulation techniques.

Summary

Why do "non-overlapping" channels overlap? There could be many answers to this question; however, it seems that the greatest cause is access points being located too close together. By separating the access points by a greater distance, the overlap between theoretically non-overlapping channels is reduced. Watching this configuration on a spectrum analyzer, you can see that for close-quarters co-location, there needs to be a channel separation larger than 3 MHz; however, since that is what we, as administrators, have to work with, we have to find a workaround.

We can either physically separate the radios by a further distance or we can use channels further than 3 MHz apart (hence the suggestion of using channels 1 & 11 only for close-quarters co-location). It also seems that co-location of different vendors' equipment makes a difference as well. Using the same vendor's equipment for close-quarters co-location has less severe overlapping than does using multiple vendors' equipment. Whether this phenomenon is due to inaccuracies in the radios, or just due to each vendor's implementation of hardware around the radio, is unknown.

Idiosyncrasies like non-overlapping channels overlapping one will not be tested on the CWNA exam. For the exam it is important to know the theory of how co-channel throughput is theoretically supposed to work.

Types of Interference

Due to the unpredictable behavioral tendencies of RF technology, you must take into account many kinds of RF interference during implementation and management of a wireless LAN. Narrowband, all-band, RF signal degradation, and adjacent and co-channel interference are the most common sources of RF interference that occur during implementation of a wireless LAN. In this section, we will discuss these types of interference, how they affect the wireless LAN, how to locate them, and in some cases how to work around them.

Narrowband

Narrowband RF is basically the opposite of spread spectrum technology. Narrowband signals, depending on output power, frequency width in the spectrum, and consistency, can intermittently interrupt or even disrupt the RF signals emitted from a spread spectrum device such as an access point. However, as its name suggests, narrowband signals do not disrupt RF signals across the entire RF band. Thus, if the narrowband signal is primarily disrupting the RF signals in channel 3, then you could, for example, use Channel 11, where you may not experience any interference at all. It is also likely that only a small portion of any given channel might be disrupted by narrowband interference. Typically, only a single carrier frequency (a 1 MHz increment in an 802.11b 22 MHz channel) would be disrupted due to narrowband interference. Given this type of interference, spread spectrum technologies will usually work around this problem without any additional administration or configuration.

FIGURE 9.12 Handheld digital spectrum analyzer showing a narrowband signal

To identify narrowband interference, you will need a spectrum analyzer, shown above in Figure 9.12. Spectrum analyzers are used to locate and measure narrowband RF signals, among other things. There are even handheld, digital spectrum analyzers available that cost approximately $4,000. That may seem like quite a bit of money to locate a narrowband interference source, but if that source is disabling your network, it might be well worth it.

As an alternative, some wireless LAN vendors have implemented a software spectrum analyzer into their client driver software. This software uses a FHSS PCMCIA card to scan the useable portion of the 2.4 GHz ISM band for RF signals. The software graphically displays all RF signals between 2.400 GHz and 2.4835 GHz, which gives the administrator a way of "seeing" the RF that is present in a given area. An example of the visual aid provided by such a spectrum analyzer is shown in Figure 9.13.

FIGURE 9.13 Screenshot of a spectrum analyzer showing narrowband interference

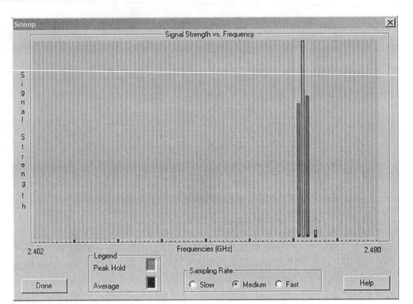

In order to remedy a narrowband RF interference problem, you must first find where the interference originates by using the spectrum analyzer. As you walk closer to the source of the RF signal, the RF signal on the display of your spectrum analyzer grows in amplitude (size). When the RF signal peaks on the screen, you have located its source. At this point, you can remove the source, shield it, or use your knowledge as a wireless network administrator to configure your wireless LAN to efficiently deal with the narrowband interference. Of course, there are several options within this last category, such as changing channels, changing spread spectrum technologies (DSSS to FHSS or 802.11b to 802.11a), and others that we will discuss in later sections.

All-band Interference

All-band interference is any signal that interferes with the RF band from one end of the radio spectrum to the other. All-band interference doesn't refer to interference only across the 2.4 GHz ISM band, but rather is the term used in any case where interference covers the entire range you're trying to use, regardless of frequency. Technologies like Bluetooth (which hops across the entire 2.4 GHz ISM band many times per second) can, and usually do, significantly interfere with 802.11 RF signals. Bluetooth is considered all-band interference for an 802.11 wireless network. In Figure 9.14 a sample screen shot of a spectrum analyzer recording all-band interference is shown.

FIGURE 9.14 Screenshot of a software spectrum analyzer showing all-band interference

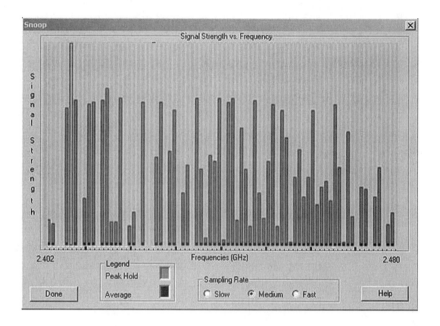

A possible source of all-band interference that can be found in homes and offices is a microwave oven. Older, high-power microwave ovens can leak as much as one watt of power into the RF spectrum. One watt is not much leakage for a 1000-watt microwave oven, but considering the fact that one watt is many times as much power as is emitted from a typical access point, you can see what a significant impact it might have. It is not a given that a microwave oven will emit power across the entire 2.4 GHz band, but it is possible, depending on the type and condition of the microwave oven. A spectrum analyzer can detect this kind of problem.

When all-band interference is present, the best solution is to change to a different technology, such as moving from 802.11b (which uses the 2.4 GHz ISM band) to 802.11a (which uses the 5 GHz UNII bands). If changing technologies is not feasible due to cost or implementation problems, the next best solution is to find the source of the all-band interference and remove it from service, if possible. Finding the source of all-band interference is more difficult than finding the source of narrowband interference because you're not watching a single signal on the spectrum analyzer. Instead, you are looking at a range of signals, all with varying amplitudes. You will most likely need a highly directional antenna in order to locate the all-band interference source.

Weather

Severely adverse weather conditions can affect the performance of a wireless LAN. In general, common weather occurrences like rain, hail, snow, or fog do not have an adverse affect on wireless LANs. However, extreme occurrences of wind, fog, and perhaps smog can cause degradation or even downtime of your wireless LAN. Smog, due to chemicals and layering of the air can cause problems for wireless LANs.

A *radome* can be used to protect an antenna from the elements. If used, radomes must have a drain hole for condensation drainage. Yagi antennas without radomes are vulnerable to rain, as the raindrops will accumulate on the elements and detune the performance. The droplets actually make each element look longer than it really is. Ice accumulation on exposed elements can cause the same detuning effect as rain; however, it stays around longer. Radomes may also protect an antenna from falling objects such as ice falling from an overhead tree.

2.4 GHz signals may be attenuated by up to 0.05 dB/km (0.08 dB/mile) by torrential rain (4 inches/hr). Thick fog produces up to 0.02 dB/km (0.03 dB/mile) attenuation. At 5.8 GHz, torrential rain may produce up to 0.5 dB/km (0.8 dB/mile) attenuation, and thick fog up to 0.07 dB/km (0.11 dB/mile). Even though rain itself does not cause major propagation problems, rain will collect on the leaves of trees and will produce attenuation until it evaporates. This problem is not as big a concern when the trees in question are Pine trees as they do not have broad leaves capable of holding the large amounts of water that other tree types have.

Wind

Wind does not affect radio waves or an RF signal, but it can affect the positioning and mounting of outdoor antennas. For example, consider a wireless point-to-point link that connects two buildings that are 12 miles (20 km) apart. Taking into account the curvature of the Earth (Earth bulge), and having only a five-degree vertical and horizontal beam width on each antenna, the positioning of each antenna would have to be exact. A strong wind could easily move one or both antennas enough to completely degrade the signal between the two antennas. This effect is called "antenna wind loading", and is illustrated in Figure 9.15.

FIGURE 9.15   Antenna Wind Loading on Point-to-point networks

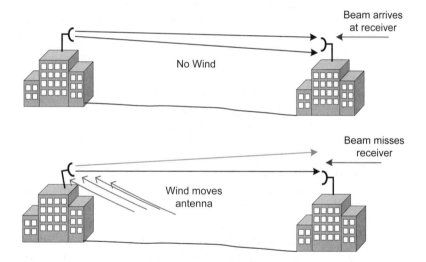

Other similarly extreme weather occurrences like tornadoes or hurricanes must also be considered. If you are implementing a wireless LAN in a geographic location where hurricanes or tornadoes occur frequently, you should certainly take that into account when setting up any type of outdoor wireless LAN. In such weather conditions, securing antennas, cables, and the like are all very important.

Stratification

When very thick fog or even smog settles (such as in a valley), the air within this fog becomes very still and begins to separate into layers. It is not the fog itself that causes the diffraction of RF signals, but the stratification of the air within the fog. When the RF signal goes through these layers, it is bent in the same fashion as visible light is bent as it moves from air into water.

Lightning

Lightning can affect wireless LANs in two ways. First, lightning can strike either a wireless LAN component such as an antenna or it may strike a nearby object. Lightning strikes of nearby objects can damage your wireless LAN components just as if these components were not protected by a lightning arrestor. A second way that lightning affects wireless LANs is by charging the air through which the RF waves must travel after striking an object lying between the transmitter and receiver. The affect of lightning is similar to the way that the Aurora Borealis Northern Lights provide problems for RF television and radio transmissions.

Adjacent Channel and Co-Channel Interference

Having a solid understanding of channel use with wireless LANs is imperative for any good wireless LAN administrator. As a wireless LAN consultant, you will undoubtedly find many wireless networks that have many access points, all of them configured for the same channel. In these types of situations, a discussion with the network administrator that installed the access points will divulge that he or she thought it was necessary for all access points and clients to be on the same channel throughout the network in order for the wireless LAN to work properly. This configuration is very common, and often incorrect. This section will build on your knowledge of how channels are used; explaining how multiple access points using various channels can have a detrimental impact on a network.

Adjacent Channel Interference

Adjacent channels are those channels within the RF band being used that are, in essence, side-by-side. For example, channel 1 is adjacent to channel 2, which is adjacent to channel 3, and so on. These adjacent channels overlap each other because each channel is 22 MHz wide and their center frequencies are only 5 MHz apart. Adjacent channel interference happens when two or more access points using overlapping channels are located near enough to each other that their coverage cells physically overlap. Adjacent channel interference can severely degrade throughput in a wireless LAN.

It is especially important to pay attention to adjacent channel interference when co-locating access points in an attempt to achieve higher throughput in a given area. Co-located access points on non-overlapping channels can experience adjacent channel interference if there is not enough separation between the channels being used, as illustrated in Figure 9.16.

FIGURE 9.16   Adjacent channel Interference

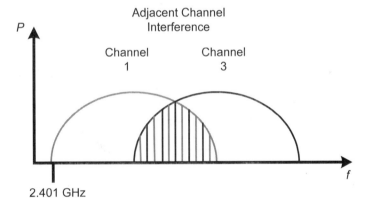

In order to find the problem of adjacent channel interference, a spectrum analyzer will be needed. The spectrum analyzer will show you a picture of how the channels being used overlap each other. Using the spectrum analyzer in the same physical area as the access points will show the channels overlapping each other.

There are only two solutions for a problem with adjacent channel interference. The first is to move access points on adjacent channels far enough away from each other that their cells do not overlap, or turn the power down on each access point enough to where the cells do not overlap. The second solution is to use only channels that have no overlap whatsoever. For example, using channels 1 & 11 in a DSSS system would accomplish this task.

Co-channel Interference

Co-channel interference can have the same effects as adjacent channel interference, but is an altogether different set of circumstances. Co-channel interference as seen by a spectrum analyzer is illustrated in Figure 9.17 while how a network configuration would produce this problem is shown in Figure 9.18.

FIGURE 9.17   Co-channel Interference

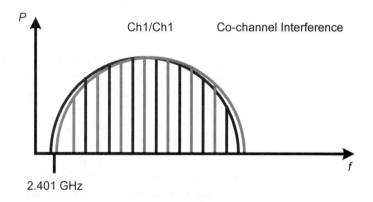

FIGURE 9.18   Co-channel Interference in a network

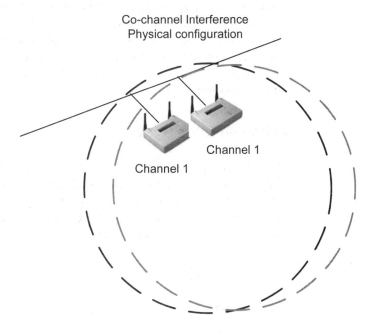

To illustrate co-channel interference, assume a 3-story building, with a wireless LAN on each floor, with the wireless LANs each using channel 1. The access points' signal ranges, or cells, would likely overlap in this situation. Because each access point is on the same channel, they will interfere with one another. This type of interference is known as co-channel interference.

In order to troubleshoot co-channel interference, a wireless network protocol analyzer will be needed. The protocol analyzer will be able to show packets coming from each of the wireless LANs using any particular channel. Additionally, it will show the signal strength of each wireless LAN's packets, giving you an idea of just how much one wireless LAN is interfering with the others.

The two solutions for co-channel interference are, first, the use of a different, non-overlapping channel for each of the wireless LANs, and second, moving the wireless LANs far enough apart that the access points' cells do not overlap. These solutions are the same remedy as for adjacent channel interference.

The best configuration for co-location of DSSS systems is on channel 1 & 11 or another pair of similarly spaced channels. For example, channels 2 & 10 or 3 & 9 would do nicely due to a large amount of frequency separation. If use of channels 1, 6, & 11 is necessary, the access points should be spaced far enough apart to where there is minimal interference between them. By adequately spacing access points while having them configured for channels 1, 6, & 11, a situation is created where the signal amplitude of each unit is so low (due to path loss and absorption by nearby objects) that by the time it reaches the other units, the adjacent channel interference is eliminated. This spacing scenario is the most common in real-world application.

In situations where seamless roaming is required, a technique called channel reuse is used in order to alleviate adjacent and co-channel interference while allowing users to roam through adjacent cells. Channel reuse is the side-by-side locating of non-overlapping cells to form a mesh of coverage where no cell on a given channel touches another cell on that channel. Figure 9.19 illustrates channel reuse.

FIGURE 9.19   Channel reuse

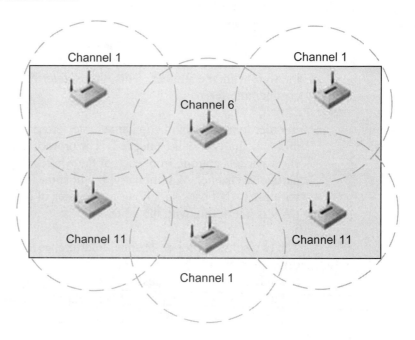

One last point of consideration when placing access points deals with configuring them for failover/hot-standby and load-balancing. Many enterprise quality access points, such as those from Cisco, now include some form of software support for hot standby and load balancing. Additionally, some access points (such as those from Orinoco) contain two separate radios that can be used for load balancing within a single access point. These points should be part of your planning and design if required.

Range Considerations

When considering how to position wireless LAN hardware, the communication range of the units must be taken into account. Generally, three things will affect the range of an RF link: transmission power, antenna type and location, and environment. The maximum communication range of a wireless LAN link is reached when, at some distance, the link begins to become unstable, but is not lost.

Transmission Power

The output power of the transmitting radio will have an effect on the range of the link. A higher output power will cause the signal to be transmitted a greater distance, resulting in a greater range. Conversely, lowering the output power will reduce the range.

Antenna Type

The type of antenna used affects the range either by focusing the RF energy into a tighter beam transmitting it farther (as a parabolic dish antenna does); or by transmitting it in all directions (as an omni-directional antenna does), reducing the range of communication.

Environment

A noisy or unstable environment can cause the range of a wireless LAN link to be decreased. The packet error rate of an RF link is greater at the fringes of coverage due to a small signal to noise ratio. Also, adding interference effectively raises the noise floor, lessening the likelihood of maintaining a solid link.

The range of an RF link can also be influenced by the frequency of the transmission. Though not normally a concern within a wireless LAN implementation, frequency might be a consideration when planning a bridge link. For example, a 2.4 GHz system will be able to reach further at the same output power than a 5 GHz system. The same holds true for an older 900 MHz system: it will go further than a 2.4 GHz system at the same output power. All of these bands are used in wireless LANs, but 2.4 GHz systems are by far the most prevalent.

Key Terms

Before taking the exam, you should be familiar with the following terms:

adjacent channel Interference

all-band interference

antenna diversity

co-channel Interference

downfade

free space path loss

narrowband interference

nulling

spectrum analyzer

stratification

upfade

Review Questions

1. Which of the following can help to overcome or solve the hidden node problem? Choose all that apply.

   A. Using RTS/CTS

   B. Increasing the power to the hidden nodes

   C. Decreasing the power to the hidden node

   D. Increasing the power on the access point

2. Antenna diversity is a solution to which one of the following wireless LAN problems?

   A. Near/Far

   B. Hidden Node

   C. Co-location throughput

   D. Multipath

3. When objects in the Fresnel Zone absorb or block some of the RF wave, which one of the following might result?

   A. Signal fading

   B. A surge in signal amplitude

   C. A change in signal frequency

   D. A change in modulation

4. What is the period of time between the main wave's arrival at the receiver and the reflected wave's arrival at a receiver called?

   A. SIFS

   B. Delay spread

   C. PIFS

   D. Signal spread

5. Which of the following could be used to remedy a near/far problem? Choose all that apply.

   A. Decrease the power of the near nodes

   B. Increase the power of the closer nodes

   C. Decrease the power of the distant node

   D. Increase the power of the far node

6. Which of the following channels on three co-located access points will result in the greatest co-channel interference?

   A. 1, 1, 1

   B. 1, 2, 3

   C. 1, 6, 11

   D. 1, 11

7. Which one of the following can cause all-band interference?

   A. Metal roof

   B. Lake

   C. Bluetooth

   D. HiperLAN

8. Why are most access points built with two antennas?

   A. Access points are half-duplex devices that send on one antenna and receive on the other

   B. Access points use one antenna as a standby for reliability

   C. Access points use two antennas to overcome multipath

   D. Access points use two antennas to transmit on two different channels

9. Using RTS/CTS can solve the hidden node problem and will not affect network throughput

   A. This statement is always true

   B. This statement is always false

   C. Depends on the manufacturer's equipment

10. Which of the following can cause RF interference in a wireless LAN? Choose all that apply.

    A. Wind

    B. Lightning

    C. Smog

    D. Clouds

11. Multipath is defined as which one of the following?

    A. The negative effects induced on a wireless LAN by reflected RF signals arriving at the receiver along with the main signal.

    B. Surges in signal strength due to an RF signal taking multiple paths between the sending and receiving stations

    C. The condition caused by a receiving station having multiple antennas which causes the signal to take multiple paths to the CPU

    D. The result of using a signal splitter to create multiple signal paths between sending and receiving stations

12. Multipath can cause signals to increase above the power of the signal that was transmitted by the sending station. This statement is:

    A. Always true

    B. Always false

    C. True, when the signal is transmitted in clear weather

    D. False, unless a 12 dBi or higher power antenna is being used

13. Multipath is caused by which one of the following?

    A. Multiple antennas

    B. Wind

    C. Reflected RF waves

    D. Bad weather

14. When can the hidden node problem occur?

    A. Only when a network is at full capacity

    B. When all users of a wireless LAN are simultaneously transmitting data

    C. Anytime, even after a flawless site survey

    D. Every time a wireless LAN client roams from one access point to another

15. Which one of the following is NOT a solution for correcting the hidden node problem?

    A. Using the RTS/CTS protocol

    B. Increasing power to the node(s)

    C. Removing obstacles between nodes

    D. Moving the hidden node(s)

16. How is the threshold set when using RTS/CTS in "On with Threshold" mode on a wireless LAN?

    A. Automatically by the access points only

    B. Manually by the user of the hidden node

    C. Manually on the clients and access points by the wireless LAN administrator

    D. Automatically by the clients only

17. A situation that results in the client(s) that are farther away from the access point and using less power to not be heard over the traffic from the closer, high-powered clients, is known as:

    A.   Hidden Node

    B.   Near/Far

    C.   Degraded throughput

    D.   Interference

18. Why should an administrator be able to co-locate 3 DSSS access points in the same area using the 2.4 GHz ISM band?

    A.   Each access point will transmit on one band and receive on another.

    B.   Each access point will use co-channel interference to stop the others from transmitting data when it is ready to send

    C.   The access points will use channels that do not overlap or cause adjacent channel interference

    D.   There are up to five non-overlapping DSSS channels in the ISM bands.

19. How many channels in the 2.4 GHz spectrum are designated for use in the United States?

    A.   3

    B.   14

    C.   10

    D.   11

20. Which one of the following is an advantage of 5 GHz (802.11a) equipment over 802.11b equipment?

    A.   The lower 5 GHz UNII band is wider than the 2.4 GHz ISM band

    B.   The 802.11a equipment is less expensive than 802.11b

    C.   The 5 GHz UNII bands allows for more non-overlapping channels than the 2.4 GHz ISM band

    D.   802.11a equipment is backwards compatible with 802.11g equipment

Answers to Review Questions

1. A, B. Sometimes increasing the power on the nodes is enough to transmit through or around the obstacle blocking the RF signals from stations and sometimes it is not. When increasing the power is not enough, the best course of action is use of the RTS/CTS protocol in order that stations broadcast their intention to transmit data on the network.

2. D. By having two antennas and supporting antenna diversity, most access points can overcome multipath problems. Antenna diversity works by separating the two antennas by a distance greater than the wavelength of the frequency in use thereby reducing the changes that both spots will have exactly the same detrimental effects from reflected waves.

3. A. Signal fading can refer to upfade, downfade, or nulling of an RF transmission. This type of fading is sometimes referred to as Rayleigh fading, but most often it is simply deemed *fading*. No matter what type of fading happens, it's generally detrimental to the main RF wave.

4. B. The delay spread is the amount of time between the arrival at the receiver of the main RF wave and the arrival of the last reflected wave. This amount of time is typically 4 nanoseconds or less.

5. A, D. The near/far problem is normally remedied by the wireless protocols in use such as CSMA/CA. When these protocols are ineffective, increasing power to remote nodes, moving the remote nodes closer to the local nodes, or decreasing power to the local nodes are some available remedies.

6. A. Co-channel interference is the interference experienced between systems using the same channel. In this question, only answer 'A' meets the criteria of all access points being on the same channel.

7. C. All band interference is interference that spans the width of the frequency band in use. This type of interference cannot be avoided by a wireless LAN system, leaving the administrator one option: a different frequency band must be used, which often means use of a different set of wireless LAN technologies. Bluetooth spans the width of the 2.4 GHz ISM band disrupting 802.11, 802.11b, and

802.11g data transmissions.

8.   C. Access points use two antennas in order to implement antenna diversity to overcome multipath. The radios used in wireless LANs are half duplex meaning they can either transmit or receive at any given time. Multipath is an effect caused by reflected RF waves and can disrupt or corrupt data transmissions. Access points sample inputs from both antennas and use the best signal. Access points normally transmit on the antenna last used for receiving.

9.   B. Use of the RTS/CTS protocol always adds overhead to the network, decreasing throughput. Use of the RTS/CTS protocol, when used appropriately, can help reduce a high rate of collisions on a wireless network, but does not *solve* the hidden node problem. Solving the hidden node problem would consist of all nodes being able to hear one another's transmissions.

10.   A, B, C. Wind can load antennas, breaking RF links or at least causing degraded throughput. Lightning can destroy wireless LAN equipment and can introduce high levels of RF interference due to power surges around the transmission path between the transmitter and receiver. Smog can have intermittent effects on wireless LANs depending on the severity and makeup of the smog. Generally smog causes degraded throughput for a long-distance RF link.

11.   A. Multipath is the set of negative effects that multiple RF signals arriving at the same destination at almost the same time from the same source has on a wireless LAN. These reflected signals can have numerous effects on the main signal. Multipath is especially disruptive when there are many reflective objects in area around the signal path from transmitter to receiver.

12.   B. Due to Free Space Path Loss, an RF wave arriving at a receiver will never be as strong as the transmitted wave. Multipath can cause an increase in the received signal over what it would have been had there been no multipath due to reflected waves being in phase with the main wave, but the main signal will never be increased in amplitude beyond the transmission power.

13.   C. If there were no reflective objective near the signal path between transmitter and receiver, multipath would not exist. The lack of any reflective object is rarely the case since anything metal and many smooth things (like a body of water or a flat stretch of earth) reflect

RF waves. Multipath almost always exists in any wireless LAN connection; hence, the use of dual antennas on most access points.

14. C. The causes of the hidden node problem are numerous. Typical causes are obstructions through which RF waves cannot penetrate and low power on client stations. A good site survey might help in reducing the occurrences of hidden node problems, but eliminating them would only be possible in an unchanging environment. The main use and advantage of a wireless LAN is mobility, which creates an ever-changing environment.

15. A. The RTS/CTS protocol is not a cure for the hidden node problem, but a tool used to reduce the negative effects that hidden nodes have on the network: collisions.

16. C. The network administrator must manually configure the access points and clients for use of RTS/CTS regardless of the setting. The three settings are *Off*, *On*, and *On with Threshold*. The *Off* setting is used by default to reduce unnecessary overhead on the network.

17. B. The near/far problem is one that is addressed by the access protocols used by wireless networks. This problem is seen in both cellular and wireless LAN networks. When the problem is severe, it might be necessary to move distant nodes closer, increase power to distant nodes, or to decrease power to closer nodes.

18. C. There are three non-overlapping DSSS channels specified by the FCC in the 2.4 GHz ISM band. Each of these bands is separated by 5 MHz. These channels are 1, 6, & 11 as numbered by the FCC.

19. D. The FCC specifies 14 channels for use with wireless LANs, 11 of which can be used in the United States. Each channel is 22 MHz wide, and the channel is specified as a center frequency +11 MHz and -11 MHz.

20. C. The lower 5 GHz UNII band and the 2.4 GHz ISM band are the same width - 100 MHz. 802.11a equipment is new and significantly more expensive than 802.11b equipment and is not compatible with 802.11b or 802.11g equipment in any capacity. The UNII bands (all three of them) allow for a larger useable portion than does the 2.4 GHz ISM band, yielding a maximum of 4 non-overlapping DSSS channels.

Wireless LAN Security

CWNA Exam Objectives Covered:

❖ Identify the strengths, weaknesses and appropriate uses of the following wireless LAN security techniques
  - WEP
  - AES
  - Filtering
  - Emerging security techniques
❖ Describe the following types of wireless LAN security attacks, and explain how to identify and prevent them
  - Passive attacks (eavesdropping)
  - Active attacks (connecting, probing, and configuring the network)
  - Jamming attacks
  - Man-in-the-middle attacks
❖ Given a wireless LAN scenario, identify the appropriate security solution from the following available wireless LAN security solutions
  - WEP key solutions
  - Wireless VPN
  - Key hopping
  - AES based solutions
  - Wireless gateways
  - 802.1x and EAP

❖ Explain the uses of the following corporate security
  policies and how they are used to secure a wireless LAN

- Securing sensitive information
- Physical security
- Inventory and audits
- Using advanced solutions
- Public networks

❖ Identify how and where the following security precautions are
  used to secure a wireless LAN

- WEP
- Cell sizing
- Monitoring
- User authentication
- Wireless DMZ

Wireless LANs are not inherently secure; however, if you do not take any precautions or configure any defenses with *wired* LAN or WAN connections, they are not secure either. The key to making a wireless LAN secure, and keeping it secure, is educating those who implement and manage the wireless LAN. Educating the administrator on basic and advanced security procedures for wireless LANs is essential to preventing security breaches into your wireless LAN.

In this very important chapter, we will discuss the much-maligned 802.11 specified security solution known as Wired Equivalent Privacy, or WEP. As you may already know, WEP alone will not keep a hacker out of a wireless LAN for very long. This chapter will explain why, and offer some steps for how WEP can be used with some level of effectiveness.

We will explain the various methods that can be used to attack a wireless LAN so that as an administrator you will know what to expect and how to prevent it. Then we will discuss some of the emerging security solutions that are available, but not yet specified by any of the 802.11 standards. Finally, we will offer some recommendations for maintaining wireless LAN security and discuss corporate security policy as it pertains specifically to wireless LANs.

This chapter on wireless LAN security is by no means the end of knowledge on the subject. Rather, this chapter should serve the CWNA candidate as a basic introduction to the inherent weaknesses of wireless LANs and the available solutions for compensating for these weaknesses.

Wired Equivalent Privacy

Wired Equivalent Privacy (WEP) is an encryption algorithm used by the Shared Key authentication process for authenticating users and for encrypting data payloads over only the wireless segment of the LAN. The IEEE 802.11 standard specifies the use of WEP.

WEP is a simple algorithm that utilizes a pseudo-random number generator (PRNG) and the RC4 stream cipher. For several years this algorithm was considered a trade secret and details were not available, but in September of 1994, someone posted the source code in the cypherpunks mailing list. Although the source code is now available, RC4 is still trademarked by RSADSI. The RC4 stream cipher is fast to decrypt and encrypt, which saves on CPU cycles, and RC4 is also simple enough for most software developers to code it into software.

When WEP is used, both the sender and receiver use the stream cipher to create identical pseudorandom strings from the known shared key (WEP key). The sender XORs the plaintext transmission with the stream cipher which produces ciphertext. The receiver then takes the shared key and stream cipher and reverses the XOR process to windup with plaintext again. Figure 10.1 shows the process to encrypt traffic as explained below and Figure 10.2 shows the process to decrypt traffic.

1. The plaintext traffic is sent through an Integrity Check algorithm (CRC-32 as specified by IEEE 802.11) which produces an Integrity Check Value (ICV).

2. The ICV is appended to the end of the plaintext message.

3. A 24-bit Initialization Vector (IV) is generated and prepended to the secret key.

4. This is then put into the RC4 algorithm to create a seed value for the WEP pseudo random number generator (PRNG).

5. The WEP PRNG next outputs the encrypting cipher-stream.

6. The encrypting cipher-stream is then run through a XOR process with the plaintext/ICV message. This produces the WEP ciphertext.

7. In the last step, the WEP ciphertext is then prepended with the plaintext IV and transmitted.

FIGURE 10.1   The WEP Encryption Process

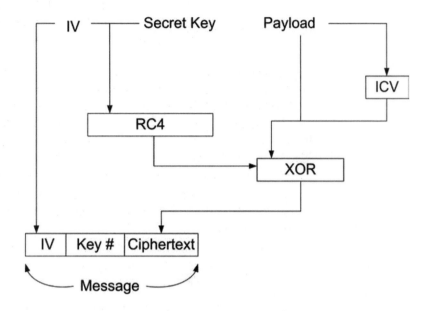

FIGURE 10.2   The WEP Decryption Process

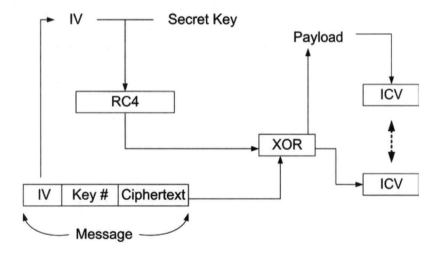

When WEP is referred to as being simple, it means that it is *weak*. The RC4 algorithm was inappropriately implemented in WEP, yielding a less-than-adequate security solution for 802.11 networks. Both 64-bit and

128-bit WEP (the two available types) have the same weak implementation of a 24-bit Initialization Vector (IV) and use the same flawed process of encryption. The flawed process is that most implementations of WEP initialize hardware using an IV of 0 - thereafter incrementing the IV by 1 for each packet sent. For a busy network, statistical analysis shows that all possible IVs (2^{24}) would be exhausted in 5 hours, meaning the IV would be reinitialized starting at zero at least once every 5 hours. This scenario creates an open door for determined hackers. When WEP is used, the IV is transmitted in the clear with each encrypted packet. The manner in which the IV is incremented and sent in the clear allows the following breaches in security:

- *Active attacks to inject new traffic*- Unauthorized mobile stations can inject packets onto the network based on known plaintext

  1. Knowledge of one packet could be used to create other, seemingly legitimate packets.
  2. Theoretically this is possible even if there is only partial knowledge of the contents of an encrypted packet.
  3. Can be used to interact with servers on the wired network (open shells, modify files, etc.).

- *Active attacks to decrypt traffic* - Can be used to "trick" the AP into revealing the plaintext of any traffic on the network.

  1. Involves capturing encrypted traffic and modifying the header information.
  2. The modified traffic is sent to some server on the Internet controlled by the attacker.
  3. The AP will decrypt any traffic before placing it on the wired network.
  4. This traffic shows up at the server in its plaintext form.

- *Dictionary-building attacks* - After gathering enough traffic, the WEP key can be cracked using freeware tools. Once the WEP key is cracked, real-time decryption of packets can be accomplished by listening to broadcasts packets using the WEP key. This type of attack can be accomplished due to the limited space in the 24-bit IV.

  1. Once the plaintext for a packet has been revealed, the RC4 stream can be computed on a "per IV" basis.

2. Given enough time and storage space an IV table could be built.

3. Once the table is built, traffic can be decrypted in near real time.

4. The Berkeley paper estimates that roughly 15GB of traffic would need to be gathered for a complete table.

- *Passive attacks to decrypt traffic* - Using statistical analysis, WEP traffic can be decrypted as follows:

1. By performing cryptographic analysis on IV collisions, the original plaintext can be determined.

2. Much of the traffic is predictable (AP beacons, ARP requests) and also includes much redundancy.

3. This redundancy can be used to eliminate certain content and increase accuracy.

4. When the plaintext for one packet is recovered, the plaintext for all similar IVs will soon follow.

5. This can be aided by sending traffic from the Internet to a specific wireless host.

Why WEP Was Chosen

Since WEP is not secure, why was it chosen and implemented into the 802.11 standard? Once the 802.11 standard was approved and completed, the manufacturers of wireless LAN equipment rushed their products to market. The 802.11 standard specifies the following criteria for security:

- Exportable

- Reasonably Strong

- Self-Synchronizing

- Computationally Efficient

- Optional

WEP meets all these requirements. When it was implemented, WEP was intended to support the security goals of confidentiality, access control, and data integrity. What actually happened is that too many early adopters of wireless LANs thought that they could simply implement

WEP and have a completely secure wireless LAN. These early adopters found out quickly that WEP wasn't the complete solution to wireless LAN security. Fortunately for the industry, wireless LAN hardware had gained immense popularity well before this problem was widely known. This series of events led to many vendors and third party organizations scrambling to create wireless LAN security solutions.

The 802.11 standard leaves WEP implementation up to wireless LAN manufacturers, so each vendor's implementation of WEP keys may or may not be the same, adding another weakness to WEP. Even the Wi-Fi Alliance's Wi-Fi interoperability standard tests include only 40-bit WEP keys. Some wireless LAN manufacturers have chosen to enhance (fix) WEP, while others have looked to using new standards such as 802.1x with EAP or Virtual Private Networks (VPN). There are many solutions on the market addressing the weaknesses found in WEP.

WEP Keys

The core functionality of WEP lies in what are known as *keys*, which are the basis for the encryption algorithm discussed in the previous section of this chapter. WEP keys are implemented on client and infrastructure devices on a wireless LAN. A WEP key is an alphanumeric character string used in two manners in a wireless LAN. First, a WEP key can be used to verify the identity of an authenticating station. Second, WEP keys can be used for data encryption.

When a WEP-enabled client attempts to authenticate and associate to an access point, the access point will determine whether or not the client has the correct WEP key. By "correct", we mean that the client has to have a key that is part of the WEP key distribution system implemented on that particular wireless LAN. The WEP keys must match on both ends of the wireless LAN connection.

As a wireless LAN administrator, it may be your job to distribute the WEP keys manually, or to setup a more advanced method of WEP key distribution. WEP key distribution systems can be as simple as implementing static keys or as advanced as using centralized encryption key servers. Obviously, the more advanced the WEP system is, the harder it will be for a hacker to gain access to the network.

WEP keys are available in two types, 64-bit and 128-bit. Many times you will see them referenced as 40-bit and 104-bit instead. This reference is a bit of a misnomer. The reason for this misnomer is that WEP is implemented in the same way for both encryption lengths. Each uses a 24-bit Initialization Vector concatenated (linked end-to-end) with a secret key. The secret key lengths are 40-bit or 104-bit yielding WEP key lengths of 64 bits and 128 bits. Note that the RC4 Stream Cipher can actually handle keys as large as 256 bits, however the implementation in WEP only makes usage of the two smaller sizes previously mentioned.

Entering static WEP keys into clients or infrastructure devices such as bridges or access points is quite simple. A typical configuration program is shown in Figure 10.3. Sometimes there is a checkbox for selecting 40- or 128-bit WEP. Sometimes no checkbox is present, so the administrator must know how many characters to enter when asked. Most often, client software will allow inputting of WEP keys in alphanumeric (ASCII) or hexadecimal (HEX) format. Some devices may require ASCII or HEX, and some may take either form of input.

 There are many HEX-ASCII conversion charts on the Internet that can be found with a simple search engine. You might have to reference such a chart if using mixed vendor hardware across your network. Some vendors include this conversion chart in their client software's HELP section.

FIGURE 10.3 Entering WEP keys on client devices

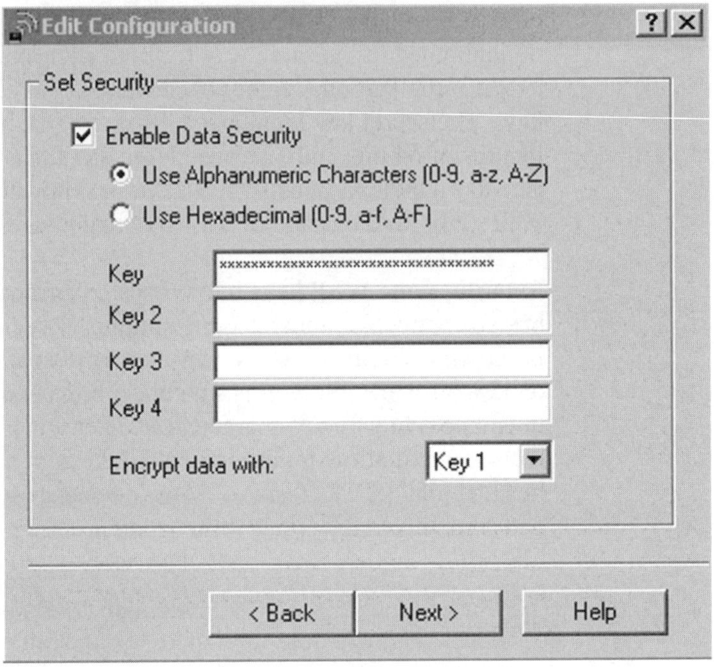

The number of characters entered for the secret key depends on whether the configuration software requires ASCII or HEX and whether 64-bit or 128-bit WEP is being used. If your wireless card supports 128-bit WEP, then it automatically supports 64-bit WEP as well. If entering your WEP key in ASCII format, then 5 characters are used for 64-bit WEP and 13 characters are used for 128-bit WEP. If entering your WEP key in HEX format, then 10 characters are used for 64-bit WEP and 26 characters are used for 128-bit WEP.

Static WEP Keys

If you choose to implement static WEP keys, you would manually assign a static WEP key to an access point and its associated clients. These WEP keys would never change, making that segment of the network susceptible to hackers who may be aware of the intricacies of WEP keys.

For this reason, static WEP keys may be an appropriate basic security method for simple, small wireless LANs, but are not recommended for enterprise wireless LAN solutions.

When static WEP keys are implemented, it is simple for network security to be compromised. Consider if an employee left a company and "lost" their wireless LAN card. Since some PC cards carry the WEP key in their firmware, the card will always have access to the wireless LAN until the WEP keys on the wireless LAN are changed.

Most access points and clients have the ability to hold up to 4 WEP keys simultaneously, as can be seen in Figure 10.4. One useful reason for having the ability to enter up to 4 WEP keys is network segmentation or departmentalization within an organization. Suppose a network had 100 client stations. Giving out four WEP keys instead of one could segment the users into four distinct groups of 25 - for use with different departments for example. If a WEP key were compromised, it would mean changing 25 stations and an access point or two instead of the entire network. Access points generally transmit using only the first key, but can receive traffic that has been encrypted with any one of the 4 keys it holds.

Figure 10.4   Entering WEP keys on infrastructure devices

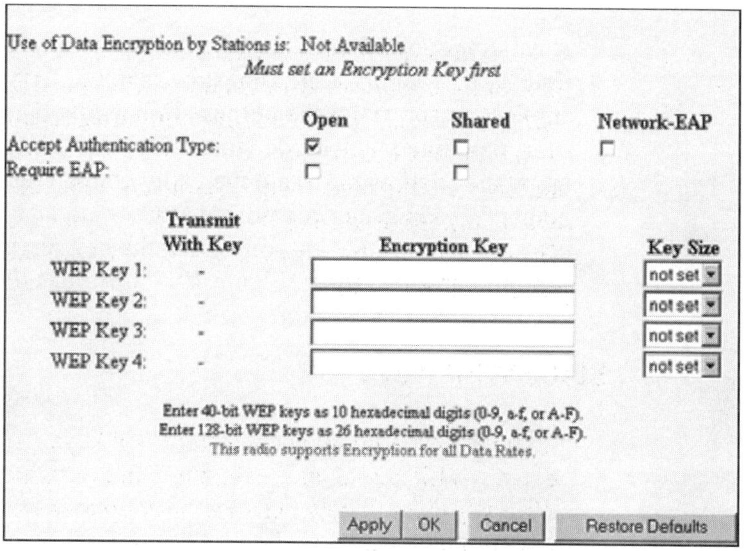

Use of Data Encryption by Stations is: Not Available
Must set an Encryption Key first

	Open	Shared	Network-EAP
Accept Authentication Type:	☑	☐	☐
Require EAP:	☐	☐	

	Transmit With Key	Encryption Key	Key Size
WEP Key 1:	-		not set ▼
WEP Key 2:	-		not set ▼
WEP Key 3:	-		not set ▼
WEP Key 4:	-		not set ▼

Enter 40-bit WEP keys as 10 hexadecimal digits (0-9, a-f, or A-F).
Enter 128-bit WEP keys as 26 hexadecimal digits (0-9, a-f, or A-F).
This radio supports Encryption for all Data Rates.

| Apply | OK | Cancel | Restore Defaults |

The problem with shared (static) WEP keys is that they are rarely changed. As with any pass phrase that is not frequently changed, static WEP keys lend themselves to easier cracking. The randomness of WEP is its weakness: the IV. Since there are only 2^{24} possible IVs, the IV is repeated after approximately 16 million packets. Most clients reset their IV back to 0 and increment by 1 for each packet, which thus yields lots of IV collisions (packets with duplicate IVs). The IV collisions make it easier for an attacker to crack your WEP key. Solutions such as TKIP or dynamic WEP keying solve this problem.

Centralized Encryption Key Servers

For enterprise wireless LANs using WEP as a basic security mechanism, centralized encryption key servers should be used if possible for the following reasons:

- Centralized key generation
- Centralized key distribution
- Ongoing key rotation
- Reduced key management overhead

Any number of different devices can act as a centralized key server. Usually a server of some kind such as a RADIUS server or a specialized application server for the purpose of handing out new WEP keys on a short time interval is used. Normally, when using WEP, the keys (made up by the administrator) are manually entered into the stations and access points. When using a centralized key server, an automated process between stations, access points, and the key server performs the task of handing out WEP keys. Figure 10.5 illustrates how a typical encryption key server would be setup.

FIGURE 10.5 Centralized Encryption Key Server

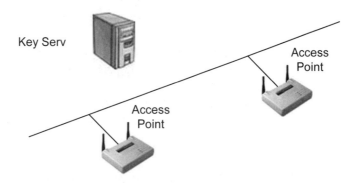

Key Serv

Access
Point

Access
Point

Centralized encryption key servers allow for key generation on a per-packet, per-session or other method, depending on the particular manufacturer's implementation. Per-packet WEP key distribution calls for a new WEP key to be assigned to both ends of the connection for every packet sent, whereas per-session WEP key distribution uses a new WEP key for each new session between nodes.

If you choose to implement per-packet WEP key distribution, be aware that it will add significant overhead to the wireless LAN.

WEP Usage

When WEP is initialized, the data payload of the packet being sent using WEP is encrypted; however, part of the packet header – including MAC address – is *not* encrypted. All layer 3 information including source and destination addresses is encrypted with WEP. When an access point sends out its beacons on a wireless LAN using WEP, the beacons are not encrypted. Remember that the beacons do not include any layer 3 information.

When packets are sent using WEP encryption, those packets must be decrypted. This decryption process consumes CPU cycles and reduces the effective throughput on the wireless LAN, sometimes significantly. Some manufacturers have implemented additional CPUs in their access points for the purpose of performing WEP encryption and decryption. Many manufacturers implement WEP encryption/decryption in software and use the same CPU that's used for access point management, packet forwarding, etc. These access points are generally the ones where WEP will have the most significant effects if enabled. By implementing WEP in hardware, it is very likely that an access point can maintain its 5 Mbps (or more) throughput with WEP enabled. The disadvantage of this implementation is the added cost of a more advanced access point.

WEP can be implemented as a basic security mechanism, but network administrators should first be aware of WEP's weaknesses and how to compensate for them. The administrator should also be aware of the fact that each vendor's use of WEP can and may be different, hindering the use of multiple vendor hardware.

Advanced Encryption Standard

The Advanced Encryption Standard (AES) is gaining acceptance as an appropriate replacement for the RC4 algorithm used in WEP. AES uses the Rijndael (pronounced 'RINE-dale') algorithm in the following specified key lengths:

- 128-bit
- 192-bit
- 256-bit

AES is considered to be un-crackable by most cryptographers, and the National Institute of Standards and Technology (NIST) has chosen AES for the Federal Information Processing Standard, or FIPS. As part of the effort to improve the 802.11 standard, the 802.11i working committee is considering the use of AES in *WEPv2*.

AES, if approved by the 802.11i working group to be used in WEPv2, will be implemented in firmware and software by vendors. Access point firmware and client station firmware (the PCMCIA radio cards) will have to be upgraded to support AES. Client station software (drivers and client utilities) will support configuring AES with secret key(s).

Filtering

Filtering is a basic security mechanism that can be used in addition to WEP and/or AES. Filtering literally means to keep out that which is *not* wanted and to allow that which *is* wanted. Filtering works the same way as access lists on a router: by defining parameters to which stations must adhere in order to gain access to the network. With wireless LANs, it is not so much what the stations do, but rather who they are and how they are configured. There are three basic types of filtering that can be performed on a wireless LAN:

- SSID filtering
- MAC address filtering
- Protocol filtering

This section will explain what each of these types of filtering are, what each can do for the administrator, and how to configure each one.

SSID Filtering

SSID (Service Set Identifier) filtering is a rudimentary method of filtering, and should only be used for the most basic access control. The SSID is used as a network name, very similar to the "WORKGROUP" name that is used in Windows by default and can be between 0 and 32 octets (bytes) in length. The SSID of a wireless LAN station must match the SSID on the access point (infrastructure mode) or of the other stations (ad hoc mode) in order for the client to authenticate and associate to the service set. Since the SSID is broadcast in the clear in every beacon that the access point (or set of stations) sends out, it is very simple to find out the SSID of a network using a sniffer. Many access points have the ability to take the SSID out of the beacon frame. When this is the case, the client must have the matching SSID in order to associate to the access point. When a system is configured in this manner, it is said to be a "closed system." SSID filtering is *not* considered a reliable method of keeping unauthorized users out of a wireless LAN.

Some manufacturer's access points have the ability to remove the SSID from beacons and/or probe responses. In this case, in order to join the service set, a station must have the SSID configured manually in the driver configuration settings. Some common mistakes that wireless LAN users make in administering SSIDs are listed below:

- *Using the default SSID* - This setting is yet another way to give away information about your wireless LAN. It is simple enough to use a protocol analyzer to see that MAC addresses originating from the access point and then look up the MAC address in the OUI table hosted by IEEE. The OUI table lists the different MAC address prefixes that are assigned to each manufacturer. Until Netstumbler came along, this process was manual, but now Netstumbler performs this task automatically. If you don't know how to use Netstumbler or are unfamiliar with network protocol analyzers, then looking for default SSIDs also works well. Each wireless LAN manufacturer uses their own default SSID, and, since there are still a manageable number of wireless LAN manufacturers in the industry, obtaining each of the user manuals from the support section of each manufacturer's website and looking for the default SSID and default IP subnet information is a simple task. *Always change the default SSID.*

- *Making the SSID something company-related* – This type of setting is a security risk because it simplifies the process of a hacker finding the company's physical location. When looking for wireless LANs in any particular geographic region, finding the physical location of the wireless LAN is half the battle. Even after detecting the wireless LAN using tools such as Netstumbler, finding where the signal originates takes time and considerable effort in many cases. When an administrator uses an SSID that names the company or organization, it makes finding the wireless LAN very easy. *Always use non-company-related SSIDs.*

- *Using the SSID as a means of securing wireless networks* – This practice is highly discouraged since a user must only change the SSID in the configuration setting is his workstation in order to join the network. SSIDs should be used as a means of *segmenting* the network, not securing it. Again, think of the SSID as the network name. Just as with Windows' Network Neighborhood, changing the workgroup your computer is a part of and is as simple as changing a configuration setting on the client station.

- *Unnecessary Broadcasting of SSIDs* - If your access points have the ability to remove SSIDs from beacons and probe responses, configure them that way. This configuration aids in deterring casual eavesdroppers from tinkering with or using your wireless LAN. By closing the network, you are disabling the broadcast of the SSID by configuring the AP to not respond to broadcast probes from clients. Clients wanting to associate with your Access Point will need to already know the correct SSID in order to become authenticated and associated. By closing the network, you prevent the popular NetStumbler (at least in its current version) from being able to see the network. NetStumbler sends out a broadcast probe approximately once per second, thus enabling it to locate open networks, meaning those networks that have not been configured not to respond to broadcast probes. Closing the network, however, is only a small part of an overall security solution and should not be considered enough to keep intruders out.

 Looking for wireless LANs is also called "netstumbling" - after the ever-so-popular wireless LAN auditing application, Netstumbler, written by Marius Milner. More information can be found on this application at www.netstumbler.com.

MAC Address Filtering

Wireless LANs can filter based on the MAC addresses of client stations. Almost all access points (even very inexpensive ones) have MAC filter functionality. The network administrator can compile, distribute, and maintain a list of allowable MAC addresses and program them into each access point. If a PC card or other client with a MAC address that is not in the access point's MAC filter list tries to gain access to the wireless LAN, the MAC address filter functionality will not allow that client to associate with that access point. Figure 10.6 illustrates this point.

Of course, programming every wireless client's MAC address into every access point across a large enterprise network would be impractical. MAC filters can be implemented on some RADIUS servers instead of in each access point. This configuration makes MAC filters a much more scalable security solution. Simply entering each MAC address into RADIUS along with user identity information, which would have to be input anyway, is a good solution. RADIUS servers often point to another authentication source, so that other authentication source would need to support MAC filters.

FIGURE 10.6   MAC Filters

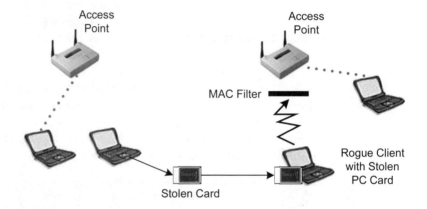

MAC filters can work in reverse as well. For example, consider an employee who left a company and took their wireless LAN card with them. This wireless LAN card holds the WEP key and MAC filters, which, for the sake of this example, are not used. The administrator could then create a filter on all access points to disallow the MAC address of the client device that was taken by the employee. If MAC filters were already being used on this network when the wireless LAN card was stolen, removing the particular client's MAC address from the *allow* list would work as well.

Although MAC filters may seem to be a good method of securing a wireless LAN in some instances, they are still susceptible to the following intrusions:

- Theft of a PC card that is in the MAC filter of an access point
- Sniffing the wireless LAN and then spoofing with the MAC address after business hours

MAC filters are great for home and small office networks where there are a small number of client stations. Using WEP and MAC filters provides an adequate security solution in these instances. This solution is adequate because no intelligent hacker is going to spend the hours it takes to break WEP on a low-use network and expend the energy to circumvent a MAC filter for the purpose of getting to a person's laptop or desktop PC at home.

Circumventing MAC Filters

MAC addresses of wireless LAN clients are broadcasted in the clear by access points and bridges, even when WEP is implemented. Therefore, a hacker who can listen to traffic on your network can quickly find out most MAC addresses that are allowed on your wireless network. In order for a protocol analyzer to see a station's MAC address, that station must transmit a frame across the wireless segment.

Some wireless PC cards permit the changing of their MAC address through software or even operating system configuration changes. Once a hacker has a list of allowed MAC addresses, the hacker can simply change the PC card's MAC address to match one of the PC cards on your network, instantly gaining access to your entire wireless LAN.

Since two stations with the same MAC address cannot peacefully co-exist on a LAN, the hacker must find the MAC address of a mobile station that is removed from the premises at particular times of the day. It is during this time when the mobile station (notebook computer) is not present on the wireless LAN that the hacker can gain access into the network. MAC filters should be used when feasible, but not as the sole security mechanism on your wireless LAN.

Protocol Filtering

Wireless LANs can filter packets traversing the network based on layer 2-7 protocols. In many cases, manufacturers make protocol filters independently configurable for both the wired segment and wireless segment of the access point.

Imagine a scenario where a wireless workgroup bridge is placed on a remote building in a campus wireless LAN that connects back to the main information technology building's access point. Because all users in the remote building are sharing the 5 Mbps of throughput between these buildings, some amount of control over usage must be implemented. If this link was installed for the express purpose of Internet access for these users, then filtering out every protocol except SMTP, POP3, HTTP, HTTPS, FTP, and any instant messaging protocols would limit users from being able to access internal company file servers for example. The ability to set protocol filters such as these is very useful in controlling utilization of the shared medium. Figure 10.7 illustrates how protocol filtering works in a wireless LAN.

FIGURE 10.7   Protocol Filtering

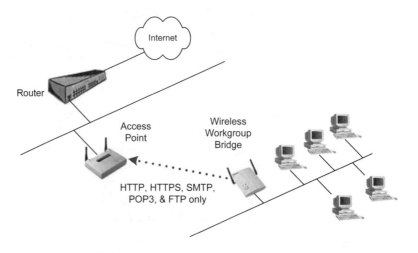

 Manufacturers vary in their implementation of protocol filters, some offering more functionality than others. Ethertype, layer 3 protocols, layer 4 ports, and layer 7 application filters are common.

Attacks on Wireless LANs

A malicious hacker can seek to disable or attempt to gain access to a wireless LAN in several ways. Some of these methods are:

1. Passive attacks (eavesdropping)

2. Active attacks (connecting, probing, and configuring the network)

3. Jamming attacks

4. Man-in-the-middle attacks

The above list is by no means exhaustive, and some of these methods can be orchestrated in several different ways. It is beyond the scope of this book to present every possible means of wireless LAN attack. This text is aimed at giving a network administrator insight into some possible methods of attack so that security will be considered a vital part of wireless LAN implementation.

Passive Attacks

Eavesdropping is perhaps the most simple, yet still effective type of wireless LAN attack. Passive attacks like eavesdropping leave no trace of the hacker's presence on or near the network since the hacker does not have to actually connect to an access point to listen to packets traversing the wireless segment. Wireless LAN protocol analyzers or custom applications are typically used to gather information about the wireless network from a distance with a directional antenna, as illustrated in Figure 10.8. This method of access allows the hacker to keep his distance from the facility, leave no trace of his presence, and listen to and gather valuable information.

FIGURE 10.8 Passive Attack Example

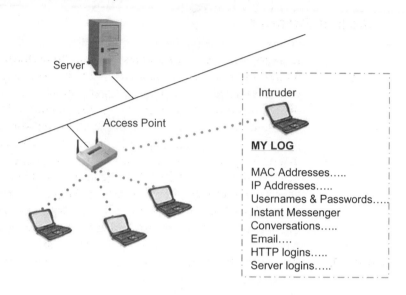

There are applications capable of gathering passwords from HTTP sites, email, instant messengers, FTP sessions, and telnet sessions that are sent in clear text. There are other applications that can snatch password hashes traversing the wireless segment between client and server for login purposes. Any information going across the wireless segment in this manner leaves the network and individual users vulnerable to attack. Consider the impact if a hacker gained access to a user's domain login information and caused havoc on the network. The hacker would be to blame, but network usage logs would point directly at the user. This breach could cost a person their job. Consider another situation in which HTTP or email passwords were gathered over the wireless segment and later used by a malicious hacker for personal gain from a remote site.

A hacker who is parked in your facility's parking lot may have a veritable toolkit for breaking into your wireless LAN. All this individual needs is a packet protocol analyzer and some shareware or freeware hacking utilities to acquire your WEP keys and to gain access to the wireless network.

Active Attacks

Hackers can stage active attacks in order to perform some type of function on the network. An active attack might be used to gain access to a server to obtain valuable data, use the organization's Internet access for malicious purposes, or even change the network infrastructure configuration. By connecting to a wireless network through an access point, a user can begin to penetrate deeper into the network or perhaps make changes to the wireless network itself. For example, if a hacker made it past a MAC filter, then the hacker could navigate to the access points and remove all MAC filters, making it easier to gain access next time. The administrator might not even notice this change for some time. Figure 10.9 illustrates an active attack on a wireless LAN.

FIGURE 10.9   Active Attack Example

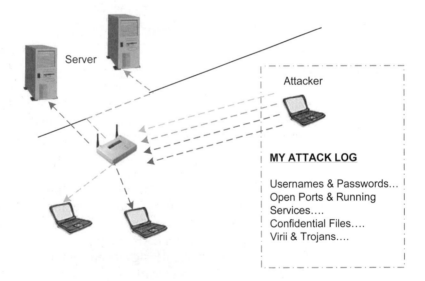

Some examples of active attacks might be a drive-by spammer or a business competitor wanting access to your files. A spammer could queue emails in his laptop, then connect to your home or business network through the wireless LAN. After obtaining an IP address from your DHCP server, the hacker can send tens of thousands of emails using your Internet connection and your ISP's email server without your knowledge. This kind of attack could cause your ISP to cut your connection for email abuse when it's not even your fault.

A business competitor might want to get your customer list with contact information or maybe your payroll information in order to better compete with you or to steal your customers. These types of attacks happen regularly without the knowledge of the wireless LAN administrator.

Once a hacker has a wireless connection to your network, he might as well be sitting in his own office with a wired connection because the two scenarios are not much different. Wireless connections offer the hacker plenty of speed and access to servers, wide area connections, Internet connections, and users' desktops and laptops. With a few simple tools, it is relatively simple to gather important information, impersonate a user, or even cause damage to the network through reconfiguration. Probing servers with port scans, creating null sessions to shares and having servers dump passwords to hacking utilities, and then logging into servers using existing accounts are all things that can be done by following the instructions in off-the-shelf hacker books.

Jamming

Whereas a hacker would use passive and active attacks to gain valuable information from or to gain access to your network, jamming is a technique that would be used to simply shut down your wireless network. Similar to saboteurs arranging an overwhelming denial of service (DoS) attack aimed at web servers, so a wireless LAN can be shut down by an overwhelming RF signal. That overwhelming RF signal can be intentional or unintentional, and the signal may be removable or non-removable. When a hacker stages an intentional jamming attack, the hacker could use wireless LAN equipment, but more likely, the hacker would use a high-power RF signal generator or sweep generator. Figure 10.10 illustrates an example of jamming a wireless LAN.

FIGURE 10.10 Jamming Attack Example

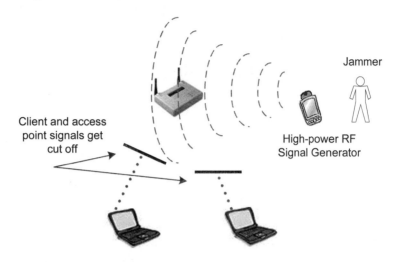

Removing this type of attacker from the premises first requires locating
the source of the RF signal. Locating an RF signal source can be done
with an RF spectrum analyzer. There are many spectrum analyzers on the
market, but having one that is handheld and battery operated is quite
useful. Several manufacturers make handheld spectrum analyzers, and a
few wireless LAN manufacturers have created spectrum analyzer
software utilities for use in wireless client devices.

When jamming is caused by a non-moveable, non-malicious source such
as a communications tower or other legitimate system, the wireless LAN
administrator might have to consider using a wireless LAN system that
utilizes a different set of frequencies. For example, if an administrator
were responsible for the design and installation of an RF network at a
large apartment complex, special considerations might be in order. If an
RF interference source were a large number of 2.4 GHz spread spectrum
phones, baby monitors, and microwave ovens in this apartment complex,
then the administrator might choose to implement 802.11a equipment that
uses the 5 GHz UNII bands instead of 802.11b equipment that shares the
2.4 GHz ISM band with these other devices.

Unintentional jamming occurs regularly due to many different devices
across many different industries sharing the 2.4 GHz ISM band with
wireless LANs. Malicious jamming is not a common threat. The reason

RF jamming is not very popular among hackers is that it is fairly expensive to mount an attack, considering the cost of the required equipment, and the only victory that the hacker gets is temporarily disabling a network.

Man-in-the-middle Attacks

A man-in-the-middle attack is a situation in which a malicious individual uses an access point to effectively hijack mobile nodes by sending a stronger signal than the legitimate access point is sending to those nodes. The mobile nodes then associate to this rogue access point, sending their data, possibly sensitive data, into the wrong hands. Figure 10.11 illustrates a man-in-the-middle attack, hijacking wireless LAN clients.

In order to get clients to reassociate with the rogue access point, the rogue access point's power must be much higher than that of the other access points in the area *and* something has to actively cause the users to roam to the rogue access point. Losing connectivity with a legitimate access point happens seamlessly as a part of the roaming process so some clients will connect to the rogue accidentally. Introducing all-band interference into the area around the legitimate access point, as with a Bluetooth device, can cause forced roaming.

FIGURE 10.11 Man-in-the-middle attack

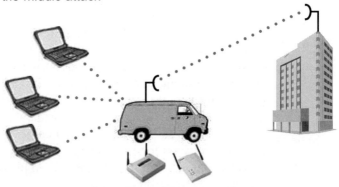

An access point and sometimes a
workgroup bridge are used to hijack users

The person perpetrating this man-in-the-middle attack would first have to know the SSID that the wireless clients are using, and, as we've discussed earlier, this piece of information is easily obtained. The perpetrator would have to know the network's WEP keys if WEP is being used on the network. Upstream (facing the network core) connectivity from the rogue access point is handled through use of a client device such as a PC card or workgroup bridge. Many times, man-in-the-middle attacks are orchestrated using a single laptop computer with two PCMCIA cards. Access point software is run on the laptop computer where one PC card is used as an access point and a second PC card is used to connect the laptop to nearby legitimate access points. This configuration makes the laptop a "man-in-the-middle", operating between clients and legitimate access points. A man-in-the-middle hacker can obtain valuable information by running a protocol analyzer on the laptop in this scenario

One particular problem with the man-in-the-middle attack is that the attack is undetectable by users. That being the case, the amount of information that a perpetrator can gather in this situation is limited only by the amount of time that the perpetrator can stay in place before getting caught. Physical security of the premises is the best remedy for the man-in-the-middle attack.

Emerging Security Solutions

Because wireless LANs are not inherently secure, and because WEP is not an end-to-end security mechanism for enterprise wireless LANs, there is a significant opportunity for other security solutions to take the forefront in the wireless LAN security market. We will discuss some of these possible security solutions that, while not yet approved and accepted into the 802.11 family of standards, can play a role in securing your wireless LAN.

As of this writing, all of the available security solutions discussed in this book are proprietary in nature. Although the IEEE has accepted 802.1x as a standard, its use as an approved part of an 802.11 series standard is not yet official. There are new standards still in draft form, such as 802.11i, that specifies use of such security mechanisms as 802.1x and EAP.

WEP Key Management

Instead of using static WEP keys, which can easily be learned or discovered by hackers, wireless LANs can be made more secure by implementing dynamic per-session or per-packet key assignments using a central key distribution system.

Per-session or per-packet WEP key distribution assigns a new WEP key to both the client and the access point for each session or each packet sent between the two. While dynamic keys add more overhead and reduce throughput, they make hacking the network through the wireless segment much more difficult. The hacker would have to be able to predict the sequence of keys that the key distribution server is using, which is very difficult.

Remember that WEP protects only the layer 3-7 information and data payload, but does not encrypt MAC addresses or beacons. A protocol analyzer could capture any information being broadcast in beacons from the access point or any MAC address information in unicast packets from clients.

In order to put a centralized encryption key server in place, the wireless LAN administrator must find an application that performs this task, buy a server with the appropriate operating system installed, and configure the application according to the organization's needs. This process could be costly and time-consuming, depending on the scale of deployment, but will pay for itself in a very short period of time in preventing liabilities due to malicious hackers.

Wireless VPNs

Wireless LAN manufacturers are increasingly including VPN server software in access points and gateways, allowing VPN technology to help secure wireless LAN connections. When the VPN server is built into the access point, clients use off-the-shelf VPN software using protocols such as PPTP or IPSec to form a tunnel directly with the access point.

First, the client would associate with the access point, and then the dial-up VPN connection would have to be made in order for the client to pass traffic through the access point. All traffic is passed through the tunnel and can be encrypted as well as tunneled to add an extra layer of security. Figure 10.12 shows a VPN configuration.

FIGURE 10.12 Wireless LAN VPN solution

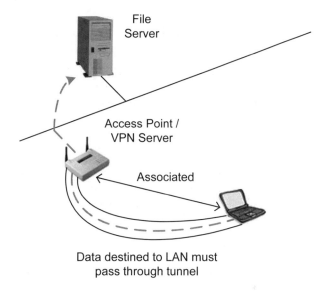

File
Server

Access Point /
VPN Server

Associated

Data destined to LAN must
pass through tunnel

Use of PPTP with shared secrets is very simple to implement and provides a reasonable level of security, especially when added to WEP encryption. Use of IPSec with shared secrets or certificates is generally the solution of choice among security professionals in this arena. When the VPN server is implemented in an enterprise gateway, the same process takes place except that, after the client associates to the access point, the VPN tunnel is established with the upstream gateway device instead of with the access point itself.

There are also vendors that are offering modifications to their existing VPN solutions (whether hardware or software) to support wireless clients and competing in the wireless LAN market. These devices or applications serve in the same capacity as the enterprise gateway, sitting between the wireless segment and the wired core of the network. Wireless VPN solutions are reasonably economical and fairly simple to implement. If the administrator has no experience with VPN solutions, it might be necessary to get training in that area before implementing such a solution. VPNs that support wireless LANs are usually designed with the novice VPN administrator in mind, which partially explains why these devices have gained such popularity among users.

Temporal Key Integrity Protocol (TKIP)

TKIP is essentially an upgrade to WEP that fixes known security problems in WEP's implementation of the RC4 stream cipher. TKIP provides for initialization vector hashing to help defeat passive packet snooping. It also provides a Message Integrity Check to help determine whether an unauthorized user has modified packets by injecting traffic that enables key cracking. TKIP includes use of dynamic keys to defeat capture of passive keys—a widely publicized hole in the existing Wired Equivalent Privacy (WEP) standard.

TKIP can be implemented through firmware upgrades to access points and bridges as well as software and firmware upgrades to wireless client devices. TKIP specifies rules for the use of initialization vectors, re-keying procedures based on 802.1x, per-packet key mixing, and message integrity code (MIC). There will be a performance loss when using TKIP, but this performance decrease may be a valid trade-off, considering the gain in network security.

TKIP starts out with a 128-bit temporal key that is shared amongst all clients and access points. This temporal key is then combined with a client's MAC address and then added to a very large 16-octet IV to produce the actual encryption key. By using this process, TKIP can effectively ensure that no two stations are using the same key stream for data encryption. RC4 is used to perform the encryption, as in WEP, thus TKIP is backwards compatible with WEP. To further ensure the security of TKIP on the network, the 128-bit temporal key is changed ever 10,000 packets--a period of time that can conceivably be reached in a very short time, under an hour in many cases.

Most hardware that is already in place can be upgraded to use TKIP through a standard firmware update. Access points running TKIP will still be able to service WEP-only clients due the aforementioned backwards compatibility, but this will introduce a security flaw into the network if utilized. TKIP looks to be a very promising solution until the 802.11i standard is ratified and included in new hardware devices. The new WPA specification from the W-Fi Alliance is actually built upon TKIP.

An important point to make note of that is that TKIP and BKR do need to be used at the same time. Since TKIP protects the integrity of the WEP key, using BKR (Broadcast Key Rotation) to dynamically rotate keys will only add further overhead to a wireless connection. It is possible to enable both, if supported on your hardware (Cisco AP 1200 for example), but not required nor recommended. It is also important to note that only devices using LEAP or EAP-TLS can use BKR.

AES Based Solutions

AES-based solutions may replace WEP using RC4, but in the interim, solutions such as TKIP are being implemented. Although no products that use AES are currently on the market as of this writing AES has undergone extensive cryptographic review and a few companies have submitted their AES-based products to NIST for review. The current 802.11i draft specifies use of AES, and, considering most wireless LAN industry players are behind this effort, AES is likely to remain as part of the finalized standard.

Changing data encryption techniques to a solution that is as strong as AES will make a significant impact on wireless LAN security, but there still must be scalable solutions implemented on enterprise networks such as centralized encryption key servers to automate the process of handing out keys. If a client radio card is stolen with the AES encryption key embedded, it would not matter how strong AES is because the perpetrator would still be able to gain access to the network.

Wireless Gateways

Residential wireless gateways are now available with VPN technology, as well as NAT, DHCP, PPPoE, WEP, MAC filters, and perhaps even a built-in firewall. These devices are sufficient for small office or home office environments with few workstations and a shared connection to the

Internet. Costs of these units vary greatly depending on their range of offered services. Some of the high-end units even boast static routing and RIPv2.

Enterprise wireless gateways are a special adaptation of a VPN and authentication server for wireless networks. An enterprise gateway sits on the wired network segment between the access points and the wired upstream network. As its name suggests, a gateway controls access from the wireless LAN onto the wired network, so that, while a hacker could possibly listen to or even gain access to the wireless segment, the gateway protects the wired distribution system from attack.

An example of a good time to deploy an enterprise wireless LAN gateway might be the following hypothetical situation. Suppose a hospital had implemented 40 access points across several floors of their building. Their investment in access points is fairly significant at this point, so if the access points do not support scalable security measures, the hospital could be in the predicament of having to replace all of their access points. Instead, the hospital could employ a wireless LAN gateway.

This gateway can be connected between the core switch and the distribution switch (which connects to the access points) and can act as an authentication and VPN server through which all wireless LAN clients can connect. Instead of deploying all new access points, one (or more depending on network load) gateway device can be installed behind all of the access points as a group. Use of this type of gateway provides security on behalf of a non-security-aware access point. Most enterprise wireless gateways support an array of VPN protocols such as PPTP, IPSec, L2TP, certificates, and even QoS based on profiles.

802.1x and Extensible Authentication Protocol

The 802.1x standard provides specifications for port-based network access control. Port-based access control was originally – and still is – used with Ethernet switches. When a user attempts to connect to the Ethernet port, the port then places the user's connection in blocked mode awaiting verification of the user's identity with a backend authentication system.

The 802.1x protocol has been incorporated into many wireless LAN systems and has become almost a standard practice among many vendors. When combined with extensible authentication protocol (EAP), 802.1x can provide a very secure and flexible environment based on various authentication schemes in use today.

EAP, which was first defined for the point-to-point protocol (PPP), is a protocol for negotiating an authentication method. EAP is defined in RFC 2284 and defines the characteristics of the authentication method including the required user credentials (password, certificate, etc.), the protocol to be used (MD5, TLS, GSM, OTP, etc.), support of key generation, and support of mutual authentication. There are perhaps a dozen types of EAP currently on the market since neither the industry players nor IEEE have come together to agree on any single type, or small list of types, from which to create a standard.

The successful 802.1x-EAP client authentication model works as follows:

1. The client requests association with the access point

2. The access point replies to the association request with an EAP identity request

3. The client sends an EAP identity response to the access point

4. The client's EAP identity response is forwarded to the authentication server

5. The authentication server sends an authorization request to the access point

6. The access point forwards the authorization request to the client

7. The client sends the EAP authorization response to the access point

8. The access point forwards the EAP authorization response to the authentication server

9. The authentication server sends an EAP success message to the access point

10. The access point forwards the EAP success message to the client and places the client's port in forward mode

FIGURE 10.13 Two Logon Processes

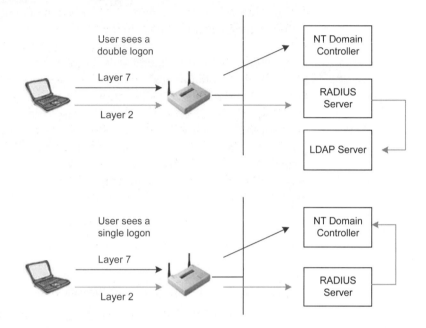

When 802.1x with EAP is used, a situation arises for an administrator in which it is possible to have a double logon when powering up a notebook computer that is attached wirelessly and logging into a domain or directory service. The reason for the possible double logon is that 802.1x requires authentication in order to provide layer 2 connectivity. In most cases, this authentication is done via a centralized user database. If this database is not the same database used for client authentication into the network (such as with Windows domain controllers, Active Directory, NDS, or LDAP), or at least synchronized with the database used for client authentication, then the user will experience two logons each time network connectivity is required. Most administrators choose to use the same database for MAC layer connectivity and client/server connectivity, providing a seamless logon process for the client. A similar configuration can also be used with wireless VPN solutions.

Corporate Security Policy

A company that uses wireless LANs should have a corporate security policy that addresses the unique risks that wireless LANs introduce to the network. The example of an inappropriate cell size that allows the drive-by hacker to gain network access from the parking lot is a very good example of one item that should be included in any corporate security policy. Other items that should be covered in the security policy are strong passwords, strong WEP keys, physical security, use of advanced security solutions, and regular wireless LAN hardware inventories. This list is far from comprehensive, considering that security solutions will vary between organizations. The depth of the wireless LAN section of the security policy will depend on the security requirements of organization as well as the extent of the wireless LAN segment(s) of the network.

The benefits of having, implementing, and maintaining a solid security policy are too numerous to count. Preventing data loss and theft, preventing corporate sabotage or espionage, and maintaining company secrets are just a few. Even the suggestion that hackers could have stolen data from an industry-leading corporation may cause confidence in the company to plummet.

The beginning of good corporate policy starts with management. Recognizing the need for security and delegating the tasks of creating the appropriate documentation to include wireless LANs into the existing security policy should be top priority. First, those who are responsible for securing the wireless LAN segments must be educated in the technology. Next, the educated technology professional should interact with upper management and agree on company security needs. This team of educated individuals is then able to construct a list of procedures and requirements that, if followed by personnel at every applicable level, will ensure that the wireless network remains as safely guarded as the wired network.

Keep Sensitive Information Private

Some items that should be known only by network administrators at the appropriate levels are:

- Usernames and passwords of access points and bridges
- SNMP strings
- WEP keys
- MAC address lists

The point of keeping this information only in the hands of trusted, skilled individuals such as the network administrator is important because a malicious user or hacker could easily use these pieces of information to gain access into the network and network devices. This information can be stored in one of many secure fashions. There are now applications using strong encryption on the market for the explicit purpose of password and sensitive data storage.

Physical Security

Although physical security when using a traditional wired network is important, it is even more important for a company that uses wireless LAN technology. For reasons discussed earlier, a person that has a wireless PC Card (and maybe an antenna) does not have to be in the same building as the network to gain access to the network. Even intrusion detection software is not necessarily enough to prevent wireless hackers from stealing sensitive information. Passive attacks leave no trace on the network because no connection was ever made. There are utilities on the market now that can see a network card that is in promiscuous mode, accessing data without making a connection.

When WEP is the only wireless LAN security solution in place, tight controls should be placed on users who have company-owned wireless client devices, such as not allowing them to take those client devices off of company premises. Since the WEP key is stored in the client device's firmware, wherever the card goes, so does the network's weakest security link. The wireless LAN administrator should know who, where, and when each PC card is taken from the organization's facilities.

Because such knowledge is often unreasonable, an administrator should realize that WEP, by itself, is not an adequate wireless LAN security solution. Even with such tight controls, if a card is lost or stolen, the person responsible for the card (the user) should be required to report the loss or theft immediately to the wireless LAN administrator so that necessary security precautions can be taken. Such precautions should include, at a minimum, resetting MAC filters, changing WEP keys, etc.

Having guards make periodic scans around the company premises looking specifically for suspicious activity is effective in reducing netstumbling. Security guards that are trained to recognize 802.11 hardware and alerting company personnel to always be on the lookout for non-company personnel lurking around the building with 802.11-based hardware is also very effective in reducing on-premises attacks.

Wireless LAN Equipment Inventory & Security Audits

As a complement to the physical security policy, all wireless LAN equipment should be regularly inventoried to account for authorized and prevent unauthorized use of wireless equipment to access the organization's network. If the network is too large and contains a significant amount of wireless equipment, periodic equipment inventories might not be practical. In cases such as these, it is very important to implement wireless LAN security solutions that are not based on hardware, but rather based on usernames and passwords or some other type of non hardware-based security solution. For medium and small wireless networks, doing monthly or quarterly hardware inventories can motivate users to report hardware loss or theft.

Periodic scans of the network with protocol analyzers, in a search for rogue devices, are a very valuable way of keeping the wireless network secure. Consider if a very elaborate (and expensive) wireless network solution were put in place with state-of-the-art security, and, since coverage did not extend to a particular area of the building, a user took it into their own hands to install an additional, unauthorized access point in their work area. In this case, this user has just provided a hacker with the necessary route into the network, completely circumventing a very good (and expensive) wireless LAN security solution.

Inventories and security audits should be well documented in the corporate security policy. The types of procedures to be performed, the tools to be used, and the reports to be generated should all be clearly spelled out as part of the corporate policy so that this tedious task does not get overlooked. Managers should expect a report of this type on a regular basis from the network administrator.

Using Advanced Security Solutions

Organizations implementing wireless LANs should take advantage of some of the more advanced security mechanisms available on the market today. It should also be required in a security policy that the implementation of any such advanced security mechanism be thoroughly documented. Because these technologies are new, proprietary, and often used in combination with other security protocols or technologies, they must be documented so that, if a security breach occurs, network administrators can determine where and how the breach occurred.

Because so few people in the IT industry are educated in wireless technology, the likelihood of employee turnover causing network disruption, or at least vulnerability, is much higher when wireless LANs are part of the network. This turnover of employees is another very important reason that thorough documentation on wireless LAN administration and security functions be created and maintained.

Public Wireless Networks

It is inevitable that corporate users with sensitive information on their laptop computers will connect those laptops to public wireless LANs. It should be a matter of corporate policy that all wireless users (whether wireless is provided by the company or by the user) run both personal firewall software and antiviral software on their laptops. Most public wireless networks have little or no security in order to make connectivity simple for the user and to decrease the amount of required technical support.

Even if upstream servers on the wired segment are protected, the wireless users are still vulnerable. Consider the situation where a hacker is sitting at an airport, considered a "Wi-Fi hot spot." This hacker can sniff the wireless LAN, grab usernames and passwords, log into the system, and then wait for unsuspecting users to login also. Then, the hacker can do a ping sweep across the subnet looking for other wireless clients, find the users, and begin hacking into their laptop computer's files. These vulnerable users are considered "low hanging fruit", meaning that they are easy to hack because of their general unfamiliarity with leading edge technology such as wireless LANs.

Limited and Tracked Access

Most enterprise LANs have some method of limiting and tracking a user's access on the LAN. Typically, a system supporting Authentication, Authorization, and Accounting (AAA) services is deployed. This same security measure should be documented and implemented as part of wireless LAN security. AAA services will allow the organization to assign use rights to particular classes of users. Visitors, for example, might be allowed only Internet access whereas employees would be allowed to access their particular department's servers and the Internet.

Keeping logs of users' rights and the activities they performed while using your network can prove valuable if there's ever a question of who did what on the network. Consider if a user was on vacation, yet during the vacation the user's account was used almost every day. Keeping logs of activity such as this will give the administrator insight into what is really happening on the LAN. Using the same example, and knowing that the user was on vacation, the administrator could begin looking for where the masquerading user was connecting to the network.

Security Recommendations

As a summary to this chapter, below are some recommendations for securing wireless LANs.

WEP

Do not rely solely on WEP, no matter how well you have it implemented as an end-to-end wireless LAN security solution. A wireless environment protected with only WEP is not a secure environment. When using WEP, do not use WEP keys that are related to the SSID or to the organization. Make WEP keys very difficult to remember and to figure out. In many cases, the WEP key can be easily guessed just by looking at the SSID or the name of the organization.

WEP is an effective solution for reducing the risk of casual eavesdropping. Because an individual who is not maliciously trying to gain access, but just happens to see your network, will not have a matching WEP key, that individual would be prevented from accessing your network.

Cell Sizing

In order to reduce the chance of eavesdropping, an administrator should make sure that the cell sizes of access points are appropriate. The majority of hackers look for the locations where very little time and energy must be spent gaining access into the network. For this reason, it is important not to have access points emitting strong signals that extend out into the organization's parking lot (or similar unsecure locations) unless absolutely necessary. Some enterprise-level access points allow for the configuration of power output, which effectively controls the size of the RF cell around the access point. If an eavesdropper in your parking lot cannot detect your network, then your network is not susceptible to this kind of attack.

It may be tempting for network administrators to always use the maximum power output settings on all wireless LAN devices in an attempt to get maximum throughput and coverage, but such blind configuration will come at the expense of security. An access point has a cell size that can be controlled by the amount of power that the access point is emitting and the antenna gain of the antenna being used. If that cell is inappropriately large to the point that a passerby can detect, listen to, or even gain access to the network, then the network is unnecessarily vulnerable to attack. The necessary and appropriate cell size can be determined by a proper site survey (Chapter 11). The proper cell size should be documented along with the configuration of the access point or bridge for each particular area. It may be necessary to install two access points with smaller cell sizes to avoid possible security vulnerabilities in some instances.

Try to locate your access points towards the center of your house or building. This will minimize the signal leak outside of the intended range. If you are using external antennas, selecting the right type of antenna can be helpful in minimizing signal range. Turn off access points when they are not in use. This will minimize your exposure to potential hackers and lighten the network management burden.

User Authentication

Since user authentication is a wireless LAN's weakest link, and the 802.11 standard does not specify any method of user authentication, it is imperative that the administrator implement user-based authentication as soon as possible upon installing a wireless LAN infrastructure. User authentication should be based on device-independent schemes like usernames and passwords, biometrics, smart cards, token-based systems, or some other type of secure means of identifying the user, not the hardware. The solution you implement should support bi-directional authentication between an authentication server (such as RADIUS) and the wireless clients.

RADIUS is the de-facto standard in user authentication systems in most every information technology market. Access points send user authentication requests to a RADIUS server, which can either have a built-in (local) user database or can pass the authentication request through to a domain controller, an NDS server, an Active Directory server, or even an LDAP compliant database system.

A few RADIUS vendors have streamlined their RADIUS products to include support for the latest family of authentication protocols such as the many types of EAP.

Administering a RADIUS server can be very simple or very complicated, depending on the implementation. Because wireless security solutions are very sensitive, care should be taken when choosing a RADIUS server solution to make sure that the wireless network administrator can administer it or can work effectively with the existing RADIUS administrator.

Something else to think about when user authentication is considered is that wireless security has many faces – man-in-the-middle attacks, eavesdropping, "free rides", etc. -and you have to think about all of them. One way to ensure the ongoing security of your network when users are mobile is to ensure that users are re-authenticated every time their IP address or network attachment point changes.

Security Needs

Choose a security solution that fits your organizations' needs and budget, both for today and tomorrow. Wireless LANs are gaining popularity so fast partly because of their ease of implementation. That means that a wireless LAN that began as an access point and 5 clients could quickly grow to 15 access points and 300 clients across a corporate campus. The same security mechanism that worked just fine for one access point will not be as acceptable, or as secure, for 300 users. An organization could waste money on security solutions that will be quickly outgrown as the wireless LAN grows. In many cases, organizations already have security in place such as intrusion detection systems, firewalls, and RADIUS servers. When deciding on a wireless LAN solution, leveraging existing equipment is an important factor in keeping costs down.

Use Additional Security Tools

Taking advantage of the technology that is available, such as VPNs, firewalls, intrusion detection systems (IDS), standards and protocols such as 802.1x and EAP, and client authentication with RADIUS can help make wireless solutions secure above and beyond what the 802.11 standard requires. The cost and time to implement these solutions vary greatly from SOHO solutions to large enterprise solutions.

Monitoring for Rogue Hardware

To discover rogue access points, regular access point discovery sessions should be scheduled but not announced. Actively discovering and removing rogue access points will likely keep out hackers and allow the administrator to maintain network control and security. Regular security audits should be performed to locate incorrectly configured access points that could be security risks. This task can be done while monitoring the network for rogue access points as part of a regular security routine. Present configurations should be compared to past configurations in order to see if users or hackers have reconfigured the access points. Access logs should be implemented and monitored for the purpose of finding any irregular access on the wireless segment. This type of monitoring can even help find lost or stolen wireless client devices.

Switches, not hubs

Another simple guideline to follow is always connecting access points to switches instead of hubs. Hubs are broadcast devices, so every packet received by the hub will be sent out on all of the hub's other ports. If access points are connected to hubs, then every packet traversing the wired segment will be broadcast across the wireless segment as well. This functionality gives hackers additional information such as passwords and IP addresses.

Wireless DMZ

Another idea in implementing security for wireless LAN segments is to create a wireless demilitarized zone (WDMZ). Creating these WDMZs using firewalls or routers can be costly depending on the level of implementation. WDMZs are generally implemented in medium- and large-scale wireless LAN deployments. Because access points are basically unsecured and untrusted devices, they should be separated from other network segments by a firewall device, as illustrated in Figure 10.15.

FIGURE 10.15 Wireless DMZ

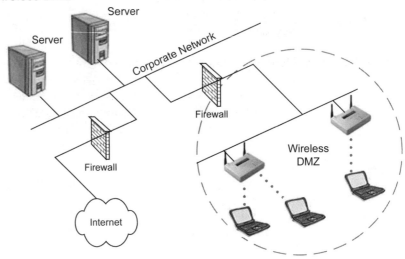

Firmware & Software Updates

Update the firmware and drivers on your access points and wireless cards. It is always wise to use the latest firmware and drivers on your access points and wireless cards. Manufacturers commonly fix known issues, security holes, and enable new features with these updates.

Mutual Authentication

It is possible that a rogue client could be placed on your network configured with the correct SSID and subsequently hijack your clients, thus creating a DOS situation for them. The clients are prevented from reaching the real network and thus are being denied service. By implementing a mutual authentication solution using a RADIUS server with the Access Point between the client and the RADIUS server, you can provide a means for both the client and the network to verify each other's identity. The client authenticates the network via a RADIUS server; likewise, the RADIUS server authenticates the client as shown in Figure 10.16. The two sides of the authentication scheme are decoupled on separate secure channels, with the access point in the middle. Many mutual authentication solutions have been developed which can be quickly and easily implemented to greatly enhance the security of your wireless network design. Solutions from Cisco (LEAP) and Funk Software have been well tested and ready to implement in a network of any size.

FIGURE 10.16 Mutual Authentication

1. Client associates
   with Access Point

2. Access Point blocks
   all user requests
   to access LAN

3. User performs
   network logon
   (Username &
   Password)

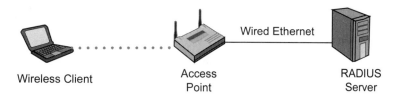

Wired Ethernet

Wireless Client

Access
Point

RADIUS
Server

Key Terms

Before taking the exam, you should be familiar with the following terms:

Initialization Vector

key server

RC4

Rijndale

Wi-Fi hot spot

Review Questions

1. Which one of the following is NOT one of the criteria for WEP implementation, according to the 802.11 standard?

    A. Exportable

    B. Reasonably Strong

    C. Self-Synchronizing

    D. Computationally Efficient

    E. Mandatory

2. Centralized encryption key servers should be used if possible. Which one of the following reasons would NOT be a good reason to implement centralized encryption key servers?

    A. Centralized key generation

    B. Centralized key distribution

    C. Centralized key coding and encryption

    D. On-going key rotation

    E. Reduced key management overhead

3. Typical key rotation options implemented by various manufacturers for encryption key generation include which of the following? Choose all that apply.

    A. Per-packet

    B. Per-session

    C. Per-user

    D. Per-broadcast

    E. Per-frame

4. A WEP key using a 40-bit secret key concatenated with the initialization vector to form the WEP key, creates what level of encryption?

    A. 24-bit

    B. 40-bit

    C. 64-bit

    D. 128-bit

5. Which piece of information on a wireless LAN is encrypted with WEP enabled?

    A. The data payload of the frame

    B. The MAC addresses of the frame

    C. Beacon management frames

    D. Shared Key challenge plaintext

6. AES uses which one of the following encryption algorithms?

    A. Fresnel

    B. NAV

    C. Rijndale

    D. Rinehart

7. What are the three types of filtering that can be performed on a wireless LAN?

    A. SSID filtering

    B. MAC address filtering

    C. Protocol filtering

    D. 802.11 standard filtering

    E. Manufacturer hardware filtering

8. SSID filtering is a basic form of access control, and is not considered secure for which of the following reasons? Choose all that apply.

    A. The SSID is broadcasted in the clear in every access point beacon by default

    B. It is very simple to find out the SSID of a network using a protocol analyzer

    C. The SSID of a wireless LAN client must match the SSID on the access point in order for the client to authenticate and associate to the access point

    D. SSID encryption is easy to break with freeware utilities

9. Using a _____, the network administrator can reduce the time it takes to rotate WEP keys across an enterprise network.

    A. Distributed Encryption Key Server

    B. Centralized Encryption Key Server

    C. Router Access Control List

    D. Filter Application Server

10. MAC filtering is NOT susceptible to which one of the following intrusions?

    A. Theft of a PC card

    B. MAC address spoofing

    C. Protocol analyzer collecting the MAC addresses of all wireless LAN clients

    D. MAC filter bypass equipment

11. Which of the following are types of wireless LAN attacks? Choose all that apply.

    A. Passive attacks

    B. Antenna wind loading

    C. Access point flooding

    D. Active attacks

12. The following statement, "MAC addresses of wireless LAN clients are broadcasted in the clear by access points and bridges, even when WEP is implemented," is which of the following?

    A. Always true

    B. Always false

    C. Dependent upon manufacturer WEP implementation

13. The best solution for a jamming attack would be which one of the following?

    A. To use a spectrum analyzer to locate the RF source and then remove it

    B. Increase the power on the wireless LAN to overpower the jamming signal

    C. Shut down the wireless LAN segment and wait for the jamming signal to dissipate

    D. Arrange for the FCC to shut down the jamming signal's transmitter

14. Why should access points be connected to switches instead of hubs?

    A. Hubs are faster than switches and can handle high utilization networks

    B. Hubs are full duplex and switches are only half duplex

    C. Hubs are broadcast devices and pose an unnecessary security risk

    D. Access points are not capable of full-duplex mode

15. Which of the following protocols are network security tools above and beyond what is specified by the 802.11? Choose all that apply.

    A. 802.1x and EAP

    B. 8011.g

    C. VPNs

    D. 802.11x and PAP

16. An enterprise wireless gateway is positioned at what point on the wired network segment?

    A. Between the access point and the wired network upstream

    B. Between the access point and the wireless network clients

    C. Between the switch and the router on the wireless network segment

    D. In place of a regular access point on the wireless LAN segment

17. Networks using the 802.1x protocol control network access on what basis? Choose all that apply.

    A. Per–user

    B. Per–port

    C. Per-session

    D. Per-MAC Address

    E. Per-SSID

18. Which of the following is NOT true regarding wireless LAN security?

    A. WEP cannot be relied upon to provide a complete security solution.

    B. A wireless environment protected with only WEP is not a secure environment.

    C. The 802.11 standard specifies user authentication methods

    D. User authentication is a wireless LAN's weakest link

19. Which of the following demonstrates the need for accurate RF cell sizing? Choose all that apply.

    A. Co-located access points having overlapping cells

    B. A site survey utility can see 10 or more access points from many points in the building

    C. Users on the sidewalk passing by your building can see your wireless LAN

    D. Users can attach to the network from their car parked in the facility's parking lot

20. For maximum security wireless LAN user authentication should be based on which of the following? Choose all that apply.

    A.   Device-independent schemes such as user names and passwords

    B.   Default authentication processes

    C.   MAC addresses only

    D.   SSID and MAC address

Answers to Review Questions

1. E. The 802.11 standard specified that the use of WEP is to be optional. If a manufacturer is to make its hardware compliant to the standard, the administrator must be able to enable or disable WEP as necessary.

2. C. Encryption key servers are useful in performing the same tasks as an administrator (changing WEP keys), except that the server can do it much faster and more efficiently. Servers of this type bring value to the network security architecture by being able to create and distribute encryption keys quickly and easily.

3. A, B. Most centralized encryption key servers have the ability to implement key rotation on a per-packet or a per-session basis. Be careful when implementing per-packet key rotation that you don't add more overhead to the network than the network can withstand.

4. C. The initialization vector (IV) is a 24-bit number used to start and track the wireless frames moving between nodes. The IV is concatenated with the secret key to yield the WEP key. With a 40-bit secret key added to a 24-bit IV, a 64-bit WEP key is generated.

5. A. Any station on the wireless segment can see the source and destination MAC addresses. Any layer 3 information such as IP addresses is encrypted. The data payload (layer 3-7 information) is encrypted. Shared Key authentication issues the plaintext challenge in clear text - only the response is encrypted.

6. C. The Rijndale algorithm was chosen by NIST for AES. There were many candidates competing for use as part of AES, but Rijndale was chosen and no backup selection has been specified.

7. A, B, C. Filtering based on SSIDs should be aimed toward segmentation of the network only, as SSID filtering does not present any real level of security. MAC addresses can be spoofed, though it's not a simple task. MAC filters are great for home and small office wireless LANs where managing lists of MAC addresses is feasible. Protocol filters should be used as a means of bandwidth control.

8. A, B. The SSID is sent as part of each beacon frame and probe response frame. Protocol analyzers, wireless LAN client driver software, and applications such as Netstumbler easily see SSIDs.

9. B. Having a single server generate and rotate encryption keys across the entire network reduces the amount of time the administrator has to devote to managing WEP on a wireless LAN.

10. D. There's no such thing as MAC filter bypass equipment, although it is possible to get past MAC filters using software applications and custom operating system configurations.

11. A, D. By passive listening to the wireless network or by connecting to access points and performing scanning and probing of network resources, a hacker is able to gain valuable information if the right precautions and security measures are not in place.

12. A. MAC addresses must always be sent in the clear so that stations may recognize both who the intended recipient is and who the source station is. Using WEP does not change this.

13. A. Depending on whether the jamming signal was originating from a malicious hacker or an unintentional nearby RF source, finding and removing the RF source is the best solution to this problem. It may not be possible to remove it, so in this case you might have to use a wireless LAN in another frequency spectrum in order to avoid the interference. Waiting on a government agency such as the FCC to respond to your complaint of a possible hacker jamming your license-free network, could take a considerable amount of time. If you locate such a malicious attacker, contacting the local law enforcement authorities is the proper procedure for eliminating the attack.

14. C. Hubs are broadcast devices that pass along all information passing through them to all of their ports. If access points are connected to hub ports, all packets on the wire will also be broadcasted across the wireless segment giving hackers more information about the network than is absolutely necessary.

15. A, C. 802.1x using EAP and VPNs both comprise good wireless LAN security solutions. There are many other solutions, and many versions of both EAP and wireless VPN solutions. Care should be taken when choosing a wireless LAN security solution to assure it both meets the needs of the network and fits the organization's

security budget.

16.   A. An enterprise wireless gateway has no wireless segments. These gateways have a downstream wired connection and a wired connection upstream that allows them to act as a gateway or firewall of sorts. Wireless LAN clients must be authenticated through this device before it may pass packets upstream into the network. Through the use of VPN tunnels, clients can even be blocked from accessing each other over the wireless segment.

17.   B. The 802.1x standard provides port-based access control. It functions by stopping a port (a connection between the edge device and the client) until the edge device authenticates the client. After authentication, the port is forwarded so that clients can establish a connection with the edge devices and pass packets across the network.

18.   C. No user authentication is specified in the 802.11 standard. User authentication is left up to the manufacturer to implement making user authentication a wireless LAN's weakest link. Never rely on WEP as an end-to-end wireless LAN security solution.

19.   B, C, D. Being able to see many access points in a given area is indicative of cell sizes being too large. Anytime someone can see or connect to your wireless LAN from outside your building without this being the specific intent of the network designer, the cell sizes are too large.

20.   A. Basing user authentication on username and passwords or other appropriate user knowledge instead of the hardware itself is a better way of securing wireless LANs.

Site Survey Fundamentals

CWNA Exam Objectives Covered:

❖ Understand the importance of and processes involved in conducting an RF site survey

❖ Identify and understand the importance of the necessary tasks involved in preparing for an RF site survey

- Gathering business requirements

- Interview management and users

- Defining security requirements

- Site-specific documentation

- Documenting existing network characteristics

❖ Identify the necessary equipment involved in performing a site survey

- Wireless LAN equipment

- Measurement tools

- Documentation

❖ Understand the necessary procedures involved in performing a site survey

- Non-RF information

- Permits and zoning requirements

- Outdoor considerations

- RF related information

- Interference sources

- Connectivity and power requirements

❖ Understand and implement RF site survey reporting procedures

- Requirements
- Methodology
- Measurements
- Security
- Graphical documentation
- Recommendations

In this chapter, we will discuss the process of conducting a site survey, also known as a "facilities analysis." We will discuss terms and concepts that you have probably heard and used before if you have ever installed a wireless network from the ground up. If wireless is new to you, you might notice that some of the terms and concepts carry over from traditional wired networks. Concepts like throughput needs, power accessibility, extendibility, application requirements, budget requirements, and signal range will all be key components as you conduct a site survey. We will further discuss the ramifications of a poor site survey and even no site survey at all. Our discussion will cover a checklist of tasks that you need to accomplish and equipment you will use, and we will apply those checklists to several hypothetical examples.

What is a Site Survey?

An RF site survey is a *map* to successfully implementing a wireless network.

There is no hard and fast technical definition of a site survey. You, as the CWNA candidate, must learn the process of conducting the best possible site survey for the client, whether that client is internal or external to your organization. The site survey is not to be taken lightly, and can take days or even weeks, depending on the site being surveyed. The resulting information of a quality site survey can be significantly helpful for a long time to come.

 If you do not perform a thorough site survey, the wireless LAN, installed according to the site survey, might never work properly, and you (or your client) could spend thousands of dollars on hardware that doesn't do the intended job.

A site survey is the most important step in implementing any wireless network.

A site survey is a task-by-task process by which the surveyor discovers the RF behavior, coverage, interference, and determines proper hardware placement in a facility. The site survey's primary objective is to ensure that mobile workers – the wireless LAN's "clients"– experience continually strong RF signal strength as they move around their facility. At the same time, clients must remain connected to the host device or other mobile computing devices and their work applications. Employees who are using the wireless LAN should never have to think about the wireless LAN. Proper performance of the tasks listed in this section will ensure a quality site survey and can help achieve a seamless operating environment every time you install a wireless network.

Site surveying involves analyzing a site from an RF perspective and discovering what kind of RF coverage a site needs in order to meet the business goals of the customer. During the site survey process, the surveyor will ask many questions about a variety of topics, which are covered in this chapter. These questions allow the surveyor to gather as much information as possible to make an informed recommendation about what the best options are for hardware, installation, and configuration of a wireless LAN.

A site survey is an attempt to define the contours of RF coverage from an RF source (an access point or bridge) in a particular facility. Many issues can arise that prevent the RF signal from reaching certain parts of the facility. For example, if an access point were placed in the center of a medium-sized room, it would be assumed that there would be RF coverage throughout the room. This is not necessarily true due to phenomena such as multipath, near/far, and hidden node. There may be "holes" in the RF coverage pattern due to multipath or stations that cannot talk to the network due to near/far.

Though a surveyor may be documenting the site survey results, another individual (possibly the RF design engineer) may be doing the site survey analysis to determine best placement of hardware. Therefore, all of the results of the entire survey must be documented. The surveyor and the designer may be the same person, or in larger organizations they may be different people. Organized and accurate documentation by the site surveyor will result in a much better design and installation process.

A proper site survey provides detailed specifications addressing coverage, interference sources, equipment placement, power considerations, and wiring requirements. Furthermore, the site survey documentation serves as a guide for the network design and for installing and verifying the wireless communication infrastructure.

If you *don't* do a site survey, you will not have the knowledge of your clients' needs, the sources of interference, the "dead" spots (where no RF coverage exists), where to install the access point(s), and, worst of all, you won't be able to estimate for the client how much the wireless LAN will cost to implement!

Finally, although performing RF site surveys is the *only* business that some firms engage in, a good site survey can be the best sales tool that a network integration firm has at its disposal. Performing a quality site survey can, and many times should, lead to your organization performing the installation and integration of the wireless LAN for which the site survey was done.

Preparing for a Site Survey

The planning of a wireless LAN involves collecting information and making decisions. The following is a list of the most basic questions that must be answered before the actual physical work of the site survey begins. These questions are purposely open-ended because each one results in more information being passed from the client to the surveyor, thus making the surveyor better prepared to go on-site and do the site survey. Most, if not all, of these questions can be answered via phone, fax, or email, assuming the people with the answers to the questions are available. Again, the more prepared one is before arriving at the site (with a site survey toolkit), the more valuable the time on-site will be. Some of the topics you may want to question the network management about before performing your site survey:

- Facilities Analysis
- Existing Networks
- Area Usage & Towers
- Purpose & Business Requirements
- Bandwidth & Roaming Requirements
- Available Resources
- Security Requirements

Facility Analysis

What kind of facility is it?

This question is very basic, but the answer can make a big impact on the site survey work for the next several days. Consider the obvious differences that would exist in conducting a site survey of a small office with one server and 20 clients versus performing a site survey of a large international airport. Aside from the obvious size differences, you must take into account the number of users, security requirements, bandwidth requirements, budget, and what kind of impact jet engines have on 802.11 RF signals, if any, etc.

All that and more comes from this one question. Your answers could come in the form of pictures, written descriptions, or blueprints whenever possible. The more you know before you get to the facility, the better prepared you will be when you actually arrive. Depending on the facility type, there will be standard issues to be addressed. Knowing the facility type before arrival will save time on-site.

To demonstrate the standard issues discussed above, we will consider two facility types. The first example is a hospital. Hospitals are subject to an act of Congress known as HIPAA. HIPAA mandates that hospitals (and other like healthcare organizations) keep certain information private. This topic alone demonstrates that, when doing a site survey for a hospital, security planning must be of prime importance.

Hospitals also have radiology equipment, mesh metal glass windows, fire doors, very long hallways, elevators, mobile users (nurses and doctors), and X-ray rooms with lead-lined walls. This set of criteria shows the surveyor some obvious things to consider, like roaming across large distances, a limited number of users on an access point due to mandated security (which means much security protocol overhead on the wireless LAN), and medical applications that are often connection-oriented between the client and server. To ensure only the necessary amount of coverage for certain areas, semi-directional antennas may be used instead of omni antennas. Semi-directional antennas tend to reduce multipath since the signal is being broadcasted in less directions. Elevators are everywhere, and cause signal blockage and possibly RF interference. Elevators are basically "dead" RF zones. A hospital site survey is good training ground for individuals wanting to get immersed in wireless LAN technology.

The second facility type is a real estate office with approximately 25 agents. In this environment, security is important, but not mandated by law, so rudimentary security measures might suffice. Coverage will likely be adequate with only 1 or 2 centrally-located access points, and bandwidth requirements would be nominal since most of the access is Internet-based or transferring small files back and forth to the file server.

These two scenarios are quite different, but both need site surveys. The amount of time that it will take to perform a site survey at each facility is also very different. The real estate office may not even take a full day, whereas the hospital, depending on size, might take a week or more. Many of the activities of the users in each facility, such as roaming, are very different. With nurses and doctors in a hospital, roaming is just part of the job. In the relatively small, multi-room facility of the real estate firm, users sit at their desks and access the wireless network from that one location, so roaming may not be necessary.

Existing Networks

Is there already a network (wired or wireless) in place?

This question is also basic, but you must know if the client is starting from scratch or if the wireless LAN must work with an existing infrastructure. If there is an existing infrastructure, what it consists of must be known. Most of the time there is an existing infrastructure, which opens the door to a myriad of questions that need answering. Documentation of existing wireless LAN hardware, frequencies being used, number of users, throughput, etc., must be taken into account so that decisions can be made on how the new equipment (if needed) will fit in. It may also be the case that the customer did the initial installation, and has since outgrown the initial installation. If the existing setup functions poorly, this poor performance must also be noted so the problems are not repeated.

Questions commonly asked of the network administrator or manager include:

- What Network Operating Systems (NOS) are in use?
- How many users (today and 2 years from now) need simultaneous access to the wireless network?
- What is the bandwidth (per user) requirement on the wireless network?
- What protocols are in use over the wireless LAN?
- What channels and spread spectrum technologies are currently in use?
- What wireless LAN security measures are in place?
- Where are wired LAN connection points (wiring closets) located in the facility?
- What are the client's expectations of what a wireless LAN will bring to their organization?
- Is there a naming convention for infrastructure devices such as routers, switches, access points, and wireless bridges in place (Figure 11.1)? If not, who is responsible for creating one?

FIGURE 11.1   Naming Conventions

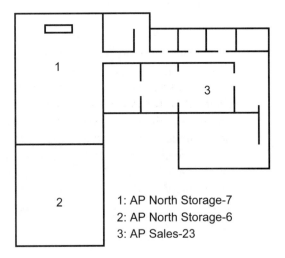

1: AP North Storage-7
2: AP North Storage-6
3: AP Sales-23

Obtain a detailed network diagram (topology map) from the current network administrator. When one or more wireless LANs are already in place, the site survey will become all the more difficult, especially if the previous installations were not done properly. Doing a site survey with an ill-functioning wireless LAN in place can be almost impossible without the cooperation of the network administrator to disable the network where and when needed. Upgrades of existing wired infrastructure devices might also be necessary to enhance throughput and security on the wireless LAN.

 It may be necessary to sign a confidentiality agreement in order to obtain network diagrams or blueprints from your client.

Where are the network wiring closets located?

It is not uncommon to find that what seems like the most appropriate location for installing an access point ends up being too far from a wiring closet to allow for upstream network connectivity. Knowing where these wiring closets are ahead of time will save on time later on. Locations of these wiring closets should be documented on the network topology map, blueprints, or other facility maps. There are solutions for these problems such as using access points or bridges as repeaters, but this method of connectivity should be avoided where possible. Connecting bridges and access points directly into the wired distribution system is almost always favored.

Has an access point/bridge naming convention been devised?

If a wireless LAN is not currently in place, a logical naming convention may need to be devised by the network manager. Using a logical naming convention with access points and bridges on the wireless network will make managing them, once they are in place, much easier. For the site surveyor, having logical names in place for each access point and bridge will facilitate the task of documenting the placement of units in the RF Site Survey Report.

Area Usage & Towers

Is the wireless LAN going to be used indoors, outdoors, or both?

Are there frequent hurricanes or tornadoes occurring in this site's locale? Outdoor usage of wireless LAN gear creates many situations and potential obstacles to installing and maintaining a wireless LAN. As we discussed in prior sections, a strong wind can eliminate the signal on a long distance wireless link. If inclement weather such as ice or strong rain is often present, radomes (a domelike shell transparent to radio-frequency radiation, used to house RF antennas) might be considered for protecting outdoor antennas. If bridges or access points need to be mounted outdoors as well, a NEMA-compliant weatherproof enclosure might be considered, as shown in Figure 11.2.

FIGURE 11.2   NEMA Enclosure

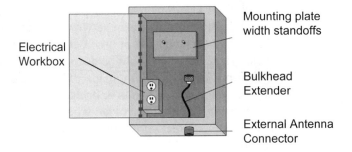

Outdoor wireless connections are vulnerable to security attacks, since the intruder would not have to be inside the building to get into the network. Once it is determined that the survey is for indoors, outdoors, or both, obtain any and all property survey documents and diagrams that are available. Indoors, these documents will show you the floor layout, firewalls, building structure information, wiring closets, and other valuable information. Outdoors, these documents will show how far the outdoor wireless LAN can safely extend without significant chance of intrusion.

When outdoors, look for RF signal obstructions such as other buildings, trees, mountains, etc. Checking for other wireless LAN signals at the point where outdoor antennas will be installed is a good idea. If channel 1 in a DSSS system were to be used, and subsequently it was found that channel 1 is in use by a nearby outdoor system using an omni-directional antenna, document in the report that a channel that does not overlap channel 1 should be used for this bridge link.

Remember that trees not only pose a potential problem in regards to Fresnel Zone blockage, but may also be a source of attenuation problems during periods of rainy weather. Tree leaves collect rainwater and this will produce attenuation of your signal until the water has evaporated. If the trees in question are Pine trees, this issued becomes much smaller because Pine trees do not have the broad leaves capable of holding large amounts of water like other types of trees.

Is a tower required?

When performing a site survey, a 30-foot tower might be needed on top of a building to clear some trees that are in the direct signal path of an outdoor wireless link. If a tower is required, other questions that need to be asked might include:

- *If the roof is to be used, is it adequate to support a tower?*
- *Is a structural engineer required?*
- *Is a permit necessary?*

A structural engineer may be required to determine if a tower can be placed on top of a building without safety risks to the occupants of the building. Permits may also be necessary to install a tower.

Permits or government approval may be necessary to install a tower. For example, for towers that are more than 200 feet (61 meters) above ground level, the FCC requires that the FAA be notified prior to constructing or modifying an antenna structure (tower, pole, building, etc.). A 190-foot tall building with an 11-foot tall tower would fall into this category for example because the building (antenna structure) has been modified and exceeds 200 feet. Local municipalities must approve the building of any type of structure (antenna structures or otherwise), thus the installer/designer of such a structure should obtain proper permissions or licenses.

Purpose & Business Requirements

What is the purpose of the wireless LAN? What are the business requirements?

From a temporary office to complete data connectivity for the Olympics, the answer to this question will drive many decisions. Using the extreme example and contrast of a temporary office versus the Olympics, dozens of issues might come up such as budget, number of users, outdoor connectivity, temporary network access, and security.

Recommending a high-speed 802.11a installation for an organization that is only using a few wireless PDAs would be a poor judgment, so the needs of the users must be determined. As much information as can be gathered will be helpful in understanding how the wireless LAN is to be used. This information gathering may require interviews with some network users as well as network management.

Find out exactly what the client expects to do with the wireless LAN and what applications are going to be used over this new network. There might be several distinct and independent purposes for the wireless LAN. Thoroughly documenting the client's needs enables the network architect to design a solution that will meet all of the client's needs, and may also assist the client in their network management.

In order for the site surveyor, and subsequently the design engineer, to keep the business requirements as a main focus, the site surveyor must have a solid understanding of how the network will be used and for what reasons. By knowing how the wireless network affects the business goals of the organization, the site surveyor will be able to create a better, more thorough RF Site Survey Report.

For example, at a ski resort, skiing instructors and ski instructor supervisors use wireless handheld PDAs to coordinate skiing classes across several slopes at once. Since these handhelds are used over a vast stretch of land, range is very important, but the small amount of data being carried over the wireless network means that many of these wireless PDAs can be used on a single access point at any given time without degraded performance. In contrast, a small workgroup of graphic designers, sitting in one room needing access to file servers to which they transfer large images over the wireless network, need high-speed access, but range is minimal. Only a small number of this type of user (high bandwidth) should be connected to an access point at any given time.

These scenarios show how uses of wireless LANs can vary substantially. The site surveyor must know the business needs of the organization in order to effectively perform a site survey.

Bandwidth & Roaming Requirements

What bandwidth and roaming requirements are there?

The answer to this question can determine the actual technology to be implemented, and the technology to be used when doing the site survey. For example, if the client is a warehouse facility and the only purpose that the wireless LAN will serve is scanning data from box labels and sending that data to a central server, the bandwidth requirements are very small. Most data collection devices require only 2 Mbps (such as a computer on a forklift in a warehouse), but require seamless connectivity while moving. However, if the client requires that the wireless LAN will serve 35 software developers who need high-speed access to application servers, test servers, and the Internet, consider using 802.11a equipment.

The necessary speed, range, and throughput per user must be determined so that when the site survey is given to the RF design engineer, the design engineer can create a solution that is cost effective and meets the needs of the users. Figure 11.3 shows a survey diagram that will allow for 2 Mbps per user, while Figure 11.4 allows for 5.5 Mbps per user. Most companies are broken into several departments such as engineering, accounting, marketing, human resources, etc. Each department type may have different uses of the wireless LAN in their area.

FIGURE 11.3 2 Mbps data rate

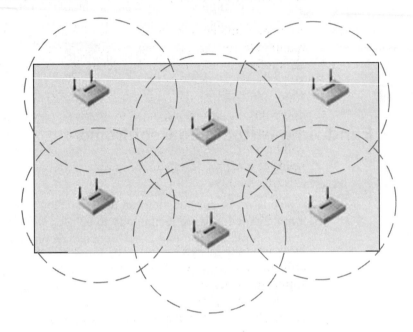

FIGURE 11.4 5.5 Mbps data rate

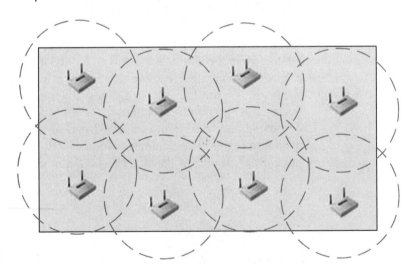

How many users are typically in a given area?

An understanding of how many users will be located in a given area is required to calculate how much throughput each user is going to have. This information is also used to determine which technology, such as 802.11b or 802.11a, would be most well suited to the needs of the users. If the network manager is not able to provide this information, the person doing the site survey will need to interview the actual users to be able to make an informed decision. Different departments within an organization will have different numbers of users. It is important to understand that the needs of one part of a facility might be different from the needs of another part of a facility.

What type of applications will be used over the wireless LAN?

Find out if the network is being used to transmit non time-sensitive data only, or time-sensitive data such as voice or video. High bandwidth applications such as voice or video will require greater throughput per user than an application that makes infrequent network requests. Connection-oriented applications will need to maintain connectivity while roaming. Analyzing and documenting these application requirements before the site survey will allow the site surveyor to make more informed decisions when testing areas for coverage.

Are there any non-typical times in which network needs may change for a particular area?

Changes in network needs could be something as simple as more users being on a particular shift or something as difficult to discover as seasonal changes. For example, if a building-to-building bridge link were being surveyed in winter, the trees would be without leaves. In the spring, trees will fill with leaves, which in turn fill with water, which could possibly cause problems with the wireless link.

What mobility or roaming coverage is necessary?

Users may want to roam indoors, outdoors, or both. Roaming may also have to incorporate crossing of router boundaries, maintaining VPN connectivity, and other complex situations. In this case, it would be important for the site surveyor to document these facts so that the wireless network design engineer would have all of the facts before presenting a solution to the customer. There may be areas within or around a facility that require special connectivity solutions, due to blockage of RF coverage or to special security requirements, in order to provide roaming.

Available Resources

What are the available resources?

Among topics to discuss with the network manager regarding available resources are the project's budget, the amount of time allotted for the project, and whether or not the organization has administrators trained on wireless networks. If documentation of previous site surveys, current topology and facility maps, and current design plans are available, the site surveyor should request copies of these plans. It is possible that the network administrator may not give access to all of these resources, citing security reasons. If so, then the site survey may take additional time.

Are facility blueprints available (electronic or printed)?

Among the first items to request from a network manager are blueprints or some kind of map showing the layout of the facility, as shown in Figure 11.5. Without the official building or facility schematics, a diagram must be created that shows the dimensions of the areas, the offices, where the walls are located, network closets, power outlets, etc.

FIGURE 11.5 Blueprints or floor plans

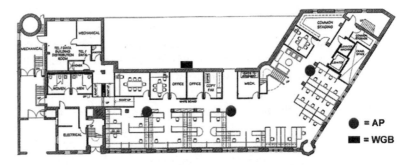

Creating a facility drawing can be a time-consuming task. If it is necessary to manually create such a document, simple things like notebook paper with grid lines are helpful in being efficient as the site survey is performed. This information can later be put into Visio, AutoCAD, or other such applications for professional presentation to the customer as part of the RF Site Survey Report.

Are there any previous site survey reports available?

If a company has previously had a site survey performed, having that site survey report available can cut down on the time it takes for the new survey to be completed. Be sure that the previous report does not bias the decisions made regarding the current site survey.

Is a facilities escort or security badge required?

A security badge or an escort may be required to move throughout the facility freely. When performing a site survey, every square foot of the facility is usually covered in order to answer all of the questions needed to define the RF coverage.

It has been said that RF site surveying is 90% walking, and 10% surveying. This is usually true, so one should wear very comfortable shoes and make sure that an escort (if necessary) has plenty of time while the survey is being performed.

Is physical access to wiring closets and the roof available if needed?

Physical access to both the roof and to wiring closets may be needed to determine antenna placement and network connection points.

Security Requirements

What level of network security is necessary?

Customers may have very strict demands for data security, or in some cases, no security may be required. It should be explained to the customer that WEP should not be the only wireless LAN security method used because WEP can be easily circumvented. Briefly educating the customer on available security options is an important step in getting started with a site survey. A discussion with the customer will provide them enough information to feel informed and will allow them to better understand the solutions likely to be presented by the design engineer. After this discussion, the customer may likely have several questions involving wireless network security that may aid the site surveyor in properly documenting the customer's business needs.

What corporate policies are in place regarding wireless LAN security implementation and management?

The network manager may not have any security policies in place. If the customer already has a wireless LAN in place, the existing security policies should be reviewed before the site survey is started. If corporate security policies relating to wireless LANs do not exist, ask questions about security requirements regarding installations of wireless LANs.

During the design phase (design is not part of the site survey itself) the RF design engineer could include a security report detailing security suggestions for this particular installation. The network administrator could then take this information and form a corporate policy based on the suggestions. Security policies may differ slightly between small, medium and enterprise installations, and can sometimes be re-used. There are general security practices that are common to all installations of wireless LANs. These policies may also include how to manage the wireless network once it is installed.

Preparation Exercises

As a thought-provoking exercise, consider some of the hypothetical examples mentioned earlier (small office wireless LAN, international airport wireless LAN, and a wireless LAN for connecting all the computers at the Olympics), and then ask the following questions:

- Are the users mobile within the facility (e.g., do they have portable computers or desktops)?

- How far – inside or outside – will the users roam and still need connectivity?

- What level of access do these users need to sensitive data on the network? Is security required? How secure is "secure enough"?

- Will these users be able to take their laptop computers away from the wireless LAN where the wireless LAN cards could be stolen?

- Do these users use any bandwidth-intensive, time-sensitive, or connection-oriented applications?

- How often do these users change departments or locations?

- Will any or all of these users have Internet access, and what are the policies regarding email and downloads?

- Does the office/work environment of these users ever change for special events that could disrupt a wireless LAN?

- Who currently supports these users on the existing network, and are they qualified to support wireless users?

- If the users are mobile, what type of mobile computing device do they use? (e.g., PDA or Laptop)

- How often and for how long will the users with laptops work without A/C power?

There are many specific questions about the users of the wireless LAN and their needs, and this information is vital to the site survey. The more information that can be gathered about who will be using the wireless LAN and for what purposes the easier it will be to conduct the site survey.

Preparation Checklist

Below is a general list of items that should be obtained from or scheduled with the client prior to visiting the site for the purpose of doing the site survey, if possible.

- ❑ Building blueprints (including power source documentation)

- ❑ Previous wireless LAN site survey documentation

- ❑ Current network diagram (topology map)

- ❑ A meeting with the network administrator

- ❑   A meeting with the building manager
- ❑   A meeting with the security officer
- ❑   Access to all areas of the facility to be affected by the wireless LAN
- ❑   Access to wiring closets
- ❑   Access to roof (if outdoor antennas are anticipated)
- ❑   Future construction plans, if available

Now that all of these questions are answered and complete documentation of the facility has been made, you are ready to leave your office and go on site.

Site Survey Equipment

This section will cover the wireless LAN equipment and tools required for a site survey. In the most basic indoor cases, you will need at least one access point, a variety of antennas, antenna cables and connectors, a laptop computer (or PDA) with a wireless PC card, some site survey utility software, and <u>lots</u> of paper. There are some minor things that can be added to your mobile toolkit such as double-sided tape (for temporarily mounting antennas to the wall), a DC-to-AC converter and batteries (for powering the access point where there's no source of AC power), a digital camera for taking pictures of particular locations within a facility, a set of two-way radios if working in teams, and a secure case for the gear. Some manufacturers sell site survey kits already configured, but in many cases, the individual prefers to select the tool kit and wireless LAN equipment piece by piece to assure that they get all of the pieces they need. A more comprehensive list of equipment required during a site survey is provided in a checklist at the end of this section.

Access Point

The access point used during a site survey should have variable output power and external antenna connectors. The variable output power feature allows for easy sizing of coverage cells during the site survey. This tool is particularly useful for situations involving long hallways such as in a hospital.

Very few manufacturers have a variable output power feature in an access point, but more vendors are expected to add this feature in the future. It is not hard to see how changing output power in software is more convenient than adding, mounting, and then dismounting and removing antennas with different amounts of gain.

Many experienced site survey professionals have an access point that operates on AC power connected to a DC-to-AC converter, which, in turn, is connected, to a battery pack. This configuration makes the access point mobile, and able to be placed anywhere the site surveyor needs to perform testing. This group of components can be tie-strapped together, or put into a single, portable enclosure. There are companies that have pieced together such a "kit" for the sole purpose of making site surveying easier. Many times the access point will be placed on a ladder or on top of the ceiling tiles while the antenna is temporarily mounted to a wall. Having completely portable gear with no need for AC power makes the site survey go much faster than it would otherwise.

Mobile access points mounted to battery packs and DC-to-AC converters may tend to look like some sort of dangerous device, and may be confiscated at airports. Make sure you disclose to all security, airports, and otherwise, exactly what this configuration is, and what it is for. Placing such devices in a hard-shell travel case and checking the case is likely a better scenario than having it as a carry-on item.

PC Card and Utilities

High quality wireless pc cards will come with site survey utility software, as shown in Figure 11.6. The site survey utilities from the different manufacturers will vary in their functionality, but most offer a link speed indicator and signal strength meter at a minimum. These two tools will provide general indications of coverage. To perform a quality site survey, the following actual quantitative measurements should be recorded:

- Signal strength (measured in dBm)

- Noise floor (measured in dBm)

- Signal-to-noise ratio ("SNR") (measured in dB)

- Link speed

Only a few vendors offer this complete set of tools in their client utility software. An additional tool that can be utilized is a spectrum analyzer, which is used for finding sources of RF interference. With quality site surveying software (whether using one or more wireless PC cards), site survey measurements can be efficiently completed with accuracy.

FIGURE 11.6   Site Monitor application

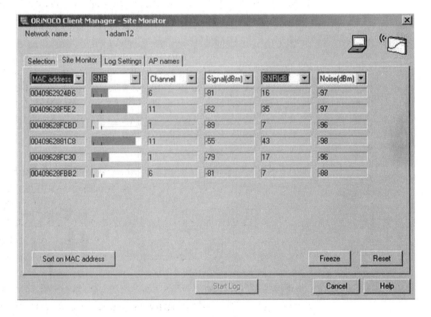

While walking around the intended coverage area, pay particular attention to the SNR measurement because this measurement shows the strength of the RF signal versus the background noise. This measurement shows the viability of the RF link, and is a good indicator of whether or not a client will connect and remain connected. Many experts agree that an SNR measurement of 22 dB or more is a viable RF link, but there is no hard and fast rule for this measurement. Whether a link is actually viable or not depends on factors other than just SNR, but as long as a link is stable and the access point provides the client with a level of RF power significantly above its sensitivity threshold, the link can be considered viable.

Having a utility that can measure the signal strength, the SNR, and the background RF noise level (called the "noise floor") is very useful. Knowing the signal strength is useful for finding out if an obstacle is blocking the RF signal or if the access point is not putting out enough power. The SNR measurement lets the site surveyor know if the link is clean and clear enough to be considered viable. Knowing the noise level is useful in determining if RF interference is causing the link a problem or if the level of RF in the environment has changed from the time that a baseline was established. An engineer can use all three of these measurements to make design and troubleshooting determinations.

One function of a wireless PC card that is particularly useful is the ability to change the power output at the client station during the site survey. This feature is useful because a site surveyor should test for situations in which near/far or hidden node problems might exist. Not all site surveyors have the luxury of taking the time to do this sort of testing, but this feature is useful when time permits.

Third party utilities such as Netstumbler are valuable utilities during a site survey in which there are already access points and bridges in place. These utilities enable the site surveyor to find all of these units quickly and record their information (such as MAC address, SSID, WEP status, signal strength, SNR, noise, etc.). These utilities can replace what the driver software and manufacturer utilities miss in many cases.

Link speed monitor utility software can be used to measure the wireless link speed. This information is useful in case part of the site survey requirement is to size or shape the cells for 11 Mbps usage by clients. As we learned earlier, Dynamic Rate Shifting (DRS) allows a client to automatically downshift link speeds as range increases. If the business requirements are for all clients to maintain 11 Mbps connectivity while roaming, then proper coverage patterns must be documented during the site survey.

Laptops & PDAs

A laptop computer or PDA unit is used by the site surveyor for checking for signal strength and coverage while roaming around the facility. Many site survey professionals have begun using PDAs instead of laptop computers to perform the site survey because of battery life and portability. PDAs can report the same information and connect to the network in the same way as the laptop without the 3 - 7 pounds of extra weight that a laptop weighs. Three to seven pounds might not seem like much weight, but after carrying a laptop of this weight around a facility that measures over a million square feet (which is a common facility size), a PDA that supports the functionality you need to do your site survey may seem like a trivial purchase. Most manufacturers make Pocket PC and Windows CE drivers and utilities (including the site survey utilities) for their PCMCIA cards.

There are miniature laptops available on the market weighing as little as 1.5 pounds, which also serve the same purpose of having a more portable unit for site surveying. However, these ultra-portable laptops tend to cost many times as much as a PDA.

Simple screen-capture software is also beneficial. For reporting purposes, screenshots show the actual results that the site monitoring software displayed. These screenshots will be presented to the customer as part of the RF Site Survey Report, which is why custom screen capture software is useful. Screen capture software packages are available for Windows, Pocket PC, and Linux operating systems.

Laptop batteries rarely last more than 3 hours, and a site survey might last 8-10 hours per day. Always having fresh batteries on hand will keep you productive while on-site. Without the luxury of extra laptop batteries, the only alternative is to charge the batteries during a break, which might not be a good alternative since many laptop batteries charge slowly. Another solution would be to find a very small, power-efficient laptop whose batteries are specified to last much longer than the typical 2-3 hours. As mentioned before, PDA batteries tend to last longer than do laptop batteries.

Paper

Both the surveyor and the network designer should make hard copy (paper) documentation of all findings in great detail for future reference. Digital photographs of a facility make finding a particular location within the facility much easier and serve as graphical information for the RF Site Survey Report as well. During most surveys scratch paper, grid paper, and copies of blueprints or floor plans are necessary. When added to the amount of equipment that will be carried around, this amount of paper and documentation tends to become a burden. For this reason, a sufficiently large mobile equipment cart that can contain all the necessary gear is quite useful while moving through a facility.

There are no industry standard forms for recording all the data that will be necessary during even the smallest site survey. However, it will prove very useful to create a set of forms that suits your style of work and recording, and to use these same forms on every site survey. Not only will this type of uniformity help you communicate your findings to the client, but it will also help maintain accurate and easy to understand records of past site surveys. These forms will be used during the creation of your site survey report as a reference for all readings taken during the site survey.

Outdoor Surveys

Outdoor site surveys will take more time, effort, and equipment than will indoor surveys, which is another reason that planning ahead will greatly improve productivity once on site. If a survey to create an outdoor wireless link is being done, obtain the appropriate antennas, amplifiers, connectors, cabling, and other appropriate equipment before arriving. Generally, the more experienced site surveying professionals do the outside site surveys because of the more complex and involved calculations and configuration scenarios that are necessary for outdoor wireless LANs.

Knowing characteristics of the wireless link (distance, link speed required, power output required, etc.) beforehand will aid in determining whether just an omni antenna or an entire outdoor testing lab will be required. Remember that it takes *two or more* antennas to create a wireless link depending on the number of locations involved in the link. Binoculars, comfortable walking shoes, rain gear, different lengths of cables, different types of connectors, and some method of communicating with someone at the other end of the link (i.e., a cell phone or walkie-talkie) will also make outdoor site surveys more efficient.

Spectrum Analyzer

Spectrum analyzers come in various types. The two main categories might be considered software and hardware spectrum analyzers. Hardware spectrum analyzers are made by many different manufacturers and may cost many thousands of dollars, depending on resolution, speed, frequency range, and other parameters.

There are companies in the wireless LAN industry who have created software capable of scanning the entire 2.4 GHz range and providing a graphical display of the results, as shown in Figure 11.7. These products give a user the effective equivalent of a hardware spectrum analyzer, which, although it may not produce precisely accurate quantitative measurements, can give a user a general idea of what sources of RF are in use in the area.

As part of the spectral analysis, have all the users turn their equipment off, if possible, so that any sources of background interference can be detected, such as low power sources of narrowband interference. Low power narrowband interference is easily located while there are no other sources of RF in use, but is quite difficult to locate when many sources of RF are in use. High power narrowband is easily located with the proper test equipment regardless of additional RF sources.

FIGURE 11.7   Spectrum Analyzer screenshot

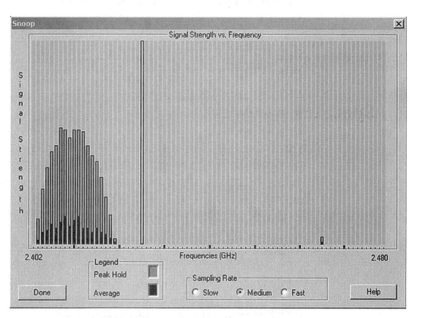

Part of a spectrum analysis should be to locate any 802.11b or 802.11a networks in use in the area around the implementation area of the proposed wireless LAN. If current or future plans involve installation of 802.11a products, it would be advantageous to both the site surveyor and the customer to know of any 5 GHz RF sources, especially if they are part of a wireless LAN.

Network Analyzer

After spectrum analysis is complete, a protocol analyzer can be used to find other wireless LANs that are present in the area (perhaps on another floor of a building), which can affect the wireless LAN implementation. The protocol analyzer will pick up any packets being transmitted by nearby wireless LANs and will provide detailed information on channels in use, distance, and signal strength, as shown in Figure 11.8.

FIGURE 11.8 Wireless Protocol analyzer screenshot

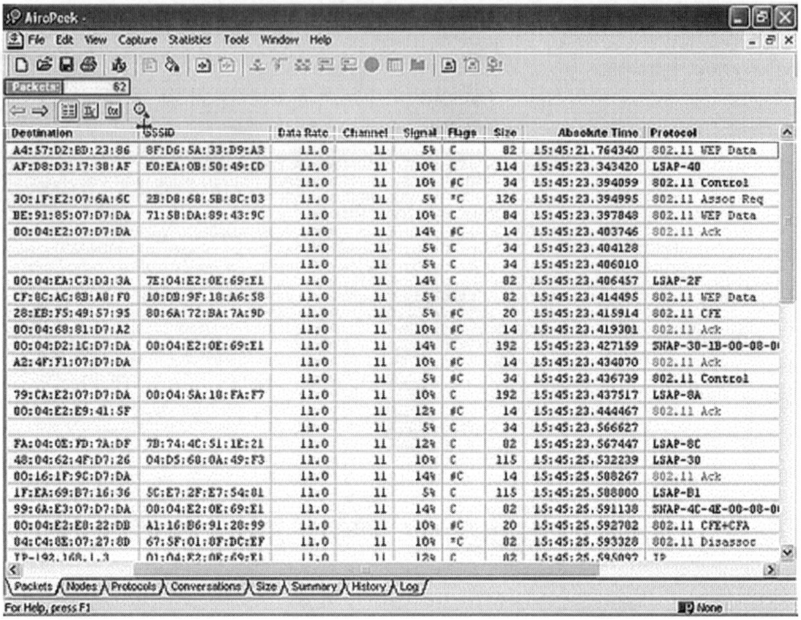

Site Survey Kit Checklist

A complete site survey kit should include:

- ❑ Laptop and/or PDA
- ❑ Wireless PC card with driver & utility software
- ❑ Access points or bridges as needed
- ❑ Battery pack & DC-to-AC converter
- ❑ Site survey utility software (loaded on laptop or PDA)
- ❑ Clipboard, pen, pencils, notebook paper, grid paper, & hi-liter
- ❑ Blueprints & network diagrams
- ❑ Indoor & outdoor antennas
- ❑ Cables & connectors
- ❑ Binoculars and two-way radios

- ❑ Umbrella and/or rain suit

- ❑ Specialized software or hardware such as a spectrum analyzer or protocol analyzer

- ❑ Tools, double-sided tape, and other items for temporary hardware mountings

- ❑ Secure and padded equipment case for housing computers, tools, and secure documents during the survey and travel to and from the survey site

- ❑ Digital camera for taking pictures of particular locations within a facility

- ❑ Battery chargers

- ❑ Variable attenuator (Figure 11.9)

- ❑ Measuring wheel (Figure 11.10)

- ❑ Appropriate cart or other mechanism for transporting equipment & documentation

FIGURE 11.9   Variable attenuator

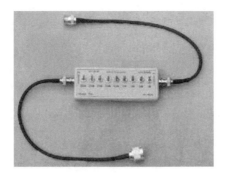

FIGURE 11.10 Distance wheel

FIGURE 11.11 Access point with a battery pack

If frequent site surveys are part of your business, create a toolkit with all this gear in it, so that you will always have the necessary site survey tools on hand. The last item in the above list – a cart – will become a valued possession after making a few dozen trips back and forth across a large facility moving the hardware and site survey support gear. Figure 11.12 shows the type of cart that can be used to carry gear.

FIGURE 11.12 Site Survey travel case

Conducting a Site Survey

Once on site with a complete site survey toolkit, walking several miles throughout the client's facility is common. RF site surveying is 10% surveying and 90% walking, so comfortable shoes should be worn when performing site surveys in large facilities. However, the general task has not changed: collecting and recording information. Beginning your site survey with the more general tasks of recording non-RF related information is usually the best course of action.

Indoor Surveys

For <u>indoor</u> surveys, locate and *record* the following items on a copy of the facility blueprints or a drawing of the facility.

- AC power outlets and grounding points

- Outdoor power receptacles and weatherproof enclosure availability

- Wired network connectivity points

- Ladders or lifts that will be needed for mounting access points

- Potential RF obstructions such as fire doors, metal blinds, metal-mesh windows, etc.

- Potential RF sources such as microwave ovens, elevator motors, baby monitors, 2.4 GHz cordless phones, etc. Figure 11.13 shows a spectrum analysis of a 2.4 GHz phone.

- Cluttered areas such as office cubical farms

FIGURE 11.13 2.4 GHz DSSS phone as seen by a spectrum analyzer

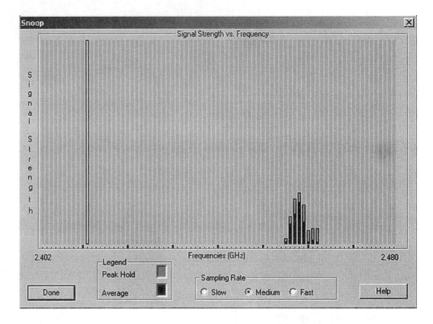

Outdoor Surveys

For <u>outdoor</u> surveys, record the following items on a copy or sketch of the property:

- Trees, buildings, lakes, or other obstructions between link sites

- If in winter, locate trees that will grow leaves during other seasons and may interfere with the RF link

- Visual and RF line of sight between transmitter and receiver
- Link distance (note: if greater than 7 miles (11.7 km), calculate compensation for Earth bulge)
- Weather hazards (wind, rain, snow, lightning) common to the area
- Tower accessibility, height, or need for a new tower
- Roof accessibility, height

Before You Begin

Once these preparatory items are checked and recorded, the next step is either to begin the RF site survey, or to obtain more information. There are several sources from the above items that could require further information from the client, including:

- Who will provide ladders and/or lifts for mounting access points on high ceilings?
- Is the client willing or able to remove trees that interfere with the Fresnel zone?
- If a new tower is needed, does the client have the necessary permits?
- Does the client have necessary permissions to install antennas on the roof and will the roof support a tower if needed?
- Do the building codes require plenum-rated equipment to be used?

Weather hazards may be easier to compensate for if you also reside in the area because you may be familiar with the area's weather patterns. If you do not live there, gathering more detailed information about local weather patterns like winds, rain, hail, tornadoes, hurricanes, and other potentially severe weather may be necessary. Remember from our troubleshooting discussion that for the most part, only severe weather causes disruption to wireless LANs. However, you must be aware of, prepare and compensate for, these types of weather before the implementation of the wireless network.

Lifts and ladders could be needed for an area where a trade show or other similar function is going to take place. The event's location may have 40-foot ceilings, and the access points may need to be mounted in the ceiling for proper coverage. OSHA has many regulations regarding ladders and ladder safety.

If a facility such as a trade show is able to provide the personnel, ladders, and lifts to do the installation, let these individuals perform the work. These individuals are familiar with OSHA regulations and have processes in place to obtain the proper permits. The RF Site Survey Report will need to reference any lifts, ladders, or permits required for installation of the wireless LAN. In many cases, a sturdy 6-foot ladder for climbing into drop-ceilings is all that is needed.

If an RF cable, Cat5 cable, access point, or any other device must be placed in the plenum (the space between the drop ceiling (false ceiling) and the hard-cap ceiling), then the item must be rated to meet building codes without being placed in a metal protective shell. This restriction applies to wiring closets as well.

RF Information Gathering

The next task will be gathering and recording data on RF coverage patterns, coverage gaps (also called "holes" or "dead spots"), data rate capabilities, and other RF-related criteria for your RF Site Survey Report.

- Range & coverage patterns
- Data rate boundaries
- Documentation
- Throughput tests & capacity planning
- Interference sources
- Wired data connectivity & AC power requirements
- Outdoor antenna placement

- Spot checks

Gather and record data for each of these areas by slowly and systematically surveying and measuring the entire facility.

Range and Coverage Patterns

Start by placing an access point in what should be a logical location. This location may not be the final location, but you have to start somewhere. The access point may get moved many times before the proper location is found, as shown in Figure 11.14. Generally speaking, starting in the center of an area is practical when using omni antennas. In contrast, when using semi-directional antennas, consider being toward one end of a stretch of intended coverage area.

When the best locations for access points are determined, mark the locations for access points and bridges with bright-colored, easily removable tape. Take a digital picture of the location for use in the site survey report. Do not make location references in the report to objects, such as a temporary desk, table, or plant that may be moved and can no longer provide a reference for locating an access point. Make sure to note orientation of your antennas because not all wireless LAN installers are familiar with antennas.

FIGURE 11.14 Access point coverage testing

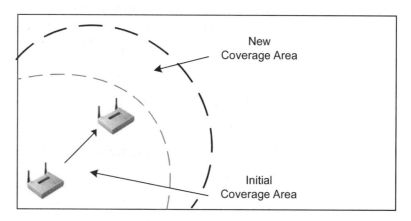

Various types of antennas can be used for site survey testing including highly-directional, semi-directional, and omni-directional. When using semi-directional antennas, be sure to take into account the side and back lobes both for coverage and security reasons. Sites may require the use of multiple antenna types to get the appropriate coverage. Long hallways might benefit from Yagi, patch, or panel antennas while omni-directional antennas would more easily cover large rooms.

There are differing opinions as to where measuring coverage and data speeds should begin. Some experts recommend starting in a corner, while some say starting in the middle of the room is best. It doesn't matter where the measurements *start* so long as every point in the room is measured during the survey and covered after installation. Pick a starting point in the room, and <u>slowly</u> walk with your laptop, PC card, and site survey utility software running. While walking, record the following data for every area of the room.

- Data rate (measured in megabits/second or Mbps)
- Signal strength (measured in dBm)
- Noise floor (measured in dBm)
- Signal-to-noise ratio ("SNR") (measured in dB)

Walking fast will speed up the survey process, but may cause you to miss dead spots or potential interference sources. Using a very simple example, Figure 11.15 illustrates what the recordings might look like on a floor plan or blueprint.

FIGURE 11.15 Marked up floor plan

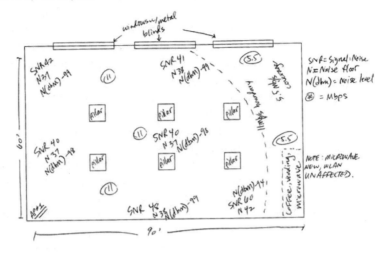

For outdoor coverage areas, be prepared to walk farther and record more. If planning an outdoor installation of an access point (to cover areas between campus buildings for example), then there are usually a very limited number of places where the access point may be mounted. For this reason, moving the access point around is rarely required. Sitting atop a building is the most common place in such an installation. There are potentially many more sources of interference or blockage to a wireless LAN signal outdoors than indoors.

Site surveying is not an exact science, which is why thoroughness and attention to detail are required. Record the measurements for the general areas of the room, including measuring the furthest point from the access point, every corner of the room, and every point in the room at which there is no signal or the data rate changes (either increases or decreases). Points of measurement should be determined by the answers to the questions that were asked before you arrived on site to do the survey. Information such as where users will be sitting in a room, where users will be able to roam, the types of users (heavy file transfer or bar-code scanning, for example), and locations of break rooms with microwave ovens in them will all help determine for which points data rate and range should be recorded.

Data Rate Boundaries

Be sure to record the data rate boundaries. These boundaries are also known as the concentric zones around the access point. If you are using an 802.11b wireless LAN, for example, record where the data rate decreases from 11Mbps to 5.5Mbps to 2Mbps to 1Mbps, as shown in Figure 11.16. These boundaries should somewhat resemble concentric circles, with the slower data rate areas further from the access point than the higher data rates. The client organization must be told that when a user roams out past the coffee machine to the mailroom, that user will not get the highest possible throughput due to the data rate decrease, which, in turn, is due to the distance increase.

FIGURE 11.16 Data rate boundaries

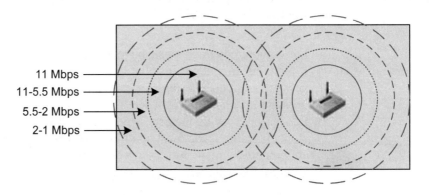

Documentation

By this point, the copy (or copies) of the facility blueprint should be well marked up, with circles, dead spots (if any), data rates, and signal strength measurements in key spots. Now another location within the facility can be documented, and the process begins again. When surveying a small office, and the entire office has facility-wide coverage with maximum throughput from the first testing location chosen, the process does not need to be repeated - the survey is finished. However, that will rarely be the case, so this chapter will prepare you for the worst-case scenario of site surveying.

Be prepared to survey and move, survey and move, again and again, until the optimum coverage pattern for a particular area has been determined. This repetition is the reason for making multiple copies of the facility blueprint or floor plan and bringing lots of paper.

The end result of this portion of the exercise should be a map of the range and coverage of the access point from various locations, with the best results and worst-case results noted. Certainly it saves much time to document only the best possible coverage pattern, so in the interest of efficiency, it is a general practice to quickly test until a "somewhat optimum" location for the access point is found, then do the complete set of documentation (drawings, recording of data, etc.). Site surveying, like anything else, takes practice to become effective. Making decisions that affect the use of time are very important because site surveying is a very time-consuming task.

Throughput Tests & Capacity Planning

There is another type of measurement (outside of the typical SNR, noise, & signal strength that we've discussed thus far) that can be performed by the site surveyor which will yield valuable information to the wireless network design engineer, and that is doing throughput testing from various points throughout the facility. The point of doing all of this coverage and data rate documentation is to understand and control what the user's experience will be on the wireless LAN. Doing live throughput tests such as file transfers to and from an FTP server will give the site surveyor a more thorough look at what the user might experience. Sometimes this test is not possible due to a lack of wired infrastructure connectivity, but it is a valuable option when it is available.

Planning for user capacity is very important if the user is to make productive use of the wireless LAN. From the answers provided by the network manager or administrator, you will know to look for locations within the facility where there are different types of user groups present. For example, if one 50' x 50' area were to house 20 people who work from desktop PCs using client/server applications, determine whether or not one access point could provide the necessary capacity, or if co-located access points would be required to provide for these users' networking needs. In this scenario, it is likely that at least two access points would be required. In contrast, if there were 30 doctors using wirelessly connected PDAs all connecting through a single access point, co-located access points would not likely be needed due to the fact that a PDA cannot transmit large amounts of data across the network very quickly.

These pieces of information will add to the markings on the blueprint in the form of specific data rates, throughput measurements, and capacity notes. With the 11 Mbps coverage circle around each access point drawn to illustrate that particular coverage area, it might be determined that there are 10 people in that area that need a minimum of 500 kbps throughput at all times. These measurements will also determine equipment needs and expenses.

Interference Sources

In this phase of the site survey process, questions are asked about potential sources of narrowband and spread spectrum RF interference.

Are there any existing wireless LANs in use in or near the facility?

Existing wireless LANs can cause hardship on a site-surveyor if permission is not provided to disable existing radios as needed. Disabling existing wireless LAN gear may not be possible due to production environments, or the surveyor may have to conduct the site survey during non-production hours.

Are there any plans for future wireless LAN installations other than the one in question?

Determine if there is another wireless LAN project that needs to be included in the analysis. These projects could affect implementation of the wireless LAN for which this site survey is being performed.

If this is a multi-tenant building, are there any other organizations within the building that have wireless LANs or sources of RF? Are any other organizations planning wireless LAN implementations?

For multi-tenant buildings, it is possible that another organization within the same building is also planning to build a wireless LAN in the future that would impact the site survey, as shown in Figure 11.17. Organizations within the same multi-tenant office building could have wireless LANs in place disrupting each other's communications. If the location is a high-rise building, try to find out if any of the neighboring high-rises have wireless LANs.

FIGURE 11.17 Multi-tenant Office Buildings

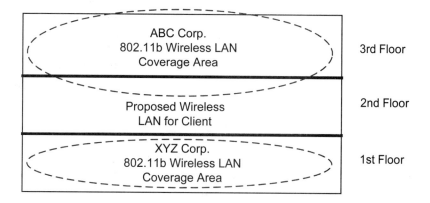

Are there any other common sources of RF interference in the 2.4 GHz band in use in the facility?

Microwave ovens, 2.4 GHz cordless phones, radiology equipment, and baby monitors are common sources of RF interference in the 2.4 GHz band. These potential interference sources need to be documented in the survey as potential problems with the installation. Microwave ovens can easily be replaced, though radiology equipment in a hospital installation may not be. 2.4 GHz phones running on the same channel as the wireless LAN can render a wireless LAN useless.

In case 802.11a networks are to be installed, are there any RF sources in the 5 GHz range?

If there were many other organizations in the area already using 802.11b, using 802.11a would avoid the interference of trying to coexist with another 802.11b network. However, it should be noted whether or not other 802.11a networks exist in the area that could interfere with an 802.11a implementation.

Obstacle-Induced Signal Loss

The chart in Figure 11.18 provides estimates on RF signal losses that occur for various objects. Using these values as a reference will save the surveyor from having to calculate these values. For example, if a signal must penetrate drywall, the range of the signal would be reduced by 50%. The loss is indicated in decibels, and the resulting range effect is shown.

FIGURE 11.18 Signal Loss Chart

Obstruction	Additional Loss (dB)	Effective Range
Open Space	0	100%
Window (non-metallic tint)	3	70
Window (metallic tint)	5-8	50
Light wall (dry wall)	5-8	50
Medium wall (wood)	10	30
Heavy wall (6" solid core)	15-20	15
Very heavy wall (12" solid core)	20-25	10
Floor/ceiling (solid core)	15-20	15
Floor/ceiling (heavy solid core)	20-25	10

Find and record all sources of interference as you map your range and coverage patterns, as shown in Figure 11.19. When measuring the coverage in the break room, for example, measure both when the microwave is running and when it is off. In some cases, the microwave could impact the entire wireless LAN infrastructure if the microwave is an older model. If this is the case, advise the client to purchase a new microwave oven and not to use the existing unit. The client and the users need to be aware of the potential interference and possible lack of connectivity from the break room (or wherever a microwave oven is operated).

FIGURE 11.19 RF Obstacles

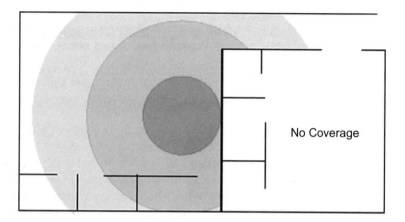

Other common sources of indoor interference to look for include metal-mesh cubicles, metal-mesh glass windows, metal blinds, inventory (what if the client *manufactures* metal blinds?), fire doors, cement walls, elevator motors, telemetry equipment, transformers, fluorescent lights, and metal studded walls (as opposed to wood studs). Piles of objects made of paper, cardboard, wood, and other similar products also serve to block RF signals.

There are standards for how a firewall (a physical fire barrier) may be penetrated. It is important to find firewalls during the site survey because they should be noted in the site survey report. When they prevent Cat5 or RF cabling from going wherever they are needed, it should be documented. Firewalls can also hamper the RF signal. Some firewalls have fire doors directly underneath. Do the site survey with the doors closed because there are locations that require fire doors to remain shut at all times. Poured concrete walls and hardcap ceilings pose the same problems as firewalls.

In a multi-tenant office building, interference could be caused by a microwave oven belonging to a company located on the same floor or possibly on floors directly above or below you. This situation can pose a difficult problem since you have no jurisdiction over the microwave oven. There are many outdoor interference sources, and some can change just by their nature. Seek out and record the effects of the following:

- Trees, buildings, lakes, or other obstructions or reflective objects

- Trees *without* leaves that will later have leaves or that will grow to interfere with the Fresnel zone.

- Automobile traffic – if linking two buildings at first-story height across a road, a large truck or bus could disable the link.

Record the interference source, its location, and its effect and potential effect on wireless LAN coverage, range, and throughput. This data should be recorded both on your copy of the blueprint as well as in a separate list for easy future reference. Taking pictures of interference sources that are permanent (e.g., lakes and buildings) will serve as a visual reference to the client. Pictures of *potential* sources of interference like young trees or future building sites will also help the client's decision making for the future.

Wired Data Connectivity & AC Power Requirements

While moving the access point around the site, indoors and out, the access point may not be able to be located in the best positions. Rather the location will be constrained to where AC power sources exist and network connectivity is within a given distance. Record on the blueprint or floor plan the locations of each AC power source and network connection point. These points will lead to the easier (not necessarily the best) locations for access points. Document and make recommendations for the best locations for all access points. Preferred access point locations may be a solid reason for the client to install new AC power sources as well as new network connectivity points. Remember that many brands of access points can utilize Power over Ethernet (PoE).

Some questions to consider when looking for the best place to install wireless LAN hardware are:

Is AC power available?

Without an available source of AC power, access points will not function. If AC power is not available in a particular location, an electrician's services may be required (added cost) or Power over Ethernet (PoE) can be used to power the unit.

Is grounding available?

Proper grounding for all wireless LAN equipment will provide added protection against stray currents from lightning strikes or electrical surges.

Is wired network connectivity available?

If network connectivity is not available, a wireless bridge may be required or an access point may need to be operated in repeater mode to provide network connectivity. Using access points as repeaters is not a desirable scenario, and the network performance would be much better if the access point could be wired to the network.

If the distance between the access point and the network connection is more than 100 meters, shielded twisted-pair (STP) cabling or an access point that supports a fiber connection can be used. However, using an access point that has fiber network connectivity negates the use of PoE and would require a source of AC power nearby. Media transceivers can be used when fiber runs are necessary. These transceivers can convert Cat5 to fiber and vice versa. When using an access point that has only a Cat5 connector, and its nearest network connection is more than 100 meters way, a media transceiver can solve the problem. Remember that in this configuration, PoE cannot be used.

Cable lengths in the site survey report should be estimated, but never "as the crow flies." Rather, estimate RF connector cable lengths using straight runs with 90-degree turns. Try to keep RF cable runs under 300 feet (91.4 m), but remember to add an extra few feet of cable in case extra length is needed in the future to move the access point or bridge.

Are there physical obstructions?

Doorways, cement ceilings, walls, or other obstructions can result in some construction costs if they need to be altered to allow for power connections or to run power or data cabling to the access points or antennas.

Outdoor Antenna Placement

For outdoor antenna placement, record the location and availability of grounding points, towers, and potential mounting locations. Outdoor antennas require lightning arrestors, which require grounding. Grounding is an easy point to miss, and the client may not be aware of this necessity. Make notes of where antennas could best be mounted and whether any special mounting materials may be required.

Keep in mind that adding network connectivity *outdoors* will be a very new concept to most companies implementing wireless LANs. Specify exactly what is required to bring the network outside the building, including cables, power, weather protection, and protection from vandalism and theft.

Spot Checks

After a wireless LAN is installed, it might not work exactly as planned, although it may be close. Spot-checking by a site surveyor after installation is complete is most helpful in avoiding troubleshooting situations during production use of the network. Items that should be checked are:

- Coverage in perimeter areas
- Overlapping coverage for seamless roaming
- Co-channel and adjacent channel interference in all areas

Site Survey Reporting

Now that you have thoroughly documented the client's facility, the necessary data is available to prepare a proper report for the client. The report will serve as the map for implementation of the wireless LAN and future reference documentation for the network's administrators and technicians.

The site survey report is the culmination of all the effort thus far, and might take days or even weeks to complete. It may be necessary to revisit the site to gather more data or to confirm some of the initial findings. Several more conversations may be needed with the decision makers and some of the people with whom you were unable to meet when you were on site.

Report Format

There is no body of standards or laws that define how a site survey report should look. The following are recommendations that will serve as a starting point and guideline. First, remember while preparing this report that this report is what the client will have after you leave. This work will represent both your knowledge and that of your company. Second, you may be doing the wireless LAN implementation, and if so, you will be working off of your own documentation. If the report is inaccurate, the implementation will not work as planned. Third, save every piece of data collected, and include everything with the report as an attachment, appendix, or another set of documentation. This information may be needed in the future.

Once the site survey is delivered and reviewed by the client, have the client sign a simple form (the site survey report is your only deliverable) that states that the client has both received and reviewed the report, and that the report is acceptable. The client may ask for additional information before signing off.

Below are the main sections of documentation that should be provided to the client in a site survey report. Include graphics that may help illustrate the data when appropriate.

Purpose and Business Requirements

The site survey report should include all contact information for the site survey company and the client company. Both the site survey company and the customer get copies of the report.

Restate the customer's wants, needs, and requirements, and then provide details on how these wireless LAN requirements can be met (item-by-item) as a result of using the site survey as a roadmap to implementing the new wireless LAN. Supplement this section with graphical representations (either sketches, or copies of actual blueprints) to *show* the client what types of coverage and wireless connectivity they requested. This section may include an application analysis where the site surveyor has tested the client's application to assure that the proper implementation of the new wireless LAN will provide appropriate coverage and connectivity for wireless nodes.

Methodology

Discuss in detail the methodology for conducting the site survey. Tell the customer exactly what was done, how it was done, and why it was done.

RF Coverage Areas

Detail RF coverage patterns and ranges specific to the requirements that were collected. If the client said that they needed 5 Mbps for all users in one particular area, correlate the findings and suggestions against that particular requirement. The concentric circle drawings on the floor plan or blueprint will be the center of attention here. It may also be helpful at this point to detail access point placements that did *not* work. Document and explain any coverage gaps.

Throughput

Detail bandwidth and throughput findings, showing exactly where in the facility there will likely be the greatest and the least of each, also using the drawings made on blueprint copies. Be sure to include screenshots of the actual numeric measurements that were recorded. These exact numbers help determine the proper solution.

Interference

Detail RF interference and obstruction findings correlating them to the particular requirements that were collected during the network management interview. Include the location and other details, such as pictures, about each source of interference. Include suggestions for removing RF interference sources where possible, and explain how the RF interference sources will affect the wireless LAN once installed.

Problem Areas

Discuss, in depth, the best possible solutions to the RF (and other networking) problems that were found and documented. The client may not be aware of problems that can surface in doing a thorough site survey. This section should include recommendations for which technologies and equipment will best serve the customer's needs. There is rarely one solution to any technology situation. If possible, present 2 or 3 solutions, so that the customer will have options. It is possible that while performing a site survey, you may find problems with the customer's wired LAN. Tactfully mention any problems you find to the network administrator, especially if those problems will directly affect implementation of the wireless LAN.

Drawings

Provide Visio, CAD, or other types of drawings and graphical illustrations of how the network should be configured including a topology map. All of the survey findings should be documented in words and pictures. It will be much easier to present a range of coverage using a floor plan than only words. Provide floor plan drawings or marked-up blueprints to the customer to graphically show RF findings and recommendations. Figure 11.20 illustrates where access points would be placed on a multi-floor installation.

FIGURE 11.20 Access point placement and coverage

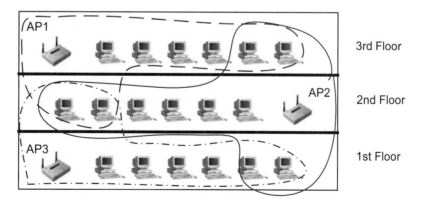

Provide screenshots of the site monitor software and digital pictures outlining locations of access points and bridges.

As mentioned earlier in this section, the site survey report could take days or weeks, and may require return visits to the site. The site survey report should be a professional technical documentation of your investigation and findings of the client's site, which can serve as a technical reference for the wireless LAN design and future network implementations.

Hardware placement & configuration information

The report should answer the following questions about hardware placement and configuration:

- *What is the name of each manageable device?*

- *Where and how should each access point and bridge be placed or mounted for maximum effectiveness?*

- *What channels should each access point be on?*

- *How much output power should each access point deliver?*

A list of facts about each access point to be installed (or already installed) should be included in the RF site survey report. This list should include at least the following:

- Name of the device

- Location within facility

- Antenna type to be used

- Power output settings

- Connectors & cables to be used

- Antenna mount type to be used

- How power should be provided to unit

- How data should be provided to unit

- Picture of location where unit is to be installed

Additional Reporting

The site survey report should be focused on informing the customer of the best coverage patterns available in the facility. Additional pieces of information that belong in the site survey report are interference findings, equipment types needed, and equipment placement suggestions.

A site survey report should not be turned into a consulting report for implementation and security. A wireless consulting firm should be able to come in, read the site survey report, and then be able to provide effective information on equipment purchasing (including vendor selection) and security solutions. The site survey report should be kept separate from implementation and security reports, which can be equally as involved as the site survey, and require as much time to complete. Often, the company that does quality work during the site survey is asked to return to perform the equipment recommendations, installation, security audits, and subsequent security solution implementations.

Consultants may charge additional fees for a report that includes information about one or more of the following:

- Which manufacturers make appropriate products for this environment and what those particular products are.

- Which security solution makes sense for this environment and how to implement that solution.

- Detailed diagrams and drawings on how to implement the suggested solutions.

- Cost and time involved to implement the suggested solutions.

- Details of how each wireless LAN requirement listed in the RF Site Survey Report will be met (item-by-item) in the suggested solution.

Recommendations for equipment vendors are very important, and require:

- Knowing what each vendor specializes in, their strengths and weaknesses

- What level of support is available from a vendor and how easy it is to get replacement hardware

- The costs and part numbers of the appropriate hardware

When a customer reads the site survey report, they may determine that another vendor offers better or cheaper hardware that can provide the same functionality. Part of the recommendation should be to include justification for the decision in choosing a particular vendor's hardware. In creating a report for the purpose of equipment recommendations and installation, create a detailed equipment purchase list (bill of materials) that covers everything needed to implement a solution that meets the customer's requirements as stated in the site survey. If you recommend three solutions (inexpensive, moderate, and full-featured, for example), three complete equipment lists should be provided. Do not omit anything, because it is better to overestimate the potential cost of a solution, and then provide ways to come in under budget. An important note here is that some customers have contractual obligations to buy a particular brand of wireless LAN hardware. In order to identify this situation, the site surveyor may choose to ask this question as part of the network manager's interview. If not, then this fact should be disclosed during the implementation consultation.

One additional point to keep in mind here is that the cost of wired and wireless installations (parts and labor combined) are roughly equivalent. Moving a wired user only once will drastically sway the cost advantage toward the wireless LAN.

Key Terms

Before taking the exam, you should be familiar with the following terms:

data boundary

data rate

dead spot

interference source

link speed

noise floor

RF coverage

signal-to-noise ratio

signal strength

site survey utility software

protocol analyzer

spectrum analyzer

Review Questions

1. Which of the following business requirements should be determined prior to beginning the site survey? Choose all that apply.

   A. Where the RF coverage areas are

   B. Where users will need to roam

   C. Whether or not users will run applications that require Quality of Service

   D. Where dead spots are

2. When determining the contours of RF coverage, site survey utilities should be used to measure which of the following? Choose all that apply.

   A. Obstructions in the Fresnel Zone

   B. Signal strength

   C. Signal-to-noise ratio

   D. Link speed

3. Which one of the following is true of an RF site survey?

   A. A site survey is not necessary in order to perform a successful wireless LAN implementation

   B. A site survey should be performed every 6 months on all wireless LAN installations

   C. A site survey is the most important step in implementing a wireless LAN

   D. Anyone who is familiar with the facility can perform a site survey

4. Which of the following would a site surveyor need to have before performing an indoor site survey? Choose all that apply.

    A. Blueprints or floor plans of the facility

    B. Permission to access the roof and wiring closets

    C. A thorough working knowledge of the existing network infrastructure

    D. Advance notice of all future construction within 5 miles (8.35 km) of the facility

5. Why is a site survey a requirement for installing a successful wireless LAN?

    A. To determine if a wireless LAN is an appropriate solution for the problem or need

    B. Because RF equipment will not operate in accordance with the manufacturer's specifications without a site survey

    C. To ensure that the client's network managers are experts at RF technology

    D. To determine the range, coverage, and potential RF interference sources

6. Which one of the following should be done prior to conducting a site survey?

    A. Interviewing network administrators

    B. Preparing a thorough site survey report

    C. Installing temporary access points

    D. Walking the entire facility with a spectrum analyzer

7. Which one of the following measurements is important to record during a site survey?

   A. The signal-to-noise ratio in a particular area

   B. The average temperature of the facility

   C. The average population of people in a given workspace

   D. The humidity in a particular area

8. A site survey can be executed using a PDA with a wireless connection as a client.

   A. True

   B. False

9. How long should an average site survey take to perform?

   A. Exactly one 8-hour day

   B. One to five hours

   C. It depends on the facility and client needs

   D. One week

10. Which of the following are pieces of information pertaining to the RF link that are gathered during a site survey? Choose all that apply.

   A. Range and coverage pattern

   B. Data rate and throughput

   C. Interference sources

   D. Wired network connectivity and power requirements

11. Which of the following items should NOT be recorded as part of an RF site survey? Choose all that apply.

   A. A/C power outlets and grounding points

   B. Wired network connectivity points

   C. Names of all wireless LAN users

   D. Potential RF obstructions such as fire doors, metal blinds, metal-mesh windows, etc.

   E. Potential RF sources such as microwave ovens, elevator motors, baby monitors, 2.4 GHz cordless phones, etc.

12. For outdoor RF site surveys, which of the following items should be recorded? Choose all that apply.

   A. Trees, buildings, lakes, or other obstructions between link sites

   B. Dimensions of all rooftops on which antennas will be placed

   C. Visual line of sight

   D. Outdoor power receptacles and weatherproof enclosure availability

   E. Link distance (note if > 7 miles (8.35 km) to calculate compensation for Earth bulge)

13. What items should be included in an RF Site Survey Report?

   A. Ranges and RF coverage pattern of particular areas

   B. Data storage details

   C. Interference sources

   D. Names and locations of all wireless LAN users

14. The Signal-to-Noise Ratio (SNR) is measured in:

    A. dBi

    B. dBm

    C. dB

    D. Mbps

15. Which two of the following should be tested during an RF site survey?

    A. RF coverage with microwave oven(s) on

    B. RF coverage with microwave oven(s) off

    C. RF coverage with 2.4 GHz phone(s) off

    D. RF coverage with 2.4 GHz phone(s) on

16. Data rate boundaries are defined as which one of the following?

    A. The line after which there is no longer any data passed to the wireless LAN infrastructure

    B. The boundary between 2 separate wireless LAN RF coverage cells

    C. The point at which the data rate is decreased or increased to the next acceptable higher or lower rate in order to maintain the fastest viable RF link

    D. Square areas of coverage denoted on the facility floor plan within which access points are installed

17. Signal strength and the noise floor are measured in:

    A. dBm

    B. dBi

    C. Mbps

    D. dB

18. To perform a site survey, you will need to record which of the following measurements? Choose all that apply.

    A. Microwave energy level on all floors with microwave ovens

    B. Signal strength

    C. Noise floor

    D. Signal-to-noise ratio

    E. Noise strength ratio

19. Which of the following are possible RF sources (that would interfere with a wireless LAN) to look for when performing a site survey in a hospital? Choose all that apply.

    A. Microwave ovens

    B. Elevator motors

    C. Baby monitors

    D. 2.4 GHz cordless phones

    E. Walkie-talkies

20. Which of the following would be NOT considered potential RF obstructions? Choose all that apply.

    A. Fire doors

    B. A large crowd of users

    C. Metal blinds

    D. Metal-mesh windows

    E. Concrete walls

    F. Metal-framed office cubicles

Answers to Review Questions

1. B, C. Determining what types of applications will be used over the wireless LAN and what those applications require from the wireless LAN infrastructure is critical in making sure the wireless LAN can meet the intended business need. Roaming requirements are no different, because where the users will use the applications can be equally as important as what applications they are using. Determining dead spots and RF coverage is required for every RF site survey.

2. B, C, D. Link speed, SNR, signal strength, and the level of RF noise are all useful pieces of information in deciding on the viability of an RF link, how to design the wireless network, meeting business requirements, and network security. There are no software utilities on the market as of this writing that can measure Fresnel Zone interference.

3. C. An RF site survey is the most important step to performing a successful wireless LAN implementation. Nobody can force an organization to do a site survey, but the results of implementing a wireless LAN without first performing a thorough site survey first can be costly in terms of both time and money.

4. A, B. It is not necessary to be intimate with a customer's wired network topology although a basic understanding might be beneficial. Having access to wiring closets and the roof and having current copies of building floor plans or blueprints is essential to performing the site survey in an efficient manner. The alternative to having this information is having to find wiring closets, guess locations of RF barriers, and create a floor plan on grid paper or in a software application.

5. D. Although part of a site survey is gathering information such as business requirements for the wireless LAN, it's important to note that these pieces of information are helpful, but not absolutely required in order to perform the site survey. In its most basic form, a site survey is simply a determination of RF coverage areas and dead spots and finding interference sources.

6. A. All of the functions listed are part of the site survey itself other than interviewing the network manager or administrator. This

function can be done before the site survey as a preparatory step that saves time on site.

7. A. The signal-to-noise ratio in a given area is important to document for the purposes of determining link viability and suitability for certain user applications. The wireless network designer can use this data to assure business requirements are met when the wireless LAN is used.

8. A. Recent advancements in client software for PDAs make it possible to do a thorough site survey using a PDA instead of a laptop. PDAs remove the burden of carrying a heavy laptop, and PDA batteries tend to last significantly longer than those in laptop computers, allowing a site surveyor to spend more consecutive hours surveying.

9. C. Site surveys can range from an hour to many days depending on client needs and the facility size, shape, and construction. For example, a multi-floor, multi-tenant building would take much longer than a single floor, small office environment.

10. A, B, C. Data rate, throughput, signal strength, SNR, range from access point, the coverage pattern generated by the access point, and RF interference sources are all pieces of information gathered during a site survey that relate directly to the RF links between clients and access points.

11. C. Names of wireless LAN users are not useful pieces of information during a site survey. Perhaps during the implementation of a wireless LAN security solution, getting the names of users for the purposes of entering them into a database would be useful, but keep in mind that a site survey consists mostly of identifying RF coverage and dead spots for particular areas.

12. A, C, D, E. Obstructions, visual line of sight and link distance are important to record during an outdoor site survey because both figure into link budget calculations. Earth bulge, Path Loss, Fresnel Zone encroachment, transmit power, and many other factors play into calculating how much power the receiving antenna will receive. Knowing where power receptacles and weatherproof enclosures are located, if they are available, helps in knowing whether they will have to be installed later or if equipment will have to be located indoors rather than outdoors.

13. A, C. Interference sources, distances from the access point where RF signals remain viable, and RF coverage pattern, including "dead spots", should all be a part of the RF site survey. There are many other items that should be included as well, such as locations of infrastructure devices, digital pictures, suggested output power and antenna selection information for access points and bridges, and channel selection information on a per-access point basis.

14. C. SNR is measured in decibels (dB). Signal-to-noise ratio is a relative measurement of the noise floor in relation to the peak of the RF data signal, which is used to determine an RF link's viability (stability and usability).

15. A, D. Always plan for the "worst case" scenario when site surveying. This method of preparatory troubleshooting is recommended for scenarios that have RF interference sources such as 2.4 GHz spread spectrum phones, baby monitors, microwave ovens, and others. Another example of this approach is to do outdoor site surveys planning for the trees between two sites to be full of leaves that are holding water. In this outdoor scenario, you would increase the height of the antennas on each side of the link planning for extra room in the Fresnel Zone.

16. C. Data rate boundaries are imaginary lines where the data rate changes speeds (either faster or slower) in order to maintain the fastest possible viable RF link between a client and an access point. Dynamic Rate Shifting (DRS) is specified by the 802.11, 802.11b, and 802.11a standards for performing this task automatically.

17. A. The RF noise floor and RF signal strength are quantifiable measurements that are measured in either milliwatts or dBm (decibels referenced to milliwatts). dB and dBi are relative units of measure used to measure changes in power, but not absolute amounts of power.

18. B, C, D. Signal strength, Signal-to-Noise Ratio (SNR), and the RF noise floor level are all valuable measurements when doing a site survey. In order for an RF design engineer to have enough information to make informed design decisions, the engineer must have a significant amount of information relating to RF levels throughout a facility.

19. A, B, C. Baby monitors are used in the nursery near the delivery

section. Microwave ovens are used in staff break rooms. 2.4 GHz cordless phones are generally not permitted in a hospital because of the interference with the wireless LAN installations. Cell phones are not normally permitted in hospitals at all. Staff throughout a hospital uses walkie-talkies; however, these units almost never use the 2.4 GHz ISM band and interfere with wireless LANs. As hard as it is to believe, elevator motors may emit RF interference across many frequency ranges including the 2.4 GHz ISM band.

20. B. People are not generally RF obstructions; however, all of the rest of these items, especially those that are metal or metal-related, are reflective of RF signals and can cause multipath or signal blockage.

RF in Perspective

Throughout this book, we have provided the technical facts, specifications, and many "how to" descriptions of wireless LANs; however, without experience working with RF networks, it may still be difficult to understand the big picture. You will spend many hours in trial and error when working with RF networks, and skill comes with experience. The following RF
Primer should help dispel some common misconceptions about wireless LANs and explain in simple terms some of the scenarios involved with forming wireless connections and optimizing wireless LAN links. Appropriate use of hardware, antenna gain, amplification, antenna use, receiver sensitivity, output power, and FCC regulations are all addressed in hopes that you will get a good perspective of what working with wireless LANs involves.

This RF Primer was authored by Michael F. Young of Young Design, Inc. (www.ydi.com), and edited by Planet3 Wireless, Inc., for use within the CWNA Study Guide.

RF in Perspective

Radio acts like light

For people who have no RF experience, it may be difficult to visualize how radio waves travel, or propagate, through the air. Even for those with RF experience, this concept is sometimes difficult to understand. An easy way to think about microwave signals (generally those frequencies above 1000 MHz or 1 GHz) is to use light as an analogy. Light is an electromagnetic signal as are radio frequency waves.

Light bulb analogy

For purposes of this light-radio analogy, we will create a hypothetical example that should help the thought process of understanding radio frequency. Imagine a dark, overcast night sky with no moon or stars shining through the high clouds, away from any city lights, where the area is totally pitch black, but closer to the ground visibility is clear. If one were to disassemble the light mechanism and remove the reflective mirror from behind the bulb of a standard flashlight with two D-cell batteries, and then set it up so that the light bulb is hanging in free space, the bulb lights up the room, but there is not even enough light to read by.

The power output of this bulb is only about 2 watts. In the license-free 2.4 GHz radio band, the most power that the FCC allows for powering an omni-directional antenna is 1 watt.

If half of the light's power is removed by removing one of the two batteries, the intensity of the bulb drops considerably. The light's output decreases because the power output is proportional to the square of the voltage, meaning that, if the voltage is cut in half, the power goes down by 25%.

The next part of the analogy is to imagine installing this 1 watt light on a tall radio tower, mountaintop, or tall building. The amount of light output represents roughly the radiation power that is present with an amplifier feeding a 6 dBi (decibel) gain omni-directional antenna.

Transmit Range Tests

At a distance of approximately ½ mile from this hypothetical tower, one should be able to see the light with the naked eye, but just barely. This arrangement using the naked eye would be analogous to a low-gain dipole antenna.

At a distance of a mile or two away, one will not likely be able to see the bulb anymore. Using a X10 (times ten) telescope and aiming it at the bulb on the tower, the light bulb is now visible. This layout would be analogous to using a 10 dBi gain directional antenna, such as a flat panel or Yagi antenna. A 10 dBi gain antenna has about ten times the focusing gain of a simple whip, or dipole, antenna.

From a distance of five or six miles out, the light is so weak that even the X10 scope cannot see it. Using a X100 scope, the light comes in clearly, but the viewing area of the telescope is much smaller, which makes aiming the telescope (analogous to an antenna) properly even more critical. This setup would be comparable to using a 20 dBi dish antenna. A 20 dBi gain directional antenna has nearly 100 times the focusing power of a dipole antenna.

From a distance of ten miles or more, presuming that the bulb is mounted high enough up so that there is clear line of sight back to it, even the X100 scope does not see the bulb. If one were to use a X100 night scope, like the ones that military and law enforcement use, the bulb would now be clearly visible, but so would everything around the bulb and the background ("background noise" as infrared light). This configuration is analogous to using a radio amplifier at the client site, which, in this example, would be where the high-powered night scope is.

In order for the bulb to be brighter, the brightness control (gain) on the night scope can be increased. As the bulb gets brighter through the night scope, so does all the background light. If the brightness control is turned up full, the light from the bulb is overcome by all the background noise created by the light amplification circuitry and the light itself gets lost in this background light.

If the gain on the night scope is turned down to the point at which the bulb is as bright as possible without an intolerable increase in the background light, this point represents the optimum "signal-to-noise" ratio for this particular configuration. Turning up the brightness (gain) did not improve the visibility of the bulb, but instead, stressed the viewer's eyes and made the viewer's iris close up to compensate for the increase in the overall light level caused by the increased brightness (gain).

The lesson from this situation is: use only as much receiver gain as is necessary because too much gain can cause less than optimum results. A delicate balance exists within the ratio of the signal to the noise when working with radio frequency.

Receive range tests

The above example explained the analysis of what the client side of the RF link would see. Below, we will look in the other direction of the signal: what the unit on the tower would see. A wireless LAN requires two-way communication, and connectivity is impossible if the client can see the tower's signal, but the tower cannot see the client's signal.

Continuing with the light analogy, if the voltage to the bulb is decreased so that, instead of radiating 1 watt, it puts out fifty-thousandths of a watt (50 mW), barely lighting the filament. Fifty milliwatts is equivalent to the transmitter power emitted by typical wireless LAN cards and access points. At this level of power, the bulb cannot be seen past several hundred feet away. Using the same X100 night scope mentioned earlier, the bulb is visible. The night scope will be the viewing mechanism, representing an amplifier, for the remainder of this example.

At a distance of a half-mile, the bare bulb can be seen with a properly adjusted night scope.

At a mile or two away, the bare bulb is not visible because the light's intensity is too weak. If the bulb were setup behind an X10 telescope eyepiece, so that the X10 eyepiece is aimed back up at the tower, this setup would be equivalent to feeding the radio signal into a directional high-gain antenna. With the X10 telescope aimed towards the tower, the bulb is visible from the tower's X100 night scope.

At five miles out, the X100 telescope is necessary in order for the client on the tower to see the bulb. The light is not strong, but it is visible. At ten miles, the bulb is not visible at all, so the voltage feeding the bulb is increased. The bulb is now radiating 250 milliwatts, which represents the maximum the FCC allows into a 24 dBi gain dish antenna. The bare bulb is still not visible from the tower. With the X10 scope in front of the bulb, the light is visible, but it is not strong. With the X100 telescope, the light is quite bright.

The lesson here is that high-gain directional antennas are needed at the client end of a wireless link.

Obstacles

If there were any obstacles in the way, the bulb would not be visible. This situation is one area in which the light bulb analogy begins to break down. A 2.4 GHz radio signal will go through walls and floors - light will not. How many walls and floors the radio signal will go through depends on the type and the thickness of the material of the walls. RF signals easily travel through sheet rock walls, such as those found in offices and homes, but are seriously attenuated (weakened) through steel reinforced concrete walls and floors.

At long distances, the analogy holds up. A large building in the way will definitely block the radio signal. At close range (a mile or less), reflection and/or refraction of the radio signal will possibly allow connectivity, but that connectivity is both unpredictable and unreliable.

Fresnel Zone

The other departure from our light analogy is the concept of the Fresnel Zone. Radio waves, unlike light, do not travel in thin laser-like lines. RF waves emanate away from an antenna like ripples in a pond when a rock is thrown in. Radio waves fan out, becoming wider toward the middle of the link. The area where radio waves spread out is called the Fresnel

Zone. Light actually has a Fresnel Zone, but because its wavelength is so small, the Fresnel Zone is microscopic. It is possible to have a situation in which there is clear or laser-like line of sight back to the base antenna, but no radio connectivity. Examples of this situation are if the base antenna is visible through a slit between two nearby buildings in the way, or if the tower is just barely visible in the distance over the visual horizon or obstacle. In both cases, the Fresnel Zone is encroached upon and the signal in both directions will be attenuated.

Depending on the distance involved and the amount of the Fresnel Zone that is encroached upon, a radio link may not be possible.

Increasing power at the tower

Wireless LAN users frequently want high-power amplifiers (for use at a tower) that exceed FCC Part 15 regulations. When asked why, they reply, "Because we want a strong signal to reach our clients." When asked if they intend to put amplifiers at their clients' sites, they invariably say "no." The next step for the wireless LAN expert is to point out that it makes no sense to put several watts of transmit power at the tower site while their clients only have perhaps 30 milliwatts of transmit power. Since a wireless LAN is a two-way system, if the base cannot hear the weak client, it does not matter how strong the signal from the base is. There must be amplification at both ends for a balanced system.

Reflection

In cases where the client is located close to the base station, it is possible to get a non line of sight connection off of a reflection from a nearby building. Once again, if everything is very close together (less than 1000 feet (305 meters)), the weak reflection from the building may have enough "illumination" to be captured by a high-gain antenna aimed at the reflecting point.

RF Summary

Below are several points to remember when implementing wireless links.

- Antennas, like telescopes, focus the signal and offer the same gain for both transmitted and received signals.

- The tower should always use an amplifier.

- Clients (except those in close proximity to the tower) need to use high-gain directional antennas when possible.

- Clients at a distance from the tower may need amplifiers.

- Clear, unobstructed line of sight is required, except perhaps for clients in close proximity to the tower.

- Fresnel Zone encroachment will reduce the strength of the radio signal.

- It is illegal, per FCC Part 15 regulations, to implement a wireless LAN that is not certified. Violation of FCC regulations can result in fines, imprisonment, and confiscation of the wireless link that violates the regulations.

- Reflected signals may be strong enough if the distances are short.

Glossary

10BaseFx - IEEE standard for 10 Mbps baseband Ethernet over optical fiber.

10BaseTx - IEEE standard for 10 Mbps baseband Ethernet over twisted-pair wire.

100BaseTx - IEEE standard for a 100 Mbps baseband Ethernet over twisted-pair wire.

5-Unified Protocol (5-UP^{TM}) – a standard proposed by Atheros Communications to enhance the features of 802.11a and HiperLAN/2 into one interoperable standard

802.1d – See Spanning Tree Protocol

802.1x – wireless LAN security implementation meant to increase security in user authentication by using RADIUS, Extensible Authentication Protocol (EAP), and LDAP for port-based authentication between an operating system and the network access device

802.2 - IEEE standard that specifies the Logical Link Control (LLC) that is common to all 802 series LANs

802.3 - IEEE standard that specifies a carrier sense medium access control and physical layer specifications for wired LANs.

802.5 - IEEE standard that specifies a token-passing ring access method and physical layer specifications for wired LANs.

802.11 - IEEE standard that specifies medium access and physical layer specifications for 1 Mbps and 2 Mbps wireless connectivity between fixed, portable, and moving stations within a local area.

10BaseFx - IEEE standard for 10 Mbps baseband Ethernet over optical fiber.

10BaseTx - IEEE standard for 10 Mbps baseband Ethernet over twisted-pair wire.

5-Unified Protocol (5-UP™) – a standard proposed by Atheros Communications to enhance the features of 802.11a and HiperLAN/2 into one interoperable standard

802.1d – See Spanning Tree Protocol

802.1x – wireless LAN security implementation meant to increase security in user authentication by using RADIUS, Extensible Authentication Protocol (EAP), and LDAP for port-based authentication between an operating system and the network access device

802.2 - IEEE standard that specifies the Logical Link Control (LLC) that is common to all 802 series LANs

802.3 - IEEE standard that specifies a carrier sense medium access control and physical layer specifications for wired LANs.

802.5 - IEEE standard that specifies a token-passing ring access method and physical layer specifications for wired LANs.

802.11b - A revision to the IEEE standard for direct sequence wireless LANs. Most 802.11b products have data rates of up to 11 Mbps, even though the standard does not specify the techniques for achieving these data rates.

802.11a - A revision to the IEEE standard that operates in the unlicensed 5 GHz band. Most 802.11a products have data rates up to 54 Mbps and must support 6, 12, & 24 Mbps.

access point (AP) - a layer-2 device that serves as an interface between the wireless network and a wired network and can control medium access using RTS/CTS. Access points combined with a distribution system (e.g. Ethernet) support the creation of multiple radio cells (BSSs) that enable roaming throughout a facility.

active scanning – method by which stations broadcast a probe frame, and all access points within range respond with a probe response frame; Similar to passive scanning, the station will keep track of the probe responses and make a decision on which access point to authenticate and associate with based on the probe responses having the strongest signal level

Address Resolution Protocol (ARP) - A TCP/IP protocol that binds logical (IP) addresses to physical addresses.

Ad Hoc network - A wireless network composed of only stations and no access point.

Advanced Encryption Standard (AES) – uses the Rijndael (pronounced Rine Dale) algorithm and was chosen by the National Information and Standards Institute (NIST) as the Federal Information Processing Standard (FIPS); it is considered uncrackable

amplifier – used to increase signal strength between the transmitter/receiver and the antenna along the antenna cable

Announcement Traffic Information Message (ATIM) – used in Ad Hoc mode to indicate to stations the presence of transmissions bound for a particular station; tells stations not to enter sleep mode before receiving their transmitted frames

antenna diversity – use of multiple antennas in order to overcome multipath

Application Layer - Establishes communications with other users and provides services such as file transfer and electronic mail to the end users of the network.

association service - An IEEE 802.11 service that an enables the mapping of a wireless station to the distribution system via an access point.

attenuation - a term used to describe decreasing the amplitude of an RF signal due to resistance of cables, connectors, splitters, or obstacles encountering the signal path

authentication - The process a station uses to announce its identity to another station. The IEEE 802.11 standard specifies two forms of authentication: open system and shared key.

authentication, authorization, and accounting (AAA) – method by which users are authenticated, authorized, and tracked to gain access and move about inside a network

automatic rate selection (ARS) – see Dynamic Rate Shifting

background noise - Extraneous noise that exists everywhere that interferes with reception of weak radio signals.

bandwidth - Specifies the amount of the frequency spectrum that is usable for data transfer. In other words, it identifies the maximum data rate a signal can attain on the medium without encountering significant attenuation (loss of power).

baseband - A transmission system in which the signals are broadcast one at a time at their original frequency (not modulated).

base station - The part of a radio network where the transceivers and antennas are located.

basic service set (BSS) - A set of 802.11-compliant stations and an access point that operate as a fully connected wireless network.

basic service set identification (BSSID) - A six-byte address that distinguishes a particular access point from others. Also know as just SSID. Serves as a network ID or name.

Bluetooth – a part of the 802.15 standard for WPANs (Wireless Personal Area Networks). Bluetooth is a close-range networking protocol primarily used for mobile devices, utilizing FHSS in the 2.4 GHz ISM band at around 1600 hops/second. Because of the high hop rate, Bluetooth devices will greatly interfere with other devices operating in the 2.4 GHz band.

bridge - A network component that provides internetworking functionality at the data link or medium access layer of a network's architecture. Bridges can provide segmentation of data frames.

Carrier Sense Multiple Access/Collision Avoidance (CSMA/CA) – a type of contention protocol. It is a set of rules determining use of the wireless medium, and it is used to prevent collisions in a wireless network. Use of this protocol means that all stations that want to transmit will listen for other transmissions in the air, and if there are transmissions, they will back off for a random period of time, and then try again. As soon as there are no transmissions detected, the station will begin transmitting. Also known as Distributed Coordination Function.

Carrier Sense Multiple Access/Collision Detection (CSMA/CD) - a type of contention protocol. It a set of rules determining how network devices respond when two devices attempt to use a data channel simultaneously (called a *collision*). Standard Ethernet networks use CSMA/CD. This standard enables devices to detect a collision. After detecting a collision, a device waits a random delay time and then attempts to re-transmit the message. If the device detects a collision again, it waits a longer period of time to attempt retransmission of the message. This is known as exponential back off.

Category 5 UTP data cable - Certified for data rates up to 100 Mbps, which facilitates 802.3 100BaseT (Ethernet) networks

Challenge Handshake Authentication Protocol (CHAP) - a type of authentication in which the authentication agent (typically a network server) sends the client program a key to be used to encrypt the username and password. This enables the username and password to be transmitted in an encrypted form to protect them against eavesdroppers.

clear channel assessment - A function that determines the state of the wireless medium in an IEEE 802.11 network.

co-location – method of installing multiple access points using different frequencies to increase throughput in a wireless LAN

coaxial cable - Type of medium having a solid metallic core with a shielding as a return path for current flow. The shielding within the coaxial cable reduces the amount of electrical noise interference within the core wire; therefore, coaxial cable can extend to much greater lengths than twisted-pair wiring. Commonly called "coax" and used in legacy Ethernet (10base2) networks.

Code Division Multiple Access (CDMA) - A spread-spectrum digital cellular radio system that uses different codes to distinguish users.

data encryption standard (DES) - A cryptographic algorithm that protects unclassified computer data. DES is a National Institute of Standards and Technology (NIST) standard and is available for both public and government use.

Data Link Layer - The OSI level that performs the assembly and transmission of data packets, including error control.

decibel gain (loss) - A unit of measurement that represents the difference between two signal levels. For example, the increased power of an active device (such as an amplifier) and the decreased power of a passive device (such as an attenuator or length of cable)

delay spread – In terms of multipath in a wireless LAN, it is the time between the first signal received and the last echoed signal received; up to 4 ns in duration

dipole antenna - The most basic type of antenna shaped like a "T"

Direct Sequence Spread Spectrum (DSSS) - Combines a data signal at the sending station with a higher data rate bit sequence, which many refer to as a chip sequence (also known as processing gain). A high processing gain increases the signal's resistance to interference. The IEEE specifies a minimum processing gain of 11 and most products operate under 20. Until May 2002, the FCC had limited processing gain to a minimum 10, however this is no longer the case.

disassociation service - An IEEE 802.11 term that defines the process a station or access point uses to notify that it is terminating an existing association.

dish antenna - A high-gain semi-spherical shaped antenna. Often used for satellite and microwave radio reception. It consists of an active element (called a feed element) and a passive spherical reflector.

distributed coordination function (DCF) – see Carrier Sense Multiple Access/Collision Avoidance

distribution service - An IEEE 802.11 station uses the distribution service to send MAC frames across a distribution system.

distribution system - An element of a wireless system that interconnects basic service sets via access points to form an extended service set.

dwell time – in FHSS wireless networks, the amount of time that a client is allowed to spend (dwell) transmitting data on a particular hopping frequency in the hop sequence

Dynamic Host Configuration Protocol (DHCP) - Issues IP addresses automatically within a specified range to devices such as PCs when they are first powered on. The device retains the use of the IP address for a specific license period that the system administrator can define. DHCP is available as part of the many operating systems including Microsoft Windows NT Server and UNIX.

dynamic rate shifting – a method by which wireless LAN clients will fall back to lower data rates when bit error rates exceed a predefined power level due to interference or radio signal attenuation. Clients will shift to higher rates when signal attenuation or interference is no longer present.

Earth bulge – the amount of rise of the earth's surface between long-distance radio links; must be calculated into tower height for radio links greater than 7 miles

Equivalent Isotropic Radiated Power (EIRP) – the actual power output, at the antenna, of a radio transmitter. EIRP can be calculated by adding the transmitter output power (in dBm) to the antenna gain (in dBi) and subtracting the cable loss (in dB): $Power_{Tx} + Gain_{Ant} - Loss_{Cable}$. "Effective" is used by many sources in the industry. The two terms have the same meaning.

Ethernet - A 10 Mbps LAN medium-access method that uses CSMA to allow the sharing of a bus-type network. IEEE 802.3 is a standard that specifies Ethernet.

Ethernet switch - An Ethernet connectivity device more intelligent than a hub, having the ability to connect the sending station directly to the receiving station in full duplex. Additionally, it has filtering and learning capabilities.

European Telecommunications Standards Institute (ETSI) - a non-profit organization whose mission is to produce the telecommunications standards that will be used throughout Europe, including HiperLAN/1 and HiperLAN/2

extended service set (ESS) - A collection of basic service sets tied together via a distribution system sharing a common network name (SSID)

Extensible Authentication Protocol (EAP) - The Extensible Authentication Protocol (EAP) is a general protocol for PPP authentication that supports multiple authentication mechanisms. EAP does not select a specific authentication mechanism at link control phase, but rather postpones this until the authentication phase. This allows the authenticator to request more information before determining the specific authentication mechanism. This also permits the use of a "back-end" server, which actually implements the various mechanisms while the PPP authenticator merely passes through the authentication exchange.

extension point - A base-station 2-radio transceiver that bridges the gap between a wireless client and an access point or between a wireless client and another extension point.

Federal Communications Commission (FCC) - The Federal Communications Commission (FCC) is an independent United States government agency, directly responsible to Congress. The FCC was established by the Communications Act of 1934 and is charged with regulating interstate and international communications by radio, television, wire, satellite and cable. The FCC's jurisdiction covers the 50 states, the District of Columbia, and U.S. possessions.

File Transfer Protocol (FTP) - A TCP/IP protocol for file transfer.

firewall - A device that interfaces the network to the outside world and shields the network from unauthorized users. The firewall does this by blocking certain types of traffic. For example, some firewalls permit only electronic mail traffic to enter the network from elsewhere. This helps protect the network against attacks made to other network resources, such as sensitive files, databases, and applications.

free-space path loss - a reference to the loss incurred by an RF signal due largely to "signal dispersion" which is a natural broadening of the wave front. The wider a wave front, the less power can be induced into the receiving antenna; this loss of signal strength is a function of distance alone and becomes a very important factor when considering link viability.

Frequency Division Multiple Access (FDMA) - A digital radio technology that divides the available spectrum into separate radio channels. Generally used in conjunction with Time Division Multiple Access (TDMA) or Code Division Multiple Access (CDMA).

Frequency Hopping Multiple Access (FHMA) - A system using frequency hopping spread spectrum to permit multiple, simultaneous conversations or data sessions by assigning different hopping patterns to each.

Frequency Hopping Spread Spectrum (FHSS) - Takes the data signal and modulates it with a carrier signal that hops from frequency to frequency as a function of time over a wide band of frequencies. For example, a frequency-hopping radio will hop the carrier frequency over the 2.4 GHz frequency band between 2.4 GHz and 2.483 GHz. A hopping code determines the frequencies it will transmit and in which order. To properly receive the signal, the receiver must be set to the same hopping code and listen to the incoming signal at the right time at the correct frequency.

Fresnel Zone – an oval-shaped zone around the main lobe of an RF transmission which must be 60 to 80 percent clear of obstacles to insure adequate signal reception between the two wireless links; gets larger as the distance between the antennas increases

full-duplex - refers to communications type in which devices can communicate in both directions at the same time; devices can transmit and receive simultaneously

gain – the process of focusing the lobes of an antenna in a specific direction

gateway - A network component that provides interconnectivity at higher network layers. For example, electronic mail gateways can interconnect dissimilar electronic mail systems.

Gaussian Frequency Shift Keying - A frequency modulation technique that filters the baseband signal with a Gaussian filter before performing the modulation; used in FHSS

Gigahertz (GHz) - One billion hertz.

half-duplex – refers to communications in which devices can communicate in only one direction at a time; devices can either be transmitting or receiving, but not both simultaneously

hidden node – occurs when two wireless clients cannot hear each other's transmissions, but both can be heard by the access point; causes excessive collisions on the wireless LAN; remedied by RTS/CTS

HiperLAN - A wireless LAN protocol developed by ETSI (European Telecommunications Standards Institute) that provides a 23.5 Mbps data rate in the 5GHz band.

HiperLAN/2 – An extension to the HiperLAN protocol developed by ETSI (European
Telecommunications Standards Institute) that provides a 54 Mbps data rate in the 5GHz band.

HomeRF - founded March 1998, this organization's charter is to establish the mass deployment of interoperable wireless networking access devices; products utilize the 2.4 GHz ISM band, FHSS technology, and SWAP to achieve data rates of up to 10 Mbps

horizontal polarization – in reference to antennas, it is the electrical field that is parallel to the surface of the earth

hub – layer-2 device that allows half-duplex communications across a network

independent basic service set (IBSS) - An IEEE 802.11-based wireless network that has no backbone infrastructure and consists of at least two wireless stations. This type of network is often referred to as an *ad hoc network* because it can be constructed quickly without much planning and has no access point with which to connect. Client stations connect directly to each other.

Industrial, Scientific, and Medical (ISM) bands - Radio frequency bands that the Federal Communications Commission (FCC) authorized for wireless LANs. The ISM bands are located at 915+/- 13 MHz, 2450+/- 50 MHz, and 5800+/- 75 MHz.

Infrared Data Association (IrDA) - founded June, 1993, this organization's charter is to create an interoperable, low-cost, low-power, half-duplex, serial data interconnection standard that supports a walk-up point-to-point user model that is adaptable to a wide range of computer devices; utilizes infrared light

infrared light - Light waves having wavelengths ranging from about 0.75 to 1,000 microns, which is longer (lower in frequency) than the spectral colors but much shorter (higher in frequency) than radio waves. Therefore, under most lighting conditions, infrared light is invisible to the naked eye.

Institute of Electrical and Electronic Engineers (IEEE) - A United States-based standards organization participating in the development of standards for data transmission systems. IEEE has made significant progress in the establishment of standards for LANs, namely the IEEE 802 series of standards.

integration service - Enables the delivery of MAC frames through a portal between an IEEE 802.11 distribution system and a non-802.11 LAN.

interframe space - Defines spacing between different aspects of the IEEE 802.11 MAC access protocol to enable different transmission priorities.

Internet protocol (IP) – layer-3 protocol that allows the assignment of IP addresses to devices in a network for routing purposes

joining – method by which wireless clients are allowed to locate, authenticate, and associate to an access point

Lightweight Directory Access Protocol (LDAP) – a set of protocols for accessing information directories conforming to the X.500 standard

line of sight (LOS) – the ability to visibly see one antenna from another antenna

lobes – the electrical fields emitted by an antenna; also called beams

local area network (LAN) – a relatively high-speed computer network that spans a relatively small area, such as a single building or a group of buildings

Logical Link Control Layer (LLC) - The highest layer of the IEEE 802 Reference Model and provides similar functions of a traditional data link control protocol.

MAC protocol data unit (MPDU) - The unit of data in an IEEE 802 network that two peer MAC entities exchange across a physical layer.

medium - A physical link that provides a basic building block to support the transmission of information signals. Most media are composed of metal, glass, plastic, or air.

medium access - A data link function that controls the use of a common network medium.

medium access control layer (MAC Layer) - Provides medium access services for IEEE 802 LANs.

Megahertz (MHz) - One million cycles per second.

Mobile IP - A protocol developed by the Internet Engineering Task Force to enable users to roam to parts of the network associated with a different IP address than what's loaded in the user's appliance.

mobility - Ability to continually move from one location to another.

modulation - The process of translating the baseband digital signal to a suitable analog form.

multipath – the composition of a primary signal plus duplicate or echoed images caused by reflections of signals off objects between the transmitter and receiver. Can cause increased amplitude (upfade), reduced amplitude (downfade), or completely cancel the radio signal (null) at the receiver. Will reduce or completely cancel throughput in a wireless LAN.

near/far – caused when network nodes in close proximity transmitting at high-power blind each other to far nodes whose power is small, effectively cuts far node off the network; can also be caused by non-wireless LAN radio interference

Network Address Translation (NAT) - an Internet standard that enables a local-area network (LAN) to use one set of IP addresses for internal traffic and a second set of addresses for external traffic. The four types are static, dynamic, overloading, and overlapping.

Network Layer - Provides the routing of packets from source to destination.

node - Any network-addressable device on the network, such as a router or network interface card.

omni directional antenna - An antenna that transmits and receives radio signals all directions.

open system authentication - The IEEE 802.11 default authentication method, which is a very simple, two-step process. First the station wanting to authenticate with another station sends an authentication management frame containing the sending station's identify. The receiving station then sends back a frame alerting whether it recognizes the identity of the authenticating station.

Orthogonal Frequency Division Multiplexing (OFDM) – A method of digital modulation in which a signal is split into several narrowband channels at different frequencies.

packet - A basic message unit for communication across a network. A packet usually includes routing information, data and (sometimes) error detection information.

passive scanning – method by which a wireless client will keep track of access points based on the reception of beacon management frames; Stations generally decide to authenticate and associate with an access point related to beacon management frames having the strongest received signal strength & lowest observed packet error rates

password authentication protocol (PAP) – The most basic form of authentication in which a username and password are transmitted over a network and compared to a database of authorized users to allow network access

peer-to-peer Network - A network where there are communications between groups of equal devices. A peer-to-peer LAN does not depend upon a dedicated server, but allows any node to be installed as a non-dedicated server and share its files and peripherals across the network. Peer-to-peer LANs are normally less expensive because they do not require a dedicated computer to store applications and data. They do not perform well, however, for larger networks.

Physical Layer - Provides the transmission of bits through a communication channel by defining electrical, mechanical, and procedural specifications.

pigtail - used for adapting proprietary connectors on bridges and access points to standard connectors

point coordination function (PCF) - An IEEE 802.11 mode that enables contention-free frame transfer based on a priority mechanism; stations are polled for the need for frame transmission. Enables time-bounded services that support the transmission of voice and video.

Point-to-Point Protocol (PPP) - A protocol that provides router-to-router and host-to-network connections over both synchronous and asynchronous circuits. PPP is the successor to SLIP.

polarization – in reference to antennas, it is the physical orientation of the antenna in a horizontal or vertical position

portal - A logical point where MSDUs from a non-IEEE 802.11 LAN enter the distribution system of an extended service set wireless network.

Post Office Protocol (POP) - a protocol used to retrieve e-mail from a mail server.

Power over Ethernet (PoE) – method of injecting DC current over the unused pairs in Cat5 cabling to power access points in remote locations; reduces difficulty in access point installation in terms of power installation

processing gain - Equal to the data rate of the spread direct sequence signal divided by the data rate of the actual data.

Radio Frequency (RF) - A generic term for radio-based technology.

Radio Frequency Line of sight – line of sight in which at least 60 to 80 percent of the Fresnel Zone is clear of obstructions; necessary for proper radio communications among wireless LANs

reassociation service - enables an IEEE 802.11 station to change its association with different access points as the station moves throughout the facility.

Remote Authentication Dial-In User Service (RADIUS) – an authentication service specified by the IETF that utilizes a computer-based database (RADIUS server) to compare usernames and passwords to allow access to a network

Request-to-Send/Clear-to-Send (RTS/CTS) – an extension to CSMA/CA, in which clients enter into a 4-way handshake with an access point to send data. (1) Client sends RTS packet to request use of the medium, (2) if the medium is free, access point sends the CTS packet to the client, (3) client sends the DATA to the receiving client, (4) receiving client sends the ACK packet to acknowledge receipt of the DATA. 4-way handshake = RTS-CTS-DATA-ACK

Resource Reservation Setup Protocol (RSVP) – a network protocol which allows a network node to reserve the transmission medium for a specified period of time for Quality of Service (QoS)-oriented applications such as video

roaming – The process of moving from one access point to another without having to re-authenticate to the wireless network.

router - A layer-3 network component that provides internetworking by allowing individual networks to become part of a WAN. It routes using logical and physical addresses to connect two or more separate networks. It determines the best path by which to send a packet of information.

Routing Information Protocol (RIP) - A common type of routing protocol. RIP bases its routing path on the distance (number of hops) to the destination. RIP maintains optimum routing paths by sending out routing update messages if the network topology changes. For example, if a router finds that a particular link is faulty, it will update its routing table, and then send a copy of the modified table to each of its neighbors.

session layer - Establishes, manages, and terminates sessions between applications.

shared-key authentication - A type of authentication that assumes each station has received a secret shared key through a secure channel independent from an 802.11 network. Stations authenticate through shared knowledge of the secret key. Use of shared key authentication requires implementation of the 802.11 Wireless Equivalent Privacy algorithm.

signal to noise ratio - A measure of the useful information being communicated relative to anything else including external noise or interference.

Simple Mail Transfer Protocol (SMTP) – protocol for sending e-mail messages between servers

Simple Network Management Protocol (SNMP) - A network management protocol that defines the transfer of information between Management Information Bases (MIBs). Most high-end network monitoring stations require the implementation of SNMP on each of the components the organization wishes to monitor.

simplex – method of communication in which data travels only in one direction

site survey - The act of surveying an area to determine the contours of RF coverage in order to ensure proper wireless LAN operation through appropriate wireless LAN hardware placement

spectrum analyzer - An instrument that identifies the amplitude of signals at various frequencies.

spread spectrum - A modulation technique that spreads a signal's power over a wide band of frequencies. The main reasons for this technique is that the signal becomes much less susceptible to electrical noise and interferes less with other radio-based systems.

Shared Wireless Access Protocol (SWAP) – a combination of CSMA and TDMA, it is a specification for wireless voice and data networking in the home

Spanning Tree Protocol (STP) - a link management protocol that is part of the IEEE 802.1 standard (802.1d) for media access control bridges. Using the spanning tree algorithm, STP provides path redundancy while preventing undesirable loops in a network that are created by multiple active paths between stations. Loops occur when there are alternate routes between hosts. To establish path redundancy, STP creates a tree that spans all of the switches in an extended network, forcing redundant paths into a standby, or blocked, state. STP allows only one active path at a time between any two network devices (this prevents the loops) but establishes the redundant links as a backup if the initial link should fail.

superframe – a special timeframe during which Point Coordination Function is allowed to have a contention free period. The superframe consists of a beacon, a contention free period (CFP) and a contention period (CP).

Telnet - A terminal emulation program for TCP/IP networks such as the Internet. The Telnet program runs on your computer and connects your PC to a server on the network. You can then enter commands through the Telnet program and they will be executed as if you were entering them directly on the server console. This enables you to control the server and communicate with other servers on the network. To start a Telnet session, you must log in to a server by entering a valid username and password. Telnet is a common way to remotely control Web servers.

Time Division Multiple Access (TDMA) - a technology for delivering digital wireless service using time-division multiplexing (TDM). TDMA works by dividing a radio frequency into time slots and then allocating slots to multiple calls. In this way, a single frequency can support multiple, simultaneous data channels. TDMA is used by HomeRF, HiperLAN/1 and /2, and cellular systems (GSM).

Traffic Indication Map (TIM) – transmitted by the access point to indicate to sleeping stations the presence of buffered transmissions for a particular station

Transmission Control Protocol (TCP) - A commonly used protocol for establishing and maintaining communications between applications on different computers. TCP provides full-duplex, acknowledged, and flow-controlled service to upper-layer protocols and applications.

Transport Layer - Provides mechanisms for the establishment, maintenance, and orderly termination of virtual circuits, while shielding the higher layers from the network implementation details.

Trivial File Transfer Protocol (TFTP) - a simple form of the File Transfer Protocol (FTP). TFTP uses the User Datagram Protocol (UDP) and provides no security features. Often used by servers to boot diskless workstations, X-terminals, and routers.

Unlicensed National Information Infrastructure (UNII) bands – a segment of RF frequencies allocated by the FCC for unlicensed data communications; the three bands are: 5.15 to 5.25 GHz, 5.25 to 5.35 GHz, and 5.725 to 5.825 GHz

vertical polarization – in reference to antennas, it is the electrical field that is perpendicular to the surface of the earth

Virtual Local Area Network (VLAN) – layer-2 functionality used to logically segment a large network into smaller domains

Voltage Standing Wave Ratio (VSWR) - caused by an impedance mismatch between connectors or devices, it is a reflected AC signal in the opposite direction of the main signal flow, usually out-of-phase with the main signal, and causes power loss on the input signal line due to the out-of-phase signal being added to the main signal

Whip antenna - A small, portable antenna often used with wireless transmitters or receivers (such as hand-held 2-way radios and cellular telephones).

Wide Area Network (WAN) - A network that interconnects users over a wide area, usually encompassing different metropolitan areas.

Wired Equivalent Privacy (WEP) - An optional IEEE 802.11 function that offers frame transmission privacy similar to a wired network. The

Wired Equivalent Privacy generates secret shared encryption keys that both source and destination stations can use to alter frame bits to avoid disclosure to eavesdroppers.

Wireless bridge – layer-2 device used to connect remote sites wirelessly to the main network; can be used as repeaters to extend the range of the segment

The Wi-Fi Alliance – Founded in 1999, this organization's charter is to certify interoperability of IEEE 802.11b products and to promote Wi-Fi™ as the global wireless LAN standard across all market segments.

Wireless Fidelity ™ (Wi-Fi™) – the Wi-Fi Alliance certification standard signifying interoperability among 802.11b products

Wireless LAN Association (WLANA) - Founded March 1996, this organization's charter is the promotion of wireless LAN education, technology, and awareness

Wireless LAN Interoperability Forum (WLIF) - founded 1996, this organization's charter was to assist manufacturers of wireless LAN equipment in interoperability testing. Vendors who participated had their equipment certified to the "OpenAir" interoperability specification.

Wireless Metropolitan Area Network (WMAN) - Provides communications links between buildings, avoiding the costly installation of cabling or leasing fees and the down time associated with system failures.

Wireless workgroup bridge – Used to connect a small group of users (normally 8 or less) from one wired network to another via a wireless link. These users connect to the wireless workgroup bridge via an 802.3 Ethernet connection. The wireless workgroup bridge then associates to an access point as a single client allowing users access to the wired network behind the access point. Users are a "collective client" on the wireless network.

INTERNATIONAL CONTACT INFORMATION

AUSTRALIA
McGraw-Hill Book Company Australia
Pty. Ltd.
TEL +61-2-9900-1800
FAX +61-2-9878-8881
http://www.mcgraw-hill.com.au
books-it_sydney@mcgraw-hill.com

CANADA
McGraw-Hill Ryerson Ltd.
TEL +905-430-5000
FAX +905-430-5020
http://www.mcgraw-hill.ca

GREECE, MIDDLE EAST, & AFRICA
(Excluding South Africa)
McGraw-Hill Hellas
TEL +30-210-6560-990
TEL +30-210-6560-993
TEL +30-210-6560-994
FAX +30-210-6545-525

MEXICO (Also serving Latin America)
McGraw-Hill Interamericana Editores
S.A. de C.V.
TEL +525-117-1583
FAX +525-117-1589
http://www.mcgraw-hill.com.mx
fernando_castellanos@mcgraw-hill.com

SINGAPORE (Serving Asia)
McGraw-Hill Book Company
TEL +65-863-1580
FAX +65-862-3354
http://www.mcgraw-hill.com.sg
mghasia@mcgraw-hill.com

SOUTH AFRICA
McGraw-Hill South Africa
TEL +27-11-622-7512
FAX +27-11-622-9045
robyn_swanepoel@mcgraw-hill.com

SPAIN
McGraw-Hill/Interamericana de España,
S.A.U.
TEL +34-91-180-3000
FAX +34-91-372-8513
http://www.mcgraw-hill.es
professional@mcgraw-hill.es

UNITED KINGDOM, NORTHERN,
EASTERN, & CENTRAL EUROPE
McGraw-Hill Education Europe
TEL +44-1-628-502500
FAX +44-1-628-770224
http://www.mcgraw-hill.co.uk
computing_neurope@mcgraw-hill.com

ALL OTHER INQUIRIES Contact:
Osborne/McGraw-Hill
TEL +1-510-549-6600
FAX +1-510-883-7600
http://www.osborne.com
omg_international@mcgraw-hill.com